Quantitative Finance

for dummies®
A Wiley Brand

by Steve Bell

Quantitative Finance For Dummies®

Published by: **John Wiley & Sons, Ltd., The Atrium, Southern Gate, Chichester,** www.wiley.com

© 2016 by John Wiley & Sons, Ltd., Chichester, West Sussex

Media and software compilation copyright © 2016 by John Wiley & Sons, Ltd. All rights reserved.

Registered Office

John Wiley & Sons, Ltd., The Atrium, Southern Gate, Chichester, West Sussex, PO19 8SQ, United Kingdom

For details of our global editorial offices, for customer services and for information about how to apply for permission to reuse the copyright material in this book, please see our website at www.wiley.com.

For general information on our other products and services, please contact our Customer Care Department within the U.S. at 877-762-2974, outside the U.S. at 317-572-3993, or fax 317-572-4002. For technical support, please visit www.wiley.com/techsupport.

Wiley publishes in a variety of print and electronic formats and by print-on-demand. Some material included with standard print versions of this book may not be included in e-books or in print-on-demand. If this book refers to media such as a CD or DVD that is not included in the version you purchased, you may download this material at http://booksupport.wiley.com. For more information about Wiley products, visit www.wiley.com.

A catalogue record for this book is available from the British Library.

Library of Congress Control Number: 2016939606

ISBN: 978-1-118-76946-1

ISBN 978-1-118-76946-1 (pbk); ISBN 978-1-118-76942-3 (ebk); ISBN 978-1-118-76943-0 (ebk)

Printed and Bound in Great Britain by TJ International, Padstow, Cornwall.

SKY10086332_093024

Contents at a Glance

Table of Contents

Introduction

Quantitative finance is about applying mathematics and statistics to finance. For maths lovers that's exciting, but for the rest of us it may sound scary and off-putting. But I guide you step by step, so no need to worry. Quantitative finance helps you to price contracts such as options, manage the risk of investment portfolios and improve trade management.

I show you how banks price derivatives contracts based on the statistics of stock and bond price movements and some simple rules of probability. Similar maths help you understand how to manage the risk of investment portfolios. Quantitative tools help you understand and manage these systems, and this book introduces you to many of the most important ones.

About This Book

This book should be helpful for professionals working in the financial sector – especially in banking. It won't take you to the level of doing the maths for pricing the latest derivative contract, but it can help you to contribute, perhaps as a programmer, data scientist or accountant. It should also be helpful for those taking a masters course in finance or financial analysis and who want help in a module on quantitative finance. Enough detail is included to really help in understanding key topics such as the Black-Scholes equation. The book also has breadth so you can discover a range of key financial instruments and how they're used as well as techniques used by traders and hedge fund managers. Whether you plan a career as a corporate treasurer, risk analyst, investment manager or master of the universe at an investment bank, this book should give you a boost.

This book isn't a traditional textbook and isn't a traditional book on quantitative finance. It is significantly different from either in the following ways:

>> The book is designed as a reference so that you can dive into the section of most importance to you. I include lots of cross references to clearly point you to other sections and chapters that may have additional or complementary information.

>> The maths is at the minimum level required to explain the subjects. I made no attempt to impress with fancy mathematical jargon, lengthy proofs or references to obscure theorems.

>> It's about applying mathematics and probability to finance. That includes derivatives but also includes tools to help you with trading and risk management. Finance is a subject centred on numbers, so maths is a natural way to help you get to grips with it.

>> It includes real-world examples so you can relate quantitative finance to your day-to-day job.

If you haven't done any algebra for a while, remember that mathematicians like to write products without multiplication signs. So P(H)P(H) is shorthand for the probability of heads multiplied by the probability of heads. For maths with actual numbers, I use the symbol * to indicate multiplication. This avoids any confusion with the variable x, which is a favourite of mathematicians to signify an unknown quantity.

Within this book, web addresses may break across two lines of text. If you're reading this book in print and want to visit one of these web pages, simply key in the web address exactly as noted in the text, pretending the line break doesn't exist. If you're reading this as an e-book, you've got it easy — just click the web address to be taken directly to the website.

Foolish Assumptions

I don't assume that you have any previous experience of quantitative finance. I don't even assume that you're familiar with the world of finance except for the apocalyptic stories you read in the press about crises, greed, bonuses and debt. However, I'm assuming that you're reading this book because you're working in a financial institution such as a bank or a hedge fund and want to know what those clever *quants* (quantitative finance professionals) are doing. Alternatively, you may be studying for a Masters in Finance and looking for help with those quantitative modules.

I assume that you're familiar with mathematics such as logarithms, exponentials and basic algebra. In some parts of the book, I also assume some knowledge of calculus both differentiation and integration. The online Cheat Sheet at www.dummies.com/cheatsheet/quantitativefinance is a good place to visit if you need to brush up on some of this maths. Some of the sections with the heaviest maths have Technical Stuff icons, which means that you can skip them if you wish.

Where I use algebra, I try to take you through it step by step and introduce all the symbols before the equations so that you know what they're about. I also include a few example calculations to help you become familiar with them and see how to use the equations in practice.

Quantitative finance is what it says it is and involves numbers and maths but you don't need to become bogged down by it. Only then will you see that the numbers are useful in real life in your job.

Icons Used in This Book

Icons are used in this book to draw your attention to certain features that occur on a regular basis. Here's what they mean:

REMEMBER

This icon is to give those grey cells a little jolt. It's so easy to forget what you learned in school.

TIP

This icon points to helpful ideas that can save you time and maybe even money.

TECHNICAL STUFF

Skip paragraphs marked with this icon if you don't want to go into the gory mathematical details. But if you do manage them, you'll really glow with achievement.

WARNING

Sometimes things can go badly wrong. Follow these sections to avoid disasters.

Where to Go from Here

The obvious answer is to start with Chapter 1. In fact, that's a good idea if you're not too familiar with quantitative finance as Chapter 1 is a bit like the book in miniature. I hope it will fire you up ready to read the rest of the book. Another obvious answer is to go to the table of contents. Just find the topic you'd like to know about and go straight there – no messing about. The book is designed to be used like that. Check out the topics you want to know about and skip what you're not interested in. A third obvious answer is to use the index, which has been conveniently arranged in alphabetical order for you. If some quantitative finance jargon is bugging you, go to the Glossary at the back. Finally, if you're really in a hurry, try Chapters 19 and 20. They give quantitative finance to you in ten bite-sized sections.

And you can use some free online material to help. The Cheat Sheet is a goldmine of handy formulae used in quantitative finance. To view this book's Cheat Sheet, go to www.dummies.com and search for "Quantitative Finance For Dummies Cheat Sheet" for additional bits of information that you can refer to whenever you need it.

1
Getting Started with Quantitative Finance

Realise that the chart of a stock price can look jumpy and rather random because market prices are indeed very close to being random.

Get to grips with the mathematics of random numbers and brush up on probability and statistics.

Enter the strange and fascinating world of random walks. Find out how you can use them as models for the price movement of financial assets such as stocks.

Use calculus to analyse random walks so that you can get going on the classic maths for option pricing.

Chapter 1

Quantitative Finance Unveiled

Quantitative finance is the application of probability and statistics to finance. You can use it to work out the price of financial contracts. You can use it to manage the risk of trading and investing in these contracts. It helps you develop the skill to protect yourself against the turbulence of financial markets. Quantitative finance is important for all these reasons.

If you've ever looked at charts of exchange rates, stock prices or interest rates, you know that they can look a bit like the zigzag motion of a spider crossing the page. However, major decisions have to be made based on the information in these charts. If your bank account is in dollars but your business costs are in euros, you want to make sure that, despite fluctuations in the exchange rate, you can still pay your bills. If you're managing a portfolio of stocks for investors and you want to achieve the best return for them at minimum risk, then you need to learn how to balance risk with reward. Quantitative finance is for banks, businesses and investors who want better control over their finances despite the random movement of the assets they trade or manage. It involves understanding the statistics of asset price movements and working out what the consequences of these fluctuations are.

However, finance, even quantitative finance, isn't just about maths and statistics. Finance is about the behaviour of the participants and the financial instruments they use. You need to know what they're up to and the techniques they use. This is heady stuff, but this book guides you through.

Defining Quantitative Finance

My guess is that if you've picked up a book with a title like this one, you want to know what you're going to get for your money. Definitions can be a bit dry and rob a subject of its richness but I'm going to give it a go.

Quantitative finance is the application of mathematics – especially probability theory – to financial markets. It's used most effectively to focus on the most frequently traded contracts. What this definition means is that quantitative finance is much more about stocks and bonds (both heavily traded) than real estate or life insurance policies. The basis of quantitative finance is an empirical observation of prices, exchange rates and interest rates rather than economic theory.

Quantitative finance gets straight to the point by answering key questions such as, 'How much is a contract worth?' It gets to the point by using many ideas from probability theory, which are laid out in Chapters 2 and 3. In addition, sometimes quantitative finance uses a lot of mathematics. Maths is really unavoidable because the subject is about answering questions about price and quantity. You need numbers for that. However, if you use too much mathematics, you can lose sight of the context of borrowing and lending money, the motivation of traders and making secure investments. Chapter 13 covers subjects such as attitudes to risk and prospect theory while Chapter 18 looks in more detail at the way markets function and dysfunction.

TECHNICAL STUFF

Just to avoid confusion, quantitative finance isn't about quantitative easing. *Quantitative easing* is a process carried out by central banks in which they effectively print money and use it to buy assets such as government bonds or other more risky bonds. It was used following the credit crisis of 2008 to stimulate the economies of countries affected by the crisis.

Summarising the mathematics

I'm not going to pretend that quantitative finance is an easy subject. You may have to brush up on some maths. In fact, exploring quantitative finance inevitably involves some mathematics. Most of what you need is included in Chapter 2 on probability and statistics. In a few parts of the book, I assume that you remember some calculus – both integration and differentiation. If calculus is too much for you, just skip the section or check out *Calculus For Dummies* by Mark Ryan (Wiley). I've tried to keep the algebra to a minimum but in a few places you'll find lots of it so that you know exactly where some really important results come from. If you don't need to know this detail, just skip to the final equation.

Time and again in this book, I talk about the Gaussian (normal) distribution. Chapter 2 has a definition and explanation and a picture of the famous bell curve.

Please don't get alarmed by the maths. I tried to follow the advice of the physicist Albert Einstein that 'Everything should be made as simple as possible, but not simpler.'

Pricing, managing and trading

Quantitative finance is used by many professionals working in the financial industry. Investment banks use it to price and trade options and swaps. Their customers, such as the officers of retail banks and insurance companies, use it to manage their portfolios of these instruments. Brokers using electronic-trading algorithms use quantitative finance to develop their algorithms. Investment managers use ideas from modern portfolio theory to try to boost the returns of their portfolios and reduce the risks. Hedge fund managers use quantitative finance to develop new trading strategies but also to structure new products for their clients.

Meeting the market participants

Who needs quantitative finance? The answer includes banks, hedge funds, insurance companies, property investors and investment managers. Any organisation that uses financial derivatives, such as options, or manages portfolios of equities or bonds uses quantitative finance. Analysts employed specifically to use quantitative finance are often called *quants*, which is a friendly term for *quantitative analysts*, the maths geeks employed by banks.

Perhaps the most reviled participants in the world of finance are *speculators*. (Bankers should thank me for writing that.) A *speculator* makes transactions in financial assets purely to buy or sell them at a future time for profit. In that way, speculators are intermediaries between other participants in the market. Their activity is often organised as a *hedge fund*, which is an investment fund based on speculative trading.

Speculators can make a profit due to

>> Superior information

>> Good management of the risk in a portfolio

>> Understanding the products they trade

>> Fast or efficient trading mechanisms

Speculators are sometimes criticised for destabilising markets, but more likely they do the opposite. To be consistently profitable, a speculator has to buy when prices are low and sell when prices are high. This practice tends to increase prices when they're low and reduce them when they're high. So speculation should stabilise prices (not everyone agrees with this reasoning, though).

Speculators also provide liquidity to markets. *Liquidity* is the extent to which a financial asset can be bought or sold without the price being affected significantly. (Chapter 18 has more on liquidity.) Because speculators are prepared to buy (or sell) when others are selling (or buying), they increase market liquidity. That's beneficial to other market participants such as hedgers (see the next paragraph) and is another reason not to be too hard on speculators.

In contrast to speculators, *hedgers* like to play safe. They use financial instruments such as options and futures (which I cover in Chapter 4) to protect a financial or physical investment against an adverse movement in price. A hedger protects against price rises if she intends to buy a commodity in the future and protects against price falls if she intends to sell in the future. A natural hedger is, for example, a utility company that knows it will want to purchase natural gas throughout the winter so as to generate electricity. Utility companies typically have a high level of debt (power stations are expensive!) and fixed output prices because of regulation, so they often manage their risk using option and futures contracts which I discuss in Chapters 5 and 6, respectively.

Walking like a drunkard

The *random walk*, a path made up from a sequence of random steps, is an idea that comes up time and again in quantitative finance. In fact, the random walk is probably the most important idea in quantitative finance. Chapter 3 is devoted to it and elaborates how random walks are used.

Figure 1-1 shows the imagined path of a bug walking over a piece of paper and choosing a direction completely at random at each step. (It may look like your path home from the pub after you've had a few too many.) The bug doesn't get far even after taking 20 steps.

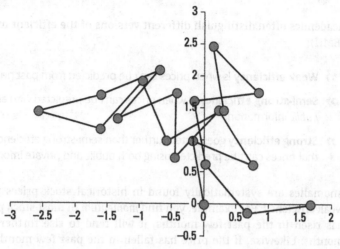

FIGURE 1-1:
A random walk.

In finance, you're interested in the steps taken by the stock market or any other financial market. You can simulate the track taken by the stock market just like the simulated track taken by a bug. Doing so is a fun metaphor but a serious one, too. Even if this activity doesn't tell you where the price ends up, it tells you a range within which you can expect to find the price, which can prove to be useful.

REMEMBER

Random walks come in different forms. In Figure 1-1, the steps are all the same length. In finance, though random walks are often used with very small step sizes, in which case you get a Brownian motion. In a slightly more complex form of Brownian motion, you get the geometric Brownian motion, or GBM, which is the most common model for the motion of stock markets. You can find out in detail about GBM in Chapter 3.

Knowing that almost nothing isn't completely nothing

The orthodox view is that financial markets are *efficient*, meaning that prices reflect known information and follow a random walk pattern. It's therefore impossible to beat the market and not worth paying anyone to manage an investment portfolio. This is the *efficient market hypothesis*, or EMH for short. This view is quite widely accepted and is the reason for the success of *tracker funds*, investments that seek to follow or track a stock index such as the Dow Jones Industrial Average. Because tracking an index takes little skill, investment managers can offer a diversified portfolio at low cost. Chapter 14 has much more about diversification and portfolios.

TECHNICAL STUFF

Academics often distinguish different versions of the efficient market hypothesis (EMH):

>> **Weak efficiency** is when prices can't be predicted from past prices.

>> **Semi-strong efficiency** is when prices can't be predicted with all available *public* information.

>> **Strong efficiency** goes a step further than semi-strong efficiency and says that prices can't be predicted using both public and private information.

Anomalies are systematically found in historical stock prices that violate even weak efficiency. For example, you find *momentum* in most stock prices: If the price has risen in the past few months, it will tend to rise further in the next few months. Likewise, if the price has fallen in the past few months, it will tend to continue falling in the next few months. This anomaly is quite persistent and is the basis for the *trend following* strategy of many hedge funds.

Somehow, though, the EMH smells wrong. Even though you can find many vendors of market information, EMH has a cost. It's no coincidence that some of these vendors are very wealthy indeed. Also, if you examine publicly available information, you soon find that such information is not perfect. Often the information is delayed, with the numbers published days or even weeks following the time period they apply to. Some exceptions exist and you can read about one of them in the sidebar, 'The impact of US employment numbers'.

It's far more likely that markets are not informationally efficient and that many participants for reasons of cost or availability are not perfectly informed. It's also highly likely that most participants are not able to instantly work out in detail the consequences of the information presented to them. This working out may take some time.

Indeed, if markets were informationally efficient, there would be no incentive to seek out information. The cost wouldn't justify it. On the other hand, if everyone else is uninformed, it would be rewarding to become informed as you can trade successfully with those who know less than you.

REMEMBER

The point that in an efficient market there's no incentive to seek out information and so therefore no mechanism for it to become efficient is the *Grossman–Stiglitz paradox*, named after the American economists Sanford Grossman and Joseph Stiglitz. The implication is that markets will be efficient but certainly not perfectly efficient.

THE IMPACT OF US EMPLOYMENT NUMBERS

One of the most widely anticipated numbers in finance is the so-called nonfarm payroll issued by the US Bureau of Labour Statistics. In fact, the nonfarm payroll isn't just a number but a report with almost 40 pages. You can find the November 2015 report at www.bls.gov/news.release/pdf/empsit.pdf. Formally, this report is called the employment situation. Its headline figure is the nonfarm payroll employment and its companion figure is the unemployment rate, so it gives a picture of the employment situation in the United States.

This number is hugely impactful globally and can move the value of currencies, stock markets and bond markets across the world within seconds of its release. In the US, though, the number is released one hour before the opening of the New York Stock Exchange so that traders get a chance to absorb the information before trading begins. Aside from the data being for the largest economy in the world, other factors make it influential:

- The nonfarm payroll is timely. It's issued on the first Friday in the month following the one it relates to. For example, the September 2015 report was issued on Friday 2 October 2015 at exactly 8:30 a.m. Eastern Daylight Time. This is no mean feat given the amount of information contained in it.

- The nonfarm payroll is comprehensive. It has surveys including small business and the self-employed so the information is credible.

- Although estimates and statistical models are used in some of the numbers, revisions are made to these numbers in subsequent months as more information becomes available. The existence of timely revisions based on a well-defined process supports market confidence in the numbers.

Be warned: If you're trading any instruments when the nonfarm payroll figures come out, you may be in for some significant turbulence!

Only with deep research into market data do markets have a chance of becoming efficient. That's the norm in financial markets, but pockets of inefficiency are always left that market traders and savvy investors can attempt to exploit. Also, attempts to use the results of deep research drive the intense trading found in many markets. In Chapter 8, I talk about techniques for analysing historical price data for patterns.

Recognising irrational exuberance

Most markets are responding constantly to a flow of news on companies, economies, interest rates and commodities. They also react to changes in the supply and demand for the financial asset in question. If more fund managers decide to buy a stock than sell it, its price tends to rise. The greater the demand for loans from companies, the higher the interest rate lenders demand.

Markets don't always behave in this sensible way, however. Sometimes, they defy gravity and keep on rising, which is called a *bubble*. Figure 1-2 shows an example of this in a chart for the share price of British Telecom, a fixed-line telecom operator. In September 1996, the Chairman of the US Federal Reserve Bank warned of *irrational exuberance* in markets. Unusual circumstances, especially low interest rates, were making markets overly excited. He was dead right. The Internet had just been invented so even traditional companies such as British Telecom saw their share price rocket upward. The market ignored Chairman Alan Greenspan when he made his warning, although the Japanese stock market respectfully dipped several per cent on the day of his speech. In a way, the market was right and farsighted: The Internet was going to be big, it was just that British Telecom wasn't Google. After rising to a very sharp peak in early 2000, British Telecom shares crashed back down to earth and continued on in their usual way.

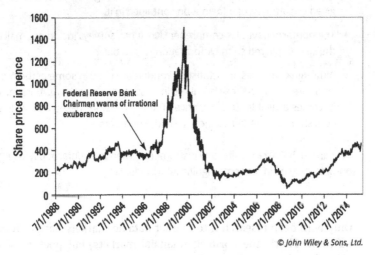

FIGURE 1-2:
Share price chart
for British
Telecom plc.

One thing for sure is that with crazy behaviour like this, the statistics of the price movements for shares don't obey Gaussian statistics. In Chapter 2, I explain quantities such as *kurtosis*, a measure of how much statistical distributions deviate from the Gaussian distribution. A large positive value for the kurtosis means that the probability of extreme events is far more likely than you'd expect from a Gaussian distribution. This situation has come to be called a *fat-tailed*

distribution. Statistics is the way of measuring and analysing the market price data used in quantitative finance, and I try to emphasise this throughout the book.

Another possibility, of course, is that prices crash rapidly downwards far more often than you'd expect. The fear of prices crashing downwards is palpable. Market participants want to protect themselves against nasty events like that. To do that, you need financial instruments such as options and futures, which I explain in detail in Chapters 5 and 6, respectively. *Options* are a form of financial insurance. For example, if you think that the stock market is going to crash, then you buy an option that compensates you if that happens. If the market doesn't crash, you've lost just the premium you paid for the option, just like an insurance contract.

TIP

George Soros, a billionaire hedge fund manager, attempted to explain these irrational market events with a concept he called *reflexivity*. He replaced the efficient market hypothesis view that the market is always right with something else:

>> Markets are always biased in one direction or another. An example of this bias is the British Telecom shares illustrated in Figure 1-2. The market thought that all things telecom would be highly profitable.

>> Markets can influence the events that they anticipate. Financial markets can be stabilising. If a recession is anticipated and the currency declines, this situation should boost exports and help prevent a recession.

George Soros's ideas are controversial, but they help to explain some major market distortions. He's been proven correct on enough occasions to have been successful using his insights.

Wielding Financial Weapons of Mass Destruction

Cash is the most fundamental of all financial assets. Economists write that money has three functions. It serves as a:

>> Store of value

>> Means of exchange

>> Unit of account

These three functions are familiar to anyone with a savings account (store of value) who has done some shopping (means of exchange) and carefully compared prices (unit of account). Whether in the form of nickel, plastic or paper, cash is the key.

Two alternatives to cash – one ancient, one modern – are good to know about:

>> **Gold** has been used for thousands of years as a store of value and also as a means of exchange. Most central banks in the world hold substantial quantities in vaults. This practice is partly a relic of the time when paper money could be exchanged for gold at the central bank. Although this ended in the United States in 1971, many investors still hold gold as part of their investment portfolios.

>> Like gold, the **bitcoin** is a currency not under the control of any government. However, bitcoin isn't physical. It's been described as a *cryptocurrency* because bitcoin is completely digital and relies heavily on encryption techniques for security. It can be used for payments just like other forms of cash, but at the moment these transactions are small compared with, say, the volume of credit card transactions.

One of the appeals of both gold and bitcoin is that they're not under government control. In the past, governments have used their power to print money, which undermined the value of the currency. The currencies then no longer function well as a store of value. By investing in gold, which is limited in supply, this undermining can't happen.

Cash exists in the form of many currencies such as the US dollar, the Japanese Yen and the Chinese renminbi. These countries all have their own central banks, and one of the key functions of these banks is to set the interest rate for the currency. This *interest* is money that you earn by depositing cash at the central bank. Normally, only other banks are permitted to use central banks in this way, but these interests rates are one of the key parameters in quantitative finance. The interest rate at a central bank is often called the *risk-free rate* because the assumption is that a central bank can't go bankrupt. Chapter 4 has some of the maths involved with interest rates that's the basis behind lots of quantitative finance calculations.

If you take out a loan to buy a house or expand your business, the loan is said to be a *floating-rate* loan if the interest rate changes when the central bank in your country changes its interest rate. The load is *fixed-rate* if it stays the same when the central bank changes the interest rate. However, given that the period over which loans are repaid can be long, locking into one type of loan gives you no flexibility. If you have a floating-rate loan, you may decide that you want to keep the interest payments fixed in future. That may help you sleep at night. The solution to this fixing is called an *interest-rate swap*. This instrument allows you to swap from a fixed-rate loan to a floating-rate loan or vice versa. Chapter 4 has a section which gives you the maths behind this.

Interest-rate swaps are one of the most important instruments used by banks to manage risk. They also use more sophisticated tools as well and Chapter 12 provides an introduction to some of the most common interest-rate derivatives. These derivatives have proved very popular with real-estate investors who typically borrow large sums of money and want to put limits on interest payments.

REMEMBER

Cash in one currency can be exchanged for cash in another currency. This transaction is called *foreign exchange*, often abbreviated as FX. The FX market isn't organised on an exchange and normally consists of dealers working in banks. This market is the largest financial market in the world with huge volumes of transactions per day.

Because different currencies have different interest rates, you can potentially make money by

>> Selling a currency with a low interest rate

>> Buying currency with a high interest rate

>> Earning a high interest rate

Such transactions are called the *carry trade* and are a big factor in influencing foreign exchange rates.

Going beyond cash

Borrowing money from a bank to expand a business is fine, but other ways are possible too:

>> **Bonds** are a form of loan to a business. The borrower (or business owner) receives the principal from the lender and in return promises to pay a regular interest payment called a *coupon*. On the bond's maturity date, the lender gets her principal back. The clever bit, though, is that this bond is a financial instrument. This means that the lender can sell it to someone else. Then the buyer is entitled to the coupon payments and the principal repayment on maturity.

>> Owning **stocks** or **shares** in a business means you're a part owner of the business, are entitled to *dividend* payments and can vote at the annual general meeting in support (or otherwise) of the managers.

Businesses issue shares in exchange for cash from investors but they have no fixed repayment date as a bond does. Dividend payments are at the discretion of the management and can vary and, in fact, be non-existent. Because of this, shares are often considered riskier than bonds.

Bonds and shares are the building blocks for most investment portfolios. Bonds are risky because the borrower can *default* and fail to pay her coupons. Shares are risky because the company may be unable to pay a dividend. Shareholders have no right to any repayment of capital so are more likely to lose everything. Chapter 4 gives you the lowdown on the bond and stock markets.

If you're thinking that you're never going to invest in shares or bonds because you may never get your money back, then you're not alone. However, the financial markets have created a solution to this, using two instruments, *options* and *futures* that can be used to control and manage the risk of investing in the stock and bond markets. They're both flexible contracts that I cover in great detail in Chapters 5 and 6, respectively. Quantitative finance developed rapidly in the 1980s after people figured out a mathematical way to price options. You can find out about pricing in Chapters 10 and 11.

Inventing new contracts

Every business likes to show off shiny new products so as to boost sales, but the financial industry has been better than most at creating new products; some would say too successful. After a long career at the heights of the financial world, the former chairman of the US Federal Reserve Bank Paul Volcker said that he'd encountered only one financial innovation in his career, and that was the automatic teller machine (ATM).

SETTING CONTRACTS IN STONE

Is anything ever written in tablets of stone? Apparently so. Some of the oldest examples of documents written in stone are Babylonian futures contracts. These were agricultural *futures* – contracts agreeing to sell or buy grain at a time in the future at a price agreed now. The point of these contracts is to reduce the impact of price fluctuations on farmers or buyers of grain such as bakers. Knowing a price in advance makes business easier. Exactly the same sort of contracts are used today, although they're mainly traded electronically on the CME (Chicago Mercantile Exchange).

Volcker's sceptical remark points out that the nature of the contracts that people enter into are not fundamentally different from ancient contracts. Energy futures were first created in the 1970s but they're similar to agricultural futures, which have been around for thousands of years. Indeed, they're now traded on exactly the same exchanges. Trading is now electronic and greatly accelerated, but the function of these contracts is exactly the same. The success of energy futures led to the introduction of financial futures contracts on interest rates and bonds. They were, and are still, a big success.

Just as in the futures market, the variety of option contracts available has proliferated. Initially, most options were share options, but they soon found use in the foreign exchange and bond markets. You can also buy commodity options such as for crude oil, which have proved very popular too.

New option styles have also been introduced. In this book, I stick to what are known as *plain vanilla contracts* which give the holder the right, but not the obligation, to buy or sell an underlying asset at a predetermined price (the *strike price*) at a specified time in the future. In the plain vanilla contract, the option *payoff* (the amount that you may get paid when the contract expires) depends only on a single strike price (the price that has to be reached for there to be any payoff to the option) whereas for barrier options, and other more complicated options, other prices are involved too.

Finally, credit derivatives give protection against defaulting loans. The most common of these derivatives are *credit-default swaps* in which the buyer of the swap makes a regular series of payments to the seller; in exchange, the seller promises to compensate the buyer if the loan defaults.

REMEMBER

Derivatives are useful because market participants who can't bear certain risks can shift them (at a price) to someone who can. As a whole though, trading in derivatives can lead to risk being concentrated in a small number of dealers with fatal consequences for the likes of Lehman Brothers. As the investor Warren Buffett presciently observed years before the 2008 crisis, 'derivatives are financial weapons of mass destruction'.

Despite the explosive possibilities inherent in the derivatives market, the use of derivatives continues because of the constant need to mitigate financial risks. Better regulation will hopefully reduce the nasty accidents that have happened.

THE 2008 BANKING CRISIS IN A NUTSHELL

In September 2008, the US investment bank Lehman Brothers filed for bankruptcy. This event was the first time in decades that a major US bank had collapsed. In the UK, major retail banks had to be bailed out by the government, and in Germany the second largest bank, Commerzbank, was partly nationalised.

These banks were deemed *too big to fail*, meaning that the government felt compelled to intervene fearing that allowing the banks to fail would create a crisis across the entire banking system.

This financial crisis was a complicated event (you can find whole books on it – not just a paragraph) but it boils down to the fact that the banks lent way too much money and lent some of it to people who were unlikely ever to pay it back. You can be forgiven for thinking they just weren't doing their job properly.

A lot of this lending was done using *mortgage-backed securities*. These securities are a bit like bonds where the coupon payments and final principal repayments come from a portfolio of residential mortgages. By ingenious methods, the banks made these securities appear less risky than they really were. These methods allowed the bank to earn yet more fees from the lending but at the expense of building a financial time bomb.

Analysing and Describing Market Behaviour

Quantitative finance is primarily about prices, but because markets are almost efficient, price changes are almost random. Also, you may be interested in not one price but many prices – all the prices in an investment portfolio, for example. I explain some of the statistical tools that you can use to deal with this problem in the next sections.

Measuring jumpy prices

The measure of the jumpiness of prices is called *volatility*. Chapter 7 is all about volatility and the different ways that you can calculate it. Normally price changes are called *returns* even if they're negative, and the volatility is the standard deviation of these returns. The higher the volatility, the jumpier the prices.

Because of the instability of financial markets, volatility is constantly changing. Prices can go through quiet spells but then become very jumpy indeed. This means that calculating volatility isn't as simple as calculating a normal standard deviation, but Chapter 7 shows you how.

Keeping your head while using lots of data

Most financial institutions are trading, selling or investing many different financial assets, so understanding the relationships between the prices of these assets is useful. In Chapter 9, I show you a special technique for gaining this understanding called *principal components analysis* (PCA). This technique helps because it can point out patterns and relationships between assets and even help you build predictive models. This is no mean feat given the almost random changes in asset prices, but PCA can do it.

Valuing your options

Black-Scholes is the equation that launched a thousand models. Technically, it's a partial differential equation for the price of an option. The reason you need such a complicated equation to model the price of an option is because of the random nature of price movements. Chapter 10 is the go-to place to find out more about Black-Scholes.

TECHNICAL STUFF

If you're a physicist or chemist, you may recognise part of the Black-Scholes equation as being similar to the diffusion equation that describes how heat moves in solids. The way you solve it is similar, too.

An *option* gives you the right, but not the obligation, to buy or sell a financial asset, such as a bond or share, at a time in the future at a price agreed now. The problem is that because prices move in random fashion you have no idea what the price will be in the future. But you do know how volatile the price is, and so from that you have an idea what range the future price is in. If the asset price is highly volatile, the range of possible future prices is large. So, the price of an option depends on the following factors:

>> The risk-free rate of interest

>> The volatility of the asset

>> The time to expiry

>> The strike price

The Black–Scholes equation makes assumptions about the statistical distribution of the asset returns. You can find the details of this geometric Brownian motion model in Chapter 3. Chapter 10, gives you an alternative way of calculating option prices using probability theory. You don't need the complicated partial differential equation to do this, but you still need the maths that you can find in Chapter 2.

You even have a third way to calculate option prices using *simulation*. With a simulation, you use the idea that asset prices follow a random walk and use your computer to generate lots of paths that the price may take in the future. From this, you can calculate the probability of the price hitting the strike price. You use this probability to work out today's price for the option.

Managing Risk

Quantitative finance and the associated futures and option contracts provide the tools for managing financial risk. With futures, you can fix the price now of purchases or sales that you know you need to make in the future. Options can give you more flexibility in protecting yourself against adverse price movements, but the drawback is that you have to pay a premium up front.

REMEMBER

To quantify the overall riskiness of a portfolio of risky financial assets, you can use the Value at Risk (VaR) number. VaR is widely used by fund managers, banks and companies using derivatives. It gives senior managers an indication of how much risk they're taking on. Regulators use VaR to figure out how much capital a bank must hold. Chapter 15 explains this measure.

Hedging and speculating

You can use options either for speculation or hedging. Options have some *leverage* built in, in other words, the returns can be similar to using borrowed money to buy shares. This similarity makes them attractive to some market participants. You can quickly earn many times more than your original premium, but you can easily end up with nought. This game is for professionals.

TIP

Options are, however, great tools for hedging. If you have a large investment portfolio, but you think that the stock market may go down, you can buy a *put option* which pays you compensation if the market goes down before the option expires.

The price of options is very much influenced by how much time is left before they expire. The sensitivity of the option price to the time to expiry is called *theta*, after the Greek letter. Chapter 11 shows you how to calculate theta and some of the other Greeks, which are useful if you're trading options.

Generating income

Most options written are worthless when they expire. That makes the business of writing them attractive – your customer pays you a premium to buy an option from you and, highly likely, it expires worthless. You can see why bankers like to sell options to their clients and why some become rich from it. Of course, a downside also exists to selling options. The option may not expire worthless. Your client may have had a great insight when buying a call option and that share price shoots up, and you have to pay your client a large payoff. Ouch!

To mitigate the risk of selling options, you can and should *delta hedge*, which means to buy or sell the underlying asset associated with your option. Chapter 11 shows you how to calculate the value of delta for a plain vanilla equity option. If you don't delta hedge and take a *naked* position, then you run the risk of large losses.

Building portfolios and reducing risk

Investment managers build large portfolios of shares, bonds and other financial assets. These portfolios are often part of pension funds or made available to private investors as mutual funds. How much of each asset should the manager buy for the portfolio? This decision depends on the manger's objective but if, like many others, she wishes to maximise returns and reduce risk, she can use a framework called *modern portfolio theory* (MPT for short). MPT is not so modern now as it was first worked out by the economist Markowitz in 1952, but the framework and concepts are still applicable today. You can read about it in Chapter 14.

REMEMBER

For your portfolio, you need to know the following:

>> The expected return of your assets

>> The volatility of your assets

>> The correlations (statistical relationships calculated from price returns) between your assets

From this, you can calculate the portfolio that meets your objectives. That may mean minimising the risk but it may also mean achieving some minimum level of return.

In practice, using MPT has proved difficult because both correlations and expected returns are hard to estimate reliably. But some timeless ideas do exist that were usefully highlighted by MPT. The main one is *diversification*, which has been described as the only free lunch in finance because of its almost universal benefits.

By placing investments over a wide number of assets, you can significantly reduce the risk for the same level of return. Equivalently, you can boost your return for the same level of risk. By paying special attention to the correlation between the assets in your portfolio you gain maximum benefit from diversification. If the correlation between your assets is small or even negative, the benefit is large. Sadly that's not easy to achieve because, for example, many stocks and shares are correlated, but at least you know what to look for. Chapter 14 talks more about tools to manage portfolios, including correlation and diversification.

Computing, Algorithms and Markets

Data can be gathered directly by monitoring activity on the Internet – especially trade data: the price, time and quantity of financial instruments bought and sold. The large amounts of data now captured means that more specialised databases are used to store it and more sophisticated machine learning techniques are used to model it. The better your models are, the more successfully you can trade, and the more data you generate for further analysis. A poet once wisely wrote that you can't feed the hungry on statistics. You can't eat data, but data is now a big industry employing – and feeding – many people. You may be one of them.

Seeing the signal in the noise

The problem with large amounts of data is what to do with it. The first thing is to plot it. Plotting allows you to spot any obvious relationships in the data. You can also see whether any data is missing or bad, which is an all-too-frequent occurrence.

Several kinds of plot are especially useful in finance:

>> **Line plot:** A line plot or chart shows how a value Y (normally shown on the vertical axis) varies with a value indicated on the horizontal axis. The Y values are shown as a continuous line. A line plot is good for showing how a price or interest rate or other variable (Y) changes with time. You can overlay several line plots to compare the movement of several assets.

>> **Scatter plot:** A plot of two variables, X and Y, against each other where each pair of values (X,Y) is drawn as a point. Scatter plots can look like a swarm of bees but are good for revealing relationships you may otherwise not spot. For example, you may want to plot the daily returns of a stock against the daily returns of a stock index to see how correlated they are.

>> **Histogram:** Also known as a *bar chart,* a histogram is great for showing the distribution of the returns of a financial asset.

In Chapter 8 I show you how to investigate a bit deeper into histograms and discover a better representation of the returns distribution.

The Gaussian distribution is so frequently encountered in quantitative finance that you can easily forget that there are often more complex distributions behind your data. To investigate this, you can use the expectation maximisation algorithm, which is a powerful iterative way for fitting data to models. Go to Chapter 8 to find out more about this.

Keeping it simple

If you build models for the expected returns of an asset you're trading or investing in, you need to take great care. If you apply a volatility adjustment to the returns of your asset, the returns look much like Gaussian random noise. Normally, Gaussian noise is what's left after you build a model. So, because markets are nearly efficient, you have little to go on to build a model for returns. Also, you certainly can't expect anything that has much predictive power.

WARNING

The temptation in building a model is to introduce many parameters so as to fit the data. But given the lack of information in the almost random data you encounter in finance, you won't have enough data to accurately determine the parameters of the model.

TIP

Always choose the simplest model possible that describes your data. Chapter 17 shows you in more depth how to fit models in these situations and statistics you can use to determine whether you have a good model or not.

Looking at the finer details of markets

In Chapter 18, you can find out more about markets in real life. Some of this information isn't pretty, but it is important. One important mechanism is *market impact,* the amount by which prices move when you buy or sell an asset. In a way, this impact is the reason markets are important – prices change with supply and demand. The example using Bayes' theorem shows how markets can take on new information and reflect it in changed prices. Doing so is the way that markets can become almost efficient.

Trading at higher frequency

More and more financial trading is completely automated. Computers running powerful algorithms buy and sell stocks and futures contracts often with holding periods of less than a second – sometimes less than a millisecond. This *high frequency trading* (HFT) must use maths and algorithms. It is part of quantitative finance and many quants are involved with the development of trading algorithms.

Chapter 2

Understanding Probability and Statistics

I f you've ever placed a bet on a horse or wondered whether your date for the evening is going to turn up, then you know a bit about probability and statistics. The concepts get more interesting if you have multiple events or events in succession.

For example, if you manage to pick both the first and second place horses in a race (an *exacta*) does that mean you have real skill? This common bet offered by bookies is almost as creative as some of the speculative products offered by bankers.

In this chapter, I start with a few ideas about probability and continue by showing you how they apply to statistical distributions. I examine applications of probability, starting with dice games.

I then look at what happens when you have many random events and a distribution of outcomes.

One distribution of special importance is the Gaussian distribution. It keeps on appearing, and I introduce you to its key properties. I also introduce you to the law of large numbers, which is a more mathematical way of looking at the outcome of a large number of random events.

Probability boils down to a number that refers to a specific situation or event. Statistics, on the other hand, is a way of reasoning from large amounts of data back to some general conclusion – a tool for dealing with data. The later sections of this chapter take you through some widely used results that help in understanding data sets.

The situations I present in this chapter come to look like financial markets, where day-by-day or even millisecond-by-millisecond prices are changing in a highly volatile fashion. So, this chapter gives you a taste of some of the key quantitative tools for understanding how modern financial markets work.

Figuring Probability by Flipping a Coin

Humans have a deep fascination for outcomes that are not certain. That may be because humans learned early that outcomes in many situations are indeed uncertain. Dice games are the most common method used to examine *probability*, which is the chance of an event taking place or a statement being true. Dice games have engaged the interest of many famous mathematicians, and because the games are played for money, studying them can be considered the birth of quantitative finance.

Archaeological evidence shows that games of chance have been played for at least the past 34 centuries. Later (well, much later in fact, only several hundred years ago) mathematicians tried to understand the results of these games of chance and that is what led to what is now called *probability theory*, the mathematical study of randomness.

Probability is the mathematician's way of analysing random events. To define *random* isn't so easy and part of what makes the study of randomness important. The rising of the sun tomorrow isn't a random event but what mathematicians (and almost everyone else) define as *certain*. Every certain event has a probability of one. An impossible event (such as having hot sunshine every day throughout the summer in England) has a probability of zero. However, whether it will be raining tomorrow or not is a random event with a probability somewhere between one and zero. That doesn't mean you have no knowledge of whether it will rain, just that even if you have looked at the most reliable forecasts, you still cannot be certain one way or the other. Equally, the flip of a coin is a random event and so is the throw of a die. The outcomes cannot be predicted, at least if the coin or die isn't loaded in some way.

Philosophers and mathematicians (for example, the French mathematician Laplace) have thought deeply about near-certain events such as the rising of the sun tomorrow. There's no day on record when the sun didn't rise, and the probability of the sun rising tomorrow is very, very close to 1, but that isn't proof that it will continue to rise every day. I'm not trying to be apocalyptic; I'm just using facts to come to conclusions.

WARNING

It's good to be wary of statements about the certainty of something happening or not happening. That can be especially true in finance where it's easy to take some things for granted. Governments and banks can go bankrupt and stock markets do crash; the probability is very small but not zero.

Mathematicians tend to evaluate the probability of a symmetrical coin turning up heads using their usual logic. It seems reasonable to assume that the likelihood of the coin turning up heads is the same as that of its turning up tails.

The probability of tossing a head, written as $P(H)$, and the probability of tossing a tail, $P(T)$, is $P(H) + P(T) = 1$. This is because the only result from tossing a coin is either heads or tails. (If you can flip a coin and make it land on its edge, please ask the publisher of this book for a refund!) Therefore, simple arithmetic shows that the probability of tossing a head is 1/2. However, you can never be sure that the coin is, in fact, symmetric. The experiment of flipping the coin can give you the estimate of the probability. Flip the coin lots and lots of times and count how many times it turns up heads. Divide this by the number of throws, and you get the estimate of the probability of getting heads. Because the number of throws is greater than the number of heads, the estimate is a number between zero and one. This number will converge to 0.5 as long as the number of flips keeps increasing. This is an empirical fact!

REMEMBER

To apply mathematics to the real world, you must make a few assumptions, so you need to be clear what these assumptions are. In this case, ignoring the possibility of a coin landing on its edge is a good one.

The sum of the probability of all possible events is one as you can be certain that one of the possibilities will happen.

A similar analysis can be applied to a fair die: There's a 1/6 probability of throwing any one of the six faces. Here again you have to put on your mathematician's hat. If the die is fair, the likelihoods of getting 1, 2, 3, 4, 5, or 6 are the same.

So, P(i) = 1/6 where i can be any integer from one to six. Now, adding up the probabilities of each way the die can land:

$$\sum_{i=1}^{i=6} P(i) = 1.$$

In common practice, I use the capital Greek letter sigma, Σ, to indicate a summation. This formula follows from the fact that the sum of the probabilities of all possible outcomes must be one.

You can also calculate the probability of a number of events. For example, if tossing a coin and turning up heads is P(H) = 0.5, then the probability of tossing two heads in succession is P(H)P(H) = 0.5 × 0.5 = 0.25. Because landing a head on the first toss is *independent* of whether you land a head on the second toss, you must multiply the probability of the individual events to get the probability of the joint event of getting two heads. Independence is an important concept in quantitative finance. You can frequently assume that the return of a financial asset on a given day is independent of the return on the previous day.

TIP

The most common definition for the return, r_n, of a financial asset on day, n, in terms of the price, p_n, on day n is:

$$r_n = \frac{(p_n - p_{n-1})}{p_{n-1}}.$$

Likewise, the probability of tossing two tails in succession is P(T)P(T) = 0.5 × 0.5 = 0.25. You need to take care in figuring the probability of tossing a head and a tail. Either the head or the tail can be tossed first, so you have two ways of getting a head and a tail. In the case of tossing a head first P(H)P(T) = 0.5 × 0.5 = 0.25 and a tail first P(T)P(H) = 0.5 × 0.5 = 0.25. Adding up these two probabilities P(T)P(H) + P(H)P(T) = 0.5 gives you the probability of a head and a tail, irrespective of which face came up first.

Applying these ideas to a die, you can calculate the probability of rolling either a three or a four, for example. To do this, you add the probabilities because the events of rolling a three or a four are *disjoint*, meaning that they're completely different and can't happen together. So the probability of rolling either a three or a four is 1/6 + 1/6 = 1/3.

When I calculated the probability of both heads and tails in two tosses, I came up with the number 0.5. I got this answer using the idea of disjoint events – the event of tossing a head first and then a tail is disjoint from first tossing a tail and then a head. So you must add the probabilities of these events to get the overall probability of getting a head and a tail in two tosses.

To make this clear in another way, use the example of a deck of cards. The probability of drawing a king or a spade isn't simply P(King)+P(Spade) because, of course, you can draw the king of spades. So the events of drawing a king or a spade are not disjoint and you need to take into account the probability of drawing the king of spades.

Probability can be summarised in a few short statements:

>> A probability is a number between zero and one.

>> For a certain event, the probability is exactly one.

>> For disjoint events, the probability of at least one event happening is the sum of the individual probabilities for the events.

>> For independent events, the probability of both of them happening is the product of the individual probabilities for the events.

You may find it amazing, but that's all you really need to know about probability.

Playing a game

Now that you're familiar with coin flipping, I'd like to challenge you to a game. I'll flip a coin again and again until it turns up heads. If it turns up heads on the first flip, I'll give you £2. If it turns up heads for the first time on the second flip, I'll give you £4. If it turns up heads for the first time on the third flip, I'll give you £2^3 = £8. And if it turns up heads on the nth flip I'll give you £2^n. How much are you prepared to pay me to play this game?

To work out how much you may win, you need to calculate some probabilities. The probability of the coin turning up heads is always 0.5, and the probability the coin turns up tails is also 0.5. If heads appears first on the nth (say, third) flip, then all previous flips must have been tails. The probability of that is $1/2^{(n-1)}$ (so 0.5^2 if n = 3). You must now multiply again by 0.5 to get the probability of heads on the nth flip preceded by tails on the previous (n−1) flips. This works out as $1/2^n$ (so 0.5 × 0.5^2 = 0.5^3 if n = 3).

So, heads turn up for the first time on the nth flip with probability $1/2^n$. If heads turns up first on the nth flip, then you win £2^n. The total *expected* pay-off (the amount, on average, you receive for winning) is then:

$$£2/2 + £2^2/2^2 + £2^3/2^3 + \ldots$$

However, this is just a series of 1s going on forever that adds up to infinity. So, then, would you pay me your life savings to play this game in the hope of a staggering return? If heads came up first, you may be disappointed at receiving a mere £2 for your savings; but if you had to wait a long time for heads to turn up but eventually it did and you were due a substantial pay off, I may not be able to pay out your winnings. I don't think that the Central Bank would print large amounts of money to help me out. This is an extreme example in which an unlikely event plays a significant role. You may notice a spooky similarity to certain recent events in financial markets even though this game was invented several hundred years ago.

Flipping more coins

Another fun experiment with a coin is to keep on flipping it again and again to see how many times heads comes up. Sometimes heads follows tails and at other times there can be long series of either heads or tails.

REMEMBER

During long sequences of heads or tails, you can easily believe that you have a higher than average probability of the other side turning up to even things up a bit. This *gambler's fallacy*, however, isn't valid. The coin has no memory. On each flip, the probability of heads remains 0.5, as does the probability for tails.

An important idea that comes out of experimenting with gambling games is the *Law of Large Numbers*. It states that the average result from a large number of trials (such as coin tossing) should be close to the expected value (0.5 for tossing heads) and will become closer as more trials are performed. I'll show you how this works.

If H_n is the total number of heads (for example, 4) in the first n tosses (for example, 8) then H_n/n should tend towards 0.5 (so, 4/8 = 0.5). Figure 2-1 graphs 1,000 coin tosses.

The chart fluctuates less and less after more coin flips and the fraction of heads *converges* (gets closer and closer) towards 0.5. This is an example of the Law of Large Numbers. You'd be surprised though at how many tosses it takes for the chart to settle down to the expected average.

I examine this further by plotting $H_n - n/2$ where n/2 is the expected number of heads after n tosses. The line in Figure 2-2 wanders about and shows that convergence isn't good. It's disconcerting that although the fraction of heads tossed tends towards 0.5 in relative terms, in absolute terms, the number of heads can wander further and further away from the expected value of n/2. You may have guessed already that this unstable sequence, called a *random walk*, can be used as a model for how share prices change with time.

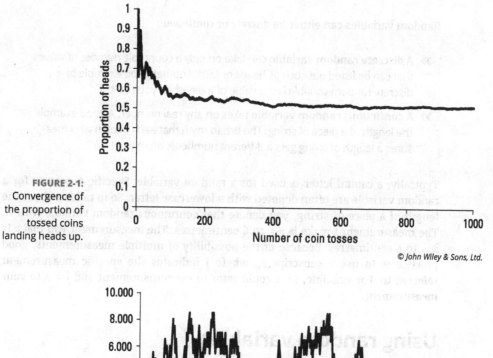

FIGURE 2-1:
Convergence of
the proportion of
tossed coins
landing heads up.

Proportion of heads (y-axis), Number of coin tosses (x-axis)

© John Wiley & Sons, Ltd.

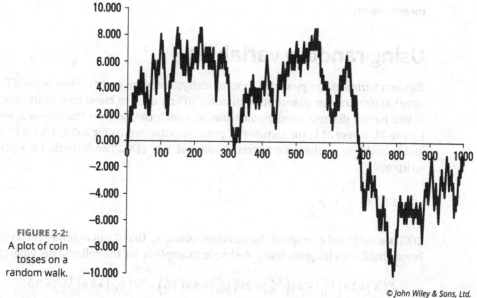

FIGURE 2-2:
A plot of coin
tosses on a
random walk.

© John Wiley & Sons, Ltd.

Defining Random Variables

A *random variable* is a measurement or characteristic that takes on its value by
chance. A random variable is different from other variables in mathematics: you
don't know what its value is before an experiment or trial has been done.

Random variables can either be *discrete* or *continuous:*

>> A **discrete random variable** can take on only a countable number of values that can be listed out such as heads or tails. Another good example of a discrete random variable is the value of a die when you roll it.

>> A **continuous random variable** takes on any real number. A good example is the length of a piece of string. The urban myth that each person who measures a length of string gets a different number is often true!

Typically, a capital letter is used for a random variable. Specific outcomes for a random variable are often denoted with a lowercase letter. So in talking about the length of a piece of string, you denote that continuous random variable with X. The measurement I make is x = 10.6 centimetres. The measurement you make is x = 10.4 centimetres. Because of the possibility of multiple measurements, good practice is to use a subscript x_j, where j indicates the specific measurement referred to. For example, j = 1 could refer to my measurement and j = 2 to your measurement.

Using random variables

Random variables are powerful tools to analyse random events. They make a frequent appearance in quantitative finance, so you need to know how to use them. If you have a discrete random variable, X, which can take on the values x_j with j = 1 to M, where M is the number of possible outcomes (6 for a die; 2 for a coin), and probability p_j, then the expected value of X is E(X). The formula for E(X) is written:

$$E(X) = \sum_{j=1}^{j=M} x_j p_j.$$

E(X) is a weighted average of the possible values, x_j, that X can assume. Each value is weighted with its probability. A simple example is for the roll of a die where:

$$E(X) = 1 \times \left(\frac{1}{6} \right) + 2 \times \left(\frac{1}{6} \right) + 3 \times \left(\frac{1}{6} \right) + 4 \times \left(\frac{1}{6} \right) + 5 \times \left(\frac{1}{6} \right) + 6 \times \left(\frac{1}{6} \right) = 3.5.$$

Clearly you will never roll a three and a half, but this number, E(X), is the expected or average value from rolling a fair die.

The formula for expected value of a continuous random variable is slightly different, and I present it in the next section on statistical distributions.

Building distributions with random variables

For statisticians, the word *distribution* is a big one. For a data set, the *distribution* is the possible values of the data and their probability or frequency of occurrence. A data set may be all the measurements of the length of a piece of string or the daily share price returns for a stock over the past ten years.

The idea is to use random variables to model or represent real data, such as the returns of a financial asset. The distribution of the returns is a property of the random variable. This is a powerful abstract idea and one used all the time in quantitative finance. It can seem very strange, especially if you believe that the past is known with certainty, although in fact it never is. You may have a great historical data set, but there's always inherent uncertainty about the future. Probability is a natural tool for understanding this uncertainty. For example, you can guess suitable probability models from past data, and assuming that the model itself doesn't change through time, you'll have at least some idea about the likely outcomes in the future, which can be useful for forecasting.

I again use the example of rolling a die and illustrate the idea of a probability distribution. Table 2-1 shows the probability distribution for a fair die. P(x) indicates the probability distribution function for a fair die.

TABLE 2-1 Probability Distribution for Rolling a Fair Die

Outcome	Probability
1	1/6
2	1/6
3	1/6
4	1/6
5	1/6
6	1/6

Continuous random variables also have a probability distribution function, also designated with p(x), but in this case, x is a continuous variable.

A simple commonly occurring continuous distribution is the uniform distribution between zero and one as shown in Figure 2-3. The value of x can be any real number between zero and one. Because each value is equally likely, the chart is a straight line.

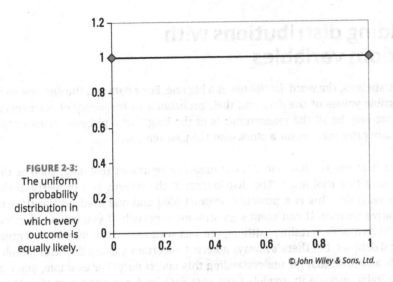

© John Wiley & Sons, Ltd.

This is a good place to explain how to use the continuous random distribution. In the previous section, I show how to calculate the expectation of a discrete random variable. To calculate the expectation for a continuous random variable, you use the probability distribution p(x). The formula is:

$$E(X) = \int_{-\infty}^{\infty} xp(x)dx.$$

The symbol ∞ indicates *infinity* – a huge number bigger than any known number.

TECHNICAL
STUFF

The formula for the expectation of a continuous random variable involves an integral, which is a way of summing over all of the possible outcomes of the random variable X. It's indicated by the extended S symbol.

For the uniform continuous distribution, the possible outcomes, x, take values only between zero and one, and p(x) = 1, so the integral takes the simpler form:

$$E(X) = \int_0^1 xdx.$$

If you can remember a bit of calculus, the value of this integral is 0.5. This makes lots of sense because the expected value for a number drawn from a uniform distribution between zero and one must surely be 0.5.

The chart in Figure 2-3 is a theoretical distribution and a perfect straight line. How does this work with real data? This isn't quite the real world of financial data. You can use a spreadsheet to generate numbers drawn from a uniform random distribution (and a normal distribution). Figure 2-4 shows the result of plotting the outputs of 200 numbers that I know follow the uniform distribution. On the vertical axis is the count of how many of the numbers pulled from the uniform random distribution lie within the ranges given on the x-axis, which is split into ten bins. These bins are metaphorical: in the same way that recycling sites have bins for green, brown and clear glass so as to separate bottles of different colours, this distribution has bins for numbers of different magnitude. In other words, after pulling a number from the distribution, it goes into a bin depending on its value. The first bin is from 0 to 0.1. The next bin is from 0.1 to 0.2 and so on.

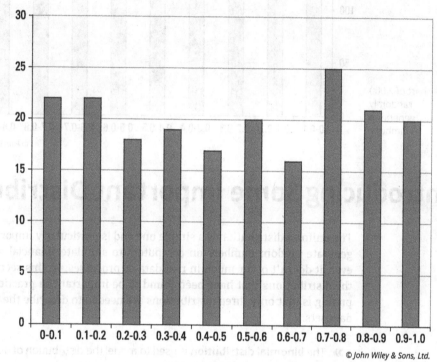

FIGURE 2-4:
A chart of 200 randomly generated numbers.

© John Wiley & Sons, Ltd.

Because you have 200 numbers and 10 bins, the expected number for each bin is 20. However, some bins have more than 20 and some less than 20, which is probably just what you expect because the 200 numbers are random. Figure 2-5 shows the chart redrawn after using 2,000 numbers in the experiment. It looks more like a straight line but has definite deviations.

REMEMBER

It can be hugely misleading to use small data sets to draw conclusions about financial variables. Many financial variables exhibit randomness and make it easy to spot a pattern that isn't really there.

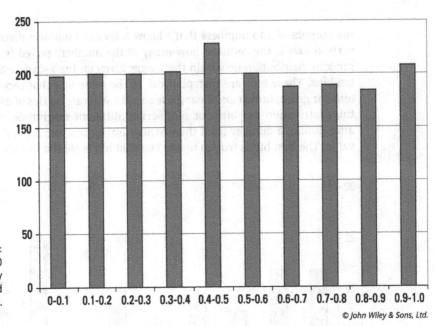

© John Wiley & Sons, Ltd.

FIGURE 2-5:
A chart of 2,000
randomly
generated
numbers.

Introducing Some Important Distributions

The uniform distribution is a simple one and is particularly important as a way to generate random numbers on computers to simulate financial variables. However, it doesn't occur much in real data or processes. In this section, I show you the distributions that have been found to be important in practice. What is surprising is that only three distributions are needed to describe the majority of real data sets:

>> The **binomial distribution** is used to model the distribution of outcomes for discrete events such as coin tosses.

>> The **Gaussian**, or **normal**, **distribution** is used to model financial returns.

>> The **Poisson distribution** is used to model the distribution of waiting times – how long you wait at a supermarket checkout or how long it takes for your trade to be executed, for example.

This distribution isn't so important in finance but it arises frequently in situations such as waiting for something – a buyer to come along for an offered contract, for example – so make sure that you know about it. The nearby sidebar, 'Describing the Poisson distribution' explains it.

The importance of these three was discovered several hundred years ago after scientists investigated many data sets from diverse fields. The most famous distribution of all is the Gaussian, or normal, distribution, named after a German mathematician. He proved a famous result called the central limit theorem, which explains why the distribution occurs so frequently. (I examine this result and its consequences in the next chapter.)

REMEMBER

Although the Gaussian distribution gives a good approximation to the returns on most financial assets such as shares and bonds, it certainly does not hold exactly. In fact, almost all traded securities systematically differ from the Gaussian distribution. The successful application of quantitative finance involves understanding how to tweak models derived using a Gaussian assumption to fit a non-Gaussian world. The expression *tail events* refers to the fact that events that occur in the tail of a Gaussian distribution – a long way from the average – actually happen more frequently than expected. The Gaussian gives a poor estimate for the occurrence of rare events such as market crashes.

Working with a binomial distribution

The most important discrete distribution is the binomial distribution, which originates more from probability than statistics. In that sense, this distribution is quite fundamental and a good place to start in discussing theoretical distributions. The binomial distribution is used in situations with two possible outcomes, such as for a coin flip or a simple yes or no such as a referendum.

If you have n trials or events, you have the probability, p, of x successes. You write this as p(x;u,n) where u is the probability of success in an individual trial. The probability of failure in an individual trial is (1 – u). (See the section 'Figuring Probability by Flipping a Coin' earlier in the chapter.) The formula for p is:

$$p(x;u,n) = u^x (1-u)^{n-x} \binom{n}{x}.$$

The u^x is the probability of success in x events, $(1-u)^{n-x}$ is the probability of failure in the remaining (n – x) events. The remaining part of the formula,

$$\binom{n}{x} = \frac{n!}{x!(n-x)!},$$

is the binomial coefficient that gives the number of ways that x objects can be arranged amongst n objects. The notation n! means n(n – 1)(n – 2) . . . 3.2·1 and is the number of ways of arranging n distinct objects. By definition 0! = 1.

The binomial distribution is a basic distribution from which others can be derived as you can sometimes model events as the result of many binary events.

DESCRIBING THE POISSON DISTRIBUTION

Although the binomial distribution isn't frequently used in quantitative finance, a special limiting case called the Poisson distribution is important. The binomial distribution is useful for discrete events (such as coin tosses), but events in continuous time such as waiting for a bus can be important as well. The timetable says busses arrive every ten minutes, but you know from hard experience that you can wait longer and that several busses can come along all at once. How do you calculate the probability of these possibilities?

You use the Poisson distribution in which you have an event rate, λ, which is the number of events in a time interval. If this interval is divided into n tiny intervals in each of which you expect an event with probability p = λ/n, you can use the binomial distribution to calculate the probability of x events in these intervals. Making n bigger and bigger so that the interval is split indefinitely, the binomial distribution becomes the Poisson distribution for x events when the expected number is λ:

$$P(x, \lambda) = \frac{e^{-\lambda} \lambda^x}{x!}.$$

This formula has many applications and is frequently used to model queues and waiting times, but also has applications to rare events such as jumps in commodity prices.

Recognising the Gaussian, or normal, distribution

The Gaussian, or normal, probability distribution function is easily the most important distribution in quantitative finance. That's because you can use it as a simple model for the returns of a financial asset. The reason it crops up so frequently in quantitative finance is based on a deep result from statistics called the *central limit theorem*, which I describe in detail in Chapter 3. What it says is that if you have a random variable that's the sum of many other random variables, then it tends towards the Gaussian distribution. So the Gaussian distribution is important whenever there are many influences on a variable (such as a financial return). This sounds like the real world and that's why the Gaussian distribution is so important. It's given by the formula:

$$p(x; \mu, \sigma) = \frac{1}{\sigma\sqrt{2\pi}} e^{-(x-\mu)^2/2\sigma^2}$$

where the parameters are the mean of the data, μ, and the standard deviation, σ. I explain more about the mean and the standard deviation and how to calculate them in the next section. Unlike the binomial distribution, the variable x here is continuous rather than discrete and so can take any value between −∞ and ∞.

REMEMBER

The *mean* is the typical or expected value for a data set and the *standard deviation* is a measure of its dispersion or spread. The more jumpy or noisy a dataset is, the higher its standard deviation.

A picture of the Gaussian probability density with various standard deviations is shown in Figure 2-6.

FIGURE 2-6: Gaussian probability density for various values of the standard deviation.

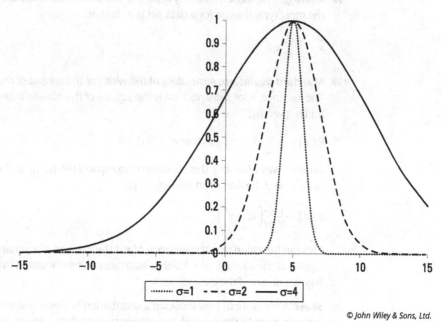

© John Wiley & Sons, Ltd.

The curves are all centred on x = 5 and have values spread around on either side.

The higher the value of sigma, the more spread the values have. The Gaussian distribution can be derived as the limiting case of a binomial distribution when n becomes larger and larger. It has been found to be widely applicable. Measurement errors in most fields of science have been found to follow a Gaussian distribution and it also proves to be a reasonable approximation to financial return data. Chapter 3 examines this in lots of detail.

Describing real distributions

In the preceding sections I examine theoretical distributions that originate from probability theory, which are useful if you know that these distributions apply to your data. In this section I show how to calculate some statistics from real data so that you can figure out what distribution your data is following.

I use the symbol xi to represent the ith element in a data set with N elements. In other words, I have a random variable, X, with samples, x_i . For example, x_i may be the exchange rate of the US dollar to pound Sterling on the ith day of the year.

A distribution can be characterised by the following statistics:

>> **Average:** The most frequently reported statistic. The average is a measure of the most typical value for a data set is as follows:

$$\bar{x} = \frac{1}{N}\sum_{i=1}^{N} x_i.$$

>> **Standard deviation:** A measure of the width or the spread of the distribution. The variance, V, of a distribution is the square of the standard deviation, σ, and is given by:

$$V(x) = \frac{1}{N}\sum_{i=1}^{N}(x_i - \bar{x})^2, \text{ so that } \sigma^2 = V(x).$$

Another way of writing this equation is to expand the terms in the bracket and to use the definition of an average to get

$$V(x) = \frac{1}{N}\sum_{i=1}^{N}\left(x_i^2 - \bar{x}^2\right).$$

This can be stated that the variance of x is the average of x squared less the square of the average of x. Further statistics can be calculated that depend on higher powers of the data values x.

>> **Skew:** A measure of how lopsided a distribution is. Positive skewed data extends more to the right while negative skewed data extends more to the left. The skew is

$$\gamma = \frac{1}{N\sigma^3}\sum_{i=1}^{N}(x_i - \bar{x})^3.$$

>> **Kurtosis:** Although it sounds like a disease, kurtosis is measure of the fatness of the distribution's tails. Almost all financial assets have *positive kurtosis* meaning that there are more values in the tails of the distribution than expected in a normal distribution. Large disruptive events are more common than expected!

Kurtosis is calculated from the fourth power of x:

$$\kappa = \frac{1}{N\sigma^4}\sum_{i=1}^{N}(x_i - \bar{x})^4 - 3.$$

For a Gaussian distribution, k is zero.

To illustrate these statistics, I downloaded 24 years of daily closing price data on the DAX from Yahoo! Finance. The DAX is an index that gives an indication of the overall level of the German stock markets by using the share price of the 30 largest companies. (Chapter 4 talks more about indices.) Figure 2-7 is a chart of the data in which I compare the DAX index with a Gaussian distribution with the same mean and standard deviation.

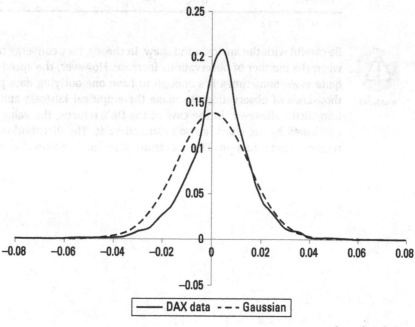

Source: Deutsche Borse

FIGURE 2-7: Comparison of empirical DAX distribution of returns and a Gaussian distribution.

Although the mean and the standard deviation of the Gaussian are the same as for the DAX data, the charts are a little bit different. The empirical DAX data has a narrower peak near the centre and, although they're not easy to see, higher values at the extremes from about ±0.04. Table 2-2 compares the statistics for the Gaussian curve and the DAX data showing that the data has slight positive skew and is reasonably kurtotic.

So, I introduce you to the Gaussian distribution and the first dataset you look at doesn't appear to follow this law. Welcome to quantitative finance! There's nothing wrong with the statistics and probability in this chapter; it's just that reality is a bit more complicated than you may anticipate as Table 2-2 shows.

TABLE 2-2

Comparing Expected and Real-World Distributions

	Expected Gaussian Distribution	Actual DAX Data
Mean	0.0004	0.0004
Standard deviation	0.014	0.014
Skew	0	0.04
Kurtosis	0	5

WARNING

Be careful with the kurtosis and skew. In theory, they converge to their true values when the number of observations increase. However, the speed of convergence is quite slow. Sometimes it's enough to have one outlying data point out of many thousands of observations to make the empirical kurtosis and skew completely unrealistic. However, in the case of the DAX returns, the value of the kurtosis is confirmed by the chart, so you can believe it. The distribution of the DAX daily returns is not Gaussian. The data from other stock indices shows a similar effect.

Chapter 3

Taking a Look at Random Behaviours

I n this chapter, I use random numbers to build what's called a *random walk*, which is a way of using probability and statistics to create models of the price movement of financial assets. As the name suggests, a random walk consists of a sequence of random steps. Random walks are a mathematical idea as well as a nice description of the stock market. You can use them to price options or to figure out how risky a portfolio of investments is. To go on a random walk, you need random numbers, so I also talk about how to generate them with a computer.

Random walks don't come in just one variety. I also explain the *mean-reverting* walk, which keeps heading back to where it began. Sometimes home is a nice place to be.

Setting Up a Random Walk

You form random walks by adding together random numbers from the same distribution. I call the random numbers X_i where the i subscript indicates that there are many numbers. In fact, I'll assume that there are N of them so that i can take the values from one up to N. To begin with, I assume that X_i has a mean value of zero. The distribution may be a binomial distribution, in which X_i is one value or another, or a normal distribution, in which X_i takes on a continuous range of values between $-\infty$ and ∞. In each of these random steps, X can represent the return of a financial asset.

In this section, I show you how to build a random walk and then make the steps smaller and smaller until the movement becomes a continuous process. This continuous process, or Brownian motion, is the basis for a model of market behaviour used in pricing options. Both the discrete and continuous versions of the motion are important and useful as they can both be used as the basis for pricing options.

REMEMBER

It may seem strange that stock prices follow a random pattern. But a number of factors affect the price of a stock or investment commodity in ways that are almost impossible to predict:

>> **Global economic news:** Because the world economy is so connected, important news from the Far East and North America has implications for Europe – and vice versa.

>> **Factors specific to a company:** New profit information can have a big impact on a stock price as can new information on a company's competitors.

>> **Sales of the stock or commodity:** Shares and commodities such as crude oil are constantly being bought and sold. Any predictable patterns in the price movement are exploited by traders to make a profit. They buy or sell immediately when new information comes to the market. The effect of this trading is to move the price. Traders even try to anticipate news so as to get their trades in before the news is announced.

The result of all this information and the frantic trading activity in which market participants try to anticipate future price movements is to make price movements random.

You can simulate these models using a computer spreadsheet such as Microsoft Excel, and I show you how to do that in the later section, 'Getting random with Excel'.

You can make the steps in a random walk smaller and smaller until they become infinitesimal so that you can use calculus to analyse the movements. Then the walk becomes what's called *Brownian motion*. When the Brownian motion is used as a model for relative or percentage returns rather than additive returns, you call it a *geometric Brownian motion*.

REMEMBER

I talk more about returns in Chapter 4 and explain several definitions. However, if the price of a financial asset today is P_n and the price yesterday was P_{n-1}, then the most common definition of *return* is $(P_n - P_{n-1})/P_{n-1}$ which is the price difference between today and yesterday expressed as a ratio to the price yesterday. It expresses how much more (or less) you have today compared with yesterday and is the quantity most investors want to know.

This random motion is the key assumption behind the most important model for the pricing of derivatives such as equity options.

TECHNICAL STUFF

Brownian motion got its name from a botanist called Robert Brown who observed pollen particles under a microscope. He saw that they jiggled about apparently moved at random by an invisible force. Mysterious! It turns out that molecules of water not visible in a microscope cause this movement. In financial markets, the frequent changes in price, up or down, are caused by many trades that move the price as the asset is bought and sold.

Stepping in just two directions

The steps in this first random walk are X_i where X_i can only be +1 or −1. You can use this assignment for X_i as the model for a walk in which only two possible outcomes exist – a person disoriented by fog can step only to the left or right. Remember though, you can use a random walk to represent the price movements of financial assets such as stock prices or commodity prices such as crude oil. (Special forms of random walks can represent interest rate movements.)

Now, in the case of the fog-bound walker, after she has taken N steps, her position is: $R_N = X_1 + X_2 + X_3 + \ldots + X_N$.

Firstly, you want to know the average or expected value of R_N. It's good to know whether your walk is getting somewhere or, on average, just staying in the same place. That's easy to discover as the value is just the sum of the expected value of each of the Xs:

$$E(R_N) = \sum_{i=1}^{N} E(X_i).$$

But each X_i has an expected value of zero because the walker can move to the left or the right with equal probability. So the expected value of R_N, which is a sum of all the X_is, is itself zero. On average, the walker stays in the same place.

Next, you want to find the expected value of the square of R_N. The reason is that although, on average, the walker gets nowhere, she certainly isn't standing at the point of origin all the time. Because the square of a number is always positive, the average of the squared distance gives you an idea of how far your subject moves out from the origin – in the example, the disoriented walker moving to the right or the left. Over time, the subject drifts away from the origin and spends an increasing time away from it. But how far away? There are lots of terms in the equation for the square of R_N, but the terms are of only two types. The first type are terms such as $E(X_i X_j)$ with $i \neq j$. These terms are all equal to zero. The four possible outcomes you have to average over are:

$$(X_i = 1, X_j = 1)$$
$$(X_i = 1, X_j = -1)$$
$$(X_i = -1, X_j = 1)$$
$$(X_i = -1, X_j = -1).$$

The sum of these products is: $1 + (-1) + (-1) + 1 = 0$.

To calculate the average of R_N squared involves only the terms of the second type, $E(X_i^2)$, for which $i = j$. But each term is equal to one and so, finally, you get the simple and memorable result:

$$E(R_N^2) = N.$$

Think of it this way: if you walk out of the pub and head briskly to the bus stop, you arrive in N steps. If you leave the pub and head to the bus stop in random fashion (perhaps you've had one too many), after N steps the average of the squared distance is N. After taking the square root, the likely distance you'll have travelled is only $\sqrt{N}$, and you may have headed in the wrong direction too. A taxi may be the better option.

Getting somewhere on your walk

In this section, I construct a random walk with *drift*. A walk with drift gets somewhere. Although each step of the walk depends on a random variable, it favours a particular direction, which means that there is a bias in the walk. This makes the walk more realistic as a description of the movement of financial assets.

Each step takes a time, Δ, so that this walk includes the idea of motion rather than just counting steps. The walker makes a jump of distance, δ, with probability, p, upwards and probability $(1-p)$ downwards. The formula that summarises this looks like the following:

$$X_i = \begin{cases} \delta \text{ with probability } p \\ -\delta \text{ with probability } 1-p. \end{cases}$$

A big difference between this random walk and the first one in this section is that the expected value of X is not zero. The walker, on average, gets somewhere. This is important when you apply these results to financial time series.

The expected value, $V(X) = E\left((X - E(X))^2\right)$, of a random variable, X, is given by the formula:

$$E(X).$$

This averages the possible values, X_i, of the distribution with the probability, p_j, for each possible value. (Chapter 2 has more details on random distributions.) The quantity X with no subscript refers to a random variable whereas X_i with a subscript refers to the specific numerical values.

The expected value of X for this walk is: $E(X) = \sum_{j=1}^{N} X_j p_j$.

V(X), the variance of X, can be calculated with the formula:

$$E(X) = \delta p + (-\delta)(1 - p) = (2p - 1)\delta.$$

This can be expanded using the probabilities, p and $(1 - p)$, for up and down moves:

$$V(X) = p(\delta - E(X))^2 + (1 - p)(-\delta - E(X))^2.$$

Sparing you the algebraic details of substituting for E(X) into the formula for V(X), the answer is: $V(X) = 4p(1 - p)\delta^2$.

At time, t, the walker arrives at point X: $X(t) = X_1 + X_2 + X_3 + \ldots + X_N$.

The Nth step is taken at the time $t = N\Delta$, because each of the steps takes a time, Δ. Using the central limit theorem (see the upcoming section), you can calculate the expected location and the variance (square of the standard deviation) of the location, X(t), from the properties of the individual steps. The expected location is just the number of steps, N, multiplied by the mean location of a single step. Likewise the variance of X(t) is N times the variance of a single step so that:

$$E(X(t)) = \frac{t}{\Delta}(2p - 1)\delta$$
$$V(X(t)) = \frac{t}{\Delta}(4p)(1 - p)\delta^2.$$

Taking smaller and smaller steps

In this section, I do something that may seem strange: I shrink the steps to smaller and smaller sizes. At the same time, I make the time, Δ, for each step shorter and shorter, and I also make the probability of an upwards or downward step close to 0.5 but not exactly. I'm not doing this on a whim, and although modern finance works on very short timescales, that's not the only reason. Using small steps allows you to use calculus to analyse these random motions which proves helpful if you wish to work out the price of options. This random walk drifts only slightly because the probability, p, is close to half. You can simplify the equations for the variance, V(X(t)), and the expected location, E(X(t)), so that the time dependence becomes clear by writing them as:

$$E\big(X(t)\big) = \mu t$$
$$V\big(X(t)\big) = \sigma^2 t.$$

Mu (μ) is the drift parameter of this random walk and sigma (σ) is usually referred to as the volatility. Comparing the two equations for the variance of X shows that $\delta^2 = \sigma^2 \Delta$ if the probability, p, is approximately equal to 0.5. This equation relates the square of the step size, δ, to the time step, Δ, via the volatility parameter, σ.

You can also compare the two equations for the expected value of X and, with a little bit of algebra, show that:

$$p = \frac{1}{2}\left(1 + \frac{\mu}{\sigma}\sqrt{\Delta}\right).$$

The probability, p, is slightly larger than 0.5 if μ is positive.

In the real world of finance, trading can happen at many different time scales: slowly with occasional trades throughout the year or at high frequency with possibly only milliseconds between trades. The time series used by these different participants can have large steps of days or weeks or tiny steps of milliseconds. The analysis here indicates that, irrespective of time scale, it can still be applied to markets. This is a special feature of the Brownian motion although other motions also have this feature of looking similar at different timescales.

Averaging with the Central Limit Theorem

The central limit theorem is an important result in probability and statistics. This result isn't easy to prove (and I don't do it here) but is quite easy to state and apply.

REMEMBER

The *central limit theorem* can be stated as:

> If $X_1, X_2, X_3, \ldots, X_N$ are independent random variables, each having the same distribution with expected value μ and standard deviation σ, then the sum $X_1 + X_2 + X_3 + \ldots + X_N$ has an approximately normal distribution with expected value $N\mu$ and standard deviation $\sigma\sqrt{N}$ when N is sufficiently large.

The central limit theorem explains why the Gaussian, or normal, distribution is so important and occurs in many different situations whether in finance, measuring the blood pressure of many people or explaining all of those near misses when you're trying to hit the bull's eye on the darts board in the pub.

A statistical distribution tells you the probability with which each value, X_i, of a random variable, X, occurs. In quantitative finance, the random variable X is usually the return of a financial asset so the return distribution is key information about what to expect from a financial asset.

The standard deviation, σ, is a measure of the amount of variation or dispersion in a random distribution. The larger the standard deviation, the more dispersed the numbers are from the average, or mean. Another way of stating the central limit theorem is that if you take the N random variables, subtract the expected value $N\mu$ and divide by the standard deviation $\sigma\sqrt{N}$, then the probability, P, of that value being less than a number, x, is given by the cumulative normal distribution:

$$P\left(\frac{X_1 + X_2 + ... + X_N - N\mu}{\sigma\sqrt{N}} < x\right) \to \Phi(x) = \frac{1}{\sqrt{2\pi}} \int_{-\infty}^{x} e^{-\frac{x^2}{2}} dx.$$

The big thing to keep in mind is that it doesn't matter what the distribution of the individual random variable X is. The process of combining random variables together leads to the normal distribution – a mathematical result that's not at first easy to grasp but explains why the normal distribution is so ubiquitous. The distribution of the random variables can be discrete, with X taking only the values ±1 or it can be a continuous distribution that isn't normal. See Chapter 2 if you're not familiar with these two types of distribution.

The central limit theorem is a bit vague (surprising for mathematicians, but nobody's perfect) about how many random variables you need before their sum becomes normal, but experience shows that N can be quite small. The following example shows the central limit theorem in action: start with 12 uniform distributions and end up with a close approximation to the normal distribution.

Take X as the uniform distribution. X can take any value between zero and one with equal probability. No value is more likely than any other. Now add together 12 of these distributions. I did this in an Excel spreadsheet, generated 5,000 numbers and calculated some statistics from them. The results are shown in Table 3-1.

Table 3-1 shows that the numbers lie between −3.25 and 3.32 and are close to a *standard normal distribution*, which has a mean of zero and a standard deviation of one.

TABLE 3-1	Statistics of 5,000 Random Numbers	
Statistic		Value
Maximum Value		3.32
Minimum Value		−3.25
Average Value		0.002
Standard Deviation		1.004

REMEMBER

Almost all – 99.7 per cent – of the numbers from a normal distribution lie within three standard deviations of the mean.

A few numbers in the example lie slightly beyond three standard deviations but that's understandable because the dataset of 5,000 is quite large. So the numbers seem to be normal.

Figure 3-1 shows the results of graphing the results by plotting them in *bins*, or ranges, of width 0.1 starting from −3 to −2.9 and ending in 2.9 to 3. The dotted line shows the data generated from the uniform distributions whilst the solid line is a plot of a normal distribution with the same mean and standard deviation as the data. Clearly, you need more than 5,000 numbers to get perfect agreement, but it's remarkable how the 12 uniform distributions approximate the normal distribution.

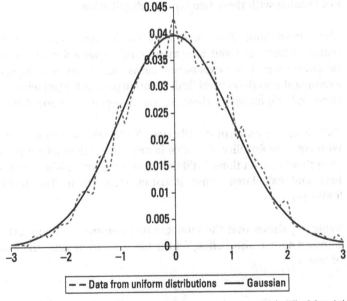

FIGURE 3-1:
Illustrating the
central limit
theorem with
random data.

© *John Wiley & Sons, Ltd.*

Moving Like the Stock Market

In this section, I construct a random walk that you can use as a model for stock market prices as well as prices of equity options and commodity future options.

The starting point is the initial price of the share or equity index which I call S_0. The price changes every Δ time units. At each time step the price changes by a factor of δ with probability, p, for an upward step and $(1-p)$ for a downward step. The share price at time, t, is: $S(t) = S(0)(1+X_1)(1+X_2) \times \cdots \times (1+X_N)$.

Notice that the random numbers, X_i, are used to multiply the current share price by a factor $(1+X_i)$ rather than to add to it.

REMEMBER

In the notation X_i, remember that i can take the value i = 1 up to the last step in the walk step N. This fact means that the fractional or percentage change in the share price is what follows a random series and not the absolute change.

The preceding equation is a bit awkward to cope with so you can use a trick well loved by mathematicians and take the logarithm. First, divide both sides of the equation by S(0):

$$\log \frac{S(t)}{S(0)} = \sum_{i=1}^{N} \log(1+X_i).$$

TECHNICAL STUFF

The logarithm of a product of numbers is equal to the sum of the logarithms: $\log(ab) = \log(a) + \log(b)$. I admit it: I had a book of log tables at school but calculators had just been invented. Some knowledge is timeless.

The going gets tough here, as you now use a result from calculus in which you expand the logarithm on the right-hand side in powers of x:

$$\ln(1+x) = x - \frac{x^2}{2} + \frac{x^3}{3} - \dots \quad \text{for } |x| < 1.$$

The absolute value of x (meaning you don't take into account the sign of x) must be less than 1 to use this formula, but because you use small steps in this random walk, that's always true. Now I can write the right side of the equation for the log of the share price as:

$$\ln \frac{S(t)}{S_0} = \sum_{i=1}^{N} X_i - \frac{1}{2} \sum_{i=1}^{N} X_i^2.$$

The first summation on the right side looks just like a random walk in the preceding section 'Taking smaller and smaller steps'. That, in fact, is the reason for using logarithms: so that the right-hand side looks familiar.

Additions are easier to handle than multiplications. The second term on the right side is new but turns out to be easy to calculate. Remember that X is a random variable that can take on the values $\pm\delta$ so that the X^2 is always δ^2 and $\delta^2 = \sigma^2\Delta$. The complicated sum becomes just:

$$\sum_{i=1}^{N} X_i^2 = N\delta^2$$

Remembering that the random walk has N steps of duration Δ, $N\Delta = t$. Finally then, you end up with an equation that looks a lot better:

$$\log\frac{S(t)}{S_0} = \sum_{i=1}^{N} X_i - \frac{1}{2}\delta^2 t.$$

REMEMBER

The random walk, $\sum_{i=1}^{N} X_i$, has a drift of γt if the probability of an upward move is:

$$\frac{1}{2}\left(1+\frac{\gamma}{\sigma}\sqrt{\Delta}\right).$$

The drift is due to the fact that you don't have an equal probability of an upward and downward move.

This new Brownian motion formed from $\ln\left(\dfrac{S(t)}{S(0)}\right)$ has a drift given by $\gamma - \frac{1}{2}\sigma^2$.

The variance for $\ln(S(t))$ is σ^2, just as for the additive random walk, because the variance is formed from the same sum of random numbers X_i.

Generating Random Numbers on a Computer

Quantitative finance can be highly theoretical with lots of abstract equations, but another side to it is where you use real financial data or simulate data in a computer. I do the latter in this section, not just because doing so is fun, but because it's useful. It can help you understand the abstract equations, but more importantly, it can help you solve problems. For example, by simulating possible future values for the price of a stock using geometric Brownian motion, you can value financial options that depend upon a future, unknown share price. Another important application of random numbers is to simulate the future value of a portfolio of assets.

These techniques of using random numbers are appropriately called *Monte Carlo methods* in deference to a casino in Monaco. The next sections show you how to generate random numbers in two different ways.

Getting random with Excel

In Microsoft Excel, you can generate a random number simply by typing =rand() into a cell. Try it! You generate a random number between zero and one. In other words, this number is a sample from the uniform distribution (which I explain in Chapter 2). This function doesn't accept any arguments, so leave the space between the brackets empty. The number changes to a different random number each time you press F9, because pressing F9 recalculates the spreadsheet.

A better way to see what many random numbers look like is to copy the formula into many cells. You can then draw plots to check that the numbers are as you expect: They should all be between zero and one and look random. To check that the numbers are uniformly distributed between zero and one, use the Histogram tool under the Data Analysis menu on the Data tab.

Generating random numbers drawn from a normal distribution isn't quite so quick and easy. You can do it by using the function called *NormInv*. This function computes the inverse of the cumulative normal distribution. Don't panic! I show you how to do this computation step by step.

The normal distribution is bell-shaped with a width determined by its standard deviation and location on the x axis by its mean. The cumulative normal distribution, $\Phi(z)$, comes from integrating the normal distribution, $\phi(x)$, from $-\infty$ to z:

$$\Phi(z) = \frac{1}{\sqrt{2\pi}} \int_{-\infty}^{z} e^{-\frac{1}{2}x^2}\, dx.$$

The cumulative normal distribution $\Phi(z)$ gives the area under the normal distribution from $-\infty$ up to z. Figure 3-2 shows a graph of this function.

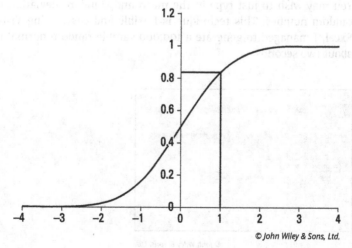

FIGURE 3-2: Cumulative normal distribution with $\sigma = 1$ and $\mu = 0$.

Notice that the cumulative distribution starts at zero and rises up to one. That's because going from left to right on the chart you're adding up probabilities so that finally, on the right-hand edge of the chart, the value is one because the sum of all probabilities must be one. Now, you find the inverse cumulative normal distribution, I(x), by turning Figure 3-2 on its side. So if you want to find I(0.8) for example, locate the x value corresponding to y = 0.8 on the cumulative normal chart, shown by the solid black lines in Figure 3-2.

Maths can help explain the *inverse-transformation* method of generating normal random numbers:

>> U is a uniformly distributed random variable between zero and one.

>> $\Phi(z)$ is the probability that a normal random number, Z, is less than z.

In other words: $\Phi(z) = P(Z < z)$.

The variable $I = \Phi^{-1}(U)$ is normally distributed just like Z. To show this, you need to prove that $P(I \le z) = \Phi(z)$. But $P(I \le z) = P(\Phi(I) \le \Phi(z)) = P(U \le \Phi(z))$. Because U is uniformly distributed – $P(U \le \Phi(z)) = \Phi(z)$ – you can prove that the inverse cumulative normal distribution is normally distributed just like Z. This proof works for other distributions too.

To generate numbers from a normal distribution, compute the inverse cumulative normal distribution with a number taken from a uniform distribution as the argument. The inverse cumulative normal distribution maps probabilities in the range zero to one onto the normal distribution. I took the screenshot in Figure 3-3 when I was typing in the formula.

You may wish to just type in the mean and standard deviation required for the random number. This technique is flexible and easy. Using Visual Basic within Excel, I managed to generate a 100,000 sample random normal numbers within about two seconds.

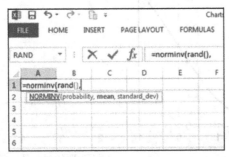

FIGURE 3-3:
Using Microsoft
Excel to generate
sample numbers
from a normal
distribution.

© John Wiley & Sons, Ltd.

WAITING FOR SOMETHING TO HAPPEN WITH POISSON

The Poisson process is used to count events that occur randomly in time, such as the arrival of trade instructions or the occurrence of power failures. It has the dual success of realism and simplicity, which makes it widely used throughout science and finance. For example, it has been successfully used to explain why just a small increase in the arrival rate of customers at a supermarket till can lead to a dramatic increase in the wait time – an all-too-familiar situation!

The Poisson process is defined by the parameter α which is the expected number of events in a given time interval and is called the *intensity*.

The Poisson process is characterised by the following properties:

- The events occur one at a time.
- The number of events in one time interval is independent of the number of events in another time interval.
- The number of arrivals during a given time interval has a Poisson distribution.

The Poisson distribution, which I explain in Chapter 2, is characterised by a single parameter, λ and gives the probability of there being exactly k successes in a sequence of trials when the average number of success is λ. The Poisson process is related to the Poisson distribution. If I take my Poisson process for a fixed time period of t seconds, then the probability of getting k orders in these t seconds is determined by the Poisson distribution with $\lambda = \alpha t$.

If the arrival rate of orders is α, then the average time between orders is $\frac{1}{\alpha}$. The probability of *no* order happening by t is $e^{-\alpha t}$, so you have an exponentially declining probability of receiving no orders as time passes. The figure shows a chart of a Poisson process with the dots indicating the arrival of orders in time. What is noticeable is the clustering of the points. Remember, though, that the arrival times of the orders are random so the clustering isn't caused by anything and despite appearances is the result of chance.

© John Wiley & Sons, Ltd.

Using the central limit theorem again

The uniform distribution is a good place to start when generating random numbers as almost all software provides a way to generate such numbers and normally does so quickly. To then transform those numbers into samples from a normal distribution, you can use the central limit theorem: simply add together N random numbers, which should start to be a good approximation to normal random numbers. N can typically be 10, but experiment with other values. If U is drawn from a uniform distribution, R is a sample from a normal distribution:

$$R = \sqrt{\frac{12}{N}} \sum_{i=1}^{N} (U_i - 0.5).$$

The factor of $\sqrt{\frac{12}{N}}$ ensures that R has a standard deviation of one. To check this, notice that $V = U - 0.5$ is a uniform distribution with a mean of zero and lies between $-\frac{1}{2}$ and $\frac{1}{2}$. To work out the variance of V, calculate:

$$\int_{-0.5}^{0.5} x^2 \, dx = \frac{1}{12}.$$

Given that the N uniform distributions are assumed to be independent, the variance of N of them is simply $\frac{N}{12}$. The standard deviation is the square root of the variance so dividing by $\sqrt{\frac{N}{12}}$ ensures that R has a standard deviation of unity. By a simple transformation, $R \to \sigma R + \mu$, you can generate random numbers from a normal distribution with mean μ and standard deviation σ.

Generating a million random numbers in this way should only take seconds using visual basic code within Microsoft Excel.

Simulating Random Walks

Simulating a random walk is a powerful thing to be able to do in quantitative finance because you can use random walks to represent the possible future price changes of financial assets such as stocks and shares. You can use them to work out the price of contracts such as options or evaluate how risky a portfolio is.

You can generate random numbers by simply using a spreadsheet or other software such as Python. The previous section 'Generating Random Numbers on a Computer' shows you how. By using these random numbers to generate random walks, you begin to get a real understanding of the processes so important in quantitative finance.

Now I show you the surprising results of generating a geometric Brownian motion. The positions in this walk are designated S_n. The following equation shows how each position follows on from the previous position by adding a step distance drawn from a normal distribution where N is the normal distribution:

$$\ln S_n = \ln S_{n-1} + N(\mu, \sigma).$$

Figure 3-4 shows a chart of ten such series each with 500 data points. I used the values $\mu = 0$ and $\sigma = 0.05$. For daily price data of a stock with 250 trading days per year, the graph in the figure represents two years of price history.

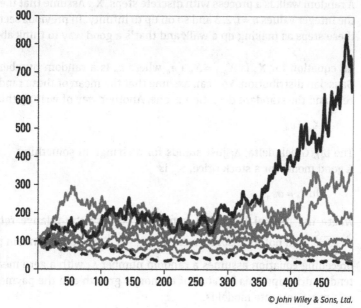

FIGURE 3-4: Geometric Brownian motion for ten simulated stock prices.

© John Wiley & Sons, Ltd.

Notice that some Brownian motions, such as the black one, rise rapidly and others, such as the dashed one, fall to a quarter of their original value. This rise and fall is a realistic feature of the stock market in which some companies prosper dramatically and others fall on hard times. But the most astonishing thing to notice is that all these ten random walks are generated from random numbers coming from exactly the same distribution.

WARNING

Any investment manager who had chosen to include the black stock in her portfolio would naturally be happy, but this rapid rise is purely the result of random chance. You can easily be fooled by randomness. Beware!

Moving Up a Gear

This section is where I get just a little bit more mathematical. That may not sound good to you, but maths is helpful. It can make it easy to see the difference between related complex ideas. It also makes it easier to work with ideas to find out what the consequences are.

Working a stochastic differential equation

A random walk is a process with discrete steps, X_n. Assume that the index, n, takes the integer values $n = 1, 2, 3$ and so on up to infinity. In previous sections, I describe these steps as making up a walk and that's a good way to think about it.

An equation for X_n is $X_{n+1} = X_n + \varepsilon_n$ where ε_n is a random number drawn from a Gaussian distribution. You can assume that the mean of these random numbers is zero and the standard deviation is one. Another way of writing this equation is:

$$\Delta X_n = \varepsilon_n.$$

The big Greek delta, Δ, just stands for a change in something – in this case X_n. A good model for a stock price, S_n, is

$$\Delta \ln S_n = \sigma \varepsilon_n$$

where the natural logarithm comes in because the relative return of a stock $\frac{S_{n+1} - S_n}{S_n}$ and not its absolute return $(S_{n+1} - S_n)$ is a stable random process. But the preceding equation assumes a random number ε_n with a zero mean. Stock prices tend to drift upwards because of economic growth and the payment of dividends so a more accurate model is:

$$\Delta \ln S_n = \mu + \sigma \varepsilon_n.$$

In this equation, I introduce a drift term of magnitude, μ, and multiply the random numbers, ε, by σ so that the second term on the right-hand side represents Gaussian random numbers with a standard deviation, σ.

But the equation so far has no notion of time. Now assume that going from the nth to the $(n+1)^{th}$ step takes a time, Δt. The equation for $\ln S_n$ then becomes:

$$\Delta \ln S_n = \mu \Delta t + \sigma \varepsilon_n \sqrt{\Delta t}.$$

You may be wondering why the second term has a square root of the time step, Δt. The reason is because the first term is for a motion where you have an expected return per unit of time μ and is the same at every time step. The second term is for the random element of the return and is much less certain, so increases only with the square root of the time step.

REMEMBER

In the section 'Setting Up a Random Walk', I show that if someone took N steps at random to the left or the right she would expect to move out about $\sqrt{N}$ steps from the origin. The square root in the equation for $\ln S_n$ happens because of exactly the same reasoning. For a moment, though, forget about the random term in this equation, which reduces it to just: $\Delta \ln S_n = \mu \Delta t$.

In the limit of smaller and smaller time steps, it becomes a differential equation:

$$\frac{dS}{S} = \mu \, dt,$$

which is solved by:

$$S = S(0)e^{\mu t}.$$

The stock price grows exponentially at a rate given by μ. This growth is exactly what you expect from compound interest.

Turning now to the equation for S_n, including the random terms, you can take the limit of smaller and smaller step sizes. In the resulting equation I write the term containing the random noise, ε, and the square root of the time step as dz. The equation for the natural logarithm of S then becomes:

$$d \ln S = \left(\mu - \frac{1}{2}\sigma^2 \right) dt + \sigma \, dz.$$

The term with σ squared arises for the same reason as in the section 'Moving Like the Stock Market' where the average of the squared terms of the random steps led to the term: $\frac{1}{2}\sigma^2 t$.

In these differential (small step sizes) forms, the equation of the natural logarithm of S is called a *stochastic differential equation*. This form of equation is widely used for the pricing of derivatives because it allows you to find relationships between option prices and variables such as a stock price.

An alternative form of the equation for dS is: $dS = \mu S \, dt + \sigma S \, dz$.

Expanding from the origin

WARNING

This section involves some fairly heavy maths, but when you're familiar with the result you're equipped to derive the famous Black–Scholes equation for pricing options. But if this level of calculus isn't your thing, don't worry: I also use another method for pricing options called binomial trees, which doesn't involve calculus, in Chapter 10.

With this formula, you look at the behaviour of a function, $F(S,t)$, where S is a random variable such as a stock price and t is time, to find out how small changes to S and t change F. For a function of two variables such as F, you need to use partial derivatives.

You can write a Taylor expansion for F:

$$\Delta F = \frac{\partial F}{\partial S}\Delta S + \frac{\partial F}{\partial t}\Delta t + \frac{1}{2}\frac{\partial^2 F}{\partial^2 S}\Delta S^2 + \frac{\partial^2 F}{\partial S \partial t}\Delta S \Delta t + \frac{1}{2}\frac{\partial^2 F}{\partial t^2}\Delta t^2.$$

In this expression, to note a small change in F you need to look at just how small each term is. The terms with just ΔS and Δt are called *first-order terms* because only one Δ is present. All the other terms are second order because two Δs exist. If you multiply a small number by another small number, you get a really small number – for example, $0.1 \times 0.1 = 0.01$. So if you make ΔS and Δt smaller and smaller, you expect all the second-order terms to become insignificant.

But something a little different happens when S is a random variable. In the stochastic differential equation for dS, the dz term is proportional to the *square root* of dt (see the section 'Working a stochastic differential equation') and so, crucially, $(\Delta S)^2$ has a term proportional to Δt. This statement means that the preceding equation has an additional linear term when you make ΔS and Δt smaller and smaller to get:

$$\Delta F = \frac{\partial F}{\partial S}\Delta S + \frac{\partial F}{\partial t}\Delta t + \frac{1}{2}\sigma^2 S^2 \frac{\partial^2 F}{\partial S^2}\Delta t.$$

All the second-order terms can be ignored when ΔS and Δt get smaller and smaller.

This type of analysis is used frequently in quantitative finance, so you need to know it if you want to understand the subject. The effort in going through the maths will be rewarded!

Reverting to the Mean

Not all markets or financial time series behave like a geometrical Brownian motion. Some series exhibit a phenomenon called *mean-reversion*. In these motions, the series doesn't shoot up to a high value or wander down to zero. Instead it tends to go back, or revert, to its original value.

For example, in the energy markets a sharp fall in the price of crude oil forces some oil companies to shut down oil wells because they become unprofitable. These shutdowns reduce supply, so the price should jump back up to its typical value.

Similarly, a sharp rise in the price of crude oil encourages explorers to drill more wells and to bring previously uneconomic finds into production. The price of oil then tends to go back down again. Of course, other factors are in play such as action by the OPEC cartel. But stability helps producers and consumers alike, so mean reversion tends to hold.

Interest rates are also thought to be mean reverting. In recent times this has probably been due to the stabilising actions of central banks. Figure 3-5 shows the yield, or interest rate, on three-month US Treasury bills, which is the short-term interest rate on loans to the US government. The vertical shaded areas indicated US recessions.

FIGURE 3-5:
Yield on
three-month US
Treasury bills.

Source: Federal Reserve Bank of St. Louis

The chart is dominated by a peak around 1980. It has taken almost 70 years from 1940 until around 2010 for the yield on three-month bills to go back down to zero percent. The chart has reverted, but slowly. This effect can be expressed in an equation:

$$\Delta x_n = \alpha \left(X - x_n \right) + \varepsilon_n.$$

Here, the term in the equation beginning with alpha forces the time series to revert back to the mean value X. It does so because if x_n is less than X, the term is positive and the next step is likely to be positive and x_n is boosted back towards X. I wrote 'likely' in the previous sentence because you also have the random variable term, ε, which means that the time series does not necessarily revert back to the mean immediately.

Likewise, if x_n is greater than X, the alpha term is negative and brings the time series back down towards X. Some examples of this kind of series are shown in Figure 3-6 with $X_0 = 1$ and for three values of α varying from 1 (strong reversion) to 0.01 (weak mean reversion).

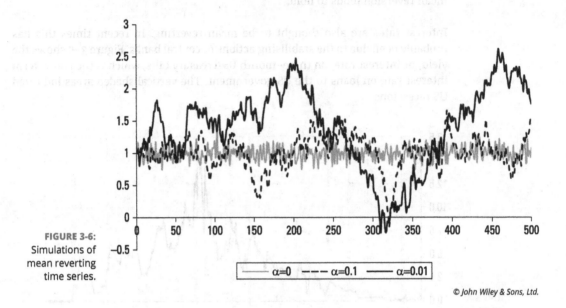

FIGURE 3-6:
Simulations of
mean reverting
time series.

—— α=0   ---- α=0.1   —— α=0.01

© John Wiley & Sons, Ltd.

Only the series with $a = 0.01$ looks at all like the real interest rate data from Figure 3-4 so the mean reversion of interest rates must be weak indeed if represented by the simple model in Figure 3-5.

2

Tackling
Financial
Instruments

Get up to speed on the most important financial instruments and find out how they work.

Understand the bread-and-butter contracts of quantitative finance – stocks and bonds.

Join the ancients in using futures contracts, which were first used for commodities such as grain, copper and oil.

Make the most of the versatility of hedges, which you can use to protect yourself against adverse price movements or to speculate.

Chapter 4

Sizing Up Interest Rates, Shares and Bonds

The most basic financial asset, and probably the most important, is money in the bank. Banks pay interest based on the amount deposited. With a little bit of maths, you can calculate the growth of an account due to the interest earned on the interest.

Stocks or *shares* are probably the next most important financial assets. These represent claims on the ownership of a company. The shareholder is entitled to receive dividend payments from the company paid from its profits, and can also vote at shareholder meetings. You may, for example, get the chance to vote against the chief executive's huge pay rise!

The third category of asset is bonds. I explain some of the many different kinds of bonds in this chapter as well as fill you in on the language used to talk about them. In all forms, bonds are a loan to the issuer. The loan can be bought or sold, a bit like a share, so its price fluctuates like share prices do.

Explaining Interest

A bank pays you interest for depositing money with it. It does this because it then lends out the money to other businesses or individuals and charges the borrowers a higher rate of interest. That's how banks make a profit. They can charge high rates of interest to some businesses because they might not get their money back if the business goes bankrupt. The high interest rate is the bank's reward for taking that risk. If you deposit an amount of money, A, in a bank, you have $A + Ar$, where r is the annual interest rate, in your account at the end of the year (assuming you don't withdraw any money). For example, if I deposit £100 and the interest rate is 10 per cent (keep dreaming, only banks earn this rate of interest), at the end of the year I have £100 + 0.1 × £100 = £110. Using simple algebra, the amount of money at the end of the year $A + Ar$ can be written as $A(1+r)$.

A percentage indicates a number out of one hundred. So, 10 per cent means ten out of a hundred or $\frac{10}{100}$ or 0.1. So 10 per cent of £100 is £10.

Compounding your interest

If you leave money and any interest it earned in the bank for another year, at the end of the second year you have the amount at the beginning, B, plus the interest rate times B, in other words $A + Ar = A(1+r)$. But B, the amount at the beginning of year two, is just the same as the amount at the end of year one and so, the amount at the end of year two is $A(1+r)(1+r)$. If you keep your money in the bank for many years, say n years, then at the end of the nth year you have $A(1+r)^n$ in the bank.

Figure 4-1 shows a chart of this formula and how the amount in the account grows exponentially. Of course, if the interest rate is only 1 per cent rather than 10 per cent, the upward curve is hard to spot.

Earning interest on both your original capital and the interest on it is called *compound interest*. Reputedly, the famous physicist Albert Einstein said that 'Compound interest is the eighth wonder of the world. He who understands it, earns it . . . he who doesn't, pays it.' Wise words worth heeding.

Not all accounts pay interest annually. Some make payments twice a year. In that case, after six months you have $A\left(1+\frac{r}{2}\right)$ in the bank. Here I use the interest rate $\frac{r}{2}$ because the rate is only for half a year. At the end of the year, you have $A\left(1+\frac{r}{2}\right)\left(1+\frac{r}{2}\right)$ in the bank. This figure isn't the same as when you received the annual payment when you ended up with $A(1+r)$. If you multiply out the brackets for the semi-annual payment, then you get $A\left(1+r+\frac{r^2}{2}\right)$, which is a little bit more.

Good to know! However, the interest rate, r, is generally small, so if it is, say, 0.1, then $\frac{r^2}{2}$ is only 0.005.

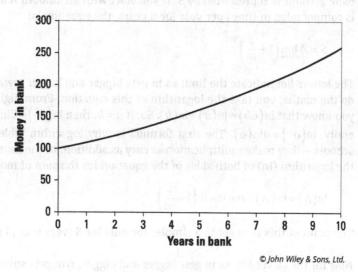

FIGURE 4-1:
Compound interest of a bank with a 10 per cent interest rate.

In practice, you don't find much difference between annual and semi-annual payments, especially if the interest rate is low.

To make things a little more complicated, banks offer accounts with interest paid any number of times throughout the year – even daily – so you do well to know about all the ways to calculate interest. If the annual rate is r, and paid m times per annum, your account receives m payments with rate $\frac{r}{m}$. At the end of the year, you have $A\left(1+\frac{r}{m}\right)^m$ in the bank, and at the end of n years, you have $A\left(1+\frac{r}{m}\right)^{mn}$ in the bank.

Compounding continuously

Money in the bank, A, earns interest at the rate of r per annum. If interest is paid in m instalments with rate $\frac{r}{m}$, then at the end of n years you have $A\left(1+\frac{r}{m}\right)^{mn}$ in the bank.

This equation looks complicated, but you can write a much simpler formula with some advanced maths. The brainy mathematicians in investment banks use the simpler formula all the time because it makes complicated valuation calculations easier.

Assume that m gets bigger and bigger – all the way to infinity, in fact (but not beyond). Now small amounts of interest are being paid all the time. This situation is called *continuous compounding*. In the next formula, the sum of money in your bank account is represented by S. If you start with an amount A and this amount is compounded m times per year for n years, the equation is:

$$S = A \lim_{m \to \infty} \left(1 + \frac{r}{m}\right)^{mn}.$$

The letters *lim* indicate the limit as m gets bigger and bigger towards infinity. To do the maths, you take the logarithm of this equation. From high school maths, you know that $\ln(ab) = \ln(a) + \ln(b)$. So, if $a = b$, then $\ln(a^2) = 2\ln(a)$. More generally, $\ln(a^n) = n\ln(a)$. The first formula is why logarithm tables were used in schools – they make multiplication as easy as addition. In the next formula, I take the logarithm (ln) of both sides of the equation for the sum of money, S:

$$\ln(S) = \ln(A) + mn \lim_{m \to \infty} \ln\left(1 + \frac{r}{m}\right).$$

The point of this is to get to a simpler formula for S (very soon, I promise).

Now for the clever bit. As m gets bigger and bigger, r/m gets smaller and smaller. This fact allows you to make a nice simplification of the term in the equation with the logarithm:

$$\ln(1 + x) = x + \frac{x^2}{2} + \frac{x^3}{3} + \frac{x^4}{4} + \ldots.$$

This formula is the Taylor expansion of the logarithm. But remember, x is small in this calculation and the square of a small number is even smaller, so you can ignore all the terms in the formula (I like that!) except the first one.

Using the approximation $\ln(1 + x) = x$, you get: $\ln(S) = \ln(A) + nr$.

Very nicely the m cancels out, and you get a formula with only n. Using the properties of logarithms again, you can write this formula as $S = Ae^{nr}$.

Here e is the base of the natural logarithm. More commonly this formula is written with t rather than n to indicate time. Just remember that the interest rate must be an annual one.

The simple exponential formula can be written backwards as $A = Se^{-nr}$. That's because the inverse of e^m is just $e^{-m} = \frac{1}{e^m}$. You may be thinking, 'So what?' or 'Why bother?' But some financial contracts, such as bonds and options, involve known payoffs at a time in the future. In that case, the backwards formula tells you how much the payoff is worth in today's money. This figure is particularly helpful if you wish to compare payoffs at different time horizons. By expressing them all in today's money using the simple exponential formula, you can make legitimate comparisons. The process of applying the simple exponential formula to find today's value of a future sum S is *discounting*. That's because today's amount is typically less than the future amount.

So it's true: money in the bank grows exponentially. Sadly, not many people can leave it there long enough to notice. Table 4-1 shows how much £100 is worth at the end of a year depending upon how often the 4 per cent interest is compounded.

TABLE 4-1   **Compounding Interest on £100 at 4%**

Interest Payment Frequency	Sum at the End of One Year
Annual	£104
Semi-annual	£104.04
Monthly	£104.0742
Weekly	£104.0795
Daily	£104.0808
Continuous compounding	£104.0811

WARNING

Central banks have been known to impose negative interest rates. The purpose may be to encourage depositors to spend the money or to exchange it for another currency. The simple exponential formula still works, but S is now smaller than A.

Sharing in Profits and Growth

Shares are one of the best known of all financial assets. A *share* is one of any number of equal portions of ownership of a company. In this book, I use the word *stocks* to mean the same as shares although it can have a more general meaning.

WARNING

In the UK, you may come across the expression *Treasury Stock*, which refers to specific UK government bonds, or gilts. Confusing!

Shares are mostly bought and sold on public venues called *stock markets* such as the New York Stock Exchange (NYSE), although large transactions are sometimes carried out on private venues called *dark pools*.

Because they're owners, shareholders have a right to a portion of a company's profits and can also vote on key matters such as appointments to the board of directors. Shareholders can also vote on large transactions, such as when a company wants to make a big takeover of a rival company.

Shares are often owned by pension funds and also insurance companies. They can also be owned by private individuals either directly or as pooled investments called *unit trusts (mutual funds)*, or *investment trusts*.

In all cases, shares of profits are paid out as dividends, typically quarterly. A company does not have to pay dividends though. Companies at the early stage of their development often pay no dividend, instead using their revenue to develop their product or acquire technology from other companies. Shareholders expect these companies to pay dividends eventually when the company matures.

Dividend payments are typically paid quarterly. By adding all the dividend payments together to get the total dividend for the year and dividing the amount by the share price, you get what's called the *dividend yield*. This number is similar to the interest rate for money in the bank and allows investments in shares to be compared with cash.

WARNING

Dividends can vary significantly from year to year depending on the profitability of the company. If a company hits a tough time, it may suspend dividends altogether. Contrariwise, if a company becomes highly profitable because of some form of windfall, such as the sale of a subsidiary, it may issue a special one-off payment to shareholders.

In the long run and on average, dividend payments rise and share prices rise because of economic growth. Interest rates, on the other hand, tend to stay fixed (Chapter 3 discusses these rates). This means that, in the long run and on average, shares offer better returns than cash, which is why pension funds frequently own so many of them.

Taking the Pulse of World Markets

The share price of any one company can be affected by many specific factors, such as the profitability of one big project or the success or otherwise of a management change. So, to get a more accurate picture of general market behaviour, it's useful to track portfolios of shares, especially of the largest companies, which represent a significant fraction of the economic activity of a country. Hypothetical portfolios, called *stock indices*, have been especially constructed for use in monitoring the overall level of the stock market.

A *stock index* is a weighted average of the components, or companies, of the index. The constituent components may vary from time to time. For example, if a company has a large share price fall, it may drop out of an index. In contrast, if a stock not in the index does well and its share price rises significantly, it may be promoted into an index. Table 4-2 shows some of the most important indices.

TABLE 4-2   **Important Stock Indices**

Index	Components
DAX	30 largest companies on the Frankfurt Xetra exchange
Dow Jones Industrial Average	30 large US companies
Hang Seng	50 largest stocks on the stock exchange of Hong Kong
London Financial Times stock exchange 100 (FTSE 100)	100 largest companies on the London Stock Exchange
Nasdaq 100	100 largest companies on the technology-oriented Nasdaq exchange in New York
Nikkei 225	225 largest companies on the Tokyo stock exchange
Standard & Poor's 500 (S&P 500)	500 of the largest companies on the New York stock exchange

Not only are these indices used for overall monitoring of a stock market but also as the basis for new financial products. In Chapter 5, I talk about stock index options and stock index futures in Chapter 6.

Figure 4-2 shows a chart of three major European stock indices. They all share common features such as the location of peaks. Over extended periods they move closely together, although in recent years the German DAX index has outperformed both the London FTSE 100 and the French CAC 40 index. This similar pattern for the indices is a result of the high correlation between the indices.

REMEMBER

Correlation is a measure of the relationship between two variables. The correlation is a number between −1 and 1. It's positive if an above-average value of one variable occurs more frequently with an above-average value of the other. On the other hand, the correlation is negative if an above-average value of one variable is associated more often with a below-average value of the other. Although stock indices are highly correlated with each other, they are often negatively correlated with bonds (which I talk about in the next section).

You can find out more about the practical importance of this common phenomenon in Chapter 14 on portfolio theory. Also, in Chapter 9 you can see the mathematical definition of correlation and its close cousin, covariance.

FIGURE 4-2:
Co-movement of
European Equity
Indices.

······ DAX — · CAC 40 − − FTSE 100

© John Wiley & Sons, Ltd.

Defining Bonds and Bond Jargon

Bonds are a form of debt. The original amount of the loan is called the *principal*. They're described as *securities* because they're tradable financial assets. That's what makes them different from regular loans. Another term used for bonds is *fixed-income security*. They're called that because, typically, bonds make interest payments that don't change once they've been issued. These interest payments are called *coupons*. The fixed interest is one of the differences between bonds and shares, because the dividends shares pay can vary from year to year. The *running yield* of a bond is the total coupon for the year divided by its market price. It allows you to make a simple comparison.

Bonds are graded according to their quality by rating agencies such as Fitch and Standard & Poor's. These agencies give bonds a score according to the likelihood of the bond defaulting. A *default* is when the issuer isn't able to pay the coupon or the principal on the bond. In this case, the holders of the bonds take legal proceedings to attempt to recover their money. The highest-quality bonds are given a triple A rating while lower-quality bonds have B and C ratings. High-quality bonds are often called *investment grade* and lower-quality bonds *junk grade*. In general, junk bonds have a higher coupon than investment grade bonds to compensate holders for the risks they're taking.

Bonds can issued by a variety of institutions:

> **National governments:** By far the most important bonds, government bonds are often referred to as *sovereign bonds.*

> **Local governments:** In some countries, local governments are permitted to issue bonds referred to as *municipal bonds.*

> **Large companies:** Companies sometimes finance debt by issuing *corporate bonds.*

Bonds are issued in the *primary market,* which is an auction. Investors bid for the bonds according to rules set by the issuing authority – in the case of sovereign bonds, a government department or agency. The outcome for the auction determines how many bonds are issued to each investor and at what interest rate.

After they're issued in the primary market, bonds can be bought and sold by market participants in the *secondary market,* which means that they're traded on exchanges just like shares. The majority are traded by broker-dealers who act as intermediaries between the buyer and seller of the bond. Many, but not all, broker-dealers are major banks.

Most bonds have a *maturity* that's fixed at the time of issuance. The maturity is the period of time between issuance and *redemption,* which is when the issuer returns the bond holder's money. The maturity of bonds can be anything from 2 years to 30 years. On redemption, the issuer returns the principal value to the holder. The *principal value* is the amount paid for the bond at issuance. Sometimes the principal value is referred to as the *face value.*

Some confusing terminology is associated with bonds. In the United States, government bonds are only called bonds if they have maturity of over ten years. Bonds with shorter maturity are called *treasury notes.* In the United Kingdom, bonds are called *gilts.* In Germany, bonds with a short maturity are called *Schatz,* middle-maturity bonds are *Bobls* and longer-maturity bonds are *Bund.*

Coupon-bearing bonds

Coupon-bearing bonds are the most common type of bond. At issuance they have a face value, F. The issuer pays a semi-annual (twice a year) coupon, C, to the holder. The most common maturities are 2, 5 and 10 years but *long* bonds with maturities of 20 or 30 years are popular too. Long bonds avoid the need for the borrower to keep on refinancing their debt by reissuing more bonds.

United Kingdom Gilt Treasury Stock 2032 4.25% (TR32). These bonds are redeemable in June 2032 and each year until then pay a yield of 4.25 per cent on the face value of 100 pence (100p). Every six months, a coupon of $2.125\,\text{p} = \dfrac{2.125\,\text{p}}{2}$ is paid for every 100p. The December 2014 price was 123.34p, so the yield for someone who has just bought TR32 is $\dfrac{4.25}{123.34} = 3.45\%$.

In June 2032, the UK Treasury will redeem the bonds at 100p so the buyer today at 123.34 will take a (near) certain loss of 23.34p. An important and useful quantity that takes into account both the semi-annual coupon payments and the repayment of the principal is the *yield to maturity*. This yield is also sometimes called the *redemption yield*, which is calculated by applying the time value of money formula to every cash flow from the bond.

The letter y represents this yield and M stands for the current market price of the bond. The current time is t and the redemption date is T. The coupon is C and is paid at times t_i. N coupons are left to be paid until redemption. So the implicit equation for yield to maturity for a coupon-bearing bond with principal, P, is $M = Pe^{-y(T-t)} + \sum_{i=1}^{N} Ce^{-y(t_i-t)}$.

This equation is an *implicit* equation for the yield to maturity y. In other words, you don't know what y is yet! You can't just plug in values for P, M and C and calculate y. In other words, this equation is saying that the current market value M of a coupon-bearing bond is equal to the sum of all the future anticipated payments from it discounted to the present day at the interest rate y. To evaluate y, you must use an iterative procedure in which you make repeated estimates of y and improve the estimate based on previous values.

In the formula for M, you see that if the yield y rises, then the price M must fall because y always appears as a negative exponential. A negative exponential looks like a downward sloping slide, so the higher y goes the lower M becomes.

Zeroing in on yield

Bonds are often called *fixed-income securities*, but curiously, some of the most important bonds do not pay a coupon. These bonds are often simply referred to as *zeroes*.

REMEMBER

A *coupon* is the interest payment made to the holder of a bond. For most government bonds, they're made as cash payments every six months.

The deal for a zero-coupon bond works as follows: You pay an amount, X, for a bond whose issuer promises to pay back an amount, Y, at a time in the future. That's it. Simple. Some of the most important zero-coupon bonds are called *bills*. These bills are issued by both the US and UK treasuries. The maturity of a bill is short being anything from 1 month to 12 months.

Normally $X < Y$; in other words, the bond is worth more at redemption than at issuance. Instead of receiving interest in the form of a coupon, the holder makes a capital gain. If the maturity of the zero bond is T, this capital gain is equivalent to an interest rate r where $X = e^{-rT}Y$ – a formula I explain in the earlier section 'Compounding continuously', which is an example of the time value of money. However, in exceptional circumstances, $X > Y$ for short-maturity bills because the issuer of the bill, frequently a government treasury, is considered a better credit risk than banks. The buyers of the bills regard their money as in safer hands than in a bank because the government treasury is less likely to default then a bank. Safety can be more important than interest payments.

TECHNICAL STUFF

SOLVING FOR Y

Equations such as $M = Pe^{-y(T-t)} + \sum_{i=1}^{N} Ce^{-y(t_i-t)}$ occur quite a lot in quantitative finance, so you benefit from knowing how to solve them. They can't be rearranged to give a simple formula for y, so the best way to solve such equations is numerically using a computer.

To show you how to solve this equation, I start with a bit of guesswork. That doesn't sound mathematical, but the important thing is to have a systematic way of improving the guess to get the correct value of y. You need to guess what the lowest possible value that the interest rate y might take – zero is a good value. Then you need to guess the highest value that y might take. A possible value may be the annual coupon, 2C, divided by the principal, P. But if the bond trades at less than P, the yield to maturity may be higher than this amount. So a possible high guess would be $\frac{4C}{P}$. I call the high guess b' and the low guess a. I also use a midpoint guess of $\frac{a+b}{2}$.

You can now write the equation as $M = f(y)$ meaning that the market price, M, is a function, f, of a yield to maturity, y. Using the guesses a and b, you can evaluate f(a) and f(b). One of these values should be higher than M and the other lower than M because the correct yield to maturity y* must lie between the lowest guess, a, and the highest guess, b. At the correct value of the yield to maturity, $M = f(y*)$.

(continued)

(continued)

By halving or *bisecting* (official maths jargon) the range from a to b with the point $\frac{a+b}{2}$, you can figure out where the correct yield to maturity might lie.

1. Make guess for lower limit, a, of y* and upper limit, b, for y*.

2. Calculate f(a), $f\left(\frac{a+b}{2}\right)$, f(b).

3. If $f(a) < M < f\left(\frac{a+b}{2}\right)$, then $b' = \frac{a+b}{2}$, and the new search range is $[a, b']$.

4. If $f\left(\frac{a+b}{2}\right) < M < f(b)$, then $a' = \frac{a+b}{2}$, and the new search range is $[a', b]$.

5. If the new search range is narrow enough to give an accurate value for y*, then stop. If not, go back to Step 1.

If the curve f(y) crosses M in the left-hand segment, then y* lies in the range $\left[a, \frac{a+b}{2}\right]$. On the other hand, if f(y) crosses M in the right-hand segment then y* lies in the range $\left[\frac{a+b}{2}, b\right]$ as shown where I plotted f(y) and the point where it intersects the line M is y*. By this process, I shrunk the range where you might expect to find the correct value y* by half. This action can be repeated or iterated, until an accurate value for y* is found. Refer to this figure for an example.

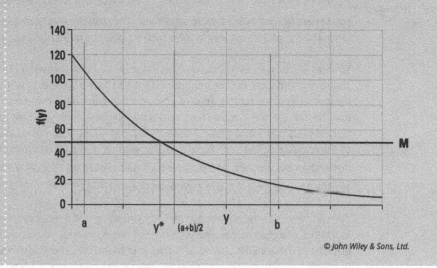

© John Wiley & Sons, Ltd.

Cleaning up prices

Accrued interest is the interest earned or built up since the last coupon payment of a bond. The prices quoted for bonds are *clean* prices that do not include the accrued interest. When you buy a bond, you have to pay both the clean price and the accrued interest, which adds up to the *dirty price*. A chart of the dirty price shows sharp drops on coupon days as the accruals fall to zero following the payment of the coupon. The clean price chart has much more continuous behaviour.

To calculate the accrued interest, you need to know the number of days elapsed since the last coupon date. Various conventions exist for doing this calculation depending on the type of bond and country of origin. They all take the form of:

$$\text{Accrued interest} = \text{Coupon} \times \frac{\text{Days since last coupon}}{\text{Days in reference period between coupons}}.$$

TECHNICAL STUFF

In some conventions, a month is always 30 days, so a year has 360 days. The half-year coupon period is then 180 days. Both the US Treasury bond market and UK gilt markets use the actual number of days when counting the days between dates and don't round months to 30 days.

Learning to like LIBOR

LIBOR is the London Interbank Offer Rate and is an essential cog in the financial system. This rate is used as a benchmark interest rate in pricing financial products such as mortgages. LIBOR is calculated for five currencies:

>> Swiss Frank

>> Euro

>> British Pound (Sterling)

>> Japanese Yen

>> US Dollar

There are seven maturities of interest rate varying from overnight to 12 months so, in total, there are 35 LIBOR rates. All these rates are calculated daily based on data from banks in London but are considered representative of global short-term interest rates. The rates are published at approximately 11:00 a.m. London time.

LIBOR rates are calculated by a poll of contributing banks. For each currency and maturity, the banks are asked 'At what rate could you borrow funds, were you to do so by asking for and then accepting interbank offers in a reasonable market size just prior to 11:00 a.m. London time?' They then compile the responses or submissions and then list these in numerical order. They then reject the highest and lowest 25 per cent of the submissions as outliers and average the remaining figures.

TECHNICAL
STUFF

An *outlier* is a statistical term for an observation or result that is distant from most of the other observations. Outliers are deemed to be sufficiently different from the population that they can't be reliably used in calculations.

Despite the apparently robust statistical procedure to calculate LIBOR, the rates were manipulated by submitting banks during the financial crisis of 2008. The stigma of making outlier submissions encouraged many, if not most, banks to make submissions lower than the then-high prevailing rate for interbank lending. The methodology is currently (December 2014) being revised.

Plotting the yield curve

The *yield curve* is the link between the yield to maturity and the maturity of a bond.

REMEMBER

The *yield to maturity* of the bond is the yield taking into account the current price, the redemption value and the coupons you'll receive. The yield to maturity is a good measure of the return of a bond if you hold it to maturity.

Bonds of different maturities have different yields. You construct a yield curve using the yield-to-maturity calculation from the section 'Coupon bearing bonds' – $M = Pe^{-y(T-t)} + \sum_{i=1}^{N} Ce^{-y(t_i-t)}$ – and repeating it for bonds with different maturity values.

To get a more accurate result, however, you do better to use the yield calculated from zero-coupon bonds because, unlike a coupon-bearing bond, payment happens only at redemption so a clear link exists between yield and the time to maturity. A resulting plot of the yield or interest rate for a given maturity is shown in Figure 4-3.

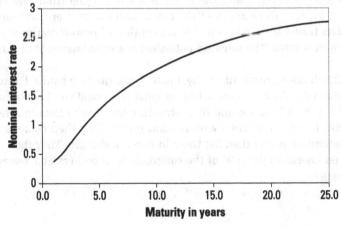

FIGURE 4-3:
Yield curve from
UK gilt data.

© John Wiley & Sons, Ltd.

The shape of this curve is typical, but in certain circumstances, the yield curve is humped or indeed downward sloping. Understanding the motion or dynamics of the yield curve is one of the hard problems of quantitative finance as you need to keep track of all the maturities at the same time. I offer a simple introduction to this subject in Chapter 12.

Swapping between Fixed and Floating Rates

Interest-rate swaps are one of the most important financial products and one of the first financial derivatives to gain widespread acceptance. An *interest-rate swap* is an agreement between two parties such as banks or large companies to trade a stream of income at a fixed rate of interest for a stream of income at a floating rate of interest. They're traded over the counter (OTC) and not on exchanges. In an OTC trade, banks enter agreements directly with other banks or with a specialist swap dealer.

Normally, if a company wishes to enter into an interest-rate swap it contacts a *swap dealer*, an intermediary specialising in buying and selling interest-rate swaps and other derivatives.

Although swaps aren't traded on exchanges, they are subject to standard contracts and documentation, which you can find at www.isda.org, the website for the International Swaps and Derivatives Association.

About a half of all derivatives trading is in interest-rate swaps. On an average day, well over a trillion dollars is traded using interest-rate swaps. So significant is the trading in swaps that their prices are often considered more reliable than other interest-rate products such as bonds. In a way, they're the tail that wags the dog.

The floating rate is most frequently the six-month LIBOR (see the earlier section 'Learning to like LIBOR').

An interest-rate swap in action:

1. **Company A borrows $10 million from a bank and agrees to pay LIBOR plus 10 basis points (LIBOR + 10 bp).**

    Basis point (bp) is a frequently used term in the bond markets and simply means one one-hundredth $\left(\frac{1}{100}\right)$ of a percentage point. So if LIBOR is 4.3 per cent, then LIBOR + 10 basis points is $4.3 + 10 \times 0.01 = 4.4\%$.

2. Company A now thinks that interest rates are going to rise sharply so it enters into an interest rate swap agreement with Company B.

3. Company B agrees to pay Company A an interest rate of LIBOR.

4. Company A agrees to pay Company B a fixed interest of F, say 4 per cent.

The overall effect of this swap is that now Company A pays a fixed interest rate of F + 10 basis points on its loan. It still makes LIBOR + 10 bp payments to the lending bank, but it receives LIBOR back from its swap agreement and pays fixed rate F. Essentially, Company A converts a floating-rate loan into a fixed-rate loan. Figure 4-4 shows the mechanics of this interest-rate swap.

FIGURE 4-4:
Cash flows for an interest-rate swap.

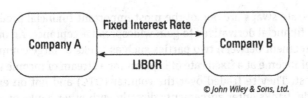

© John Wiley & Sons, Ltd.

REMEMBER

The flexibility that interest-rate swaps provide is one of the keys to their popularity. A company with a fixed-rate loan that believes the interest rate will fall can enter into an agreement to swap that loan for a floating-rate loan. Equally, the holder of a fixed-income asset such as a bond who believes that interest rates will rise can enter into an agreement to swap the fixed-coupon payments for floating-rate payments. Interest-rate swaps are therefore of great use for both investing and borrowing institutions.

Note that the principal amount of a loan or investment isn't exchanged in an interest-rate swap – only the interest. The expression *notional principal* is used for swaps to make clear that the principal amount isn't relevant to the swap.

The key number in an interest-rate swap is the fixed rate, F, as the floating rate is almost always LIBOR. F is often called the *swap rate*. The fixed rate is chosen so that the present value of the swap is zero, which means that, if you add up the discounted value of the fixed-rate payments, they equal the discounted value of the floating-rate payments. A swap constructed to have zero value when the agreement is started is called a *par swap*. Maybe this value is another reason for the popularity of interest-rate swaps. Who can argue with free?

WARNING

Although interest-rate swaps may not cost anything to enter, they can end up being costly. Each party makes the agreement with its own assumption about how interest rates are going to change during the agreement. For example, if you agree to swap fixed payments for floating payments and the interest rate goes up sharply, you will lose a lot of money over the period of the agreement.

Because interest rate swaps are over-the-counter (OTC) instruments, they can be tailored to client requirements. They're issued with a wide range of maturities – anything from a year to 30 years. Interest payments are swapped at predetermined intervals, frequently every six months, just as for many government bonds and with the floating rate set at six-month LIBOR.

For example, a three-year fixed-for-floating interest rate swap with semi-annual payments is agreed between bank A and bank B. The fixed rate is 4 per cent whilst the floating rate is six-month LIBOR. Notional capital, P, is £10 million. Bank A pays bank B $0.5 \times 4\% = 2\%$ every six months. For £10 million of notional capital, this amounts to £200,000 every six months for three years. Again, remember that the notional capital of £10 million is not exchanged. Bank A agreed to make $3 \times 2 = 6$ payments of £200,000 to bank B. In exchange, bank B will make 6 payments at the rate of six-month LIBOR. Depending on whether A's payment is greater than or less than B's payment, bank B will receive or pay a net payment.

The six-month LIBOR payment for a given six-month period is based on the LIBOR rate prevailing at the beginning of the period. This means that immediately after the agreement is set up, both parties know what the first payment in six months' time will be. But the second floating payment to be paid one year after the agreement is set up is not known. All LIBOR rates change from day to day so that, in six months' time, the six-month LIBOR rate could be very different from what it was when the agreement was set up.

Table 4-3 shows how to calculate the value of these floating rate payments at the time the agreement is set up even though you don't know the LIBOR rate at the future payment dates.

TABLE 4-3

Floating Payments and Cash Flow

Payment Day	Floating Rate Deposit	Floating Rate Withdrawal
6 months	Deposit P at agreement	Withdraw P at 6 months
12 months	Deposit P at 6 months	Withdraw P at 12 months
18 months	Deposit P at 12 months	Withdraw P at 18 months
24 months	Deposit P at 18 months	Withdraw P at 24 months
30 months	Deposit P at 24 months	Withdraw P at 30 months
36 months	Deposit P at 30 months	Withdraw P at 36 months

Look at a sample payment day such as for the one in 18 months' time. The interest payment is at six-month LIBOR, which is known at 12 months, and is based on notional capital of P. The cash flow from the floating leg is just the interest payment, so is equivalent to a deposit of P at 12 months and a withdrawal of P at 18 months. If you add up all the cash flows in the table, you notice that all withdrawals, apart from the last, are cancelled by a deposit. Handy! So the equivalent cash flow for all the floating-rate payments is a deposit of P at the time of the agreement and a withdrawal of P at the end of the agreement. A withdrawal at the end of the agreement has to be discounted using the interest rate for a maturity of three years. There are no LIBOR rates for this maturity, so typically a value is taken from the yield curve constructed from zero-dividend bonds (see the section 'Plotting the yield curve').

Valuing the fixed-rate payments is a bit simpler because they're all known in advance. For semi-annual payments, $P \times F/2$ is paid every six months, in which P is the principal amount and F is the fixed rate. Each of these payments has to be discounted by a factor taken from the yield curve. Call the payment times τ_i with $i = 1$ up to the last payment N. For the example above $N = 6$. The interest rate with maturity τ_i is $r(\tau_i)$. By equating the present value of the fixed-rate payments to the present value of the floating-rate payments, you get:

$$P\left(1 - e^{-\tau_N r(\tau_N)}\right) = xFP \sum_{i=1}^{N} e^{-\tau_i r(\tau_i)}.$$

Notice that the principal, P, is a common factor throughout so it can be cancelled. You can then simply solve the equation for the fixed rate F that gives the interest-rate swap zero or par value initially. The term x in the equation takes account of the frequency of the interest payments. For example, if the payments are semi-annual, then $x = 0.5$.

Cancelling P from both sides and solving for the fixed rate F gives you

$$F = \frac{1 - e^{-\tau_N r(\tau_N)}}{x \sum_{i=1}^{N} e^{-\tau_i r(\tau_i)}}.$$

This is the swap rate to give the contract zero value at initiation.

An interest rate swap is in two parts so they're often referred to as legs: the *floating leg* and the *fixed leg*.

Chapter 5

Exploring Options

E veryone likes to have options and financial people are no different. A *financial option* does exactly what it says: it gives the holder the right to buy or sell an asset as she determines the situation is favourable for her to do so. The downside to this nice feature is that options cost money. Contracts that create obligations to buy or sell something, such as futures (which I cover in Chapter 6), are effectively free.

One of the reasons for the enormous popularity and importance of options is the great expansion in the range of underlying assets. Options are now available on interest rates, bonds, equity indices, individual stocks and foreign exchanges. You can even have an option on a futures contract for commodities such as gold and oil.

In this book, I focus on equity and interest rate options, but the concepts I explain can be applied to the other kinds of options too. Because of their versatility, options play a big role in many significant financial transactions such as business lending, the management of large portfolios of stocks used in pensions and in international transactions in different currencies.

Examining a Variety of Options

Options are often called *derivatives* because their price is derived from an underlying asset such as a stock or a bond. If you need a reminder about stocks and bonds please have a look at Chapter 4 which delves into the details about these assets.

Normally, options are traded as separate contracts from the underlying asset. However, sometimes options are embedded into other contracts and occur as a little twist in the terms of a contract. Figuring out the value of such contract terms is an important part of quantitative finance. The most common types of embedded options include the following:

>> **Callable bond:** A bond in which the issuer has the option of calling in the bond and giving the investors their money back if the interest payments become large compared with current market rates. Nice for the issuer of the bond to have that option, but it benefits the purchaser because she pays less for a bond because she isn't guaranteed to receive the attractive interest rate offered at the time of issue.

>> **Convertible bond:** This type of bond gives the holder the right to convert it into the equity of the issuing company.

Starting with plain vanilla options

Options are now available in huge variety – so many in fact that you may find it hard to get your head around the number or understand the need for so many. Think of options as a bit like ice cream flavours: they're always coming up with something more exotic to sell more product. And, just like ice cream, the most basic options are referred to as *plain vanilla options*. A *plain vanilla option* has a single underlying asset and a simple payoff based on the final price.

The most common type of option is one traded separately from an underlying asset. That asset may be a stock such as Vodafone or a government bond such as a ten-year US Treasury Note. However, whatever the underlying asset, options come in two distinct types:

>> A **call option** gives the holder the right, but not the obligation, to buy a particular asset for an agreed price at a specified time in the future.

>> A **put option** gives the holder the right, but not the obligation, to sell a particular asset for an agreed price at a specified time in the future.

This flexibility to buy options that give you rights to buy *or* to sell at a future price is an important part of their appeal. Option contracts have value because they define a price now for an unknown price in the future. The more uncertain the future price the more value an option has. The measure of the uncertainty in the price of an asset is called its *volatility*. (Chapter 7 is where to go to find out about the important concept of volatility and how to measure or calculate it.)

Aiming for a simple, binary option

A *binary* or *digital option* has a simpler payoff than a plain vanilla option. If the asset price ends higher than the strike price, then the binary call has a payoff, Q, irrespective of how much higher the asset price ends up compared with the strike price. The payoff is therefore *discontinuous*. Likewise, a binary put pays off an amount, Q, if the asset price ends up lower than the strike price and irrespective of how much lower it ends up. (Chapter 10 shows you how simple it is to work out how much to pay for a binary option.)

Branching out with more exotic options

Many different kinds of non-standard or *exotic* options are available. I can offer just a small selection here. In fact, such a variety of options exist that it can be hard even to categorise them.

However, one category that's become particularly popular is the *path-dependent option*. The value of these options depends on the price path the underlying asset takes up to the expiry date and not just the value at expiry.

REMEMBER

Barrier options depend on hitting a particular price, the barrier price, before expiry. They come in two types:

>> **Knock-in options** pay off only if the barrier is reached before expiry.

>> **Knock-out options** pay off only if the barrier isn't reached before expiry.

It turns out that the price of a barrier option can be determined in a way not too different from that for plain vanilla options but with a bit of extra mathematics.

Lookback options are yet another form of path-dependent option, but they depend on the maximum or minimum asset price reached during the life of an option. So a lookback call option has a payoff that depends on how much the final asset price exceeds the minimum price reached during the life of the option. Similarly, a lookback put option has a payoff that depends on how much the maximum price reached during the life of the option exceeds the final asset price.

I provide only a short summary of just one category of exotic option here. Much more detailed information can be obtained from textbooks such as *Options, Futures and other Derivatives* by John C Hull, published by Prentice Hall.

Reading Financial Data

Along with the two words of option jargon I define in the preceding section – call and put – I now introduce you to the other key words used to describe options. Having this vocabulary enables to you to examine the websites of option exchanges and understand the figures you see there.

Figure 5-1 is taken from the website of the Intercontinental Exchange, or ICE, and shows options for the British supermarket group Tesco as of 12 November 2014 (which is when I wrote this section). It shows the parts of a financial statement that I explain in the following sections.

NOVEMBER 2014 PRICES - 12/11/14   EXTENDED VIEW

Calls							Strike		Puts					
Settl.	O.I.	Day Vol	Last	Bid	Ask	C		P	Bid	Ask	Last	Day Vol	O.I.	Settl.
15.75	3,004	-	-	10.00	12.50	C	180.00	P	1.00	1.75	-	-	306	0.75
11.25	197	12	7.25	6.75	8.00	C	185.00	P	2.00	2.75	-	-	392	1.25
7.50	3,530	12	3.75	4.00	4.75	C	190.00	P	4.00	4.75	4.50	12	238	2.50
4.50	445	45	3.25	2.00	2.75	C	195.00	P	6.25	8.75	-	-	120	4.50
2.50	219	-	-	1.00	1.50	C	200.00	P	10.00	12.75	-	-	58	7.50

FIGURE 5-1: Tesco put, call and strike prices in November 2014.

Source: Intercontinental Exchange (ICE)

Seeing your strike price

The *strike price* or sometimes *exercise price* is the price at which you have the right to buy or sell the underlying asset of an option. The *expiration date*, or *expiry*, is the date by which you must exercise your option.

Most options are *traded* (bought and sold) on exchanges, so the holder of an option doesn't necessarily have to exercise the option herself. She can simply sell it on an exchange before its expiration date.

Options traded on an exchange are offered for a range of both strike price and also expiration date, as shown in Figure 5-1. The price of the underlying shares for Tesco is 191pence(p). The table shows two halves with call prices on the left and put prices on the right. The strike price is given in the centre column. Note that strike prices apply to both puts and calls.

Abbreviating trading information

The prices at which an option has been bought and sold on the exhange are listed under the heading *Last* in Figure 5-1, meaning the last available price as information is updated throughout the day. The other columns in the table are not specific to options but this is as good a place as any to explain them.

>> **Settl. (settlement):** The price at the close of business on the previous working day. In Figure 5-1, the previous day is 11 November 2014.

>> **O.I. (open interest):** The number of option contracts in existence for that expiry date and strike price.

>> **Day vol (daily volume):** The trading volume indicating how many option contracts are bought and sold. Notice that a Last price only exists for contracts with trading volume because only with trades can prices truly be discovered.

>> **Ask:** The amount it costs to buy a contract.

>> **Bid:** The amount you can sell a contract for.

The ask price is always higher than the bid price as the exchange intends to make money by offering a platform to trade options.

REMEMBER

As the strike price increases, the call prices goes down. That's because buying at higher prices isn't so attractive as buying at low prices. Contrariwise, the settlement price for a put option rises as the strike price increases as selling at higher prices is attractive.

Valuing time

The options shown in Figure 5-1 have an expiration date in November 2014 – at 16:30 p.m. on the third Friday in that month, 21 November, to be precise. For plain-vanilla options the expiry date is set when you buy the option, but there's normally a choice of expiry dates. Near months such as December 2014 and January 2015 also trade.

In general, equity options are available in cycles with expiry months in March, June, September and December. For the Tesco options traded on ICE in November 2014, the longest expiry available was for December 2017.

The prices in Figure 5-2, showing December 2014 prices for Tesco options, are all higher than those in Figure 5-1, which shows November prices. This is an example of *time value*, meaning that the longer an option has to reach its strike price the more expensive it is. The price change is due to the fact that the longer the option exists, the more probable it is that it reaches or exceeds the strike price and gives investors a good payoff.

DECEMBER 2014 PRICES - 12/11/14   **EXTENDED VIEW**

				Calls						Puts				
Settl.	O.I.	Day Vol	Last	Bid	Ask		Strike		Bid	Ask	Last	Day Vol	O.I.	Settl.
18.00	554	-	-	14.00	16.75	C	180.00	P	3.50	4.25	-	-	1,437	3.00
14.50	343	-	-	11.75	12.50	C	185.00	P	5.00	5.75	-	-	36	4.25
11.50	2,097	25	9.75	8.75	9.75	C	190.00	P	7.00	8.00	7.75	20	295	6.25
8.50	294	27	6.00	6.50	7.25	C	195.00	P	9.75	10.50	11.75	15	205	8.50
6.25	972	8	4.50	4.50	5.25	C	200.00	P	12.75	13.75	-	-	737	11.25

Source: Intercontinental Exchange (ICE)

FIGURE 5-2: Tesco option prices in December 2014.

The option exchange, such as the Intercontinental Exchange (ICE), provides other important information about these options on other pages of its website. The *unit of trading*, for example, is the number of shares over which the holder of the option has rights. The ICE website indicates that one option gives the holder rights over 1,000 shares. This number is important to know when you're calculating how much you can potentially gain or lose from owning an option.

The price of an option is often referred to as the *premium*. This language is similar to that used by insurance companies, which is no coincidence as options can be used as a form of financial insurance. I explain this in the upcoming section 'Hedging your risk'.

Getting Paid when Your Option Expires

If you write the price of a share (or any other underlying asset) as S and the strike price of an option as X, you can write the *payoff* of a call option as: Max(S–X,0). The notation means 'the maximum of the share price, S, minus the price of the option, X, or 0'. This is the amount you receive from exercising the option at its expiry.

REMEMBER

You won't find it encouraging to see a zero in there for the payoff, but that's reality: a call option has value only if the share price, S, is greater than the strike price, X, on the expiration date. Because if S is less than X at expiry, then nobody wants the right to buy at a higher price than that available in the market. I show this in the form of a chart in Figure 5-3.

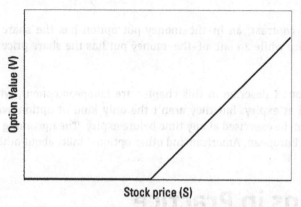

FIGURE 5-3:
Influence of call-option value at expiry on the share price.

© John Wiley & Sons, Ltd

The payoff for a put option can be written as Max(X–S, 0) where the share price now has to be *less* than the strike price for the option to have value at expiry. Only then would anyone want the right to sell at the higher strike price, X.

Figures 5-3 and 5-4 show charts of the value of call and put options at expiry, but options traded on an exchange have prices quoted before expiry. Enabling you to figure the valuation of options before expiry is one of the objectives of this book, and the chapters in Part 4 go into option pricing in detail.

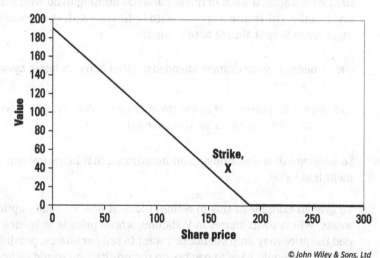

FIGURE 5-4:
Influence of put-option value at expiry on share price.

© John Wiley & Sons, Ltd

TECHNICAL STUFF

If, at times before expiry, a share price is above the strike price of a call option, then the call option is said to have *intrinsic* value and to be *in the money*. Contrariwise, if at times before expiry a share price is below the strike price of a call option, then the call option is said to be *out of the money*. If the share price is far below the strike price, it's said to be *deep out of the money* and the option has a low price. By contrast, an in-the-money put option has the share price below the strike price while an out-of-the-money put has the share price above the strike price.

REMEMBER

The options I describe in this chapter are *European options*, which can only be exercised at expiry. But they aren't the only kind of option available. *American options* can be exercised at any time before expiry. The upcoming section, 'Distinguishing European, American and other options' talks about other options.

Using Options in Practice

In this section, I show you how to put your knowledge of options (which I explain in the preceding sections) into practice. This type of information could easily be a chapter or a book all on its own, but I shrink it down to four subsections. I look at how options can be used to control, or hedge, risk. I also show you how they can be used to speculate and attempt to make money.

Hedging your risk

Hedging is a special word in finance and has nothing to do with gardening or topiary. Equally, *risk* is also a special word in finance with subtle variations in meaning. I try to keep it simple here though:

>> A **hedge** is an investment intended to offset potential losses by another investment.

>> **Risk** is the potential of an investment to lose value. (Chapter 7 on volatility has a more elaborate discussion about risk.)

So *hedging risk* is about buying an investment that helps prevent another investment lose value.

To give an example of this in action, I look at how an equity option for Vodafone works. Wilma owns shares in Vodafone, whose price is 205pence (p). She's worried the price may drop but doesn't want to sell her shares, possibly because if she did sell she would have to pay tax on the profits. She would rather insure against a capital loss and continue to receive dividends. So, she buys a December put option with a strike price of 210p. This means that in December she has the right to sell Vodafone at 210p. That's cool – a higher price than for today, but she has to pay 15.25p for this option. What happens if Vodafone takes a dive down to 170p by December? Wilma loses 35p on every share she owns – almost 15 per cent. On top of this, she paid 15.25p for the option, so that's a painful 50.25p of loss per share. However, her option to sell Vodafone at 210p is rather useful given that she can buy Vodafone at 170p in the stock market. Her options are worth 40p each (210p – 170p) so her overall loss is just 10.25p. That doesn't eliminate the loss but makes it much smaller than it would have been. It may even be the case that between October and December, when Vodafone was declining in value, she could have bought a further option to get closer to a zero loss in December.

But what would have happened if the price of Vodafone had risen to 240p by December? Wilma would have made a nice 35p per share profit (240p – 205p), but her options would have been worthless. Nobody would want the right to sell Vodafone shares at 210p if they can be sold at 240p on the stock market. Overall then, Wilma would have made a profit of 35p – 15.25p = 19.75p per share.

This example shows an imperfect example of *hedging*, when you use a put option to protect, or hedge, against the fall in the price of a share you already own. It didn't work perfectly for Wilma, but with a few techniques that I show you in Chapter 11, you can improve on this.

Placing bets on markets

You can look at options as bets on the future price of an asset. Because both put and call options are available, you can place bets on both a falling and rising asset value. Options can therefore be used for purely speculative purposes as well as for more defensive hedging purposes.

In this example, I explain how this works. Tesco supermarket has just gone through a hard time and its share price is down more than 40 per cent on the year. I don't think that this price is justified and believe that the share price is going to rise sharply in the new year after trading results for Christmas are announced. Current share price is 195p. For 5p, I can buy a March 2015 call option with a strike price of 220p. That looks like a bad idea as the current price is less than the strike and this option has no intrinsic value. In other words, if it were expiry day, the option would be worthless. But the point is that if by March 2015 the price is higher than 220p, my option has value.

Now, in Scenario A, the price of Tesco continues to struggle but ends slightly up at 200p by March 2015. That's still below the strike price of 220p so the call option is worthless. In Scenario B, imagine that Santa Claus decided to do all of his shopping at Tesco. Sales were fantastic, and the share price shot up to 240p by March. The option is worth 240p – 220p = 20p but I only paid 5p for it. The percentage return is 100 per cent × (20 – 5)/5 = 300 per cent. If instead, I had simply bought Tesco shares at 195p and sold them in March at 220p, my return would have been 100 per cent × (220 – 195)/195 = 12.8 per cent, which is a nice return but far smaller than that from buying the option.

The potential percentage return has been greatly amplified by buying the deep out-of-the-money option. The probability of achieving this return is low, though, and Scenario A with its 100 per cent loss is more likely than Scenario B.

TIP

Don't try this kind of hedging at home, however many seductive adverts you see from derivatives brokers! Look back at Figure 5-2 and notice that the difference between the bid and ask prices is considerable. If a speculative bet starts to go wrong, even if you wisely decide to get out, you still lose a lot of money. Option trading is for professionals taking a disciplined approach and using good risk management across a portfolio.

Writing options

If you buy a put or call option, someone on the other side of the trade issued, or *wrote*, that option. The writer receives the option premium. If you sell a call option, you're said to have a *short position in a call option*. Likewise, if you sell a put option, you're said to have a *short put position*.

If you sell a call option and the share price on its expiration date is above the strike price, then the option is exercised, and you have to deliver the underlying shares to the buyer of your call. Sadly, you have to buy the shares in the market at price S, which is above the exercise price, X. So you lose an amount (S – X) for each of the underlying shares. Potentially, your losses can be extremely large if the share price soared.

Writing a call means that you're guaranteed to receive the premium up front, but you risk huge potential losses. Simply writing a call option is often referred to as a *naked position* because of the potential for embarrassment.

I show this in a payoff diagram Figure 5-5. Notice that the value is never positive so the only reason to write a call option is to receive the premium from the buyer. In the second chart in Figure 5-5(b), I show the payoff for a short put position. Again the value is never positive and the only reason to write a put option is to receive the premium.

Earning income from options

Writing a naked call option is a risky business, but an alternative strategy, *covered-call writing* is much safer. In this strategy, the writer – a fund manager, for example – already owns the shares she writes calls on. The writer receives the premium up front. Only if the share price exceeds the strike price does the writer have to deliver shares to the buyer of the call option. As the writer already owns the shares, she doesn't have to buy them in the market.

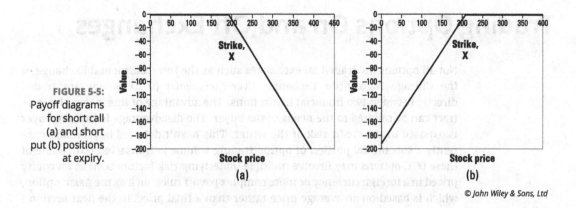

FIGURE 5-5:
Payoff diagrams
for short call
(a) and short
put (b) positions
at expiry.

In effect, writing the call option limits the up side to the fund manager's portfolio: if the price of the shares she writes a call on rises, she has to cede the shares to the option buyer at the strike price. But in compensation she receives the premium income.

Writing a naked call option may be a good course of action for a fund manager who believes that the market is going to decline but doesn't want to sell her shares or simply wants to increase the cash return from her portfolio. If she's correct and the market declines, then she earns a steady income from the premiums.

Distinguishing European, American and other options

The options I describe in this chapter generally are *European options*, which can only be exercised at expiry. But other options have different policies. *American options* can be exercised at any time before expiry. Because the American option holder has more rights than a European option holder, American options are more valuable. Also, because the holder has more flexibility, American options tend to be harder to price than European options. Note that American options can trade in Europe and vice versa. The names are an historical curiosity.

A third style is the *Bermuda option*, which is halfway between an American and European option in that it can be exercised on some days but not all days like an American option. In this book I cover only at the two simpler types of option – European and American.

To complete the range of options with geographical names, you also find Asian options where the payoff is based on an average price over a certain time period rather than the final price.

Trading Options On and Off Exchanges

Not all options are traded on exchanges such as the Intercontinental Exchange or the Chicago Mercantile Exchange. *Over-the-counter (OTC) options* are traded directly between two financial institutions. The advantage of this is that the contract can be tailored to the needs of the buyer. The disadvantage is that the buyer is exposed to the credit risk of the writer. This hasn't deterred buyers, and currently a substantial portion of option trading volume is transacted OTC. Some of these OTC options may involve multiple underlying risk factors such as an equity priced in a foreign currency or more complex payoff rules such as the Asian option, which is based on an average price rather than a final price. In the next section I explain a few more of these non-standard options.

Although OTC options are typically tailored to client requirements, the International Swaps and Derivatives Association (ISDA) has pioneered standardised documentation for OTC options. This can significantly reduce both legal and credit risks surrounding these kinds of options. Some derivatives contracts such as swaps (covered in Chapter 4) are exclusively traded OTC and, in those cases, the ISDA agreements play a key role in the market.

Exchange-traded options are highly standardised instruments although, as Figure 5-2 earlier in the chapter indicates, they come in a range of both strike and expiry dates. The advantage of this standardisation is that it attracts trading volume and, because the exchanges report on trades, market participants have a clearer view of what is happening in the market than for OTC markets. This clearer view is often referred to as *transparency*.

In addition, options traded on an exchange always have bid and ask prices so that the holder can rapidly and reliably assess the value of their holding. By contrast, OTC derivatives may not have any publicly available pricing. In that case they can be *marked to model*, a process in which mathematical models are used to value them. An introduction to the development of these models is given in Chapter 10.

Relating the Price of Puts and Calls

An important part of quantitative finance lies in valuing options. The plain vanilla options come in two varieties (or should that be flavours?) – puts and calls – and it's nice to be able to relate the price of these two types so that you need just one formula to price them both.

Calculating the price or value of an option at its expiration date is easy (see the section 'Getting Paid when Your Option Expires' earlier in the chapter); sorting out the price before expiry is harder. The value depends certainly on the underlying asset price, S, the time, t, and other factors too. (I go into more detail on this formula in Chapter 10.)

For European options, which you can exercise only on their expiry date at time T, I represent the call and put prices as $c(S,t)$ and $p(S,t)$ to indicate the dependence on the underlying asset price S and time t. Options can be bought and sold before their expiry so it's important to have pricing formulae for all of these times t and not just at expiry at time T. Sometimes I abbreviate these formulas as c and p if the dependencies aren't important.

In Chapter 4 I explain the wonder of compound interest and how money accumulates at an exponential rate. Sounds fantastic, but sadly the rate, r, at which the interest is calculated is often small. The rate I use is the *risk-free rate r*, which is the interest rate offered by the central bank or treasury. Using the exponential function signified by the letter e a sum of money U now, at time t, is worth $Ue^{r(T-t)}$ at a time, T, in the future.

In the following examples, I create two small portfolios containing options and show that they have the same value:

>> **Portfolio A:** A European call option and cash to the value of $Xe^{-r(T-t)}$ where X is the strike price.

>> **Portfolio B:** A European put option plus one share.

The value of both of these portfolios is $Max(S_T, X)$ where S_T is the share price at expiry at time, T, and X is the strike price. I come to this formula because in Portfolio A the cash is worth X at the expiry by the rule for compound interest (check Chapter 4). At expiry I will have the cash, X, to exercise my call option if S (share price) is greater than X (strike price). In this case, the portfolio is worth S_T, the price of the share at expiry. If not, then I just have my cash, X, because the call option is worthless. So the portfolio is worth $Max(S_T, X)$.

For Portfolio B, if the share ends up greater than the strike price at expiry, $(S > X)$ the option is worthless, and the portfolio value is just the value of the one share. If, on the other hand $S < X$, I can exercise my put option and sell the share for the strike price, X, so the portfolio has value X. So, again the portfolio has value $Max(S_T, X)$.

But if Portfolios A and B have the same values at expiry, they must have the same value at any time, t, as European options can't be exercised prior to expiry. In that case, I can equate the portfolio values to get $c + Xe^{-r(T-t)} = p + S$, in which I include time, t, in the compound interest factor to show that the formula is valid for any time between buying the option and its expiration date T.

This formula relates the call and put values for European options, but it doesn't work for American options as they can be exercised before expiry.

Chapter 6

Trading Risk with Futures

Futures contracts are one of the oldest forms of financial contract. They originated thousands of years ago in the agricultural markets. Before a crop was harvested – or even planted – a buyer agreed to pay a farmer a certain amount for the grain or produce. With this contract in hand, the farmer could then budget for expenses related to growing the crop.

Futures markets have evolved significantly, and this chapter explains their modern form. They're some of the most heavily traded financial instruments used by industrial producers, sophisticated hedge funds and banks.

Surveying Future Contracts

A *futures contract* is an agreement to buy or sell an asset at a specified price and at a specified time in the future. Futures are traded on organised exchanges.

If you buy a futures contract, you're said to have a *long position*, and if you sell a contract, you have a *short position*. Most futures contracts are specified by a *delivery month*, also called the *expiry*, which is when the holder of a long position must take delivery of the asset and when the holder of a short position must make a delivery of the asset. Typically, many delivery months are available for each asset.

A hedger can have a long or short position depending on whether he's a producer or consumer of a commodity. Likewise, speculators can have long or short positions.

TECHNICAL STUFF

All futures contracts come in standardised sizes. For example, for corn traded on the Chicago Mercantile Exchange (CME), the standard trading amount is 5,000 bushels, or approximately 127 metric tonnes. For crude oil traded on the Intercontinental Exchange (ICE), the amount is 1,000 barrels, which is approximately 136 metric tonnes.

Because a futures contract is an agreement that creates obligations on the holder – to make or take delivery at a given price – the contract is, in effect, free of charge.

WARNING

Free of charge sounds great but is dangerous. For example, if you enter into a short position in corn at 350 cents per bushel and the harvest is bad that year, the price on the open market may rise to 700 cents a bushel. In that case, you lose 350 cents a bushel on 5,000 bushels, or $17,500. In principle, the losses are unlimited as the price could have gone even higher.

By the way, exchanges such as the CME specify their contracts in exacting detail (nobody likes to take delivery of thousands of tons of the wrong kind of wheat) including how prices are quoted. For corn, you need to use price per bushel. Needless to say, it's fine to use dollars when you finally calculate your gain or loss.

Because futures contracts are traded on an exchange, you can purchase additional contracts that offset your existing position. So, if you have one short position on corn at 350 cents per bushel and see the price rising to 500 cents per bushel, you can buy a long contract with the same delivery month as the first contract so that your *net position* (the balance of your short and long positions) is zero, or flat. This process of creating a net position of zero is called *closing your position*. Going back to the example, in practical terms, you've lost 150 cents per bushel, or $7,500 because you sold 5,000 bushels at 350 cents per bushel and bought 5,000 bushels at 500 cents. Sometimes this calculation in which you consolidate two positions into a single position (in this case a flat position) is called *netting*.

Futures contracts don't have just financial implications – they can involve physical delivery of a commodity. Say that you're a farmer with 5,000 bushels of corn in your barn. You have a futures contract to sell your corn at 350 cents a bushel (you were concerned that the price would go down), but when the open-market price rises, you aren't too concerned. You can simply hold the contract until the delivery month and deliver the corn to a warehouse or grain elevator managed by the futures exchange. You miss out on selling your corn at 700 cents a bushel, but you haven't lost any cash. You notice a big difference between selling something you own and selling something you don't own.

Trading the futures market

Because of the possibility of going either long or short, the futures market is attractive to many market participants.

Markets exist primarily for *hedging*, which is a method to protect yourself against a price movement in the future. If you're the producer of a commodity, price drops are bad news so you go short. On the other hand, if you're a consumer of a commodity, price rises are bad news so you go long.

Other market participants called *speculators* hope to make a profit by buying and selling futures contracts. They may do a detailed statistical analysis of historical price movements or use information relevant to the market – weather forecasts when trading agricultural futures, for example.

REMEMBER

Although speculators have no interest in the deliverable commodity or asset, by making many transactions in the futures market, they make it easier for hedgers to operate in the futures market. In other words, a speculator is often on the other side of a hedger's position.

Finally, large commodity-trading companies are engaged in the purchase, shipment, storage and sale of commodities. In the agricultural market, the largest companies have become known as ABCD because of the first letters in their names: Archer Daniels Midland, Bunge, Cargill and Dreyfus. These companies actively use the futures market in conjunction with their physical trading activity. There are equivalent companies in the oil and gas markets.

Marking to market and margin accounts

Futures are risky, so brokers require users of the exchange to open a *margin account* – money or other assets in an account to offset possible losses.

Each day at the end of trading, the exchange announces a *settlement price* for each contract. Based on your profit or loss (P&L) for the day, the broker adds or deducts an amount from your margin account. This process is known as *marking to market*. If the balance on your margin account falls below a maintenance margin level, you will be *margin called* and asked to pay more money into the account. The margin call is the broker's way of ensuring that even if a client has large losses the broker still gets paid.

Minimum margin levels are set by the exchange based on the volatility of the contract. The higher the volatility, the higher the margin as a greater probability exists of a large return throwing the client into a loss. (I talk about volatility in Chapter 7.)

Say that you think that the price of crude oil is going to go up. On Day 1, you buy one futures contract (1,000 barrels) for West Texas Intermediate (WTI) crude oil at a price of $45. (WTI is the benchmark price for crude oil in the United States.) So, you're committed to paying $45,000 to take delivery of your 1,000 barrels. The initial minimum margin account level is $2,200. So, by depositing $2,200 into a margin account, you're able to realise the profit and loss (P&L) from $45,000 worth of crude oil. When the WTI price rises by $1 on Day 2 to $46, your margin account is credited with $1,000. And when the futures price goes down to $45.5 on Day 3, you decide to close out the position by going short one contract of WTI. Your account is debited $500 for that day so that its balance is $2,700. This process is summarised in Table 6-1.

TABLE 6-1   Marking to Market with Oil Futures

	Futures Price	Action Taken	P&L	Margin Account Balance
Day 1	$45	Buy one contract		$2,200
Day 2	$46		$1,000	$3,200
Day 3	$45.5	Close out	–$500	$2,700

Hedging – buying a position opposite to one you already hold – isn't always as safe as it may seem. Dramatic price changes can make your margin account balance fall precipitously, prompting a margin call, and you may have financial problems long before your delivery date!

Dealing in commodity futures

Futures contracts first evolved for agricultural products such as wheat, corn and even live cattle. As the usefulness of these contracts to manage risk became evident, exchanges introduced futures contracts for other commodities as well, including metals, crude oil and natural gas. All these futures contracts have developed into important markets that attract hedgers and speculators alike. Futures for gold and copper are closely followed: gold because it continues to be regarded almost as a currency and is held by central banks; copper because its use in electrical cables means that its price is a good indicator of economic activity.

Common to all these commodity contracts is the possibility of physical delivery. The detailed mechanics of the commodity and delivery method are specified in the contract documents:

» **Product quality:** The contract spells out the industry standards the commodity must meet. For example, the gold futures contract trading on CME 'must assay to a minimum of 995 fineness' meaning that delivering bars of gold that have been melted down and blended with copper isn't permitted. Purity specifications are also used for natural gas so that pipelines are not contaminated.

» **Product form:** The form of the commodity is clearly specified. For example, gold must be delivered as bars; orange juice must be frozen. As you'd expect, for coffee there's a testing for flavour.

» **Delivery location:** Exchanges such as the London Metal Exchange use a global network of licenced warehouses where deliveries can be made. But energy contracts typically have a more specific location. The ICE gasoil contract is specified for ARA delivery where ARA stands for Amsterdam, Rotterdam or Antwerp. (*Gasoil* is a distillate of crude oil similar to heating oil and diesel.) All these cities are near the mouth of the river Rhine and delivery is typically by barges, which can travel up and down the river.

» **Delivery date:** Most commodity futures contracts are available in a wide range of delivery months. Whereas for agricultural contracts the contract months are focused on times near harvest, energy contracts are available for all calendar months and sometimes for as many as ten years in the future. The most frequently traded contracts are always the contracts near to delivery. Equally, the open interest is always highest for contracts coming up for expiry. The prospect of delivery focuses the mind and speculators normally close out their position before then.

REMEMBER

Open interest refers to the total number of contracts taken out. Unlike shares, which are generally limited in number, futures can increase in number as market participants take out more contracts.

Figure 6-1 shows the open interest and trading volume in the ICE Brent crude oil futures contract by delivery month. Note that open interest declines exponentially the farther away the delivery month. The trading volume also declines exponentially but at a faster rate than open interest does. Nonetheless, this market clearly has great *depth*, meaning that large trades can take place with relatively small impact on the price. The maturity nearest to the delivery month, also called the *front month*, has over 300,000 contracts open with almost as much trading volume. Bear in mind that each contract is for 1,000 barrels, so this trading volume comfortably exceeds global daily production of oil which, in 2015, stands at about

90 million barrels. This liquidity is needed in the market to give participants the confidence to enter large trades with the knowledge that they will be able to exit their position with ease.

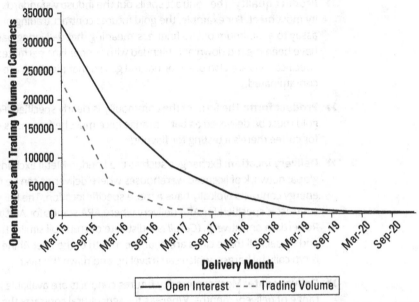

Source: Intercontinental Exchange (ICE)

FIGURE 6-1:
Open interest and trading volume in Brent crude oil futures contracts.

This high level of financial trading (speculation) in commodities such as oil isn't always comfortable. But the same is true, for example, in the foreign exchange (FX) markets where the amount of currency traded in a day often greatly exceeds the economic output of a country. In the oil market, large trading volume means that hedgers can put on positions with ease without changing prices too much. The high volume of transactions and the large number of participants in the market gives credence to the prices. Financial speculation clearly has a role in short-term price movements but commodity futures are connected to real life by delivery and so supply and demand of the commodity will be the dominant influence on price.

REMEMBER

Few commodity futures contracts are held until delivery. Most are closed out by placing an opposing trade as explained in the previous section 'Marking to market and margin accounts'. Many participants *roll* their position, meaning that they close out their position and then replace their original position with a position one month farther out. I explain this topic in more detail in the upcoming section 'Rolling a Position'. Because futures contracts expire, rolling is a good way of maintaining a position in the market. The high level of trade in the front month makes this easily possible.

Index futures

The futures market isn't restricted to physical commodities. A good, and highly successful, example of financial innovation is the introduction of *stock index futures*, which are futures contracts in which the deliverable is an amount of cash determined by the value of a stock index on the delivery date. They're available for most of the world's major stock indices such as the DAX and the S&P 500. (Chapter 4 gives the lowdown on indices.) The DAX is the main index for the German stock market. The name comes from **D**eutscher **A**ktien Inde**X**, which, in English, means German stock index.

An index future is traded on a futures exchange. Contracts are expressed as a cash amount per index point. One of the most liquid contracts is for the S&P 500; its settlement is based on $250 per index point. You can also trade a smaller contract that is only $50 per index point. The DAX futures contract trades on the Eurex exchange on 25€ per point. On its delivery date, the future is settled in cash.

Like all futures contracts, you can go long or short for speculative or hedging purposes.

Imagine that you're the manager of a $100 million portfolio of stocks that's diversified across the large companies represented in the S&P 500 – a pension portfolio, for example. You believe that the portfolio will do well in the long run because you chose the stocks carefully after much research. But you're concerned about the performance of the S&P 500 in the short term. For example, there's anxiety in the market about an election result. What do you do? You could sell a fraction of your portfolio and wait until the short term uncertainty in the market as a whole has passed. The snag with this are the transaction costs associated with selling and buying back shares. A good alternative is to hedge your portfolio using S&P 500 futures because of the low cost of buying and selling these contracts. You can sell some contracts so as to put on a short position. This position will profit if the S&P 500 goes down and will compensate you for losses in your portfolio.

To discover how many contracts you need to hedge your portfolio, follow these steps:

1. **Calcuate the value of one futures contract, which is the index value (I'm assuming the S&P 500 is at 2,000) times the cost per point.**

   For this example, the formula is 2,000 × $250 = $500,000.

2. **Determine the number of contracts you need by dividing your portfolio value by the value of the futures contract.**

   The formula is: $100 million ÷ $500,000 = 200 contracts.

So, you sell 200 of the front month S&P 500 futures contract at 1,990. Notice that the futures price isn't the same as the cash index price – I explain why in the upcoming section 'Seeing into the Future'. Several weeks later, the S&P 500 drops to 1,800. The front month future has dropped down to 1,790 so your futures position has gained a cool $10 million. Calculate this from 200 (contracts) times the difference between the initial and current index value $(1{,}990 - 1{,}790)$ times $250 per point – or $200 \times 200 \times \$250 = \$10$ million.

But your portfolio has declined at the same rate as the index. The index declined by 10 per cent and so your portfolio lost 10 per cent of $100 million, which is $10 million. At the end of the three weeks, you manage to retain the value of your portfolio. Your clients are happy and you've saved yourself some of the transaction costs involved in selling shares.

I made several assumptions in this example. If the portfolio is more volatile than the S&P 500, then the calculated amount of futures contracts will be insufficient to maintain its value. That's because the portfolio will decline more than the index in percentage terms. Equally, if the portfolio is less volatile than the S&P 500 then you will buy too many contracts.

In Chapter 14, I talk about the capital asset pricing model and its constants α and β. To more accurately calculate the number of contracts to hedge your portfolio, you must multiply the answer given in the steps, 200, by β. In the calculation here I assumed your portfolio is similar to the S&P 500 and that its β is equal to 1.

Interest rate futures

Another important group of futures contracts are for short-term interest rates. Sometimes these are referred to as STIR futures. The most popular instrument is the Eurodollar future traded on the Chicago Mercantile Exchange (CME). This contract is a template for other short-term interest rate contracts such as the three-month sterling future that trades on ICE or the one-month Euroyen future that also trades on CME. *Euroyen* are Japanese Yen traded outside of Japan.

Eurodollars are US dollars deposited in a bank outside of the United States. The Eurodollar futures contract is a contract on the three-month LIBOR (London Interbank Offer Rate) for these deposits. (You can read about LIBOR in Chapter 4.) The futures contract works by cash settlement on expiry using the price $(100 - L)$ where L is the three-month LIBOR rate. This formula ensures that the futures contract has a direct connection with LIBOR and that if LIBOR changes, the futures contract will compensate the holder for any lost interest.

Interest rate contracts are defined so that a one basis point change in the futures quote results in a $25 change in the contract value. If you have a $1 million contract then a one basis point increase in the interest rate results in an increase of $0.01 \times 0.01 \times \$1,000,000 = \$100$ in the interest earned per year.

One per cent of an amount, P, is $0.01 \times P$, so one basis point, which is a hundredth of one per cent, is $0.01 \times 0.01 \times P$.

TECHNICAL STUFF

That's equivalent to $25 in three months. The Eurodollar futures contract is then able to lock in a three-month interest rate for $1 million of capital.

A *basis point* is 0.01 of a percentage point. So an interest rate of 0.06 per cent is one basis point higher than 0.05 per cent.

REMEMBER

Because the settlement is based on $(100 - L)$, a long position gains value when the LIBOR rate declines while a short position gains when LIBOR rises. Eurodollar futures contracts exist with many delivery dates going out many years. This makes them powerful tools for banks and large companies to manage their cash deposits.

You can also invest in futures contracts for government bonds such as German Bunds, British Gilts and US Treasury Notes among many others. These contracts all settle by delivering bonds rather than cash.

There are futures contracts for the different maturities of bonds so, for example, there's a two-year Treasury Note future as well as a ten-year Treasury Note future. In effect, all of these contracts allow market participants to hedge or speculate in longer term interest rates.

Seeing into the Future

A key element of the futures market is that each asset has many contracts with different delivery dates. This variation allows participants to manage risk over different time horizons. An oil refinery that wants to fix its crude oil purchase prices for the year can do so by hedging using contracts throughout the 12-month calendar. On a shorter time scale, a large company may use Eurodollar futures to fix the interest it earns on a large sum of money deposited in a bank.

Paying in cash now

The price paid for a commodity for immediate delivery is called the *spot price* or sometimes just the *cash price*. This pricing seems straightforward, but in practice the spot price is a bit more complicated than it seems. For one thing, most physical commodities can't be delivered immediately. For example, you need ships to transport crude oil and pipelines to transport natural gas, and they're not always immediately available.

REMEMBER

For commodities such as crude oil, the spot price absolutely must be assessed by an independent agency such as Argus Media, Platts or ICIS Heren, that checks the integrity of the quoted cash prices. Both Platts and ICIS Heren are owned by major publishers (McGraw Hill and Relex, respectively). The role of all of these agencies is as trusted providers of information independent of the market participants. Physical traders of crude oil such as oil companies report their traded prices to these agencies who then compile a daily index reference price.

Metals have a strong connection between the spot price and the futures price because metals are easy to store – that's one of the reasons for the popularity of gold as an investment commodity.

Even cash-settled contracts such as index futures have delivery subtleties. For financial futures, such as index futures, the underlying index is often referred to as the cash price of the index to distinguish it from the futures price.

REMEMBER

Stock index futures are cash settled using the value of the index and a multiplier defined by the exchange.

For a futures contract to reflect the reality of the cash index, it must be possible to trade the shares representing the index at the contract's expiry. This possibility doesn't exist if you try to use the closing price of the index – because the exchange just closed – so most index futures are settled using a special intra-day auction. This auction is run by the stock exchange itself and often at a random time near to the close. The purpose of that is to prevent participants manipulating the index by making cash purchases or sales of stock to change the index in a way to favour their position in the futures market.

REMEMBER

If the futures price of the stock index is higher than the cash price close to the delivery month, then it's possible to make a profit by shorting the index future and buying the underlying shares of the index. This is called *index arbitrage*. Equally, if the futures price is lower than the cash price of the index, you can buy the index future and sell the constituent shares of the index.

Connecting futures and spot prices

You can relate the spot price of a commodity to the future price using the time value of money I talk about in Chapter 4. If the futures price is F, the spot price is S, the rate of interest is r, current time is t and delivery month time is T, the equation looks like this:

$$F = Se^{r(T-t)}$$

The constant e in the equation for the futures price is the base of the natural logarithm. Its value is e = 2.718. . . The Cheat Sheet at www.dummies.com/cheatsheet/quantitativefinance has more information on the natural logarithm and the exponential function.

The future price is higher than the spot price. This equation is slightly different from the one for time value of money because a futures price is on the left side of the equation and a cash price is on the right. It's important that a futures contract can be delivered and the cash realised for this equation to hold.

The connection between the spot and futures price is made by *arbitrage trades* in which the same or similar assets are bought simultaneously to exploit price differences. It is by making these trades that this equation becomes true.

Here is how arbitrage works:

If F is greater than $Se^{r(T-t)}$, then you take certain actions now and on the delivery date:

> Now: You buy a gold bar for spot price S, taking a short position on gold futures.

> At expiry: You deliver the gold bar and receive future price F for your gold.

On expiry, you receive the amount, F, and hand over the gold bar. The present value of the futures sale is $Fe^{-r(T-t)}$ and so the condition for making a profit is that $Fe^{-r(T-t)} > S$, which can be written as $F > Se^{r(T-t)}$. This method is a sure way of making money. As people buy gold in the spot market, the price of gold rises. Eventually, the inequality becomes an equality and $F = Se^{r(T-t)}$.

However, if F is less than $Se^{r(T-t)}$, you have to do a different trade:

> Now: You borrow a gold bar from a bank. You sell it for spot price, S, and invest the proceeds at a rate, r. You take a long positon on gold futures.

> At expiry: Pay future price, F, and take delivery of your gold bar. Hand it over to the bank which lent you the gold at the start.

You make a profit if $Fe^{-r(T-t)} < S$. If this works, the spot price of gold declines as more sales of physical gold are made. Eventually, the equality $F = Se^{-r(T-t)}$ holds.

Accounting for convenience

This arbitrage trade is less straightforward than the first because you have to sell something you don't own. In fact, to borrow gold from a bank you have to pay a fee, called the *convenience yield*, represented by y in the equation expressed as $F = Se^{(r-y)(T-t)}$.

The convenience yield exists because banks may not want to lend you a commodity. This yield is a measure of the desirability or convenience of actually holding the physical commodity. If the convenience yield is high, then futures contracts are priced lower than the spot price, which happens if a shortage of the commodity is evident. By contrast, if surpluses of a commodity exist, then the convenience yield is low and futures contracts are priced higher than the spot price.

Settling storage costs

The formula $F = Se^{(r-y)(T-t)}$ is still a bit inaccurate because it doesn't account for the cost of storing a physical commodity. Grain elevators and oil storage tanks are expensive. If these costs, u, are expressed as a proportion of the spot price, your equation becomes $F = Se^{(r+u-y)(T-t)}$.

Adding in dividends

A slightly different formula applies for an index future that has no storage costs, but pays dividends. If the dividend yield is q, the formula is $F = Se^{(r-q)(T-t)}$.

Checking trading volume

Although index futures are cash-settled contracts, extensive trading occurs in the underlying shares of an index at expiry as hedgers and speculators trade futures positions to guarantee a quick profit. Figure 6-2 shows the trading volume of the DAX index. Notice the monthly pattern of sharp peaks in trading volume. These peaks are caused by arbitrage activity at expiry of the DAX index futures contracts.

Looking along the forward curve

Futures contracts all have delivery dates, and for some commodities you have a choice of delivery date extending to beyond ten years in the future. This is an important feature because it allows businesses to use futures contracts for both short- and long-term planning.

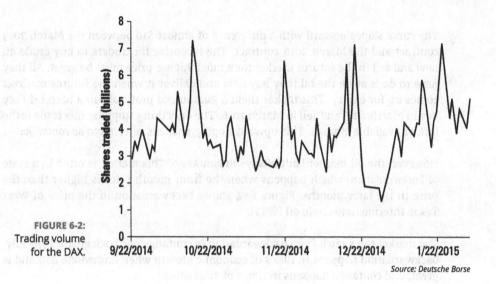

FIGURE 6-2:
Trading volume for the DAX.

Source: Deutsche Borse

Oil wells are expensive to develop, so normally oil companies borrow from banks to fund their development. The oil company can then use futures contracts to lock in the price of the produced oil not just for one month but potentially for many months or years into the future. The way these futures prices vary with the delivery date is a sensitive reflection of the state of the oil market.

Figure 6-3 plots the prices for Brent crude oil futures contracts through nearly two years. A graph like this one showing the price of a series of contracts with different maturities or delivery dates is called a *forward curve*.

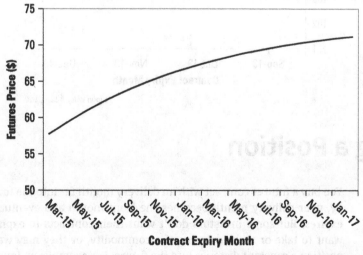

FIGURE 6-3:
Forward curve for Brent Crude Futures (February 2015).

Source: Intercontinental Exchange (ICE)

The curve slopes upward with a difference of almost $10 between the March 2015 contract and the March 2016 contract. The incentive for traders to buy crude oil now and sell in the futures market for a much higher price must be great. All they have to do is store the oil they buy now and deliver it when the futures contract comes up for expiry. This makes them a guaranteed profit of $10 a barrel if they buy in March 2015 and sell in March 2016. The only thing stopping this trade is the lack of available storage. This upward sloping shape is referred to as *contango*.

However, the oil market isn't always in contango. This market is often in a state of *backwardation*, which happens when the front month price is higher than the price in the later months. Figure 6-4 shows backwardation in the price of West Texas Intermediate crude oil (WTI).

The market can switch from backwardation to contango and back again. Typically, backwardation happens in times of economic growth when immediate demand is great, and contango happens in times of stagnation.

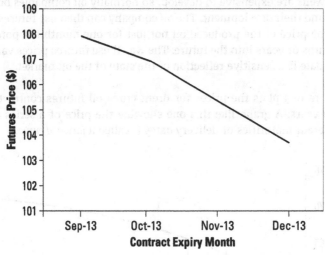

FIGURE 6-4:
Forward Curve for WTI Crude Oil Futures (August 2013)

© John Wiley & Sons, Ltd.

Rolling a Position

You buy a futures contract with an delivery month far into the future. As time goes by, your delivery month becomes the front month and eventually your contract expires. But some investors don't want their contracts to expire. They may not want to take or make delivery of a commodity, or they may want to maintain a position a constant distance into the future. For example, an investor may want to hedge a whole year's production or consumption futures.

To a speculator, a front month future is attractive. Refer to Figure 6-1 to see that both the open interest and the trading volume of the front-month contract exceeds that of all the other contracts. This liquidity means that the transaction charges are low for buying and selling the front month and allows the speculator to make the most of opportunities that come along.

Keeping a consistent position

To maintain a position a consistent distance into the future, you need to *roll* your contracts. *Rolling* means to successively sell (or buy) the front-month contract and buy (or sell) the next month contract as shown in Table 6-2:

TABLE 6-2   Maintaining a Position by Rolling

Month	Futures to Sell	Futures to Buy
February	March 2015	April 2015
March	April 2015	May 2015
April	May 2015	June 2015

The March 2015 contract is for physical delivery in March and ceases trading in February, so you want to sell this contract before the last trading day in February. If you're a hedger and have long contracts for all the months from March 2015 to March 2016, then your roll involves selling March 2015 and buying April 2016.

Adjusting backwards

If market participants are maintaining a front month position – or any other position for that matter – by rolling, then, in a sense, the front month is a new form of contract. But quantitative analysis of this new kind of contract isn't easy because it consists of many segments of data pasted together from the different monthly contracts. Frequently, you can see jumps in the price from one contract to another. The solution to this problem is to use a process of *back-adjustment,* which produces a continuous data set for a front month, second month or whatever contract you wish by splicing together data from the different monthly contracts according to a schedule – normally just before the front month comes up for expiry.

If the March 2015 contract is at price, P, on your roll date just before expiry and the April 2015 contract is at price Q, then you simply add $(Q-P)$ to all the March prices. So, on the roll date, your old front-month contract has the same price as your new front-month contract. Your front-month prices become continuous, and you can analyse trends or calculate volatility in a systematic way. Figure 6-5 shows this process.

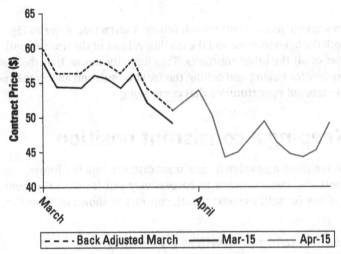

FIGURE 6-5:
Adjusting futures prices to create a continuous front-month contract.

- - - - Back Adjusted March ——— Mar-15 ——— Apr-15

Converging Futures to the Spot Price

All futures contracts have an expiry date at which time they're settled in cash or delivered or received. It makes sense then that the futures price must converge towards the spot price as the expiry date gets closer. If that did not happen, there would be opportunities to make riskless profits by arbitrage.

REMEMBER

Arbitrage is the process of taking advantage of the price difference between two similar markets – in this case, the spot and futures markets. If the spot price is high relative to the futures price as the expiry date of the futures approaches, holders of the commodity will sell it and go long on the future. When the future expires, these holders buy back the commodity for a lower price. If the spot price is low relative to the futures price, then speculators will buy the commodity in the cash market and sell futures contracts. On expiry, they deliver the commodity to their buyer for a higher price than they bought it.

Traders monitor prices as expiries approach by measuring the *basis*, which is the spot price minus the futures price, or Basis = Spot price – Futures price, which is a simple equation but useful nonetheless.

Figure 6-6 shows schematically how a futures price converges towards the spot price.

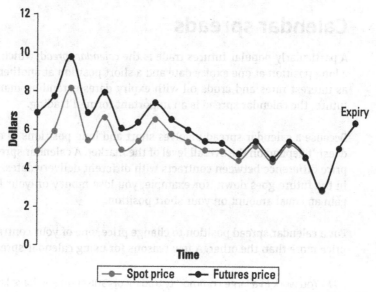

FIGURE 6-6: Convergence of spot price to the futures price at expiry.

Spot price — Futures price

© *John Wiley & Sons, Ltd.*

If you're using the futures contract to hedge the production or consumption of a commodity, monitoring the basis is crucial. It may be that you start to run out of crude oil sooner than you expected. If you then close out your hedge early and buy crude oil in the spot market, your hedge won't work perfectly because the basis hasn't converged to zero yet. This situation is called *basis risk*. Basis risk also happens because the futures contract doesn't exactly match the asset you're buying or selling.

WARNING

The futures contract doesn't have to converge to the spot price at expiry. This situation is unusual but happens if, for some reason, you cannot carry out the arbitrage trades that usually make the prices converge. For example, if the stock market crashes around expiry time and delays are imposed on trades, then convergence between an index and the index futures price may not happen.

Using Futures Creatively

Futures contracts are useful for hedging the price of commodities, insuring stock market portfolios against crashes and protecting the interest rate of your deposit in a bank. But some less straightforward uses of futures are well worth knowing about. These uses are possible because of the many different futures contracts out there in the market and the creativity of the traders who use them.

Calendar spreads

A particularly popular futures trade is the *calendar spread,* which involves placing a long position at one expiry date and a short position at another. For assets such as interest rates and crude oil with expiry dates extending many years into the future, the calendar spread is an important form of trading.

Because a calendar spread involves short and long positions in equal measure, it doesn't depend on the overall level of the market. A calendar spread is a bet on the price difference between contracts with different delivery dates. If every contract in the future goes down, for example, you lose money on your long position but gain an equal amount on your short position.

For a calendar spread position to change price, one of your contracts must change price more than the other. A few reasons for using calendar spreads are

» You work in a large commodity trading organisation and have knowledge about shipments of a commodity. You're fairly sure that supply will be disrupted in the short term but that the commodity won't be in short supply in the future. You could go long on the front month future and short the second month. If your view is correct, then a short-term supply problem causes the front month price to increase without changing the second month price. In addition, if an unanticipated event occurs that changes both prices then your position isn't affected.

» You work in a hedge fund and want to maintain a long position in a futures contract that's coming up for expiry. You roll the position by going short the current front month and buying the current second month. This action is equivalent to buying a calendar spread.

TECHNICAL STUFF

A *hedge fund* is an investment fund that uses riskier strategies than a mutual fund. Hedge fund managers normally require their investors to be accredited as having a high level of financial knowledge. The minimum investment is often quite large.

Commodity spreads

Futures contracts can be used to hedge commodity prices by producers or consumers of commodities. Using futures contracts in this way allows them to fix their input costs or their output prices so as to make running their business less risky. Slightly more complex is to hedge both input costs and output prices. Doing so can be useful if your industry converts one commodity into another. A good example of this action is the *crack spread,* which is the price difference between crude oil and the gasoline and diesel products the former is refined into.

In the following calculation I use prices from March 2015 Chicago Mercantile Exchange (CME) contracts, and assume the 321 *crack spread*, or that three barrels of crude oil is processed into two barrels of gasoline and a barrel of diesel:

>3 barrels of crude oil at $51.37 per barrel = $154.11
>2 barrels of gasoline = 84 gallons at $1.54 per gallon = $129.36
>1 barrel of diesel = 42 gallons at $1.83 per gallon = $76.86
>Crack spread = $129.36 + $76.86 − $154.11 = $52.11.

So you make a profit of $17.37 for each barrel of crude oil you process ($52.11 ÷ 3 − the crack spread divided by the number of barrels). Liking this high level of profitability, you could purchase three crude oil futures and sell two gasoline futures and one diesel future – all for April 2015. This activity would lock in high profitability for another month.

Seasonality in Futures Prices

The forward curves I explain in the 'Looking along the forward curve' section earlier in this chapter don't all look like Figure 6-3. If the market is in backwardation, the curve slopes downwards rather than upwards. However, yet another possibility exists: The forward curve can be *seasonal*. In this case, the forward curve has a wave-like pattern corresponding to the seasons of the year. The cause of this is changes in supply or demand for the commodity underlying the future. Figure 6-7 shows a seasonal curve for natural gas, but as you may expect, many agricultural commodities have seasonal curves. Natural gas is seasonal because gas is used extensively for heating in homes and commercial premises. Demand is high in winter, so prices reach a peak in January or February.

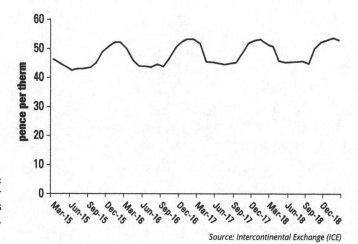

FIGURE 6-7: Forward curve for UK natural gas futures.

Source: Intercontinental Exchange (ICE)

Because of the seasonality of the forward curve, the relationships that hold for a simple forward curve (see 'Connecting futures and spot prices' earlier in this chapter) no longer hold. The simpler equations have an exponential relationship between futures price and the expiry date T that can't express a periodic relationship like that for natural gas. To adapt the formula, you can use a seasonal premium s(T) which depends on the expiry month, indicated by T. Otherwise, the formula is the same:

$$F(t,T) = S(t)e^{s(T)+(r+u-y)(T-t)}.$$

3
Investigating and Describing Market Behaviour

Chapter 7

Reading the Market's Mood: Volatility

olatility is an important quantity in quantitative finance – it's like the mood of the market. Long periods of calm can be followed by jittery markets with high volatility. This variation makes modelling volatility challenging and interesting. Volatility occurs naturally if you're trying to model financial asset prices. It's also closely connected with the idea of risk. Risk is often measured using variance (see Chapter 2 on probability and statistics), which is the square of the volatility. Because of that, volatility is often used to calculate the size of positions in financial trading so as to maintain a constant level of risk in a portfolio. In addition, the price of derivative products such as options depends very much on the volatility of the underlying asset.

You can't observe volatility in the market directly. You can only see market prices. You need to calculate volatility from a model, and in this chapter I tell you how to do this.

Defining Volatility

Volatility is a measure of how changeable market prices are. If prices frequently make large moves up and down, volatility is high. On the other hand, if the market is calm with only small price changes, volatility is low. But volatility itself is constantly changing.

REMEMBER

A_n indicates an asset with a price, A, on day n, which can be any integer, such as 1, 2, 3 or higher. A_n is a good shorthand to use. You deal with lots of historical financial data, so you need a simple way of referring to specific days. The asset price on the previous day is then: A_{n-1}.

The return on day n is written R_n and defined by the formula:

$$R_n = \frac{A_n - A_{n-1}}{A_{n-1}}.$$

The numerator of the formula is the change in asset price from day $n-1$ to day n. Divide it by the price on day $n-1$ so that the return is a relative quantity. You can then use this formula to compare the returns for one asset with another because it doesn't rely on the absolute value of the asset. If you multiply R_n by 100, you get the familiar percentage return used on many financial products.

REMEMBER

Another common way to define returns in quantitative finance is to use natural logarithms. The online Cheat Sheet at www.dummies.com/cheatsheet/quantitativefinance gives you a heads up on natural logarithms. They behave just like logarithms to base 10 except that they're to base e where e = 2.718 . . . . Using such a strange number as the base of a logarithm may seem obtuse, but as the Cheat Sheet shows, it makes other properties of the natural logarithm a lot simpler than logarithms to base 10. With this new definition, I use U_n to mean the return on the nth day:

$$U_n = \ln\left(\frac{A_n}{A_{n-1}}\right).$$

An advantage of this definition is that if you add the return for M successive days, where M is an integer such as 5, the result is equal to the multi-day return (good to know):

$$U_1 + U_2 + U_3 + \ldots + U_M = \ln\left(\frac{A_M}{A_0}\right).$$

This equation isn't true for the other definition of return, R_n. On the other hand, $U_n = \ln(1 + R_n)$, so if R_n is small, nearly equal to U_n. Plug numbers into your calculator for values such as 0.1 and 0.05 if you're sceptical, and see for yourself!

TECHNICAL STUFF

You can expand the natural logarithm of $1 + x$ using a Taylor expansion:

$$\ln(1+x) = 1 + x - \frac{x^2}{2} + \frac{x^3}{3} - \frac{x^4}{4} + \dots.$$

By using just the first term in this expansion, you get the approximation that $R_n = U_n$ if the return is small because squared returns and higher powers of the returns are even smaller.

The returns of a financial asset can be considered a random variable. (See Chapter 2 for more on random variables and distributions.) If the returns of financial assets were predictable, it would be possible to systematically make money from the markets. However, you can't do so (or if you can, you've kept it a closely guarded secret). The statistical distribution of returns is often approximately a Gaussian distribution. The volatility of a financial asset is the standard deviation of the returns and is one of the parameters in the Gaussian distribution. Although the Gaussian distribution is a good approximation to financial returns, don't forget that very large losses (and gains) occur much more frequently than predicted by this distribution. This is the phenomenon of *fat tails*.

REMEMBER

A high value of the standard deviation (σ) means that the distribution is broad and that the asset price can be expected to rise and fall a lot. By contrast, a small standard deviation means that the distribution of returns is narrow and that the asset price doesn't fluctuate much.

Financial returns are not stable, though. No single standard deviation describes the return distribution. That's why the word *volatility* is used and not just *standard deviation*. Volatility varies with time. During periods of political uncertainty or economic troubles, volatility can become high.

Figure 7-1 shows a plot of the daily returns on the Hang Seng index (HSI) – the main indicator of the Hong Kong stock exchange – from 1990 until 2014. The graph shows major bursts of activity when the index had large returns – both positive and negative – in 1997 and also in 2008. These dates correspond with Hong Kong becoming a special administrative region within China in 1997 and the global financial crisis in 2008. The standard deviation of returns during both years was high compared to, say, 2005 when it was low. Bursts of activity like this interspersed with periods of calm are typical of financial markets. The figure also shows the extent to which financial markets are connected with world events and that they can indeed be part of world events.

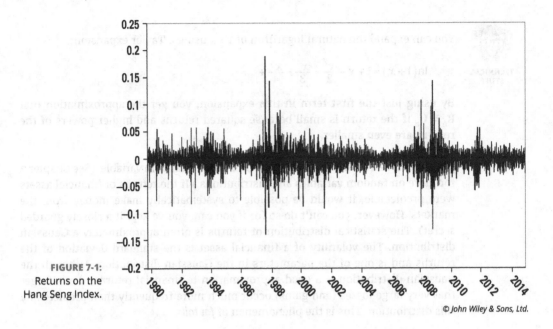

FIGURE 7-1:
Returns on the
Hang Seng Index.

© John Wiley & Sons, Ltd.

Using Historical Data

One way to calculate the volatility of a financial asset is to use historical prices. Because the volatility is constantly changing, any calculation based on historical data is only an estimate of the current volatility. Calculating a standard deviation of the returns of all the available data normally isn't adequate because it averages over periods of high and low market activity. In the following sections, I offer a variety of ways of calculating volatility.

Weighting the data equally

The simplest calculation of volatility to use is the standard deviation over M days of returns:

$$\sigma_n^2 = \frac{1}{M}\sum_{i=1}^{M} R_{n+1-i}^2.$$

In words, this formula says that the square of the volatility, σ, on day n is the average of the squared returns on the M previous days. You can choose to let M be much smaller than the total number of data points so that you can make a running chart of the volatility, such as the one shown in Figure 7-2.

Figure 7-2 uses the Hang Seng data presented in Figure 7-1 but only from 2007 until 2011. I used $M = 64$ so that the volatility is calculated from almost three months of historical data – the 64-day volatility in the figure. (Lest you be confused about 64 days being equal to 3 months, the number of days the markets operate in three months is roughly 64 days.)

Figure 7-2 shows almost a fourfold increase in volatility from 2007 to 2010 and then a subsequent steady decline. The plateau in December 2008 is artificial and due to the way the volatility was calculated using data from the 64 previous days. So it includes the days with exceptional returns towards the end of October 2008. When those days drop out of the 64-day window, the volatility starts to decline.

Although this method of calculation shows clearly the rise and fall of volatility, the method isn't as responsive as it could be to changes in market conditions.

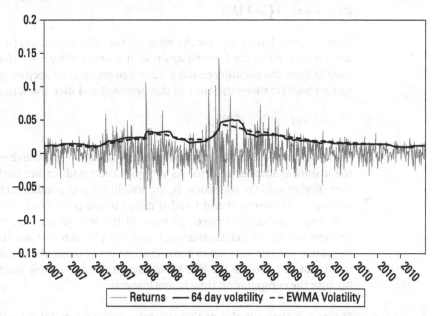

FIGURE 7-2: Comparing volatility calculations for the Hang Seng Index.

— Returns — 64 day volatility – – EWMA Volatility

© John Wiley & Sons, Ltd.

Weighting returns

The volatility of a financial asset is constantly changing, and if you use the latest returns, M, to calculate it, you'll be using some stale information. If you treat each of the M historic data points as equally important, data from M days ago have the same importance as data from today. You can avoid this by using the method of *exponential smoothing*, which is also called an *exponentially weighted moving average* (*EWMA*).

In a weighted average, you don't treat the numbers being averaged equally. Some are considered more important than others and get a higher weight. In the EWMA, recent returns get higher weight than the returns from a longer time ago. It intuitively makes sense that market participants pay more attention to recent history.

In this method, you calculate the square of the volatility on day n using a weighted average of the squared volatility on the previous day and the squared return on day n. You can choose the value of the weighting, λ, to be anything between 0 and 1. Sometimes λ is called a *smoothing parameter* because by averaging over previous values of the squared returns, the EWMA smooths out jumps in the squared returns. If you choose a value close to 0, there is very little smoothing of the squared returns. On the other hand, a value close to 1 leads to lots of smoothing and the EWMA can be used to see trends in volatility. Many market practitioners use a value of 0.95. You can see a chart in which various values of λ have been used in Figure 7-3. Finally, the formula for volatility using exponential weighting is: $\sigma_n^2 = \lambda \sigma_{n-1}^2 + (1-\lambda)R_n^2$.

However, you don't yet know the value for the volatility on day $(n-1)$. To sort that out, you can write the formula again with n replaced by $n-1$. However, then you need to know the volatility on day $n-2$ and so on. You can keep on going further and further back (mathematicians call this *iterating*) and then the formula looks like:

$$\sigma_n^2 = (1-\lambda)\sum_{i=1}^{\infty} \lambda^{i-1} R_{n-i+1}^2.$$

Now you can see that the squared volatility on day n is a weighted average of all the historical squared returns. As you go further and further back in time, however (higher value of the index, i), the weighting gets smaller and smaller. That's because λ is between 0 and 1 and if raised to the power $i-1$, it becomes smaller still. Your data set will never go back all the way to infinity, but don't worry: because the terms get smaller and smaller, you can just set the return at the beginning of your data set to zero. That means you can always calculate the formula. But to calculate the EWMA, always prefer the simple iterative calculation because the computation time is much shorter.

Figure 7-2 shows a plot of this volatility indicated as EWMA volatility. You can clearly see that after the financial crisis of 2008 the EWMA volatility drops quicker than the equally weighted 64-day volatility. In the EWMA calculation, I use the value $\lambda = 0.98$.

Exponential weighting is used to make a *running*, or day-by-day, calculation of the volatility (but you can use any time increment). A running calculation is, in effect, an update formula from the previous day's value. The first few values you calculate will be inaccurate because at the beginning of your data you're forced to use a return of zero. Sometimes this initial period with inaccurate values is called a *warm-up phase*, like a steam engine that takes time to work up to full power.

Figure 7-3 shows the effect of different values of λ on the calculation of the EWMA volatility. For the lowest value of λ = 0.875, the EWMA volatility is more reactive to big market events, but the high volatility then dies away quickly.

REMEMBER

Choosing the value of λ is probably more of an art than a science. In general, though, for longer-term models and forecasts use a value close to one so that it's not too responsive to the most recent history.

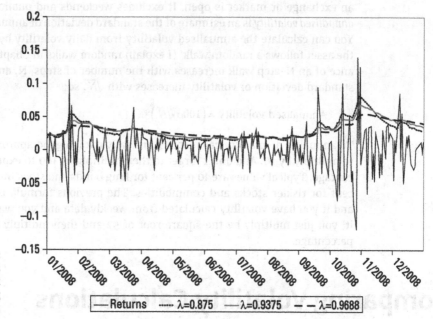

FIGURE 7-3:
EWMA volatilities using different smoothing factors.

| —Returns ⋯⋯ λ=0.875 —λ=0.9375 – –λ=0.9688 |

© John Wiley & Sons, Ltd.

WARNING

If you use a small value of lambda in a period of low volatility, the exponential smoothing method will give you a low value for volatility because the formula only uses data from that period of low volatility. This value can be misleading. Chances are that there were periods of high volatility in the past and that there will be high volatility again in the future – don't let anyone tell you otherwise! It's good practice to check your value of volatility using a high value of lambda – something close to one – and use that number to limit how low your estimate of volatility can go.

Shrinking Time Using a Square Root

Price returns data can come in many different frequencies: daily, weekly, monthly or even hourly. If you calculate a volatility from this data and then want to make comparisons with the volatility of another asset, you must calculate both at the same frequency. A common solution to this problem is to *annualise* the volatility by converting all asset returns to a yearly frequency. This conversion makes comparisons straightforward between the riskiness of different assets whether they're stocks, bonds or commodities.

To calculate an annualised volatility, you need to know how many price returns there are every year for your price return data. A generally used assumption is that there are 250 trading days per year, so $N = 250$. (*Trading days* are those days when an exchange or market is open. It excludes weekends and public holidays.) The *annualised volatility* is an estimate of the standard deviation of annual price returns. You can calculate the annualised volatility from daily volatility by assuming that the asset follows a random walk. (I explain random walks in Chapter 3.) The variance of an N-step walk increases with the number of steps, N, and therefore the standard deviation or volatility increases with $\sqrt{N}$, so:

$$\text{Annualised volatility} = \left(100\sigma\sqrt{N}\right)\%.$$

To annualise a volatility calculated from daily data, a good approximation is just to multiply by 16. And don't forget to then multiply by 100 to express it as a percentage. Typical values are 10 per cent for long bonds and stock indices and 20 per cent for riskier stocks and commodities. The previous formula is quite general, and if you have volatility calculated from weekly data and you want to annualise it, you just multiply by the square root of 52 and then multiply by 100 to get a percentage.

Comparing Volatility Calculations

Calculating volatility from historical price data, as explained earlier in the section 'Using Historical Data', isn't the only way to find a value for volatility. You can use the price of an *option*, which is the right to buy or sell an asset in the future at a price agreed to in the present. (Chapter 5 talks more about options.)

REMEMBER

Because the price of an option depends on a future unknown price for an underlying asset, an increase in volatility tends to increase an option price because it becomes more probable that the option will hit the *strike price* – the price at which the option holder can buy or sell – on its delivery date and have some value (many options expire valueless). Higher volatility means larger price moves for the underlying asset of an option and increases the chance of hitting the strike price.

The price of a call option can be written as $C = f(r, S, \tau, K, \sigma)$. This equation means that the price of a call option is a function of the risk-free interest rate, r; the underlying asset price, S; the time to expiry, τ; the option's strike price, K; and the market volatility, σ. However, for every option you can find S and C from market data feeds and τ and K from the option specification. For r, you can use the central bank base rate or the yield on a short-term (three months, for example) government bill. Using these known parameter values means that only σ is an unknown in the equation for C. In Chapter 10, I offer formulae for option prices to use as the function f, such as the solutions to the famous Black-Scholes equation. Here, I show you the results of using a few of these formulae.

To calculate σ from the formula $C = f(r, S, \tau, K, \sigma)$, you need to be consistent with the data that you put into the formula. The best way is to use annualised volatility and express τ in years. Similarly C, S and K should all be expressed in the same units and currency. The risk-free rate should be expressed as a decimal fraction. For example, use 0.03 for a 3 per cent rate.

TIP

For exchange-traded options, always check the contract specifications to find out the expiry date. Normally, this date is the third Friday of the expiry month.

To calculate the time to expiry, τ, use the formula $\tau = \dfrac{\text{Trading days until expiry}}{\text{Trading days in the year}}$ so that τ is now in fractions of a year. Most exchanges have about 250 trading days per year. Good evidence is available that trading activity itself can create volatility in asset prices, so you're better to calculate τ with this definition rather than with calendar days.

The chart in Figure 7-4 shows the results of some calculations for the implied volatility of the March 2015 Brent crude oil future. It shows that if you take data for a range of strike prices, the volatility is certainly not constant, which is a bit unsettling. The shape of the curve has been called the *volatility smile*. It may have been a joker in the City of London who thought that expression up, but it's an important feature of option markets. The nickname reflects the fact that many analyses of option prices make simplifying assumptions about volatility. In particular, the assumption that the volatility is constant is mathematically convenient but not quite right. By fitting the Black-Scholes formula – $C = f(r, S, \tau, K, \sigma)$ – to market data by adjusting σ, you violate one of the assumptions made to derive the formula for f. However, this choice is pragmatic. Making more realistic assumptions about volatility is possible but makes the mathematics of pricing options exceptionally complex.

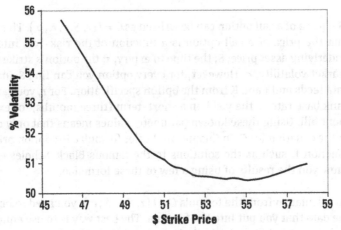

Source: Intercontinental Exchange (ICE)

The smile shape probably results from the kurtotic returns from most financial markets.

REMEMBER

Kurtosis is a measure of the fatness of the tails of a statistical returns distribution. If the kurtosis of a financial returns distribution is greater than that for a Gaussian distribution, then it is *fat tailed*. Then large price changes, both positive and negative, happen much more frequently than assumed in the Gaussian distribution.

Because of the fat-tailed nature of financial market returns, out-of-the-money options are more likely to become in-the-money options than is assumed in constant volatility Black-Scholes. The high implied volatility corrects for this situation in the only possible way.

The plot of implied volatility against strike price doesn't always look like the smile in Figure 7-4. That's a pity, but in the equity market, the chart often has a negative skew with higher implied volatilities for low strike call options and lower implied volatilities for high strike options, as shown in Figure 7-5. The chart shows the implied volatility for the Royal Bank of Scotland (RBS). The Black-Scholes model under-prices in-the-money call options, so the implied volatility has to be higher at low strike prices. The reason may be that large falls in the equity market are often associated with rising volatility. If the underlying price of an in-the-money call option falls sharply back down towards the strike price, traders may not be too concerned because they anticipate an increase in volatility associated with the price fall and are happy to pay a slightly higher price for the option.

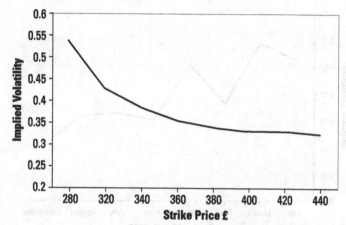

FIGURE 7-5:
Volatility skew of an equity call option.

Strike Price £

Source: Intercontinental Exchange (ICE)

However, you don't just have to use call options to calculate implied volatility. You can use put options, too. The chart in Figure 7-6 shows this use for the FTSE 100 Index. The markets smile has returned (sort of), but you can still see a sharp rise in implied volatility for out-of-the-money puts with low strike price.

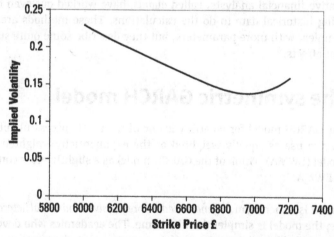

FIGURE 7-6:
Implied volatility from June 2015 FTSE 100 Index put options.

Strike Price £

Source: Intercontinental Exchange (ICE)

Yet another way to plot a chart for implied volatility is to compute it for a range of different expiry months rather than strike prices. Figure 7-7 shows an example of this possibility using call option data for RBS.

The historical volatility on the same day was 28 per cent, so the implied volatility is slightly higher and seems to be declining slowly towards the historical volatility.

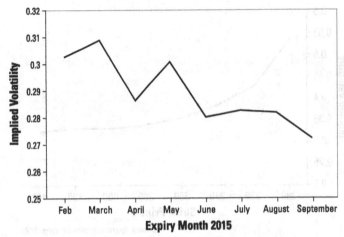

FIGURE 7-7:
Term structure of implied volatilities for RBS on 20 January 2015.

Source: Intercontinental Exchange (ICE)

Estimating Volatility by Statistical Means

Because volatility is so important for understanding the riskiness of assets, quantitative financial analysts, called *quants*, have worked out even better ways than using historical data to do the calculations. These methods are inevitably more complex, with more parameters, but they describe some quite subtle and important effects.

The symmetric GARCH model

The GARCH model for volatility is one of the most successful, although it isn't as easy to use as equally weighted or the exponentially weighted moving average model (EWMA). Think of the GARCH model as a slightly more complicated version of EWMA.

TECHNICAL STUFF

GARCH is an acronym of *generalised autoregressive conditional heteroscedastic.* Believe me, the model is simpler than its name. The academics who developed the model were probably trying to show off. In reverse order, the terms mean:

>> **Heteroscedastic** is just a big word to say that the variance of the returns isn't constant. If it were, the model would be homoscedastic (or constant), but referring to Figure 7-1 shows that the volatility clusters into regions of high volatility.

>> A probability is **conditional** if it depends on an event that's already happened. GARCH is conditional because the volatility varies over time and depends on the previous squared returns. The model does, however, have an unconditional variance (squared volatility). You can use GARCH models to forecast volatility; these forecasts show that the volatility tends towards the unconditional volatility.

>> **Autoregressive** means that the volatility at a given time step is related to the volatility at the previous time step.

>> **Generalised** because there are more parameters than in simpler volatility models such as EWMA. More accurately, there is an ARCH model in which the volatility depends on a weighted average of the earlier squared returns but not on the earlier volatility. It isn't good at modelling the volatility so I skip it and go straight to GARCH.

Many different variants of the GARCH model exist. However, especially for finance, the simplest models are the most effective, so I focus on the plain vanilla GARCH model, which is sometimes called GARCH(1,1) because, thankfully, it has only one parameter of each kind in it.

The equation has three constants: α, β and ω. The ω parameter behaves like a constant volatility you expect in a homoscedastic model while the α and β parameters are a generalisation of the parameters in an exponentially weighted moving average model. The formula is:

$$\sigma_n^2 = \omega + \alpha R_{n-1}^2 + \beta \sigma_{n-1}^2.$$

This GARCH model becomes the EWMA volatility model if $\omega = 0$ and $\alpha + \beta = 1$. It is indeed a generalised model. Sometimes the constant B is called the *persistence* because if it's large, sharp rises in volatility take a long time to die down. The constant α is sometimes called the *reaction* because it determines how the volatility is affected by the latest return data.

The difficulty with GARCH is to figure out what the value of the parameters should be. You can do this calculation using the method of maximum likelihood. (I explain this method with more detail in Chapter 17.) Using the GARCH parameters α, β and ω, the likelihood for a dataset with N independent price returns, r_i, and a probability density function of returns, P, is denoted by L and given by:

$$L = \prod_{n=1}^{N} P\left(\alpha, \beta, \omega; r_n\right).$$

The formula produces the probability density function for each of the data points. Usually, the normal probability density function is used although you can make good arguments for using functions that better model the fat tails of financial market returns. This alternative turns out to be a complex task, and so, in practice, you use the normal distribution.

The probability density for the normal distribution with standard deviation, σ, and a mean of 0 is given by:

$$P(x, \sigma) = \frac{1}{\sqrt{2\pi\sigma^2}} e^{-x^2/2\sigma^2}.$$

Taking natural logarithms of the formula for L, it becomes:

$$\ln(L) = \sum_{n=1}^{N} p_n$$

with

$$p_n = -\frac{1}{2}\left(\ln\sigma_n^2 + \frac{r_n^2}{\sigma_n^2} \right).$$

You can then substitute the GARCH formula for σ_n^2 together with its parameters α, β and ω. You can then find the maximum value of ln(L) by adjusting the GARCH parameters. To do this well, you need to use dedicated software or a programming language such as Python or R.

The GARCH model doesn't account for asymmetry in markets because it involves only squared returns and so doesn't distinguish between a market's rises and falls. The plain vanilla GARCH model only picks up on changes in magnitude of price movements irrespective of their sign.

The leverage effect

In some markets there appears to be an asymmetry between upward and downward price movements: After a sharp fall in an equity market, the volatility is higher than if there had been a sharp rise. The GARCH model doesn't incorporate this effect. However, with a small modification, you can still use a GARCH model, but you need an extra parameter: $\sigma_n^2 = \omega + \alpha\left(R_{n-1} - \delta \right)^2 + \beta\sigma_{n-1}^2$.

The extra parameter, δ, makes fitting this equation more difficult than for plain vanilla GARCH.

A reason for the existence of leverage effects often given for equity markets is that after a sharp fall in share price, a stock becomes riskier as the proportion of debt to equity in the company rises. However, it may just be that investors get spooked by price falls and start trading more and generating volatility.

Going Beyond Simple Volatility Models

Volatility is, perhaps, the most important concept in quantitative finance. Because of this, many advanced models for volatility exist, including the two in this section. The thoughts behind these more advanced models are straightforward, but the maths isn't, so the following sections contain mainly words.

Stochastic volatility

In the GARCH model, the conditional volatility depends on previous random price returns and volatilities. But there's a more general possibility called a *stochastic volatility* model in which the volatility depends on an outside random variable.

TECHNICAL STUFF

Stochastic is a fancy word to mean a process that is non-deterministic, or random. Generally *stochastic* is used for a time-dependent process that fluctuates due to a random external influence. The geometric Brownian motion I describe in Chapter 3 is an example of a stochastic process. But remember, in that model, that volatility is assumed to be constant.

Quants have tried to go beyond the limitations of a constant volatility model. By applying the Black-Scholes solution for call and put option prices to real market data, you find that the solutions fit the data only if you assume that the volatility depends both on the option strike price and the time to expiry. To get around these constraints, some quants use a much more complex model called the Heston model in which both the asset price, S, and the volatility, V, are assumed to be stochastic processes. It is the best known stochastic volatility model.

The Heston model has three equations and extra parameters:

» $dS = \mu S\, dt + \sqrt{V}\, S dz$: The first equation in the Heston model is very similar to the usual geometrical Brownian motion model for stock prices (see Chapter 3).

» $dV = \kappa(\theta - V)\, dt + \sigma\sqrt{V}\, dW$: This equation is for the volatility, V. It's assumed to be mean-reverting to a value, θ, at a rate given by k. The symbol σ is now used as the volatility of the volatility.

» $dz\, dW = \rho\, dt$: The symbols dz and dW represent the random variables that create the fluctuations in the asset price, S, and the volatility, V. They're assumed to be connected by the third equation. The parameter ρ measures the strength of this connection.

Solving these equations is an exercise in advanced mathematics. It's impressive that quants attempt to overcome the limitations of the Black-Scholes model.

Regime switching

Volatility is a measure of the magnitude of the fluctuations in the price returns of a market. In the simplest approach, volatility is assumed to be constant. With the slightly more complex EWMA model, the volatility is slowly varying as explained in the earlier section, 'Using Historical Data'.

Figure 7-8 shows the EWMA volatility calculated for the US natural gas spot price. (The *spot price* is the price to buy gas for delivery the next day.) The volatility itself is clearly volatile with frequent spikes during winter when shortages or fear of shortages emerge.

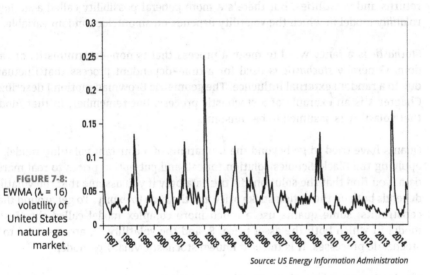

FIGURE 7-8: EWMA (λ = 16) volatility of United States natural gas market.

Source: US Energy Information Administration

The spikes don't appear every winter, and they don't always appear during the same month. Sometimes prices spike in November and at other times in December or even February.

Models that take this kind of effect into account are called *regime switching*. A fast-moving panicky winter regime and a calmer summer regime can be seen, but the market doesn't switch between them in automatic fashion. The switching time is stochastic. In the winter regime, the EWMA model needs a smaller value of λ than in summer so that it can be more responsive to the rapid changes in supply and demand.

Estimating Future Volatility with Term Structures

To forecast future volatility, you can use the GARCH model explained in the previous section 'Estimating Volatility by Statistical Means', but you can first try to use the EWMA to make a volatility forecast. Remember that the equation for the EWMA volatility is: $\sigma_{n+1}^2 = \lambda\sigma_n^2 + (1-\lambda)R_{n+1}^2$.

I shifted the subscript from n to $(n+1)$ to make it clear that you want to use the equation to make a forecast for the next step. If you take the expectation of this equation, then you can use the formula $E\left(R_{n+1}^2\right) = \sigma_{n+1}^2$.

Calculating expectations of random variables such as financial returns is explained in Chapter 2. Because I'm not calculating numbers at the moment, I don't need to specify the probability distribution of the financial returns.

The *variance*, or squared volatility, is just an expectation of the squared return. Substituting this into the EWMA volatility equation, you find that $\sigma_{n+1}^2 = \sigma_n^2$ because the λ cancels from the equation, which means that the EWMA volatility has no power to forecast volatility. It just says that the best estimate for tomorrow's volatility is today's volatility. That probably isn't a bad prediction, but isn't particularly exciting. You also find that EWMA volatility is inconsistent with calculations of implied volatility which, even for short life options, indicate volatilities different from the historical volatility.

Going back to the GARCH model for volatility, $\sigma_{n+1}^2 = \omega + \alpha R_n^2 + \beta\sigma_n^2$, and taking expectations, you get:

$$\sigma_{n+1}^2 = \omega + (\alpha + \beta)\sigma_n^2.$$

This equation can be used to estimate the variance at time step n + 1 from the variance at time step n. If you write that $\sigma_{n+1}^2 = \sigma_n^2$, then:

$$\sigma^2 = \frac{\omega}{1-\alpha-\beta}.$$

This value of σ² is the long-term value of variance that GARCH estimates converge towards provided $(\alpha + \beta) < 1$. You can also see here that ω must be greater than zero; otherwise you can't take the square root to find the volatility.

For example, if $\omega = 0.1$, $\alpha = 0.1$ and $\beta = 0.7$, then the long-term or unconditional value of the variance is:

$$\frac{0.1}{1-0.1-0.7} = 0.5.$$

Starting at an initial value of $\sigma_1^2 = 2$, you can use the GARCH variance equation $\sigma_{n+1}^2 = \omega + (\alpha + \beta)\sigma_n^2$ to calculate all the future values of the variance (squared volatility). The forecast of the variance, unsurprisingly but interestingly, converges to the unconditional variance because as the time lag advances, the process "forgets" its conditioning (initial starting value).

The chart in Figure 7-9 shows that variance quickly declines down to the long-term value of 0.5. The chart in Figure 7-7 shows a similar effect albeit calculated from implied volatilities. That curve has ups and downs because the points are calculated from real market data. In both cases, the volatility reverts back to its long-term value. This property by which the volatility returns to a long-run historical value is called *mean reversion*. The same is also true of interest rates. You can find out more about this property in Chapter 3.

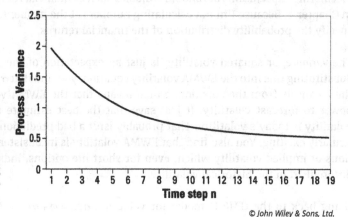

FIGURE 7-9: GARCH term structure showing convergence to long-term value.

Chapter 8

Analysing All the Data

D ata, mainly in the form of numbers, but also as text, is collected and analysed in huge quantities by banks, hedge funds, insurance companies and other financial organisations. Making sense of this data isn't easy. There may be nuggets of gold, but you have to look hard for them. I show you some of the techniques available to help analyse all this data in this chapter.

These techniques can be useful if you want to develop trading strategies or find patterns in large data sets. They involve going beyond using just the normal (Gaussian) or Poisson distributions you can read about in Chapter 2. In real life, financial markets can deviate from these distributions. By building more accurate models of returns distributions you can manage risk better.

Data Smoothing

Price returns are almost random. They can be positive or negative with almost equal probability. Sometimes they're large in magnitude; sometimes they're small. No wonder that it can be hard to detect what's really going on in financial markets.

To be able to see patterns or trends in financial data, it helps to *smooth* it, which you do by making use of averages so that the short term up and down movements in price are removed (averaged out) and longer term trends are revealed. Even for data such as trading volume in which trends and patterns are more obvious than with prices, it's helpful to smooth out random fluctuations.

Random up and down fluctuations are sometimes called *noise* because the first people to investigate them were physicists interested in sound.

Smoothing doesn't just allow you to figure out trends in the price but also to estimate the underlying statistical distribution of your data. This is useful in financial trading and in understanding the risk involved in holding a particular portfolio of financial assets.

Putting data in bins

Calculating the average value and the standard deviation of your data is a good start in understanding it. Calculating the skew and kurtosis (which I explain in Chapter 2) of your distribution is a good idea. Although risk is closely connected with the standard deviation of returns, a high value of kurtosis (over five, say) is also undesirable because it means there's an increased chance of large losses (and gains).

Knowing the distribution of your data can give you useful information. For example, it gives you an immediate idea whether the normal distribution is a good distribution to use. By calculating the histogram of your data, you may find that it's *bimodal* and has two peaks rather than the single peak of the normal distribution. This can be informative as it can be better to model financial returns as being governed by two distributions. You may have different distributions for summer and winter or for investment grade bonds and high-risk (junk) bonds.

Start with *one-dimensional data*, meaning that each piece of data is just a single number. The numbers can be any of many things: the time taken for a bond to default; the return on a stock index; the daily trading volume of a stock.

You work out the maximum value of all of your data and the minimum value. You then split this data range into bins. Each bin is a small range within the data range. You then count up how much of your data falls into each bin. Nothing could be simpler but it's nonetheless a powerful technique.

REMEMBER

The area under a probability distribution curve must add up to one. The x-axis represents all possible data values, and if you add up the probability of everything that can possibly happen the answer must be 1 because the probability of a certain event is one. It can be handy to create a histogram that does the same so that you can compare it directly with probability distributions such as the normal distribution.

TECHNICAL STUFF

If you have N data points in total and n_i data points in the ith bin, which has a width of Δ_i then you can assign the probability p_i to the probability distribution at the bin's location:

$$p_i = \frac{n_i}{N\Delta_i}.$$

Because the total number of points in all of the bins must equal the number of data points, N, if there are nb bins:

$$N = \sum_{i=1}^{nb} n_i.$$

The Greek letter sigma, Σ, indicates the sum of the quantities to the right of it. The lower index value i = 1 tells you where to start the sum, and the upper index value, nb, tells you where to end the sum. The formula shows that the total number of data points N is equal to the number of points in the first bin plus the number of points in the second bin and all the way up to the number of points in the nb^{th} bin. There are nb bins altogether.

If you're wondering where the equation for p_i comes from, try rearranging the equation and then summing the index, i, over all the bins:

$$\sum_{i}^{nb} p_i \Delta_i = \frac{1}{N} \sum_{i}^{nb} n_i = 1.$$

The right-hand side is equal to 1 because of the summation in the equations to find p_i and N. But the left-hand side is the discrete version of the equation for the normalisation of a probability distribution function:

$$\int p(x)dx = 1.$$

So the equation for p_i correctly makes the link between the discrete world of bins and the continuous world of probability distribution functions.

You can unearth the probability distribution – or at least an estimate of it – using a histogram. A *histogram* represents data in graphic form. A histogram looks like a bar chart (see Figure 8-1). They're usually used to show data that has a continuous range of values – such as financial returns. Most spreadsheets have helpful tools to build histograms.

In the histogram in Figure 8-1, the vertical axis is the probability p_i. I'm going to 'fess up: I made up this data by using 50 random numbers. I did this so that you can see how good the histogram is at showing the underlying distribution of the data. The data ranges from –2.4 to 2.4, and in the figure I put it into bins of width 0.2. Because there are only 50 data points, a lot of noise is in the histogram.

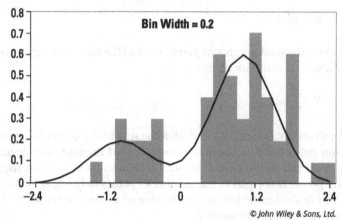

© John Wiley & Sons, Ltd.

FIGURE 8-1: Histogram of a distribution with a too-narrow bin width.

The main hump on the right doesn't look smooth at all. But if you increase the width of the bins so that you have more data in each bin, you can smooth out the hump. The new chart is shown in Figure 8-2.

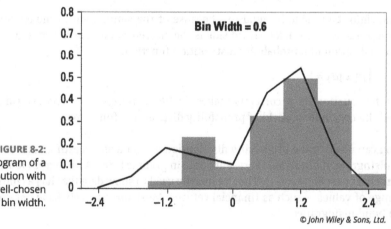

© John Wiley & Sons, Ltd.

FIGURE 8-2: Histogram of a distribution with a well-chosen bin width.

If you go a step further and increase the bin width to 1.2, you get the histogram in Figure 8-3. The black line still shows the underlying distribution with its two peaks, but the lower peak in the histogram has disappeared. The width of the bins increased too much, and the detail in the distribution was lost. Therefore, you can conclude that the best result is obtained with an intermediate value of 0.6 for the width.

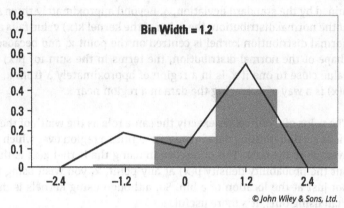

FIGURE 8-3: Histogram of a distribution with wide bins.

The sequence of histograms in Figures 8-1 to 8-3 shows a simple but effective way to determine the width of the bins in your histogram: too narrow and your histogram is noisy with lots of little peaks; too wide and detail is smoothed over.

Smoothing data with kernels

Histograms are extremely useful for getting a quick visualisation of a statistical distribution, but they have limitations. For one thing, and especially with a low value of the bin width, the histogram never produces a curve that resembles the underlying distribution. Also, with larger bin widths, you get less spiky representations, but the width of the bins means that the estimate of the location of peaks in the underlying distribution isn't accurate. A solution to this problem is to use kernels.

A *kernel* is a function, k(x), that can be used to estimate a smooth approximation to the probability density of a data set. Because the kernel is, in effect, used for counting the data in the bins for you, it must be positive and the area under the curve k(x) for the kernel must be equal to 1. These are exactly the same conditions as for a probability distribution function. In other words:

$$k(x) \geq 0 \quad \int k(x)dx = 1.$$

There are quite a few possible choices for the function k(x). A good choice is the normal distribution because it will pick out the data in a well-defined vicinity of its average value. You can estimate a probability density, p(x), using the equation:

$$p(x) = \frac{1}{N\Delta} \sum_{i=1}^{N} k\left(\frac{x - x_i}{\Delta}\right) = \frac{1}{N\Delta} \sum_{i=1}^{N} \frac{1}{\sqrt{2\pi}} e^{-\frac{(x-x_i)^2}{2\Delta^2}}.$$

REMEMBER

The normal distribution curve is hump-shaped with the width of the hump determined by the standard deviation, Δ. Beyond approximately three Δ from the mean of the normal distribution, the value of the kernel k(x) value falls almost to 0. Each normal distribution kernel is centred on the point x, and because of the humped shape of the normal distribution, the terms in the sum for p(x) will only have a value close to one if x_i is in a region of approximately Δ from x. The formula for p(x) is a way of averaging the data in a region near x.

The value of Δ here plays exactly the same role as the width of the bins in the previous section 'Putting data in bins': it defines a region over which you're taking an average of the data. The difference in using the kernel k(x) is that you can work out the probability density p(x) at any point, x, you wish using the formula and not just at the location of a bin. So, although using kernels is more complicated than using bins, it's more useful.

If you choose $x = x_j$, then n_j is the number of points in its vicinity and $p(x_j)$ becomes approximately:

$$p(x_j) = \frac{n_j}{N\Delta}.$$

This is the same equation as in the 'Putting data in bins' section, which shows that the kernel is doing the job of counting data points. To illustrate the use of kernels, I created a chart, shown in Figure 8-4, using that same data.

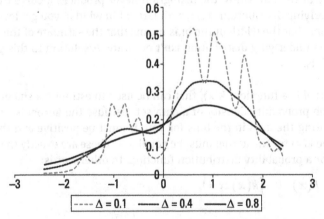

FIGURE 8-4: Kernel density estimation to a bimodal distribution.

With a small value of Δ, the kernel density estimation is quite spiky. For a large delta value, the second peak in the distribution is lost. The intermediate value of Δ = 0.4 shows that the kernel density reproduces the bimodal pattern of the underlying data.

However, if you overlay the estimated probability density using Δ = 0.4 with the actual probability density, you get the curves shown in Figure 8-5. This figure demonstrates that although the kernel density estimation is smooth and has two peaks, it's quite spread out compared with the actual distribution.

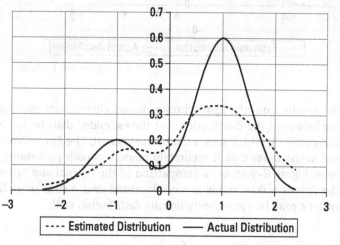

FIGURE 8-5:
Comparing an estimated kernel distribution with the true distribution.

---- Estimated Distribution — Actual Distribution

© John Wiley & Sons, Ltd.

With a larger data set, the estimated distribution is closer to the actual distribution. However, you can't always obtain more data. The choice of kernel function, k(x), is also an influence on the result. For example, you can use the Epanechnikov kernel, $k_E(x)$, instead of the normal distribution:

$$k_E(x) = \frac{3}{4\Delta}\left(1 - \frac{x^2}{\Delta^2}\right).$$

The kernel $k_E(x)$ is zero for values beyond a distance Δ from x. Figure 8-6 shows a chart of the Epanechnikov kernel. Again, Δ plays the role of the width of the bins used to build histograms of data. Now, using the Epanechnikov kernel to estimate the distribution of the data, the estimated distribution turns out better than with a normal kernel as you can see in Figure 8-6 by comparing with Figure 8-5.

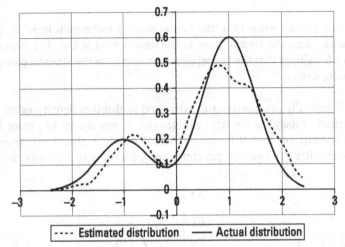

FIGURE 8-6:
Density
estimation with
Epanechnikov
kernel.

The results from the Epanechnikov kernel show closer correspondence with the two humps of the distribution, but the estimated distribution isn't as smooth as in Figure 8-5, which shows the normal kernel. The Epanechnikov kernel is optimal in the sense that it accurately models smooth probability density distributions. Figure 8-7 shows a comparison of the normal and Epanechnikov kernels. The Epanechnikov kernel is more localised near 0 so is more likely to be able to model a peak in a probability density distribution well.

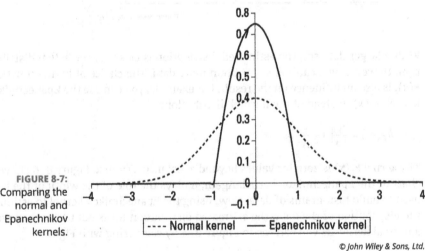

FIGURE 8-7:
Comparing the
normal and
Epanechnikov
kernels.

Using moving averages as filters

A *moving average* is an average calculated using only the latest values of a time series and not the whole of the time series. As more data become available, you can update the value of your moving average and so its value changes with time. This makes moving averages well adapted to financial time series such as prices, which are constantly fluctuating.

REMEMBER

A *time series* is data such as stock or bond prices that's updated on a regular basis. The data consists of lots of numbers, with each number associated with a different time.

Normally, the data is updated on a regular basis, be it hourly, daily, weekly or some other frequency. However, some time series are not updated regularly. For example, with individual trades on a stock exchange there can be quiet periods of the day (lunchtime?) when the time between trades is longer than the busy periods at the beginning and end of the trading day. These time series are harder to analyse as the time between trades is additional data, which makes them like two time series rolled into one.

A nice feature of moving averages is that you can update them as more data becomes available without redoing the complete recalculation of the moving average. This makes them fast and easy to use and is one of the reasons for their popularity. Moving averages provide information that you can use to take immediate action rather than waiting for an analysis of a complete data set. They're used extensively in financial trading and come in at least two distinct types:

>> Simple moving average, or SMA

>> Exponentially weight moving average, or EWMA (head to Chapter 7 for a complete discussion of EWMA)

If you calculate a simple moving average with the latest n data points, you call it SMA(n).

You choose the value of n depending on how rapidly you think your data is changing. If the data is jittery, you may have a low value with $n = 5$ while if it's varying slowly then you could choose $n = 100$. Every time a new data point in the series arrives, you shift the block of numbers that you average forward so that it always includes the latest value. Assuming that you have a price series, P_i, with N values, the formula for the SMA(n) is:

$$SMA(n) = \frac{1}{n}\sum_{i=1}^{n} P_{N+1-i}.$$

The SMA is simple, but it's effective. By averaging the latest values of a price series, the short term up and down fluctuations in the time series are removed.

You can think of the SMA as a *filter* because it removes these short-term fluctuations. The purpose is to give you an idea of the direction that the time series is heading in independent of the fluctuations present in the data. The SMA is good at uncovering signal in time series data, which is unexpected for something so, well, simple.

REMEMBER

The short-term fluctuations in price I talk about in this section are sometimes called *noise*. With speech, noise is unhelpful and masks what someone is saying. With a financial time series, the noise masks the *signal* or trend in the data.

An alternative to the simple moving average is the exponentially weighted moving average (EWMA). Chapter 7 demonstrates how to calculate an EWMA using a weighted average of the most recent time series value and the previous EWMA value. You can use an EWMA directly on price data as well, although it detects trends the same way as with an SMA. The advantage of the EWMA is that it responds better to changes in trend in the time series because of its extra weighting on recent data values.

A new possibility arises now for both the SMA and EWMA. You can calculate two moving averages with different periods and then compare them by subtraction. This situation is often called a *moving average crossover*. The purpose of this calculation is to detect changes in the trend of the data. The point where the two moving averages cross over each other can be identified as a change in trend and is often called a *signal* by traders because it indicates that it may be a good time to buy or sell the financial asset whose price you're tracking.

Figure 8-8 shows an example that charts the recent history of the price of West Texas Intermediate (WTI), a frequently traded grade of US crude oil, along with two SMAs.

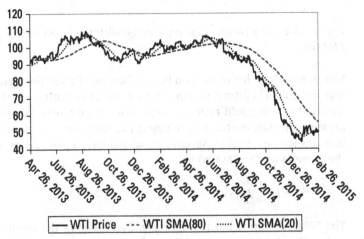

FIGURE 8-8:
WTI Crude oil price with two simple moving averages.

Source: Energy Information Administration

The chart in Figure 8-8 shows that the SMAs effectively smooth out the noise in the WTI price with the SMA(80) curve being smoother than the SMA(20) curve because of the averaging over more data points. In periods of strong price uptrends, the short-term simple moving average SMA(20) is above the long-term average SMA(80). In periods of strong downtrends, such as late 2014, SMA(20) is significantly beneath SMA(80).

REMEMBER

The usefulness of moving average crossovers is as trading signals. You can use them to identify periods of rising or falling asset prices. Traders can then take a long or short position on the asset.

You can also use the EWMA to build crossovers and, to some extent, whether you use that to smooth the data or the SMA is a case of trader preference.

Estimating More Distributions

This section looks a bit deeper into probability distributions. You discover how to generate random numbers that have some of the real-life features of financial returns such as positive kurtosis. These numbers are useful for testing out other models that need realistic data.

REMEMBER

Kurtosis is a measure of how likely high losses or gains are for a financial returns distribution. If kurtosis is positive, then high losses or gains are more likely than for the normal distribution. Distributions with positive kurtosis are often called *fat tailed*. The *tails* of a distribution are the edges, a long way from the average values. Chapter 2 is the place to go to see the mathematical definition of kurtosis and more explanation of statistical distributions.

Mixing Gaussian distributions

The Gaussian mixture is a way to create models of financial returns with positive kurtosis. The fat tails associated with positive kurtosis are a key feature of financial markets, so it's useful to create numbers with this property.

The *Gaussian mixture* is what it says it is: a mixture of Gaussian distributions, but you need to be careful in the way you generate them. By mixing Gaussian distributions, you can come up with a distribution much more like a real financial returns distribution with positive kurtosis. With realistic simulated data, you can test out how well a portfolio or trading strategy might work in the future. (Chapter 3 talks about generating random numbers, so you may wish to check there.)

Use this process to mix your distributions:

1. **Select the parameters for your Gaussians σ_1, μ_1, σ_2, μ_2 and the mixture ratio r.**

   There will be r of Gaussian 1 and (1–r) of Gaussian 2 in the mixture.

2. **Generate a uniform random number between 0 and 1.**

   If the number is less than r, generate a number from a Gaussian distribution with parameters σ_1 and μ_1.

   If the number is greater than r, generate a number from a Gaussian distribution with parameters σ_2 and μ_2.

3. **Repeat Step 2 as many times as you'd like random samples from a Gaussian mixture.**

You can see the result of generating numbers according to this scheme in the section 'Putting your data in bins' earlier in the chapter. The distribution there had $\sigma_1 = 0.5$, $\mu_1 = 1$, $\sigma_2 = 0.5$, $\mu_2 = -1$ and $r = 0.75$. Refer to Figure 8-1 and note that the two humps in the distribution are due to the fact that one of the normal distributions in the mixture has a negative average and the other has a positive average. The heights of the humps are different because the 75 per cent of the data points are for the normal distribution with a positive average.

The probability density function for the Gaussian mixture P is written as a weighted sum of the probability density functions ϕ for the constituent Gaussian distributions:

$$P(x) = r\varphi(x; \mu_1, \sigma_1) + (1-r)\varphi(x; \mu_2, \sigma_2).$$

Going beyond one dimension

Most of equations in this chapter use one-dimensional data, which means that only one piece of data exists for every time step. But, if you want to know the probability for two asset returns together, you need to build a two-dimensional distribution.

Instead of splitting a line into segments of width, Δ, and counting how many data points are in each bin, you need to split a plane into squares and work out how many data points lie in each square.

This process can be time consuming, but it's still possible in two dimensions especially if you use the kernel methods from the earlier section 'Smoothing data with kernels'. Going beyond two dimensions becomes rather difficult.

In one dimension, if your return data has a maximum value L and a minimum value –L when you create bins of width Δ, there are $\frac{2L}{\Delta}$ of them. In two dimensions, you need $\left(\frac{2L}{\Delta}\right)^2$ square bins to cover the area where your data lies. (In three dimensions, you need $\left(\frac{2L}{\Delta}\right)^3$ cubic bins.) The amount of data required to fill these bins and get a good estimate of the density distribution soon becomes prohibitive. So, in practice, you cannot use the histogram method I describe in this chapter for more than one or two-dimensional data. However, the kernel method is more powerful and you can try it for higher dimensional data.

Modelling Non-Normal Returns

In this section I show you a powerful technique called expectation-maximisation, or EM for short, that you can use to fit a Gaussian mixture model to financial returns data.

If financial returns are normal, their parameters are the mean and the standard deviation. But two random processes may determine an asset's returns with different means and standard deviations. The magic of EM is to resolve what these different averages and standard deviations are. In a way, EM is a generalisation of the usual formula to calculate the average and standard deviation of a distribution.

TECHNICAL STUFF

A *parameter* is a measurable quantity that defines the behaviour of a system. A parameter is usually constant. In the normal distribution, the mean and the standard deviation are parameters. By contrast, a *variable* is a changeable quantity often determined during a measurement. For example, time is often a variable.

The earlier section 'Smoothing data with kernels' shows how to fit a probability distribution with a general kernel smoothing function. Although the kernel has width, you have no mathematically simple function with its own parameters that you can fit the density distribution to. This kind of statistics is often called *nonparametric statistics*. You can now impress your colleagues at those cocktail parties.

Testing and visualising non-normality

A simple way to test for normality is to take the standardised returns from your distribution, plot the distribution using the method in the earlier 'Putting data in bins' section and compare it with the theoretical curve for the normal distribution.

You can test your data sample for normality by calculating the skew and kurtosis. The *skew* is a measure of how lopsided the returns distribution is whilst the *kurtosis* is a measure of how fat tailed the distribution is. For a normal distribution the skew and kurtosis should both be zero, but for real financial returns distributions they aren't. (I talk in depth about skew and kurtosis in Chapter 2.)

The standard deviation of these fluctuations in kurtosis is $\sqrt{\frac{24}{N}}$ where N is the number of data samples. Likewise, the standard deviation in the fluctuations of the skew is $\sqrt{\frac{6}{N}}$. What this means is that if the value of kurtosis that you calculate for your data is greater than three times the standard deviation of the kurtosis fluctuations, it's highly unlikely to have happened by chance. You can then say that the data isn't normal.

Another way to investigate whether your data is normal is to use the cumulative distribution rather than the probability density distribution itself. The *cumulative distribution*, P(z), is the probability that your data has a value in the interval from −∞ to z. You calculate it from the probability density p(x) using the formula:

$$P(z) = \int_{-\infty}^{z} p(x)dx.$$

The cumulative distribution can give more reliable answers because it's a bit like taking an average, and so it's less liable to be influenced by random fluctuations in the data.

To create a cumulative distribution, follow these steps:

1. **Create z values, which are simply standardised data.**

    To standardise data, calculate the average and the standard deviation, then subtract the average value from every data point and divide by the standard deviation.

2. **Order your data from smallest to largest.**

    Number the smallest $j = 1$, the next smallest $j = 2$, all the way up to the largest $j = N$.

3. **From the index j calculate the probability $p = \frac{j - 0.5}{N}$ that your data has a value less than the z value of the jth data point.**

By transforming your data, you can compare it with the cumulative normal distribution. Take the z value from your data and read off the probability that data is less than this value from your calculated table. Using the inverse cumulative normal distribution, you can use this same probability and calculate the value of z that would apply for a normal distribution. If, for example, your empirical data is kurtotic, there should be more data values less than a given small value of p than you'd find from a normal distribution.

The best way to show this situation is by a chart called the *QQ plot*. The Qs stand for *quantile*. *Quantiles* occur when you split an ordered data set into q equal parts. The values separating the parts are the quantiles. For example, the median is a quantile. It's the value of a data set with equal numbers of data values above and below it. For normally distributed data, the mean is close to the average value, but if the data isn't normal, then it may differ considerably. In an ordered data set, you can regard each data point as an equal part of the sample. For a given value of z_a such that a fraction p of the data has a value of z less than z_a, compute z_a for both the cumulative normal distribution and the financial returns data. You need to use the inverse normal cumulative distribution to calculate the z values corresponding to the probabilities in your ordered table of data.

A sample QQ plot is shown in Figure 8-9. The solid black line shows where a normal distribution would lie on the chart. The other two series are for a small oil company (IGAS) and an integrated major oil company (BP). The increased departure away from the normal distribution line indicates that the data for the smaller company has a higher kurtosis.

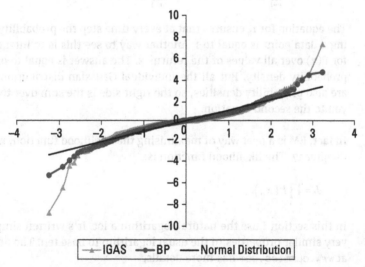

FIGURE 8-9:
QQ plot for
IGAS and BP.

Maximising expectations

If your distribution isn't normal, it's still nice to have a simple quantitative model of it. Building a histogram, which I talk about in the first section of this chapter, is a good start but may not be practical in subsequent calculations with the distribution. A formula is handy to have if you have more calculations to do. A good way to estimate a formula for your distribution is to assume that the underlying distribution is a mixture of Gaussian distributions.

In the earlier section 'Mixing Gaussian distributions', I show you how to generate random numbers from a Gaussian mixture. This process is something different – in fact, you go backwards! Taking real-life financial returns data, you can figure out the parameters of a Gaussian mixture that best fits the data. These parameters include the standard deviation, the mean and percentage weight given to each distribution. The algorithm to do this is called Expectation Maximisation (EM), which consists of two stages which are simply called E and M.

An *algorithm* is a well-defined sequence of steps for coming up with an answer to a mathematical problem.

To keep things simple, I only consider a single return time series. The starting point of the technique is the probability P(x) used in the earlier section 'Mixing Gaussian distributions'. I write the equation more generally assuming that there are K Gaussian distributions in the mixture, each with weight r_k, average μ_k and standard deviation σ_k:

$$P(x) = \sum_{k=1}^{K} r_k \varphi(x; \mu_k, \sigma_k) \qquad \sum_{k=1}^{K} r_k = 1.$$

The equation for r_k ensures that at every time step the probability of actually having a data point is equal to 1. Another way to see this is to integrate the equation for P(x) over all values of the returns x. The answer is equal to one because P is a probability density. But all the individual Gaussian distributions in the mixture are also probability densities, so the right side is the sum over the r_k, which takes you to the second equation.

In fact, EM is a neat way of maximising the likelihood function, which I explain in Chapter 17. The likelihood function is:

$$L = \prod_{n=1}^{N} P(x_n).$$

In this section I use the natural logarithm a lot. It's written simply as ln and has very similar properties to the usual logarithm to base ten. The online Cheat Sheet at www.dummies.com has more details.

Using the property that the logarithm of a product is the sum of the logarithms, the equation becomes:

$$\ln L = \sum_{n=1}^{N} \ln \left[\sum_{k=1}^{K} r_k \varphi(x_n; \mu_k, \sigma_k) \right].$$

This equation is often just referred to as the *log likelihood*. To maximise the log likelihood, you must now do some calculus and differentiate this equation with respect to the parameters μ_k and σ_k and set the resulting equations to zero.

Remember that you're trying to find the values of μ and σ that maximise the natural logarithm of the likelihood, ln L so x_n isn't differentiated.

TIP

To find the maximum value of a function, f(a), with respect to a, differentiate the equation with respect to a and set the resulting equation to zero. When you then solve that equation for a, you find the location of the maximum value. The *maximum value* of a function is the point where the function turns horizontal and changes from going up in value to going down in value. The slope of the function is therefore zero at the maximum and located by where the first derivative is zero. You may also find a minimum value by this process because it also has zero slope. To tell the difference, you need to calculate the second derivative at the turning point. A maximum value has a negative second derivative while a minimum value has a positive second derivative.

So, differentiating with respect to μ_k:

$$\sum_{n=1}^{N} \frac{r_k \varphi(x_n; \mu_k, \sigma_k)}{\sum_{j=1}^{K} r_j \varphi(x_n; \mu_j, \sigma_j)} (x_n - \mu_k) \sigma_k^{-1} = 0.$$

To stop the algebra getting messy, I introduce another function, g, which I define as:

$$g(x_n; \mu_k, \sigma_k) = \frac{r_k \varphi(x_n; \mu_k, \sigma_k)}{\sum_{j=1}^{K} r_j \varphi(x_n; \mu_j, \sigma_j)}.$$

Using this new function, you can rewrite the first equation as:

$$\sum_{n=1}^{N} g(x_n; \mu_k, \sigma_k)(x_n - \mu_k) = 0.$$

With one more definition:

$$N_k = \sum_{n=1}^{N} g(x_n; \mu_k, \sigma_k),$$

you can now write an equation for the mean of the kth Gaussian distribution as:

$$\mu_k = \frac{1}{N_k} \sum_{n=1}^{N} g(x_n; \mu_k, \sigma_k) x_n.$$

Similar calculations after differentiating with respect to σ_k gives you:

$$\sigma_k^2 = \frac{1}{N_k} \sum_{n=1}^{N} g(x_n; \mu_k, \sigma_k)(x_n - \mu_k)^2.$$

The nice thing about these equations is that the mean and standard deviation of the components of the Gaussian mixture have the same form as the usual equations for a mean and standard deviation. The difference is that here the sums are weighted by the function g.

The function g depends on the data point x_n, and the mean and standard deviation of the kth Gaussian in the mixture. It takes the form of a probability divided by the sum of all of those probabilities in the denominator.

You may have guessed that g itself is a probability. It can be interpreted as, given the data x_n, the probability that the Gaussian distribution k is responsible for the data point x_n. This statement sounds strange, but if you go back to the 'Mixing Gaussian distributions' section, each data point is generated by a random choice between two Gaussians with a ratio of r in one Gaussian and $(1-r)$ in the other. Now, though, you're trying to figure out how the mixture was created after the event, and g is your best guess of which Gaussian distribution was used to create the data point x_n. Mathematicians call this situation a *posterior probability*.

TECHNICAL STUFF

A good way to think about the Gaussian mixture is that it has an extra random variable, z. The value of z determines which of the K Gaussian distributions was used to create the data point x_n. Because you can't tell the value of z by looking at the data, it's called a *hidden* or *latent variable*. Its probable value is inferred from the data.

REMEMBER

Maths can be a bit confusing sometimes. I use capital K to indicate how many Gaussian functions are in my mixture. I use lowercase k to indicate a specific Gaussian function. For example, μ with a subscript k indicates the average value of the kth Gaussian in the mixture.

You use the Bayes' theorem to explain a bit more about g. Write the probability of k, given that x has happened, as P(k|x). Bayes' theorem then says that:

$$P\left(k|x\right) = \frac{P\left(x|k\right)P\left(k\right)}{P\left(x\right)}.$$

P(x) can be broken down into a sum depending on the Gaussian k so that:

$$P\left(k|x\right) = \frac{P\left(x|k\right)P\left(k\right)}{\sum_{j=1}^{K}P\left(x|k\right)P\left(k\right)}.$$

But P(k) is just the probability of the kth Gaussian in the mixture and so r_k. P(x|k) is the probability of x given that Gaussian k generated that point so:

$$P\left(k|x\right) = \varphi\left(x; \mu_k, \sigma_k\right).$$

Now you can see that P(k|x) is the function $g\left(x; \mu_k, \sigma_k\right)$. Sometimes the probability r_k is called the *prior probability* of k because it's the probability you would apply if you were generating the data yourself.

The final equation you need for EM is the one for the probabilities r_k. You can do this calculation mathematically using calculus, but given some of the interpretation you now have of g, you can see intuitively what the answer must be. If you go back to the equation for N_k, you see it's a sum over all the functions g. Therefore, this equation is the best estimate you have of how many of the data points were generated by the Gaussian k. Given that you have N data points in total, it follows that the best estimate of r_k is:

$$r_k = \frac{N_k}{N}.$$

You now have all three equations for the parameters of the Gaussian mixture. But you have a snag to deal with. The equations for μ_k, σ_k and r_k all contain those same parameters on the right-hand side of the equation because the function g depends on those parameters. So you can't just work out the parameters from those equations. It looks as though you have to do some heavy maths to solve them, but in fact you don't. The EM algorithm allows you to work out μ_k, σ_k and r_k iteratively by first guessing some values and then successively improving them.

TIP

The beauty of EM (expectation maximisation) is that the iterations always improve the estimates, so EM is a powerful and simple technique to use. Here's how in five steps:

1. **Guess the initial values for μ_k, σ_k and r_k.**

2. **Calculate the log likelihood.**

   This is the expectation, or E, step. Use the values from Step 1.

3. **Compute $g(x; \mu_k, \sigma_k)$ for all the data points x_n.**

4. **For the M, or maximisation, step, improve your values for the parameters using the equations:**

   $$\mu_k(\text{new}) = \frac{1}{N_k}\sum_{n=1}^{N} g(x_n; \mu_k, \sigma_k) x_n$$

   $$\sigma_k^2(\text{new}) = \frac{1}{N_k}\sum_{n=1}^{N} g(x_n; \mu_k, \sigma_k)(x_n - \mu_k)^2$$

   $$r_k(\text{new}) = \frac{N_k}{N}$$

   Remember that $N_k = \sum_{n=1}^{N} g(x_n; \mu_k, \sigma_k).$

5. **Calculate the log likelihood function again.**

   If the log likelihood has converged to a value close to the one you previously calculated, then stop. Otherwise, go back to Step 2 using your improved values for the parameters.

Figure 8-10 shows the log likelihood as a continuous black line. After almost 30 iterations, the curve levels out and the log likelihood is at its maximum. The two dashed lines show the convergence of the values for the standard deviations of the two normal distributions towards their value of 0.5. The chart has two y axes with the values for likelihood shown on the right-hand axis and the values for the standard deviations on the left-hand axis.

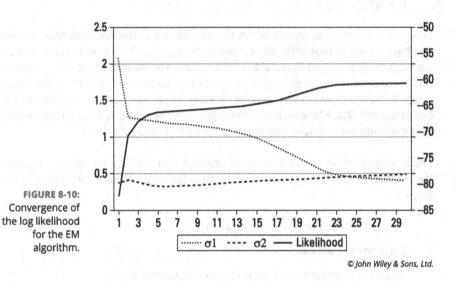

FIGURE 8-10: Convergence of the log likelihood for the EM algorithm.

Figure 8-11 shows the convergence of the values for the averages to their values of +1 and −1 and the mixture ratio to its value of 0.25.

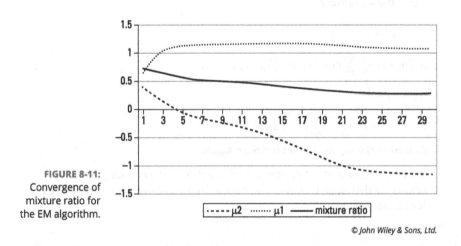

FIGURE 8-11: Convergence of mixture ratio for the EM algorithm.

Chapter 9

Analysing Data Matrices: Principal Components

rincipal components analysis, or PCA for short, is a powerful mathematical technique for analysing large data sets. Think of historical price data on a large portfolio of stocks, bonds or other financial assets. With PCA you can figure out which linear combinations of prices explain as much as possible about your data set. These combinations are called *principal components*. You can then use these principal component values to visualise your data. That's not possible with the raw data because of the large numbers. But typically only a few principal components are needed to accurately model your data. This reduction in the complexity of your data set is useful because you can then quickly do further calculations such as working out how risky your portfolio is.

PCA is especially useful if you're getting duplicate information in different parts of a large dataset. Historical prices from one asset may be telling a similar story to historical prices from another asset. Bond yields of 20-year maturity may follow closely those for 30-year maturity. In these situations other statistical techniques such as linear regression can fail because they're confused between the similar asset prices or yields. In contrast PCA gives you a few combinations of prices or yields that explain the majority of your data.

Reducing the Amount of Data

Numbers – and lots of them – are the lifeblood of quantitative finance. Sometimes this fact can be a problem: the overabundance of numbers can prevent you from understanding what they mean. You end up not seeing the wood for the trees. Often financial data is set out as a table or a *data matrix*. Each row of the matrix may have the price of many assets on a given day. Therefore, for a large portfolio, you can have hundreds of columns.

TIP

Spreadsheets are perhaps the most common way of analysing this kind of data. But they're by no means the best way. The computer languages R and Python both have dedicated ways to handle data matrices which they call *data frames*. They're well suited to this job because both languages have built-in tools that make handling data in this form easy. These tools include standard operations such as importing data from other sources such as databases or text files, sorting data into alphabetical or numerical order and joining data matrices together.

Table 9-1 shows a snapshot of a data matrix containing the share prices for some of the stocks from the Dow Jones Industrial Average (DJIA) Index. I downloaded the data from Yahoo Finance, which is one of the best sources for free stock-market data. The first row identifies the stocks whose prices are contained in the given column. Stock exchanges are brief when it comes to naming stocks so that traders can place orders quickly. Short ticker codes also help when you're searching databases or displaying data. In this example, the ticker codes are AXP for American Express, BA for Boeing Company, CAT for Caterpillar Inc., CSCO for Cisco Systems Inc. and CVX for Chevron Corporation. The first column shows the dates for the share prices, which are normally in chronological order.

TABLE 9-1 **Date Matrix with DJIA Numbers**

	AXP	BA	CAT	CSCO	CVX
04/01/2010	38.11	50.65	52.47	22.53	68.01
05/01/2010	38.02	52.31	53.1	22.43	68.49
06/01/2010	38.64	53.9	53.26	22.29	68.5
07/01/2010	39.27	56.08	53.48	22.39	68.24
08/01/2010	39.24	55.54	54.08	22.51	68.36
11/01/2010	38.79	54.88	57.47	22.44	69.57
12/01/2010	39.3	54.48	55.78	22.09	69.17

	AXP	BA	CAT	CSCO	CVX
13/01/2010	39.42	55.14	55.86	22.49	68.65
14/01/2010	39.92	55.5	55.55	22.77	68.43
15/01/2010	39.65	54.83	54.25	22.27	68.15
19/01/2010	40.18	54.68	54.98	22.68	68.54
20/01/2010	40.2	54.27	53.92	22.28	67.23
21/01/2010	39.43	53.37	51.3	21.88	65.58

The data shown in Table 9-1 is only a corner of a larger matrix with the prices for all 30 stocks in the DJIA Index and for dates going all the way up to the present day. (I know you're glad I didn't fill this book with all those numbers.) Although large enough that it won't fit onto the page of this book, this data matrix is comparatively small. My computer says that the file containing the whole table is 300 kilobytes in size. Financial institutions are used to dealing with data in gigabytes or more. That's because they're concerned with far more than 30 assets and may be looking at prices as they fluctuate throughout the day.

TECHNICAL STUFF

The quantity of data is measured in bytes. One byte is sufficient to store a character such as *a*. A thousand bytes is called a *kilobyte* (often abbreviated to kB, at least on my computer); a million bytes is a *megabyte* (MB); a billion bytes a *gigabyte* (GB).

As a first step in understanding the properties of a large amount of data, such as the sample in Figure 9-1, you can calculate summary statistics for each of the columns. The *summary statistics* are numbers that describe the columns of a data matrix as a statistical distribution. (Chapter 2 explains statistical distributions.) These statistics are calculated from the entire time series in each column and are a compact way of saying something useful about the data for each of the stocks.

A *time series* is a range of data values at different points in time such as stock prices on every trading day of the year. Each column of the Dow Jones data matrix is a time series. Before you calculate the summary statistics, you need to transform the prices into returns.

REMEMBER

Prices are important, of course, but anyone holding a financial asset is looking for a return. To calculate this, divide the price change between today and yesterday by the price yesterday. In maths this is $r_n = \left(p_n - p_{n-1} \right) / p_{n-1}$ in which r_n is the return on day n and p_n is the price on day n. I'm assuming that you have price data for many days and the index n indicates which one. Using returns is important because it allows you to compare one asset with another on the same scale.

Price returns also have statistical properties that are much more stable than prices over time and that, on average, are close to zero. This stability over time is called *stationarity*. It doesn't mean that the returns don't change. It means that the summary statistics don't change. In contrast, prices meander similar to the geometric Brownian motion I describe in Chapter 3 and so are much harder to measure.

Figure 9-1 shows a chart of the annualised volatility of the stocks that make up the DJIA Index.

REMEMBER

The *volatility* is the standard deviation of the returns of a financial asset such as a stock. Often it's calculated using daily price data but then annualised so that you can compare the number with the annualised volatility of other assets. Chapter 7 gives more detail on how to do this. If the annualised volatility is 20 per cent, then you can fully expect the asset price to rise or fall by 20 per cent over a year.

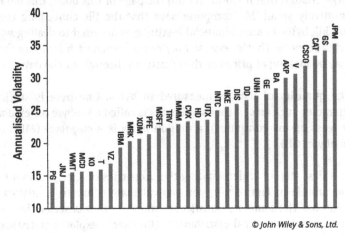

FIGURE 9-1:
Annualised
volatility of stocks
in the Dow Jones
Industrial
Average.

© John Wiley & Sons, Ltd.

Companies that provide for life's necessities, such as Proctor and Gamble (PG), which makes nappies, or McDonalds (MCD), which flips hamburgers, have a low volatility. By contrast, high-rolling investment banks such as Goldman Sachs (GS) and JP Morgan (JPM) have high volatility. The chart in Figure 9-1 was created using the latest five years of data on the stocks, and it's unlikely the order of the stocks in the bar chart will change much in the future. In five years' time (that'll be in 2021), making nappies will probably still be less risky than investment banking. By knowing the volatility of individual stocks, you can build portfolios tailored to the needs of a client's risk tolerance.

The ticker codes for all the stocks in the DJIA Index are shown in Table 9-2.

TABLE 9-2 **Ticker Codes for DJIA Companies**

Ticker Code	Company	Ticker Code	Company	Ticker Code	Company
AXP	American Express Co.	IBM	International Business Machines Corp.	PFE	Pfizer Inc.
BA	Boeing	INTC	Intel Corp.	PG	Proctor & Gamble Co.
CAT	Caterpillar Inc.	JNJ	Johnson & Johnson	T	AT&T Inc.
CSCO	Cisco Systems	JPM	JPMorgan Chase & Co.	TRV	The Travelers Companies Inc.
CVX	Chevron	KO	Coca-Cola Co.	UNH	UnitedHealth Group Inc.
DD	DuPont	MCD	McDonald's Corp.	UTX	United Technologies Corp.
DIS	Walt Disney Co.	MMM	3M Co.	V	VISA Inc.
GE	General Electric Co.	MRK	Merck & Co. Inc.	VZ	Verizon Communications Inc.
GS	Goldman Sachs Group Inc.	MSFT	Microsoft Corp.	WMT	Walmart
HD	Home Depot Inc.	NKE	Nike Inc.	XOM	Exxon Mobil Corp.

Understanding collinearity

Frequently, close connections between the prices of assets are evident. The 30 stocks of the DJIA Index tend to move together, whether up or down, because as the US economy does well, most stocks rise, and if the United States goes into recession, most stock prices fall.

Figure 9-2 shows the way the DJIA stocks moved together from April 2010 through April 2014.

Most of the stocks move up from the bottom left of the chart to the top right, and most experience a sharp downturn in 2011. This similar movement in the price of financial assets is called *collinearity*. One way to characterise collinearity is using the correlation matrix. It's a matrix because a correlation exists between each of the 30 stocks in the DJIA Index. So it's a 30-by-30 matrix.

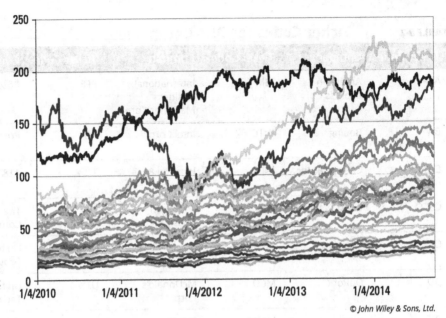

FIGURE 9-2:
Price movement
of the DJIA stocks.

250

200

150

100

50

0
1/4/2010   1/4/2011   1/4/2012   1/4/2013   1/4/2014

Before calculating a correlation, you need to calculate the covariance. As the name suggests, covariance is like a variance (see Chapter 2) but connects two different stocks. The following formula uses x_i to refer to the returns of the first stock and y_i to refer to the returns of the second stock. The index, i, is used to show that the returns are a time series and so i is used to indicate each time there is a quoted price. Working with data for N days of returns in my data matrix. In other words, it has N rows.

The formula for the covariance, C, between these returns is:

$$C(x, y) = \frac{1}{N} \sum_{i=1}^{N} (x_i - \bar{x})(y_i - \bar{y})$$

The bars over x and y indicate the average value. If you put $x_i = y_i$ in this formula, it becomes the formula for the variance of a stock's returns. The covariance C(x,y) is large and positive when the stocks x and y behave in similar ways and is large and negative if they behave in dissimilar ways. For example, if the stock x tends to fall in value when stock y is rising, then the covariance is negative.

REMEMBER

You can use this formula with a small value of m such as ten but you're likely to get a misleading value for the covariance. You're better advised to use a large value in the hundreds to get a more reliable figure. Also, you can use data over any timeframe. You're fine to use intraday data (for example every minute) or daily, weekly or monthly data.

The covariance is a useful quantity to know about, but a more frequently quoted value is the correlation between the two stocks x and y because the correlation can only be a number between –1 and 1. It places the degree of connectedness between the price returns of x and the price returns of y on a simple scale. You find the correlation by dividing C(x,y) by both the standard deviation of x and the standard deviation of y. So, if you calculate the correlation between the same two stocks, you divide the variance by the square of the standard deviation. In other words, you divide the variance by the variance, which is just 1. So stocks that move in exactly the same way have a correlation of 1.

If the standard deviation of x is σ(x) and the similar formula for the standard deviation of y is σ(y), the formula for the correlation is:

$$\text{Corr}(x, y) = \frac{\frac{1}{m} \sum_{i=1}^{m}(x_i - \bar{x})(y_i - \bar{y})}{\sigma(x)\sigma(y)}.$$

REMEMBER

The formula for the standard deviation σ(x) is:

$$\sigma(x) = \sqrt{\frac{1}{N} \sum_{i=1}^{m}\left(x_i^2 - \bar{x}^2\right)}.$$

Figure 9-3 shows the result of using the formula for Corr(x,y) on the returns for the stocks in the DJIA. The correlation is indicated on the chart by shades of grey as well as numerical values. Dark shades indicate low or negative correlation whilst d shades indicate high correlations near one. The majority of the values are high around 0.8 to 0.9 indicating that most of the stock prices move in unison with each other. The stock marked CSCO, the internet hardware company Cisco Systems, is a bit of an exception with some low and even slightly negative correlations. The correlations on the top left to bottom right diagonal of the matrix are all equal to one because every stock is perfectly correlated with itself.

	AXP	BA	CAT	CSCO	CVX	DD	DIS	GE
AXP	1	0.962463	0.558762	0.539088	0.896254	0.924036	0.977894	0.957923
BA	0.962463	1	0.491091	0.60514	0.809885	0.907549	0.948154	0.929371
CAT	0.558762	0.491091	1	−0.06746	0.716657	0.760181	0.56061	0.576245
CSCO	0.539088	0.60514	−0.06746	1	0.288784	0.366277	0.57947	0.514313
CVX	0.896254	0.809885	0.716657	0.288784	1	0.889716	0.878803	0.91753
DD	0.924036	0.907549	0.760181	0.366277	0.889716	1	0.920053	0.904253
DIS	0.977894	0.948154	0.56061	0.57947	0.878803	0.920053	1	0.962416
GE	0.957923	0.929371	0.576245	0.514313	0.91753	0.904253	0.962416	1

FIGURE 9-3: Correlation matrix (part) for the DJIA Index.

High correlations are also normal in other situations such as for the yield curve for bonds.

WARNING

Check the data you use from any source for errors – a process called *data cleaning*. If you're working for a company that already has a team doing data cleaning and has built a clean database, great. Otherwise, plotting data as I did in Figure 9-3 and calculating summary statistics as in the previous sections are good ways to check for errors. Bad data should show up clearly on a plot and is likely to produce some summary statistics way out of line. You should also check that all the data is actually there. This check may need to be automated with a computer program for a large data matrix. If you have missing data, you're okay to estimate it. In fact PCA is a good tool to do this.

Another way to look at data is to mark data points on a scatter plot in which you show the returns of one asset on the X axis and the returns of another on the Y axis. Figure 9-4 shows a scatter plot.

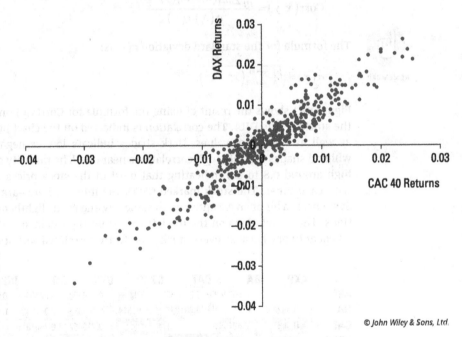

FIGURE 9-4: Scatterplot of the returns for the DAX and CAC 40 stock indices.

© *John Wiley & Sons, Ltd.*

Note that most of the data points lie along a line. If the return on the DAX is high, the returns on the CAC 40 is very likely to be high, too.

Standardising data

Another helpful (I hope) way to look at principal components analysis is to calculate a correlation matrix Z from the data matrix with the formula $Z = X^T X$. For this calculation to work, you must first take each column of your data matrix X and *standardise* it. To standardise data, follow these steps:

1. **Find the mean of every column of the data matrix and subtract it from every element in that column.**

   The *mean* is the sum of the numbers divided by the number of entries in the column.

2. **Divide every column by the standard deviation of that column.**

   REMEMBER

   If the N elements in the column are x_i, the standard deviation σ is

   $\sigma(x) = \sqrt{\frac{1}{N}\sum_{i=1}^{m}\left(x_i^2 - \bar{x}^2\right)}$ where the mean of the column is $\bar{x}$.

   The result is that every column of the data matrix has a mean of zero and a standard deviation of one. Having every variable start off on an equal footing can be useful. This *pre-processing* of the variables often helps to reduce the number of principal components you need. Standardising isn't the only way of pre-processing the data matrix, but it is a common one.

   WARNING

   A potential problem with standardising your data matrix is that you use all of each column to work out your standard deviations. Because the columns are often in chronological order, you process the data at the top of a column with information from the bottom of the column, which belongs to a future time. It doesn't make sense to do this processing if you eventually use your principal components model to try to predict, say, how a yield curve may change in the next few days because your model itself contains information about the future.

Brushing up some maths

To size up and analyse data matrices, it's helpful to be familiar with the maths of matrices. This section is designed to remind you of those bits of maths you've forgotten. If you're an expert on matrices, then please feel free to skip this section.

I start with matrices with only one row or column. Sometimes such matrices are called *vectors* because they can be used to indicate directions in space. I indicate a vector with a bold lower case letter like this:

$$\mathbf{a} = \begin{pmatrix} 1 \\ 1 \end{pmatrix}.$$

The individual elements of vectors are often referred to using subscripts. So, for the vector **a** above the elements are $a_1 = 1$ and $a_2 = 1$. Taking things simply I now introduce a second vector:

$$\mathbf{b} = \begin{pmatrix} 1 \\ -1 \end{pmatrix}.$$

If you like to think of vectors as directions in space, then **a** represents one step to the right and one step up whereas **b** represents one step to the right and one step down.

You can multiply vectors in a special way called a *dot product*. For vectors with just two elements, it's written like this:

$$\mathbf{a}.\mathbf{b} = a_1b_1 + a_2b_2$$

Doing the maths, you find that for the two vectors **a** and **b**, the dot product **a**.**b** is equal to 0. Vectors that have a dot product of 0 are called *orthogonal*.

But vectors don't have to have just two elements; they can have many more. You can think of these vectors as being in an N dimensional space and not just a two-dimensional piece of paper. This idea may seem like a stretch (mathematicians are known for their flights of fancy), but the idea is to use familiar ideas and thoughts from ordinary geometry to better understand larger data sets. I call these two vectors $\mathbf{p}_i$ and $\mathbf{p}_j$. In N dimensions, the dot product is:

$$\mathbf{p}_i \cdot \mathbf{p}_j = p_{i,1}p_{j,1} + p_{i,2}p_{j,2} + p_{i,a}p_{j,a} + \cdots + p_{i,N}p_{j,N}.$$

If the vectors $\mathbf{p}_i$ and $\mathbf{p}_j$ are orthogonal, then $\mathbf{p}_i \cdot \mathbf{p}_j = 0$ if $i \neq j$. If $i = j$, then the dot product is the sum of the squares of the components of $\mathbf{p}_i$. If you divide $\mathbf{p}_i$ by $\sqrt{\mathbf{p}_i \cdot \mathbf{p}_i}$, then **p** becomes *normalised* to a length of one. The sum of the squares of the elements of the normalised vector is equal to one. It's often useful to use vectors like this because they're like the axes of a diagram.

I turn now to matrices with more than one row or column, which I indicate in bold and in capitals. In this chapter, you frequently see the data matrix **X**. The individual elements of the matrix are $X_{i,j}$. The notation using bold letters is handy because it gets annoying looking at lots of subscripts. But sometimes you want to see the detail, so it's worth knowing both ways to write a matrix.

With matrices you can pretty much do what you want with numbers but also lots more. I start with multiplication. To multiply two matrices, you need to work out the dot product of each row of the first matrix with each column of the second matrix. The example here shows how this works for two-by-two matrices where I multiply **T** by **Q** to get:

$$\mathbf{X} = \mathbf{TQ} = \begin{pmatrix} t_{1,1} & t_{1,2} \\ t_{2,1} & t_{2,2} \end{pmatrix} \begin{pmatrix} q_{1,1} & q_{1,2} \\ q_{2,1} & q_{2,2} \end{pmatrix} = \begin{pmatrix} t_{1,1}q_{1,1} + t_{1,2}q_{2,1} & t_{1,1}q_{1,2} + t_{1,2}q_{2,2} \\ t_{2,1}q_{1,1} + t_{2,2}q_{2,1} & t_{2,1}q_{1,2} + t_{2,2}q_{2,2} \end{pmatrix}.$$

Later in this chapter I show that you can write the data matrix **X** as the product of two large matrices, **T** and **Q**. I show the formula for this using a dummy index, k, to indicate the sums needed for each element. I assume that the matrix, **T**, has M columns:

$$X_{i,j} = \sum_{k=1}^{M} t_{i,k} q_{k,j}.$$

This formula means that every element of **X** is calculated by working out the sum of the products of a row of **T** and a column of **Q**. To do this, the number of columns in **T** must be the same as the number of rows in **Q**. The summation, indicated by the big Greek sigma, goes from one up to the integer M.

You can do things with matrices that you can't do with numbers – this is where the fun begins. The *transpose* of a matrix is found by just switching around the indices – so $P_{i,j}^T = P_{j,i}.$ As an example:

$$\text{If } \mathbf{P} = \begin{bmatrix} 2 & 3 \\ 1 & 4 \\ -3 & 0 \end{bmatrix}, \text{ then } \mathbf{P}^T = \begin{bmatrix} 2 & 1 & -3 \\ 3 & 4 & 0 \end{bmatrix}.$$

Because the number of columns of a transposed matrix always equals the number of rows of the original matrix, you can always multiply them together:

$$\mathbf{Z} = \mathbf{P}^T \mathbf{P} = \begin{bmatrix} -4 & 10 \\ 10 & 25 \end{bmatrix}.$$

The matrix **Z** is said to be *symmetric* because the top-right element is equal to the bottom-left element. The covariance matrix and the correlation matrix are both symmetric. A matrix is symmetric if it's the same as its transpose. Check with the matrix **Z** that $\mathbf{Z}^T = \mathbf{Z}$.

Another special case of matrix is the *diagonal matrix*. In a diagonal matrix, all the elements equal zero except along the diagonal line from the top left to the bottom right. The matrix Λ is diagonal:

$$\Lambda = \begin{bmatrix} 15 & 0 \\ 0 & 2 \end{bmatrix}.$$

One last special matrix is the *identity matrix*, which is a diagonal matrix with all its diagonal elements equal to one.

A special kind of equation that only exists for matrices is called an *eigenvalue equation*. For a square matrix, **Z**, the eigenvalue equation is:

$$\mathbf{Z}\mathbf{P} = \mathbf{P}\lambda.$$

The constant λ is called the *eigenvalue* whilst the vector **p** is the *eigenvector*. For a square matrix with M rows and M columns, there are M values for λ, each with their own eigenvector.

Computer languages such as Python have built-in software to calculate eigenvalues and eigenvectors of a square matrix. In Python, it's part of the NumPy (Numerical Python) module that you can download, along with the Python language itself, from www.python.org. In the NumPy reference manual on the Python website is the eigenvalue routine within the linear algebra section.

If you're wondering, *eigen* is a German word meaning 'own' or 'self'. The eigenvector is the own vector of a matrix because if you multiply the eigenvector by the matrix, you get back to a multiple of the eigenvector.

Decomposing data matrices into principal components

Principal components analysis starts with a data matrix, **X**. This matrix may contain the returns for a stock market in each of its columns or it may contain the daily changes in yields for bonds of different maturities.

Assume that **X** has N rows of data and M columns where N and M are integers. Remember that M can be any integer – it may be as few as 5 or as large as 500 or greater. Principal components analysis is especially useful with cumbersome data matrices with lots of columns (large M). Sometimes these columns are called variables because they're the quantity of interest to you such as a share price return. So there are M variables in principal component analysis.

The big idea of principal components analysis is to write the data matrix **X** as the product of two other matrices, **T** and **P**:

$$X = TP^T.$$

The superscript, T, on **P** indicates that it's the transpose of **P**.

The matrix **T** has N rows and M columns – M is the number of principal components. The matrix **P** has M rows and M columns, so it's a square matrix. This kind of equation is called a *decomposition* because the matrix **X** is broken down into two parts.

At the moment, you don't know what **T** and **P** are. In the next section, 'Calculating principal components' I show you how to calculate them, even if you're working with a very large data matrix. If you're itching to find out how to calculate **T** and **P** for your own data matrix, then please go straight to that section. For the moment, I tell you more about **T** and **P**. You can also see an example of how to use principal components analysis in the upcoming section 'Applying PCA to Yield Curves'.

Here's a clever bit about principal components analysis: The matrix P is *orthonormal*, which is short for *orthogonal* and *normalised*. Think of P as made up of column vectors, which I call p_i. The index, i, can take the values from one to M – the number of rows and columns in P. Each of these vectors has a length of one and is orthogonal to the other column vectors. The same, in fact, is true of the row vectors of P. As a result, $\mathbf{P^TP = I}$ where i is the identity matrix. Because P has a length of 1, it can be used to rotate vectors and to find new combinations of variables that are more useful than the old variables. Here's how: you can rewrite the decomposition of **X** using the elements of **P**, $p_{i,j}$ and the columns of **T** which I call t_i.:

$$\mathbf{x}_i = p_{i,1}\mathbf{t}_1 + p_{i,2}\mathbf{t}_2 + \ldots + p_{i,M}\mathbf{t}_M$$

(The lowercase x indicates a single column of **X**.)

This is the *principal components representation* of the ith column vector of the data matrix X. The matrix **T** is, then, the matrix of the M principal components. The ith principal component is t_i.

At the moment, this equation for x_i doesn't look useful because I just rewrote the data matrix **X** in terms of M new variables t_i . Hold on though – I show you how it's helpful in a minute.

Another helpful way to write these equations is to multiply the matrix decomposition equation for **X** on the right side by **P**, which gives you the equation **T = XP**. This follows by using the property $\mathbf{P^TP = I}$ since **P** is orthonormal. Remember that in this equation, **I** is the identity matrix which has ones on its diagonal and zero everywhere else. This equation for **T** can be written using the elements of the **P** and **X** matrices as:

$$\mathbf{t}_i = p_{1,i}\mathbf{x}_1 + p_{2,i}\mathbf{x}_2 + \ldots + p_{M,i}\mathbf{x}_M.$$

Each principal component, t_i, is a linear combination of the columns of the data matrix. The elements of the matrix **P** tell you how much of each of the variables (columns of **X**) to use in each principal component. Because of that, the columns of **P** are sometimes called *weight vectors*.

If you substitute for **X** in the matrix decomposition equation for the correlation matrix $\mathbf{Z = X^TX}$, you get that $\mathbf{Z = PT^TTP^T}$. Now multiply both sides of the equation by **P** on the right to get $\mathbf{ZP = PT^TTP^TP}$. Because **P** is orthonormal, you can simplify this equation to get $\mathbf{ZP = PT^TT}$. This kind of equation is called an *eigenvalue equation* in mathematics. The previous section "Brushing up some maths" explains eigenvalues and eigenvectors if you're a bit hazy on them.

A matrix eigenvalue equation such as $\mathbf{ZP} = \mathbf{PT^{T}T}$ looks a bit funny because an *eigenvector* $\mathbf{P}$ is on each side of it. The product $\mathbf{T^{T}T}$ is a diagonal matrix often written using the capital Greek letter lambda, Λ. The elements along the diagonal are the eigenvalues.

I'm not going to prove it, but the sum of the eigenvalues of a correlation matrix is equal to the number of variables. For example, for the Dow Jones Industrial Average Index data matrix I use in Figure 9-3, the sum of the value of the eigenvalues is equal to 30. Figure 9-5 shows the first 20 eigenvalues of the correlation matrix.

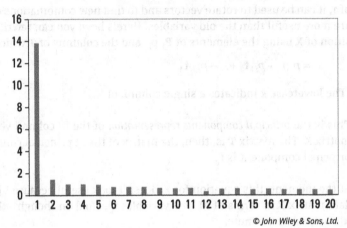

FIGURE 9-5: Eigenvalues of the DJIA Index correlation matrix.

The figure shows one particularly large, or dominant, eigenvalue followed by much smaller ones. This is the main point of principal components analysis: Normally only one or two eigenvalues are large, and you can ignore the others. Because the variance of each principal component is given by its eigenvalue, the first principal component, t_1, explains a very large fraction of the variance in the data matrix $\mathbf{X}$. In the principal components representation of $\mathbf{X}$ you only need to retain a small number of principal components. This can lead to important simplifications for calculations on large portfolios. In the upcoming section "Checking your model with cross-validation" I show you how to decide how many principal components to retain in your model of the data matrix.

Going back to the Dow Jones data matrix in Table 9-1, the large eigenvalue is connected to an eigenvector (a column of the matrix $\mathbf{P}$) that combines all the DJIA components in almost equal measure. So this first principal component is similar to the Dow Jones Index itself. It means that most of the variability that can be explained in the DJIA stocks is explained by the overall market. However, there are still some residual, smaller amounts of variability explained by the smaller principal components.

Calculating principal components

In this section, I show you how to calculate the matrices **T** and **P** from **X** in a principal components analysis (finally, I hear you say).

REMEMBER

In principal components analysis, you write a $N \times M$ data matrix, **X**, as the product of two other matrices, **T** and $\mathbf{P^T}$.

One way is to use specialised software to compute the eigenvalues and eigenvectors of the correlation matrix **Z** calculated from the data matrix using $\mathbf{Z = X^T X}$. However, you can use a simpler method that makes use of the fact that often only a few eigenvalues of significance are present. A big advantage of this second method is that if your data matrix is large with maybe hundreds of variables, you can still do the calculations in a short amount of time on an ordinary computer.

TECHNICAL STUFF

This second method is called non-linear iterative partial least squares which is quite a mouthful and is often abbreviated to NIPALS.

The algorithm in the following steps works out the eigenvalues and eigenvectors one at a time starting from the largest eigenvalue first. That's good news as it starts with the most important principal components, and you can stop when your decomposition is accurate enough. The calculations are *iterative*, which means that you go through a loop time and again, each time improving the accuracy of your estimates of t and p until you're happy with them.

To build a PCA representation, follow these steps:

1. **Start with a guess for the first principal component, t_1.**

A good guess is the values in first column of the data matrix.

2. **Calculate an estimate of the first weight vector p_1 using $p_i = \mathbf{X^T} t_j$.**

3. **Normalise p_1.**

To do so, calculate the length, L, of $\mathbf{p_1}$. If the components are $\mathbf{p_{i,1}}$, then the length is:

$$L = \sum_{i=1}^{n} p_{i,1}^2.$$

You can write your normalised $\mathbf{p_1}$ as $\mathbf{p_j^*} = \dfrac{\mathbf{p_j}}{\sqrt{L}}$.

4. **Update your guess for t_1 by calculating your new value: $t_j = \mathbf{X}_j \mathbf{p_j^*}$.**

5. **You now have a new value of t_1 that you need to compare with the old value that you guessed at the beginning if this calculation.**

Do this by calculating $\Delta = \left(\mathbf{t_{old}} - \mathbf{t_{new}} \right)^2$. Remember that the square of a vector is calculated using the sum of the squares of the components.

If Δ is less than a small number, say 0.001, then you're finished with this iteration. Mathematicians like to say that your iterations have *converged*. Continue to Step 6. If not, go back to Step 2 and use your new updated vector, $\mathbf{t}_1$. Each time you go back to Step 2, you should see a drop in Δ and finally you'll get through to Step 6.

6. **Shrink the data matrix by calculating $\mathbf{X}_{shrunk} = \mathbf{X} - \mathbf{t}_1 \mathbf{p}_1^T$.**

   This formula uses your new value for $\mathbf{t}_1$. Remember that $\mathbf{X}$ is a matrix and the product $\mathbf{t}_1 \mathbf{p}_1^T$ is also a matrix calculated from a column vector $\mathbf{t}_1$ and a row vector $\mathbf{p}_1^T$. Shrinking happens when the information about a principal component is peeled off from the data matrix and you get ready to calculate the next principal component.

7. **Go back to Step 1 to calculate the next principal component.**

You can calculate as many principal components as you wish with this process.

TIP

Try this process for yourself using Excel VBA, Python or R. Each step is straightforward to code. Find some financial data and try building your own model. Good sources of data are the Federal Reserve Economic Database (FRED), which has excellent interest-rate data, and Yahoo Finance, which has many historical stock price quotes.

The procedure in the numbered steps is an example of an *algorithm*, which is just a set of step-by-step operations. Algorithms are what you need for many of the calculations in quantitative finance and this is a good example of one.

Checking your model with cross- validation

Building a PCA model involves decomposing the data matrix $\mathbf{X}$ into a product of the principal components $\mathbf{T}$ and the weights $\mathbf{P}$. You need to make the important decision of how many principal components to retain in your model. I call this number MC. By leaving out many principal components from your model, you're saying that they don't contain useful information. Another way of saying this is that PCA splits the data matrix into useful information and noise like this:

$$\mathbf{X} = \mathbf{TP}^T + \mathbf{E} = \text{Useful information} + \text{Noise}.$$

Noise most commonly means an unwanted sound, but in financial analysis, it's used to refer to data containing little information. *Noise* is random data; you can assume that it has a Gaussian distribution. (Chapter 2 gives you more information on random variables and the Gaussian distribution.)

The principal components decomposition of your data matrix uses only a few principal components, and because it doesn't perfectly reconstruct the data matrix, you also have a noise term, E. To work out exactly how many principal components to use, you can use a technique in which you split your data set into two parts. The data matrix is split into a region for building the models and a region of withheld test data. There's no hard-and-fast rule about how to do this, so just splitting your data set in two halves is fine.

The models are then used to predict the data for the test region. None of the test data is used to build models. This technique is therefore called *out-of-sample testing*. In fact, you need to carry out two principal component analyses. The first analysis uses data for all the assets (variables) but not for all the time. The second analysis uses data for all the time but not all the assets. I show this in Figure 9-6 where the regions of data used for each principal component analysis are shown in light grey. The overlap region common to both the PCA models shows as dark grey and the withheld data is in white as it isn't used in either model.

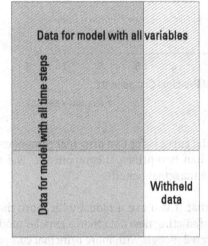

FIGURE 9-6:
Defining calibration and test data regions for cross-validation.

© John Wiley & Sons, Ltd.

Using the results (the **T** and **P** matrices) from the two principal components analyses, you can predict the withheld data. You do this using the usual decomposition formula, $\mathbf{X} = \mathbf{TP}^T$, but this time you use the principal components **T** from the analysis with all the time steps and the weights **P** from the analysis with all the assets. Then, the formula for the predicted data matrix values is $\mathbf{X}_{pred} = \mathbf{T}_1 \mathbf{P}_2{}^T$ where the subscripts 1 and 2 indicate the two different principal component analyses.

Using the predicted values for the withheld test part of the data matrix, you can compare them with the actual values. Take the difference between them and then calculate the sum of the squared values to get a statistic, Δ.

$$\Delta = \sum_{j=1}^{P} \left(X - X_{pred} \right)^2.$$

The chart in Figure 9-7 shows a plot of how delta varies as the number of principal components is increased from zero. To begin with, it drops sharply, and then it starts to rise again.

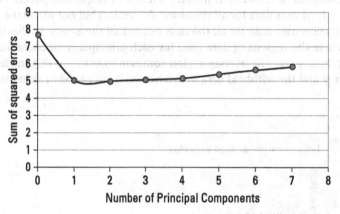

FIGURE 9-7:
Calibrating a PCA
model using
out-of-sample
predictions.

© John Wiley & Sons, Ltd.

The lowest point (just) on the curve is for two principal components, so there's no good reason to use more than two principal components. The second principal component gives you only a marginal benefit.

What this chart shows is that if you use a model with more than two principal components, it's worse at predicting new data than a smaller model with only two components. More complicated models with more principal components are models of noise rather than useful information. When such a model is used to make predictions, it does poorly.

This technique of using a model to make predictions for data not used in its construction is widely applicable. It enables you to figure out how complicated to make a model and to get a good idea of what its performance might be in real life.

Going back to the Dow Jones example, the first principal component is closely connected with the overall market. A PCA model with two components gives a good parsimonious description of the DJIA Index.

Applying PCA to Yield Curves

PCA can be applied to yield curves because the different maturities of bonds are highly correlated. Figure 9-8 shows the yield from US Treasuries at constant maturity. Notice the clear similarity among the curves, although the period during the onset of the 2008 financial crisis associated with the collapse of the investment bank Lehman Brothers is a bit chaotic. Also notice that the 3-month yield (indicated as a dotted line) is almost always the lowest, and the 20-year yield is almost always the highest. In the past two decades, only during the so-called dot-com bubble in 2000 and the financial crisis of 2008 has the 3-month yield risen above the 20-year yield.

The unstable relationship in time for these bond yields means that you're well advised to take the difference between yields from one day to another as the basic variable in the PCA.

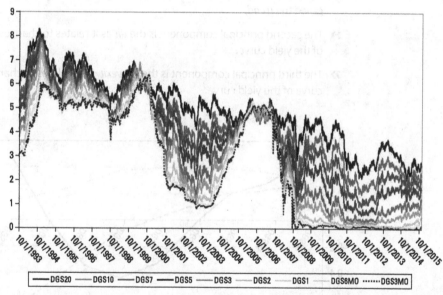

FIGURE 9-8:
Constant
maturity US
Treasury yields.

— DGS20 — DGS10 — DGS7 — DGS5 — DGS3 — DGS2 — DGS1 — DGS6MO ······ DGS3MO

Source: Federal Reserve Economic Database

Figure 9-9 shows a chart of the correlation matrix between the different maturities of US Treasury bonds. It shows the typical behaviour for a yield curve with positive correlations that tend to get close to one for close maturities. The lowest correlation at 0.105 is between the 1-month and 30-year maturities.

	1 Month	3 Month	6 Month	1 Year	2 Year	Year	5 Year	7 Year	10 Year	30 Year
1 Month	1									
3 Month	0.702725	1								
6 Month	0.538376	0.787159	1							
1 Year	0.515779	0.669882	0.857081	1						
2 Year	0.284917	0.366075	0.5208	0.748357	1					
Year	0.245001	0.322481	0.477994	0.693006	0.938008	1				
5 Year	0.191042	0.248156	0.383581	0.586027	0.858767	0.935631	1			
7 Year	0.161249	0.204892	0.325185	0.509917	0.776199	0.872159	0.968647	1		
10 Year	0.133831	0.16705	0.279772	0.446028	0.701494	0.806043	0.925091	0.968632	1	
30 Year	0.105271	0.120933	0.214922	0.349796	0.554013	0.658634	0.794014	0.866483	0.929197	1

Source: Federal Reserve Economic Database

FIGURE 9-9:
Correlations of US constant maturity Treasury yields.

The chart in Figure 9-10 shows the weights (or eigenvectors) from the first three principal components. The weights for the first principal components all show quite different patterns:

» The first principal component, which belongs to the largest eigenvalue, is called the *trend*.

» The second principal component is the *tilt* as it relates to changes in the slope of the yield curve.

» The third principal component is the *convexity* and relates to changes in the curve of the yield curve.

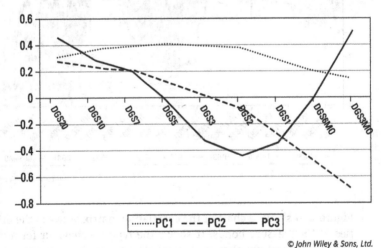

FIGURE 9-10:
Trend, tilt and convexity for the US Treasury yield curve.

© John Wiley & Sons, Ltd.

These principal components give an idea of the main ways a yield curve can move. The first component, the trend, which has the largest eigenvalue, is the dominant one, and is associated with a shift of the entire yield curve up or down because all the weights are positive. The second component is associated with a change in the slope of the yield curve. The weights are positive for short maturities less than two years and negative for longer maturities greater than two years. These movements can happen when an increase in the short-term interest rates by the central bank reduces the prospect for long-term rates and so tilts the yield curve. The third component is associated with a more complex movement in which the weights are positive for short-term maturities less than six months, negative for medium-term maturities and positive again for long-term maturities greater than three years.

The importance of these three movements can be evaluated using the R^2 value after each of the principal components has been calculated and comparing with the sum of the squared values S^2 for the data matrix. The R^2 value is the sum of the squares of all the elements of the data matrix after principal components have been peeled off using the iterative algorithm described in the 'Calculating principal components' section earlier in the chapter. The cumulative R^2 is called C^2 and is calculated from both R^2 and S^2:

$$C^2 = 1 - \frac{R^2}{S^2}.$$

Before any iterations of the PCA algorithm, C^2 is equal to zero, as you may expect. However, after all the principal components are calculated and the data matrix has been shrunk to zero, then $R^2 = 0$ and $C^2 = 1$. So the cumulative R^2 ranges from zero to one as a principal components representation is built up. Table 9-3 shows the values for the yield curve analysis.

TABLE 9-3

Sample R^2 Ranges

Principal Component	Cumulative R^2
PC1	0.79
PC2	0.90
PC3	0.95

After calculating three principal components, 95 per cent of the variation in the data matrix is explained. Given that nine maturities are in the data matrix, this high percentage shows the efficiency of the principal components representation.

Using PCA to Build Models

The PCA decomposition of a data matrix can help you do a couple things with data:

» Identify clusters of similar assets.

» Build predictive models. You can use the principals components as new variables to predict related quantities. In the case of the yield curve, because interest rates are so important to the economy as a whole, you can even consider trying to predict stock index returns.

Identifying clusters of data

To discover how your data is grouped, you can graph your numbers in a chart of the principal components weights, as shown in Figure 9-11. The x-axis value for the jth stock in the Dow Jones index is the value $p_{1,j}$, whilst the y-axis value is $p_{2,j}$. So you can construct your own charts from your data after you do your principal components analysis.

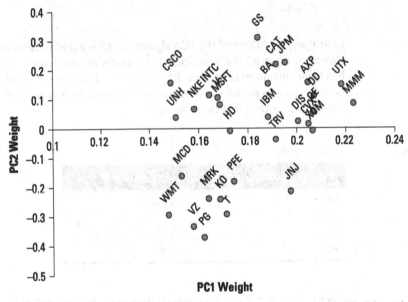

FIGURE 9-11:
PCA weight plot for the DJIA Index.

The x-axis is the PC1 weight. All the values are positive and close to 0.18 so this principal component is putting approximately equal weight on all the constituents of the Dow Jones Index. This principal component is effectively the index itself. It's not surprising that PC1 explains a lot of the variability in the data matrix.

The second principal component separates the Dow Jones constituents into clusters above and below the x-axis. The cluster below contains *defensive stocks* that are expected to do fine even if the economy does badly because they sell essential goods and services. Examples are Walmart (discount stores), Proctor and Gamble (nappies and other household goods) and Verizon (telecom).

The cluster above the line contains companies that depend more on the economy doing well. These companies include investment banks and major industrials such as General Electric. This classification has happened because the principal components are calculated to be orthogonal. The second principal component of the DJIA data matrix is therefore characterising stocks by dissimilarity to the index and so naturally picks out defensive stocks. You can use this application of PCA to gain insight into the construction of investment portfolios with particular risk characteristics.

Principal components regression

Principal components analysis is highly versatile and can be used to build predictive models. If your data matrix is **X**, then you may have a quantity, **Y**, that depends on the variables in **X**. A good technique to find a relationship between **X** and **Y** is linear regression, which I explain in more detail in Chapter 16. In this section, I tell you how to adapt linear regression to use the results from a principal components analysis as input. Because PCA reduces the dimensionality of a data matrix, you can use far fewer predictor variables than in a normal linear regression model.

To do a principal components regression, follow these steps:

1. **Set up your data matrix X with pre-processing so as to standardise the variables.**

    Check the 'Standardising data' section for information on how to do this.

2. **Use out-of-sample validation to figure out how many principal components you need.**

    The 'Checking your model with cross-validation' section covers this.

3. **From your PCA, find the T matrix.**

    You obtain the T matrix from the algorithm in 'Calculating principal components'.

4. **For your Y values, you treat the T matrix as a matrix of predictor variables, so you're trying to find a relationship, $Y = TC$, where C is a vector of constants.**

You can now do this using standard software for calculating a linear regression such as the function linest in Excel.

It may be that even with the reduced number of variables from your PCA, you don't need all of them in your regression model. You can detect how many you need by examining the t statistics.

REMEMBER

The *t-statistics* are the ratios of the estimated coefficients, **C**, in your regression and the standard error of the coefficients. The larger they are in magnitude, the more significant is that variable. Typically, if the t-statistic for a variable is less than three, leave it out of the model.

After leaving out variables that do not have large t-statistics, you can rebuild your model with the remaining significant variables.

WARNING

If you change your pre-processing step, the results for your PCA change. Deciding not to use standardised data, which has a mean of zero and standard deviation of one, may mean that you need an extra principal component to represent your data matrix.

Option Pricing

IN THIS PART . . .

Make pricing clearer with the Black-Scholes equation.

Build pricing trees as an alternative method of working out the price of options.

Go to the Greeks (letters used in maths terms) for ratios that come in handy when you're using options.

Use interest-rate options as banks and real estate investors do.

Chapter 10

Examining the Binomial and Black-Scholes Pricing Models

O ptions are versatile financial instruments that derive their price from an underlying asset such as a share or a bond. In this chapter, I show you how to price them, relating this price to the price of the underlying asset and other factors such as the interest rate.

You benefit from having more than one tool at your disposal, so I explain two main methods to price options and add a third method that's useful for valuing some of the more exotic kinds of option.

Looking at a Simple Portfolio with No Arbitrage

A simple but big idea is the basis of most option pricing: if you set up a portfolio that includes the option but has no risk, the portfolio return must be given by the risk-free interest rate.

REMEMBER

You hear a lot about the risk-free rate in this chapter, but what exactly is it? A good definition of the *risk-free rate* is the interest rate offered by short-term government bills such as the three-month US Treasury bill. Short-term bills are frequently traded so their interest rates reflect market conditions. Governments are unlikely to go bust, so the interest rate they offer can be considered to be risk free. On the other hand, if you lend money to a bank, you may earn a higher interest rate called LIBOR (London Interbank Offered Rate) but you're subject to the risk of the bank going under. This risk is real – during the 2008 financial crisis, queues of worried depositors formed outside some banks.

If you hold a *call option*, which is a right to buy an underlying share at a strike price, X, at some time in the future, you're exposed to the risk of the share price going down. To make your option riskless, you must short the underlying share so that you make money as the share price declines. A *short position* is one in which you borrow shares and then sell them in the market. This position is equivalent to holding a negative amount of shares.

Shorting is a way of gaining when share prices decline but losing when they rise. For example, say you borrow 10 shares worth £100 each and promptly sell them for £1,000. The shares then decline in price to £90. You buy 10 shares for £900 and return them to your lender. You made £100, or £10 per share. If the share price had gone up by £10, you would have lost £100 because you would have had to buy them back at a higher price than you sold them for. Finance is a topsy-turvy world sometimes!

REMEMBER

By holding a call option together with a short position in the underlying stock, you can make your overall position riskless. Likewise, if you hold a put option, you can make your position riskless by buying the underlying stock. A *put option* is a right to sell an underlying share at the strike price, X, at some time in the future.

You can compensate for any loss or gain in an option position with a market position in the underlying asset.

The fact that the payoffs from options can be replicated by stocks and cash is referred to as the *completeness of markets*. In a way, options aren't needed, but they prove to be convenient instruments. Crucially, the completeness means that options can be hedged using the underlying stock and that is the idea that allows them to be priced.

Pricing in a Single Step

In this section, I show you how to price an option using a portfolio constructed to be risk free using a simple model for the behaviour of stock prices called the *binomial model*. In this model, time is discrete – it goes in steps. You can think of it as a price quoted at the close of business every day rather than having prices quoted continuously throughout the day.

I write the time today as t = 0 and the time tomorrow as t = 1. In addition, at every time step, the price can only end up in one of two possible states: it can go up by a specified amount or it can go down by a specified amount. This seems simplistic, but it incorporates the key characteristic of stock prices – they're random. At t = 0 you don't know what the price will be at t = 1. Figure 10-1 shows a diagram that illustrates a binomial model of prices for an underlying stock.

Now I show you how to use the underlying stock to hedge an option by creating a riskless portfolio. To make things easy (if that seems soft, then please skip ahead to 'Branching Out in Pricing an Option'), start with a call option that has only one day left until expiry. Today the underlying stock is worth £100; tomorrow it will be worth either £102 or £98. You short a quantity, Δ, of this stock to hedge the option. At the moment you don't know the value of Δ. The option has a strike price of £100, so if the stock goes up to £102, the option is worth £2. On the other hand, if the stock goes down to £98, then the option is worthless. For this little portfolio to be riskless, its value must be the same regardless of whether the stock goes up or down. You can write an equation for this, remembering that the value of the shares is their price multiplied by the quantity Δ:

$$2 - 102\Delta = -98\Delta.$$

The equation has the form: (Value if stock price goes up) = (Value if stock price goes down). Remember that you're short the stock, so that the terms in the equation for the stock are negative.

Solving for Δ, you get that $\Delta = \frac{1}{2}$, so you need to short one stock for every two options you hold.

TIP

This quantity, Δ – the amount needed to make your investment risk free – keeps coming up in quantitative finance. It gives its name to *delta hedging,* which means to hedge an option by holding an amount Δ of the underlying asset.

So if the stock goes up to £102, your portfolio is worth –£49, and likewise if the stock goes down, your portfolio is worth –£49. The negative portfolio value is because you're short the stock.

The calculation for Δ involves equating the portfolio values for the up and down states of the stock at the end of the time step. It's good to know Δ, but you really want to know V – the option price. The value of the portfolio today, when the stock is worth £100, is $V - 100\Delta$ – using subtraction for the short position in Δ of stock. However, if the interest rate is zero, the portfolio value must be equal to –£49, the portfolio value at t = 1. Because the portfolio is hedged and risk free, its value at t = 0 must be the same as its value at t = 1, assuming the interest rate is zero. This means that $V - 100\Delta = -49 \implies V = -49 + \frac{100}{2} = 1$. You now have the price of the option at t = 0. The graph in Figure 10-1 summarises this calculation.

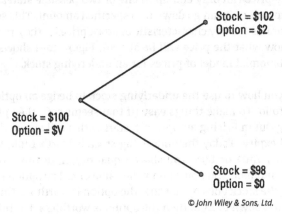

Stock = $102
Option = $2

Stock = $100
Option = $V

Stock = $98
Option = $0

FIGURE 10-1:
Calculating the price, V, of an option using a one-step binomial tree.

© *John Wiley & Sons, Ltd.*

REMEMBER

The calculation for V depends in a big way on the range of possible values for the stock. This, in turn, depends on the volatility of the stock. So the volatility is a key quantity in calculating option prices. V also depends on the *strike price* (the price at which you can exercise your option) for the option because that determines the payoff at expiry. Although I assumed here that the interest rate is zero, this too influences option prices.

Entering the world of risk neutral

In the preceding section, I show you how to price an option in a world with a single time step, from t = 0 to t = 1 by constructing a hedged portfolio with no risk.

Notice that I didn't have to specify the probability of the stock going up or down at t = 1 to find that the option value, V, is V = 1. But you can calculate the probability, p, of the stock going up that is consistent with the option price of V = 1. If the stock goes up, the option payoff is £2, and if the stock goes down the payoff is zero. The expected value of the option at t = 1 is $2p + 0 \times (1 - p) = V$. But this expected value at t = 1 must be equal to the option value at t = 0 because the interest rate is zero, so 2p = V = 1. Using simple algebra, p = ½.

The correct pricing of the option implies a probability of 0.5 for the stock to move up. This probability is called the *risk-neutral probability* because it's the probability consistent with the risk-free portfolio I constructed.

Now, to make the calculations more realistic, I stick with a single time step but introduce the interest rate, r, and use algebra for the stock and option prices so that you can do the option price calculation no matter what the initial price of the stock is and no matter what the possible prices for the stock are at t = 1.

Figure 10-2 shows the portfolio with more general prices.

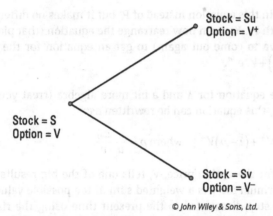

Stock = Su
Option = V⁺

Stock = S
Option = V

Stock = Sv
Option = V⁻

FIGURE 10-2:
Binomial tree
with general
prices.

© John Wiley & Sons, Ltd.

Now the stock price, S, can rise by a factor, u, or fall by a factor, v. I make no assumption about the final price of the option, so this analysis is correct no matter what the strike price of the option is. The portfolio is the same as in the previous section with a call option hedged by a short position in the underlying stock. The value of this portfolio, P, is given by the option value, V, minus (because you're short) the stock price multiplied by the amount of stock you hold. As always, while hedging options the amount of stock is denoted by Δ: $P = V - S\Delta$.

At the end of the time step, the portfolio changes value to:

$$P^+ = V^+ - Su\Delta \quad \text{or} \quad P^- = V^- - Sv\Delta.$$

However, to be riskless, P⁺ must equal P⁻ so that the portfolio value is independent of whether the share price rises or falls. These two equations can then be combined and rearranged (you may need to get a pencil and piece of paper out to check the combination for yourself) to give an equation for Δ:

$$\Delta = \frac{V^+ - V^-}{S(u-v)}.$$

Riskless by construction, the portfolio at the end of the time step must have a present value equal to the value of the portfolio at the beginning. The riskless portfolio of option and shares must be valued using the risk-free rate, otherwise there would be an arbitrage opportunity against a portfolio holding just cash. To calculate the present value of the expected portfolio value, I use the time value of money formula from Chapter 4 which uses the risk-free interest rate, r. Remember that in this formula, e (for exponential) is the base of the natural logarithm: $V - S\Delta = P^+ e^{-rt}$.

You can use P⁻ in this equation instead of P⁺ but it makes no difference because of the equality with P⁺. You can now rearrange the equation (that piece of paper and pencil may have to come out again) to get an equation for the option price V: $V = S\Delta(1 - ue^{-rt}) + V^+ e^{-rt}$.

Now, using the equation for Δ and a bit more algebra (treat yourself to a fresh sheet of paper), this equation can be rewritten as:

$$V = e^{-rt}\left[pV^+ + (1-p)V^- \right] \quad \text{where } p = \frac{e^{rt} - v}{u - v}.$$

TIP

This equation for the option price, V, tells one of the big results of quantitative finance. The formula for V is a weighted sum of the possible values of the option after one time step discounted to the present time using the risk-free interest rate, r. I use a new variable, p, which looks suspiciously like it may be a probability. The equation for p involves only the risk-free interest rate r and the numbers u and v, which determine the possible future values of the share price; u and v depend on the volatility of the underlying share.

Nowhere in the formula is there reference to the probability of the share price rising or falling, which means that the formula for V does not depend on the expected return of the share. To check this, you can calculate the expected return of the share using the probability given by p. In Chapter 2, I show you how to calculate expected values for random variables. The expected return for the share price E(S) is $E(S) = pSu + (1-p)Sv$. Then substitute: $p = \frac{e^{rt} - v}{u - v}$ to get that the expected return for the share price is: $E(S) = Se^{rt}$.

What this shows is that if you use the formula for p given here, you're essentially assuming that the share price rises at a rate given by the risk-free interest rate. In the real world, the expected value of a share price is more likely to be given by $E(S) = Se^{\mu t}$ where μ is the growth rate of the share. The reason you find an expected return given by the risk-free rate in this calculation is that risk has been eliminated from the hedged portfolio of share and option. The formula you use for the probability, p, is the correct one if the share price drifts with an expected growth rate given by the risk-free interest rate, r.

In a risk-neutral world, options can be valued as the expected present value of the option using probabilities assuming that the underlying share drifts at the risk-free rate.

Calculating the parameters

The constants u and v, used to indicate by how much the share can rise and fall in the time step, can be related to the share price volatility. Now assume that the time step in the binomial tree is small. (Later in this chapter, I create binomial trees with many steps so that they more realistically model financial assets. It makes sense to have many small steps to build the path taken by the share price in time.)

You have some freedom in calculating the values of u and v provided that the resulting tree of prices reflects the correct volatility, σ, of the share. Making use of this freedom, write that $u = 1 + R$ and $v = 1 - R$ so that R is the return of the share in the time step. $S \times u$ is now $S + SR$, so the absolute price of the share increases by SR in the time step. The steps in this binomial tree are just like the steps in the geometric Brownian motion explained in Chapter 3. In that case, the change in the price of the share in a single step must be $S\sigma\sqrt{\delta t}$, so $R = \sigma\sqrt{\delta t}$. Now you can use the formula:

$$u = 1 + \sigma\sqrt{\delta t}, \quad v = 1 - \sigma\sqrt{\delta t}$$

in binomial tree calculations. Substituting these values into the formula for p, you get:

$$p = \frac{1}{2} + \frac{r\sqrt{\delta t}}{2\sigma}.$$

 To work this formula out from the equation for p, I use the fact that the time step is small – δt – so I can use the approximate formula: $e^{r\delta t} \approx 1 + r\delta t$, which is valid provided that rt is small (much less than one).

TIP

The formula for the probability, p, is saying that in the limit of a very small time step, δt, the probability of the stock going up is slightly more than 0.5 and the probability of it going down is slightly less than 0.5. And if the risk-free rate is high, then the probability of the stock going up increases.

Branching Out in Pricing an Option

Pricing an option in a world with a single time step is a bit unrealistic. In these sections, you can see how to grow your tree of prices into many steps so that you can price options more accurately.

Building a tree of asset prices

So far in this chapter, the binomial tree has only two branches. After the price rises by a factor, u, the tree can rise again by a factor u or fall by a factor v. Thus, each branch can branch out farther. These branches build up a tree that shows the range of possible outcomes of moving forward in time from the present, as shown in Figure 10-3. The root of the tree at time t = 0 is on the left side. On the right side of the diagram are all the possible prices of the share and beneath each is the probability of reaching that price. The factors of three in the probabilities are due to the three different paths that can arrive at the middle points.

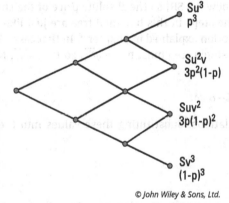

FIGURE 10-3:
A binomial tree model showing stock prices and the probability of reaching that value.

Su^3
p^3

Su^2v
$3p^2(1-p)$

Suv^2
$3p(1-p)^2$

Sv^3
$(1-p)^3$

© John Wiley & Sons, Ltd.

Building a tree of option prices by working backwards

The key step in using the binomial tree to price an option is to work from the expiry date all the way back to the root. First, you need to work out the option prices. Doing so is easy because you've worked out the stock prices and, because you're using the expiry date, you calculate the option price from the payoff function.

REMEMBER

The payoff function tells you how much an option is worth at expiry given the stock price and the strike price for the option.

To go backwards, you must now use the equation:

$$V = e^{-rt}\left[pV^+ + (1-p)V^-\right].$$

This equation relates an option price, V, to the two prices, V^+ and V^-, closer to expiry. Using the formula for p from the preceding section, 'Calculating the parameters', you can work your way backwards all the way to the current time at the root. In this way, you can calculate the current value of the option. Notice that by calculating the option prices backwards, you never need to use the stock prices. You need the stock prices only to calculate the option payoff at the expiry.

To show how this works, take this numerical example: You want to value a European call option that has two months left until expiry. The strike price is £180 and the underlying stock is currently at £200. The annual risk-free interest rate is 1 per cent, so: $r = 0.01$. The annual volatility is 30 per cent, so: $\sigma = 0.3$.

TECHNICAL STUFF

To convert percentages to fractions, divide the percentage by 100 – simple to do; easy to forget.

Always use the same units throughout any calculation. In this example, time is measured in years, so I use annual volatility and an annual interest rate.

Using two time steps of one month each should give you a reasonable estimate of the option value. Because I'm measuring time in years, the time step is one month:

$$\delta t = \frac{1}{12} = 0.0833.$$

You need the factors u and v calculated to build up your tree of stock prices:

$$v = 1 - 0.3 \times \sqrt{0.0833} = 0.913 \quad \text{and} \quad u = 1 + 0.3 \times \sqrt{0.0833} = 1.0866.$$

Figure 10-4 shows the result. The numbers in the box show the stock price at the top and the option price at the bottom. So, at the root, the stock price is £200. At the top right, after the stock has risen for two months in a row, the price is $£200 \times u \times u = £236$. The option price in the top right is £56 because the option is a call option with a strike price of £180. The option holder then has the right to buy the stock at £180 which she will promptly do and then sell at £236 to make a profit of £56. By contrast, in the bottom right, the stock price is only £167, which is lower than the strike price. Buying at £180, above the market price, is pointless, so the option expires worthless.

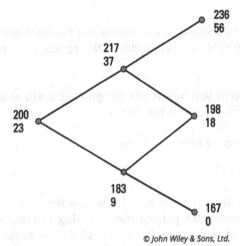

FIGURE 10-4:
Sample pricing of
call option in two
time steps.

236
56

217
37

200
23

198
18

183
9

167
0

© John Wiley & Sons, Ltd.

The probability, p, is calculated using the formula:

$$p = 0.5 + \frac{0.01 \times \sqrt{0.0833}}{2 \times 0.3} = 0.505.$$

With this, you can start calculating more of the option prices. When the stock price rises, the option price one time step beyond the root is:

$$V = e^{-0.01 \times 0.0833} \left(0.505 \times 56 + 0.495 \times 18 \right) = 0.999(28 + 8.9) = 37.15.$$

The other two prices are calculated in similar fashion. The price for the option turns out to be £23.

Pricing an American option

The binomial tree can be applied to American options. (Chapter 5 explains about the different types of American options.) Unlike a European option, an American option can be exercised at any time during its life, not just at expiry.

With a few simple changes, the binomial tree method can be adapted to work for American options. Here's how it goes.

1. **Build the binomial tree of prices just as for a European option.**

   Start with the stock price S at the root on the left hand side. At the end of an upward branch, multiply by u to get the price and at the end of a downward branch multiply by v. Go all the way to the right-hand side of your diagram.

2. **Work out the option prices at expiry just as for a European option by using the payoff function.**

   For a call option with strike price X, the payoff is S – X if S is greater than X and zero otherwise. For a put option with strike price X, the payoff is X – S if S is less than the strike price and zero otherwise.

3. **Work backwards by calculating the option prices at the time step before expiry using the equation $V = S\Delta\left(1 - ue^{-rt}\right) + V^{+}e^{-rt}$ just as for a European option.**

4. **Check all the option prices at each *node* (points on the tree where it branches in two) from Step 3 to see whether the option price is greater or less than the payoff from exercising the option.**

   Remember, an American option can be exercised at any time before expiry, so any node on the tree where the option price is below the payoff will be arbitraged. So, if the payoff is higher than the option price you just calculated, you must replace that option value with the payoff.

5. **Continue going backwards in the tree, checking at each node whether early exercise is optimal.**

   When you get down to the root at the left side of the tree, you've calculated the current price of the American option.

This procedure is a simple but powerful one and is good to know because it's the only way to price American options other than using simulation (see the final section in this chapter 'Valuing Options Using Simulations').

It turns out that for non-dividend paying stocks, American call options have the same price as European call options. However, American put options are always more valuable than European put options. This makes sense because American options give the holder, well, more options because she can exercise them when she likes.

Making Assumptions about Option Pricing

Like all mathematical theories, option pricing makes assumptions that may or may not be true:

>> **The stock price follows the geometric Brownian motion process.** In Chapter 3, I emphasise that the statistical properties of markets are similar to geometric Brownian motion but that real markets have fat tails. The greater chance of large returns in the real world than in the geometric Brownian motion model is usually accommodated by using an implied volatility.

>> **Both the volatility, σ, and the interest rate, r, are constant in time.** The assumption of constant volatility is clearly not true. Chapter 7 should persuade you of that. However, in some models this assumption is relaxed, but those models are complex. In practice, option traders use an *implied volatility*, a volatility fitted to make the option value correct. Using option pricing models has evolved as a bit of an art form to adapt to market realities.

>> **Short selling of stock is permitted.** Remember that the no-arbitrage argument used to price options (and covered in the first section in this chapter) relies on a portfolio with short positions. The argument is invalid if it isn't possible to short stock.

Restrictions indeed exist on short selling, but in practice they don't invalidate the construction of the riskless portfolio that shorts stock.

>> **You incur no transaction costs.** The risk-free portfolio I use to price options has to change from time step to time step, but I assume that this change doesn't cost anything.

Clearly, you incur transaction costs in the real world. The construction of a riskless portfolio with delta hedging definitely has costs. For the most heavily traded stocks, this cost may be low but for others it may lead to an inaccuracy.

>> **Dividends don't apply.** Most stocks do pay dividends, and they can be included in the analysis if required. Dividends are usually treated as fixed, just as interest is, but in reality are random. But this complication is one for experts.

Introducing Black-Scholes – The Most Famous Equation in Quantitative Finance

In this section, I explain the Black–Scholes equation for option pricing. The Black–Scholes equation is the basis for a lot of what quantitative analysts do. Although this section is highly technical, the ideas of no-arbitrage and risk neutrality are the same as those in the binomial model. Check out the section 'Looking at a Simple Portfolio with No Arbitrage' at the beginning of this chapter if you missed it.

Just as in the binomial model, I set up a portfolio with positions in an option and a short position in stock. The value of the portfolio is P where $P = V(S,t) - \Delta S$.

THE ECONOMISTS BEHIND BLACK-SCHOLES

The Black-Scholes equation was derived by economists Fischer Black and Myron Scholes in 1973. It allowed a mathematical way of pricing options for the first time.

Its success meant that banks became confident enough to invent new forms of financial derivatives in the knowledge that they could be priced accurately using the ideas and analyses pioneered by Black and Scholes. Quantitative finance flourished and became an accepted new subject. Soon *quants,* or quantitative analysts, became regular employees of investment banks. Typically quants have PhDs in mathematics or physics and are good at coding their mathematics as computer programs. Now, many specialist masters courses are run at universities for those wishing to become expert in quantitative finance.

In 1997, Myron Scholes and a fellow economist Robert Merton were awarded the Nobel Prize for their work on option pricing. Sadly, Fischer Black died several years earlier but would almost certainly have been included in the prize had he survived.

The brackets after the V indicate that the option price, V, depends both on the stock price, S, and time, t. Delta, Δ, is a constant that tells you how much stock you need to make the portfolio riskless. Assume that the stock price, S, follows a geometric Brownian motion (GBM), which I talk about in depth in Chapter 3, and use the equation:

$$dS = \mu S\, dt + \sigma S\, dz.$$

The two terms on the right side tell you that the movement of the stock price drifts in time, t, at a rate, μ, but that it also has a random component dz with a volatility determined by σ. The statistical distribution of this random component is described by the normal distribution. Now, for the portfolio to be riskless, you need to work out the changes in the portfolio value, P, so as to relate them to changes in a riskless portfolio with only cash in it. As always, the position size for the stock is given by Δ:

$$dP = dV - \Delta dS.$$

In Chapter 3, I show how you can work out how small changes in V depend on the small changes in S and t that drive changes in option prices. The equation is:

$$dV = \frac{\partial V}{\partial t}\, dt + \frac{\partial V}{\partial S}\, dS + \frac{\sigma^2 S^2}{2}\frac{\partial^2 V}{\partial S^2}\, dt.$$

In other books, this equation is called *Ito's lemma*. Please don't ask what a lemma is, but it often seems to be a handy equation.

You can now use the equation for dV in the equation for the portfolio change dP to get:

$$dP = \frac{\partial V}{\partial t}dt + \frac{\partial V}{\partial S}dS + \frac{\sigma^2 S^2}{2}\frac{\partial^2 V}{\partial S^2}dt - \Delta dS.$$

Two terms in this equation represent dS, the small change in the stock price. Because you're constructing a hedged portfolio that should be risk free, dP shouldn't depend on dS, which is a random variable. Notice, though, that by a careful choice of Δ, the terms in dS disappear! Do this using

$$\Delta = \frac{\partial V}{\partial S}.$$

It's that simple. But it means that to maintain a riskless portfolio, you have to keep the option hedged with an amount of stock, Δ. Remember that $V = V(S, t)$, so the option price is constantly changing with time and with the price of the underlying stock. This fact means that Δ also constantly changes, and you need to buy and sell stock continuously to keep your portfolio riskless. If transaction costs are low, it should be possible to periodically rebalance your portfolio and keep it close to riskless.

The next step in the derivation of the Black-Scholes equation is to make use of the fact that the portfolio, P, is riskless. Any small change in its value over time can only be due to the risk-free rate of interest. If the returns to the portfolio were different from the returns on cash, there would be arbitrage opportunities. For example, if the portfolio earned less than cash, it could be shorted and the proceeds invested in a cash account earning more. That would generate riskless profits and so should not be possible.

And so:

$$dP = Pr\,dt.$$

This equation is just saying that the interest, dP, earned on an amount of money, P, can be calculated by multiplying by the interest rate, r, and the length of time in the bank, dt. Putting together the two equations for dP you get:

$$Pr\,dt = \frac{\partial V}{\partial t}dt + \frac{\sigma^2 S^2}{2}\frac{\partial^2 V}{\partial S^2}dt.$$

But now you can use the defining equation for P at the top of this section and cancel the dt throughout. You also need to use the equation for Δ in terms of the partial derivative of V with respect to S:

$$\frac{\partial V}{\partial t} + \frac{\sigma^2 S^2}{2} \frac{\partial^2 V}{\partial S^2} + rS \frac{\partial V}{\partial S} - rV = 0.$$

This is the world-famous Black-Scholes equation for the price of an option. The equation is a partial differential equation because the option price, V, is a function of both the underlying stock, S, and time, t.

Solving the Black-Scholes Equation

The Black-Scholes equation isn't simple and solving it is less so. Whole books have been devoted to solving partial differential equations in two variables. It's possible to solve the Black-Scholes equation analytically (using algebra) for some special cases such as European puts and calls.

But the Black-Scholes equation has many solutions depending on the final conditions. Many of these solutions can be found only by numerical methods – computer calculations that rely on creating a grid of values for the stock price and time and finding numbers that satisfy the equation itself, the final conditions and the initial value of the underlying. In a way, this is similar to the binomial tree method (see 'Pricing in a Single Step' earlier in this chapter) in which the life of an option is split into discrete time steps and the possible values of the underlying stock are explored at each step by considering up and down moves in the stock.

Black-Scholes applies only to a non-dividend paying stock, but it applies to both put and call options whether they're European or American style. With small modifications, the Black-Scholes equation can be used for future options, currency options and index options. It does not apply to bonds, however, because they don't follow the geometric Brownian motion. As a bond comes to close redemption, its value fluctuates less and less because it's soon to be paid back as cash. (Chapter 12 has an equation that applies for bonds.)

To make use of Black-Scholes, you need to know the *final conditions*, a maths expression for knowing what happens at expiry. The final conditions are the payoff function. For a call option, the final condition is that $V(S, T) = \max(S - X, 0)$, while for a put option it's $V(S, T) = \max(X - S, 0)$. In both cases, X is the strike price for the option.

A third way to solve the Black–Scholes equation is by using the *Monte Carlo simulation*, a method in which you generate random numbers to mimic the geometric Brownian motion assumed in the Black–Scholes analysis. By creating many possible paths for the underlying asset between the current moment and expiry, you can value options using the concept of risk neutrality. The upcoming section 'Valuing Options Using Simulations' has more on this.

The solution for the Black–Scholes equation for a European call option at time t, with strike price, X, and expiry date, T, is given by the formula:

$$V = C = SN(d_1) - Xe^{-r(T-t)}N(d_2).$$

C indicates that this is the price of a call option. The parameters d_1 and d_2 are given by the formulae:

$$d_1 = \frac{\ln\left(\frac{S}{X}\right) + \left(r + \frac{1}{2}\sigma^2\right)(T-t)}{\sigma\sqrt{T-t}}$$

$$d_2 = \frac{\ln\left(\frac{S}{X}\right) + \left(r - \frac{1}{2}\sigma^2\right)(T-t)}{\sigma\sqrt{T-t}} = d_1 - \sigma\sqrt{T-t}.$$

Sigma, Σ, is the volatility of the stock, and r is the risk-free rate of interest. The function N(x) is the cumulative normal distribution function. This function is defined by an integral over the normal distribution:

$$N(x) = \frac{1}{\sqrt{2\pi}} \int_{-\infty}^{x} e^{-\frac{1}{2}x^2} dx.$$

By integrating the normal distribution from minus infinity up to x, the equation calculates the probability that the variable is less than x.

The formula for a put can be expressed using the same parameters:

$$V = P = Xe^{-r(T-t)}N(-d_2) - SN(-d_1).$$

Deriving these formulae for call and put options analytically using algebra is no small task. The Black–Scholes equation itself can be simplified by changes of variable but advanced maths is still required to solve it. An alternative approach is to directly use the risk-neutral concept introduced in the section on the binomial method 'Looking at a Simple Portfolio with No Arbitrage'. The value of an option is the expected value of the payoff at expiry, assuming the asset followed geometric Brownian motion with an expected return equal to the risk-free rate.

For a call option, you can write this phrase mathematically, using E to indicate the expected value:

$$C = e^{-r(T-t)}E\left(\max(S-X,0)\right).$$

The payoff for a call option is $S - X$, if $S > X$ and is zero otherwise, so it can be written in the form shown. The payoff is the maximum of the two values indicated in brackets. To calculate the expected value, you need to know the statistical distribution of the stock prices. In Chapter 3, I show that a stock price follows a geometric Brownian motion:

$$\ln \frac{S(t)}{S_0} = \sum_{i=1}^{N} X_i - \frac{1}{2}\sigma^2 t.$$

The additive motion given by the sum of the steps, X_i, has a drift given by γ if the probability of an up move is:

$$p = \frac{1}{2}\left(1 + \frac{\gamma}{\sigma}\sqrt{\Delta}\right).$$

When pricing options, you must work in the risk-neutral world so you must replace γ by the risk-free interest rate, r. Then the equations for probability are identical and correspond with the correct probabilities for the risk-neutral process. As shown in Chapter 3, $\ln(S(t))$ (ln is the natural logarithm) has a normal distribution but with a mean and standard deviation given by:

$$\ln S + \left(r - \frac{\sigma^2}{2}\right)T, \; \sigma\sqrt{T}.$$

In a risk-neutral world, the value of an option can be expressed as the discounted value of the expected value of the option at time, t. The formula in the first section of this chapter for the value of an option, V, working backwards through the binomial tree is exactly this form. Here you use the probability distribution for the natural logarithm motion of S. Also, you need to use a formula from Chapter 2 for the expectation, E, of a random variable distributed according to a continuous distribution such as the normal distribution. Putting all these formula together, you get this formula:

$$C = e^{-r(T-t)}E\left[\max\left(S_T - X, 0\right)\right].$$

Note: In this formula, the time to expiry of the option is T whilst the current time is t.

The expectation, E, is an integral over a normal probability distribution, which I denote by Φ, but with $\ln S_T$ as the argument. The arguments of Φ indicate the mean and standard deviation:

$$C = e^{-r(T-t)}\int_{-\infty}^{\infty} \Phi\left(\ln S + \left(r - \frac{\sigma^2}{2}\right)(T-t), \sigma\sqrt{T-t}\right)\max\left(S_T - X, 0\right)\frac{dS_T}{S_T}.$$

Because $\ln S_T$ is normally distributed, the differential is $d\ln S_T$, which equals dS_T/S_T, which explains the last part of the integral.

TECHNICAL STUFF

To calculate an integral requires a few tricks. You'll find it awkward integrating over a normal distribution if the variable is a logarithm of another variable. A good idea is to introduce a new variable, $\max\left(S_T - X, 0\right)$. If you remember that the differential of a logarithm, ln S, is equal to $\frac{1}{S}$, then $dy = \frac{dS}{S}$. (Remember that the lowercase d indicates a differential from calculus.)

Rearrange this calculation to get $dS = S\,dy$ and then use the fact that $e^y = S$ to get $dS = e^y\,dy$. I made use of properties of the exponential function indicated with the e. The online Cheat Sheet at www.dummies.com has more about the exponential function. Doing so allows you to change the variable in the integral from S to y and life gets a little easier.

REMEMBER

The exponential function is the inverse of the natural logarithm. So if $y = \ln S$, then $S = e^y$. Also, keep in mind that $e = 2.718\ldots$ is the special base of the natural logarithm.

If that wasn't enough, here's more: the integral for C is over the payoff function, which is non-zero only if $S > X$. This fact means that you can replace the lower limit of the integral with X and no longer need to use the max function. After the change of variable using the natural logarithm, this lower limit becomes ln(X).

REMEMBER

The normal distribution probability density with a mean, μ, and standard deviation, σ, is given by the formula:

$$\Phi\left(\mu, \sigma\right) = \frac{1}{\sigma\sqrt{2\pi}}e^{-\frac{1}{2}(x-\mu)^2/\sigma^2}.$$

Using the formula for the normal distribution and making the change of variable, the integral for the value of a call option becomes:

$$C = \frac{e^{-r(T-t)}}{\sigma\sqrt{2\pi(T-t)}}\int_{-\ln X}^{\infty} e^{-\left(y - \ln S - \left(r - \frac{1}{2}\sigma^2\right)(T-t)\right)^2 / 2\sigma^2(T-t)}\left(e^y - X\right)dy.$$

Properties of the Black-Scholes Solutions

Although the solutions to the Black–Scholes equations look complicated, they have some properties that are quite straightforward. First, I look at how the price of a put option depends on the time to expiry. This dependence is shown in Figure 10-5 for an option with strike price $X = 200$.

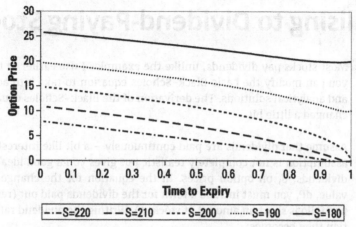

FIGURE 10-5:
Put option price
for strike of 200
and various
underlying stock
prices.

S=220   S=210   S=200   S=190   S=180

© John Wiley & Sons, Ltd.

The price of the put options declines towards expiry. For a randomly moving underlying stock, time is what you need to achieve a favourable outcome, so as time runs out, the option price declines, and at-the-money $S = 200$ and out-of-the-money options $S > 200$ expire worthless, as Figure 10-6 shows.

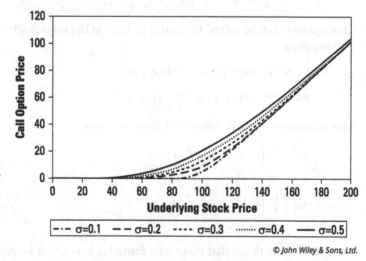

FIGURE 10-6:
Call option price
for a variety of
volatilities, strike
of 100 and time
to expiry of one
year.

$\sigma=0.1$ $\sigma=0.2$ $\sigma=0.3$ $\sigma=0.4$ $\sigma=0.5$

© John Wiley & Sons, Ltd.

The option price always rises as a function of the underlying stock price. The dispersion in prices due to volatility has a maximum effect when the option is at-the-money for which $S = X$. Deep out-of-the-money options with $S \ll X$ are effectively valueless.

Generalising to Dividend-Paying Stocks

Most stocks pay dividends, unlike the examples I use earlier in this chapter, and you can modify the basic Black–Scholes equation to take into account dividends and analytical solutions. The derivation of the Black–Scholes equation needs to be changed a little bit.

Assume that dividends are paid continuously – a bit like interest payments. This assumption is not completely realistic but gives you a good idea of the impact of dividends, d, on option prices. In the equation for the change in the portfolio value, dP, you must include a term for the dividends paid out (remember that the portfolio is short an amount of stock, Δ). Writing the dividend rate as q, the equation then becomes:

$$dP = \frac{\partial V}{\partial t}dt + \frac{\sigma^2 S^2}{2}\frac{\partial^2 V}{\partial S^2}dt - \Delta qS\,dt.$$

Substituting for the value of Δ and equating to Prdt, you get a modified Black–Scholes equation:

$$\frac{\partial V}{\partial t} + \frac{\sigma^2 S^2}{2}\frac{\partial^2 V}{\partial S^2} + (r-q)S\frac{\partial V}{\partial S} - rV = 0.$$

This equation can be solved in similar fashion to the non-dividend paying equation resulting in

$$V = C = Se^{-q(T-t)}N(d_1) - Xe^{-r(T-t)}N(d_2) \text{ and}$$

$$V = P = Xe^{-r(T-t)}N(-d_2) - Se^{-q(T-t)}N(-d_1).$$

The parameters d_1 and d_2 are now slightly changed:

$$d_1 = \frac{\ln\left(\frac{S}{X}\right) + \left(r - q + \frac{1}{2}\sigma^2\right)(T-t)}{\sigma\sqrt{T-t}} \text{ and}$$

$$d_1 = \frac{\ln\left(\frac{S}{X}\right) + \left(r - q - \frac{1}{2}\sigma^2\right)(T-t)}{\sigma\sqrt{T-t}} = d_1 - \sigma\sqrt{T-t}.$$

An intuitive way to see that these new formulae are correct is that an option on a stock with a continuous dividend of q must have the same value as a non-dividend paying stock of value: $Se^{-q(T-t)}$.

TECHNICAL STUFF

When a stock goes ex-dividend, someone who buys the stock isn't eligible to receive the latest dividend. On the ex-dividend date, the stock drops in value by an amount equal to the dividend payment. The day before, buyers of the stock were eligible to receive the dividend. So in the real world of discrete dividend payments, the stock price declines by an amount equal to dividend payments. In the approximate, but convenient, world of continuous dividend payments, the stock price declines continuously with a factor determined by the dividend rate, q.

Substituting in $Se^{-q(T-t)}$ to the Black-Scholes solutions for C and P results in the equations in this section.

Defining other Options

So far in this chapter, I talk about how to price call and put options with a payoff that depends on how far above or below the strike price the stock price ends up at expiry. You may also have options that pay off depending only on whether the stock price ends up above or below the strike price. These options are called *binary options* because the only thing that matters for the expiry price is the above or below strike price outcome. The payoff function can be written using the *Heaviside function, H(x)*, which is zero for x values less than zero and one for positive x values as shown in Figure 10-7.

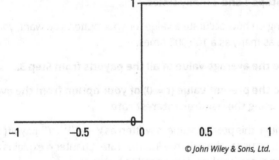

FIGURE 10-7: Heaviside function used to define binary option payoff.

Using this function, the payoff for a binary call option is $H(S-X)$; for a binary put option the payoff is $H(X-S)$. These options can be valued in similar fashion to the calculations in the section 'Solving the Black-Scholes Equation'. The results are simpler and can be written using exactly the same definition of parameter d_2:

$$C = e^{-r(T-t)}N(d_2) \quad \text{and} \quad P = e^{-r(T-t)}\left(1-N(d_2)\right).$$

Valuing Options Using Simulations

A third way to value options that's good to know about is called the Monte Carlo simulation, which I introduce in Chapter 3. Exactly as for the binomial tree and Black–Scholes equation, this method uses the idea that the value of an option is the present value of the expected payoff using a risk–neutral random walk. The method works like this:

1. **Simulate a risk-neutral random walk starting from today's price and going up until expiry of the option.**

   If the expiry time is T and the current time, t, equals zero, and you use N time steps, then the time steps are $\delta t = T / N$. Starting at t = 0, you calculate the stock price, S(t), at every time step up to the expiry at t = T. Use the formula $S(t+\delta t)=S(t)+rS(t)\delta t+\sigma S(t)\sqrt{\delta t}\varphi$ to calculate the stock price at any given time step from the price at the previous time step. The volatility of the stock is σ, and r is the risk-free interest rate; φ is a random number drawn from a normal distribution with mean zero and a standard deviation of one.

2. **Calculate the option payoff using the strike price and the equation $\max(X - S_T, 0)$ for a put or $\max(S_T - X, 0)$ for a call.**

3. **Repeat Steps 1 and 2 many times.**

   Depending on how accurate a value for your option you want, you can repeat the steps as many as a 100,000 times.

4. **Calculate the average value of all the payoffs from Step 3.**

5. **Calculate the present value (t = 0) of your option from the average of the pay-offs using the risk-free interest rate.**

   As a formula, this present value is written as $V = e^{-r(T-t)}E\left[\text{payoff}(S_T, X)\right]$ where r is, as usual, the risk-free interest rate. Chapter 4 explains about calculating present values if you need to brush up.

TIP

Instead of the time step formula given in Step 1, you can use instead:

$$S(t+\delta t)=S(t)e^{\left(\left(r-\frac{1}{2}\sigma^2\right)\delta t+\sigma\sqrt{\delta t}\varphi\right)}.$$

This formula is slightly more complicated, but it's more accurate so you may get away with using far fewer time steps.

Chapter 3 gives some details about these time–step formulae for a geometric Brownian motion and also how to generate random numbers. Monte Carlo simulation is easy to implement using a computer, especially if you use a language such as Python or R, but it can be time consuming because of the large number of walks needed to get a good answer.

A big advantage of the Monte Carlo simulation is that it's flexible enough to value some exotic options such as barrier options. *Barrier options* have a payoff that depends on the path taken by the stock price as time passes towards expiry – not just on the final stock price at expiry. Typically, barrier options depend on the stock price breaching a specific value prior to expiry or the opposite – the stock price *not* breaching a specific value prior to expiry. Both of these payoffs are easy to calculate given the simulated risk-neutral walk. You just need to check every walk to see if specific barrier values are breached or not.

IN THIS CHAPTER

Understanding the solutions of Black-Scholes

Managing risk by delta hedging

Meeting the other Greeks

Seeking portfolio balance

Preventing possible errors

Chapter **11**

Using the Greeks in the Black-Scholes Model

I n this chapter, I talk about more solutions to the Black-Scholes equation. (I talk about Black-Scholes in Chapter 10 as well.) The Black-Scholes model for the pricing of vanilla options has limitations, but the solutions to the model equation provide a good framework for understanding the behaviour of options.

I introduce the Greeks here – not the ancient philosophers but the quantities that show how sensitive the Black-Scholes solutions are to variations in parameters such as the interest rate and volatility and in variables such as time and the underlying asset price. For banks that sell or write option contracts, using the Greeks is a way of working out how the value of their portfolio of options may change and to hedge portfolios of options.

Using the Black-Scholes Formulae

The price of a European style call option, C, with strike price X and time to maturity T on a non-dividend paying stock with price S and volatility σ is $C = SN(d_1) - Xe^{-rT}N(d_2)$, where

$$d_1 = \frac{\ln\left(\frac{S}{X}\right) + \left(r + \frac{1}{2}\sigma^2\right)T}{\sigma\sqrt{T}} \text{ and } d_2 = d_1 - \sigma\sqrt{T}.$$

The parameter, r, is the risk-free rate of interest, which is set to one per cent in the following example, so $r = 0.01$.

The constant e = 2.718. . . in the formula for C is the base of the exponential function. You can find out more about it in the Cheat Sheet at www.dummies.com. The function N(x) is the cumulative normal distribution, and I explain more about it just below.

REMEMBER

The two constants d_1 and d_2 occur a lot in this chapter. They're used to make the algebra of the Black-Scholes solutions simpler but they don't have any simple interpretation. The formulas for them show you how to calculate them from simpler parameters such as the volatility and the risk free rate.

As an example, I set $S = 200$ with a strike price of $X = 220$. You can think of this example in any currency you want, but you must use the risk-free rate appropriate to that currency. Given that the interest rate is expressed as a return per annum, you must express the time to maturity in years. As an example, I use $T = 0.5$ so that there are six months to go until the option expires. The volatility, σ, must also be expressed on an annual basis.

REMEMBER

To convert a volatility calculated using daily returns data, multiply by the square root of the number of trading days in the year, which is normally about 250. So, multiply a daily volatility by approximately 16 to get the annual volatility:

$$d_1 = \frac{\ln\left(\frac{200}{220}\right) + (0.01 + 0.5 \times 0.2 \times 0.2) \times 0.5}{0.2 \times \sqrt{0.5}} = -0.568$$

$$d_2 = d_1 - 0.2 \times \sqrt{0.5} = -0.568 - 0.2 \times 0.707 = -0.709.$$

N(x) is the cumulative normal distribution function that I explain more fully in Chapter 10. N(x) is defined by an integral that can't be expressed as a simple formula. If you've forgotten your school calculus then think of an integral as representing the area under a curve. So N(x) is the area under a normal distribution from minus infinity up to x. The calculation has to be done numerically or by using an approximation. I used the function Norm.Dist provided in Excel.

If you use the Norm.Dist function, opt for the cumulative normal distribution by choosing the fourth argument as True. Doing so, I get that $N(d_1) = 0.285$ and that $N(d_2) = 0.239$.

This calculation means that I can now write for the option price:

$$C = 200 \times 0.285 - 220e^{-0.01 \times 0.5} \times 0.239 = 4.68.$$

The option is quite cheap because it starts with the share price less than the strike price so it's out of the money.

Hedging Class

Many options are traded on exchanges such as the Chicago Board Options Exchange and Eurex. However, most are sold by banks to clients wanting a more tailored product. The bank is left with the problem of managing the risk in its option portfolio. It may earn a good premium for selling the option but that may be more than wiped out if a change in the price of the underlying asset means that the bank has to pay the buyer of the option a substantial payoff at expiry. In principle, this problem doesn't matter. The bank may lose badly on one sale but do well on the next. If it prices the options correctly and charges clients higher prices than given by the Black-Scholes formula, in the long run it should make a profit.

The problem is that the short-run profit and loss can look nasty, which means that the bank has to hold a lot of capital in reserve to stay solvent during unprofitable periods. In practice, this isn't an acceptable way of running a business. If the bank sold many options, the effect of occasional large losses is reduced because of the constant profit gains from options that are worthless at expiry. But despite that, these so-called *naked positions*, in which options are sold without being hedged, gives plenty of scope for an embarrassing profit and loss account. In contrast a *covered position* is much safer. It involves hedging an option with an equal and opposite position in the underlying asset.

TECHNICAL STUFF

Sometimes selling an option is referred to as *writing an option*. That's because the buyer receives a document. It doesn't matter which word you use.

The solution adopted by banks to reduce the riskiness of selling options is *hedging*. Hedging means to buy (or sell) some other asset that offsets the risk taken in selling (or buying) an option. I talk about hedging options in Chapter 5.

A bank that has sold an option can hedge by buying or selling the underlying shares. The simplest form of hedging is *static hedging*. In a static hedge, the bank buys (or sells) the underlying asset and leaves it in place until the option expires. For example, the bank sells a call option on a stock it can simultaneously buy. If the option expires in the money, the bank has no problem, it just sells its stock position to settle up with the client. The bank doesn't experience the big loss that a naked position would have caused. The snag, though, is if the stock price drops and the option expires worthless. The bank was paid the premium for the option but it lost money on the stock used to hedge the option.

In the following list, I consider several scenarios involving basic hedging strategies. A bank sells call options on 10,000 shares for £47,000. The strike price is £220 while the share price is £200. The risk-free rate is 0.01 and the annual volatility of the shares is 0.2. The option has a time to maturity of 6 months, or 0.5 years. For a non-dividend paying stock, the Black–Scholes formula for this gives a price of £4.70 (check the preceding section for the calculations).

>> **Scenario 1:** The bank adopts a naked position. At the end of the six months, the share price ends at £170 and the option is worthless because the share price is less than the strike price. The bank receives £47,000 in premium income.

>> **Scenario 2:** The bank adopts a naked position, but at the end of six months the share price is £230. The share ends up £10 higher than the strike price and so the bank has to pay $10,000 \times £10 = £100,000$ to the client. This loss is big given the £47,000 premium.

>> **Scenario 3:** The bank adopts a covered position and purchases 10,000 shares at £200 for £2 million. The share drops to £170 by the end of the six months. The bank received the £47,000 premium but lost $£30 \times 10,000 = £300,000$ on its hedge, which makes the net loss £253,000.

>> **Scenario 4:** The bank adopts a covered position, but the share price rises to £230 at the end of the six months. The client exercises her option at expiry and buys the shares at the strike price of £220. The bank made $£20 \times 10,000 = £200,000$ on the hedge and £47,000 premium income for a total of £247,000.

You can certainly conclude from these scenarios that simple covered or naked positions are risky and can produce large losses. Static hedging is not a good idea. The solution is dynamic hedging in which the size of the hedge is adjusted according to changes in the price and volatility of the underlying assets. To do this you need to be able to calculate the sensitivity of the option price to the underlying asset price – otherwise known as delta, or Δ. Please read on in the next section to find out more.

That's Greek to Me: Explaining the Greek Maths Symbols

A bank uses the Greeks to work out how sensitive its overall option position is to change. Probably the most important change is a change in the underlying asset price. That Greek is called *delta* and is written Δ. Other important Greeks are also in evidence, such as theta, or Θ, which gives the sensitivity of option value to time to expiry. Then you have a quantity called vega, which isn't a letter in the Greek alphabet but was carefully thought up to sound like one. *Vega* measures the sensitivity of option value with respect to changes in volatility. Vega is often denoted using ν, the symbol for the Greek letter nu.

Delta

The most important Greek is *delta*, which measures the change in the value of options as the underlying asset price changes. Delta measures the sensitivity of the option value, V, with respect to changes in the underlying asset price, S:

$$\Delta = \frac{\partial V}{\partial S}.$$

Using the cumulative normal distribution, $N(x)$, calculations show that for a non-dividend paying European call option, $\Delta_{Call} = N(d_1)$, where d_1 is the same quantity as in the first section in this chapter, 'Using the Black–Scholes Formulae'.

To work out the formula for Δ, you need a bit of algebra. However, Δ is such an important quantity that it's good to know where it comes from.

The formula for the price of a call option, C, is:

$$C = SN(d_1) - Xe^{-rT}N(d_2).$$

REMEMBER

In this formula, S is the underlying asset price whilst X is the strike price of the option. The risk-free interest rate is r and the time to expiry of the option is T. Lowercase e indicates the exponential function and has the value e = 2.718 . . . .

To differentiate this formula with respect to the stock price S, remember that the quantities d_1 and d_2 both depend on S. Also, the cumulative normal distribution is defined by an integral so that:

$$\frac{\partial N}{\partial x} = \varphi(x)$$

where ϕ is the standard normal distribution. That's the normal distribution with mean = 0 and standard deviation = 1. You can now use the chain rule of calculus so that:

$$\frac{\partial N}{\partial S} = \frac{\partial N}{\partial d_1}\frac{\partial d_1}{\partial S} = \phi(d_1)\frac{\partial d_1}{\partial S}.$$

The derivatives of both d_1 and d_2 can be found by remembering that the derivative of the natural logarithm $\ln(x)$ is simply $\frac{1}{x}$. Using the definition of d_1 again you get that:

$$\frac{\partial N(d_1)}{\partial S} = \phi(d_1)\frac{1}{S\sigma\sqrt{T}}.$$

The same formula applies for d_2 because d_1 and d_2 differ by an amount that doesn't depend on S, so their derivatives are the same. To differentiate the first term of the formula for the call option price, you need to use the product rule from calculus giving you:

$$\Delta = \frac{\partial C}{\partial S} = N(d_1) + \frac{1}{S\sigma\sqrt{T}}\Big[S\phi(d_1) - Xe^{-rT}\phi(d_2)\Big].$$

The term in square brackets turns out to be equal to zero. To see this, you need to use the formula for d_2 and for the standard normal distribution $-\phi(x)$. The argument x in brackets shows the point at which you need to calculate the normal distribution function:

$$d_2 = d_1 - \sqrt{T}$$

$$\phi(x) = \frac{1}{\sqrt{2\pi}}e^{-x^2/2}.$$

Substitute the expression for d_2 into the second term in the square brackets to get:

$$Xe^{-rT}\frac{1}{\sqrt{2\pi}}e^{-\frac{(d_1-\sigma\sqrt{T})^2}{2}}.$$

Expanding the squared term, you can rewrite this formula as:

$$Xe^{-rT}\phi(d_1)e^{d_1\sigma\sqrt{T}-\sigma^2T/2},$$

which uses the definition of ϕ.

Going back to the first section in this chapter, you can now substitute in the definition for d_1 to get:

$$Xe^{-rT}\phi(d_1)e^{rT+\ln(S/X)+(r+\sigma^2/2)T-\sigma^2T/2}.$$

The formula looks complicated but, remarkably, almost all the terms cancel out leaving:

$$X\varphi(d_1)e^{\ln(S/X)} = S\varphi(d_1).$$

Going back to the formula for Δ with the square brackets, the whole term in square brackets cancels out so that finally you have:

$$\Delta_{Call} = N(d_1)$$

as stated at the beginning of this section.

Similar calculations show that for a European put option on a non-dividend paying stock: $\Delta_{Put} = N(d_1) - 1$.

Delta is positive for a call option but negative for a put option. If delta is positive, the option price rises with the underlying stock price. A short position in a call option is then hedged by a long position of the stock. If the stock price rises, the drop in value of the short call position is exactly compensated for by the rise in the long stock position. By contrast, with negative delta, a short position in a put option is hedged by a short position of the stock. Then, if the stock price rises, the rise in the value of the short put position is exactly matched by the fall in the value of the short position in the stock. A plot of delta is shown in Figure 11-1.

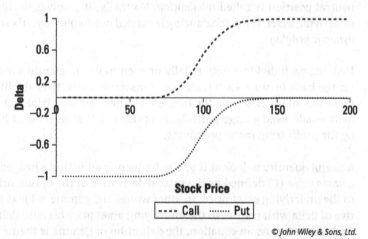

FIGURE 11-1: Delta for calls and puts with strike price of £100 in any currency.

© John Wiley & Sons, Ltd.

The figure shows that if the stock price is substantially below the strike price, you don't need to hedge. Only when the stock price rises towards the strike price do you need to start hedging with stock.

REMEMBER

Delta is at the heart of option pricing. The concept of delta neutral was introduced so as to create a riskless position that could be valued using the risk-free interest rate. A position is *delta neutral* if its overall value doesn't alter with changes in the price of the underlying asset.

This is the way banks like to manage their option portfolios so as not to lose money (or, in fact, to gain money) with sudden changes in asset markets. The plan is to make a steady income from the option premiums and to remove risk from their positions with hedging. Like all good plans, a snag can be found: the delta of an option changes as the price of the underlying asset changes, which you can see plotted in Figure 11-1. This variation means that the amount of underlying asset used in the hedge has to change from time to time to keep the overall position delta neutral.

Dynamic hedging and gamma

Delta allows you to figure out how to hedge an option position using the underlying asset. A great start, but delta varies with the price of the underlying asset and, in fact, with the passage of time. That variation is because delta, through the quantity d_1 defined earlier in this chapter, depends upon the underlying asset price and its volatility. So, as time goes by delta changes even if the underlying asset price does not. The process of adjusting a portfolio so as to maintain a delta neutral position is called *rebalancing*. Normally, it involves buying or selling the underlying asset. If the rebalancing is carried out frequently, it's sometimes called *dynamic hedging*.

Hedging an individual option daily or even more frequently would be expensive for the bank because each trade has transaction costs. Over the life of the option, these mount up. Reducing the frequency of hedging may help, but realistically the bank would need a large portfolio of options so that the cost of hedging is offset by the profit from many premiums.

A useful quantity to look at if you're frequently adjusting a hedged portfolio is the *gamma value* (Γ) defined as the second derivative of the option price with respect to the underlying asset price. In other words, the gamma value is the first derivative of delta with respect to the underlying asset price because delta is already the first derivative. As an equation, the definition of gamma is then:

$$\Gamma = \frac{\partial \Delta}{\partial S} = \frac{\partial^2 V}{\partial S^2}.$$

For a European call option on a non-dividend paying stock with price S, volatility σ and time to expiry T, the gamma is given by the formula:

$$\Gamma = \frac{\varphi(d_1)}{S\sigma\sqrt{T}}.$$

Phi is the standard normal distribution, and d_1 is a complicated function of the underlying asset price and volatility. Figure 11-2 shows a chart of gamma and how it varies with the stock price for a call option with a strike price of 100 in any currency, time to expiry of 0.5 and annualised volatility of 0.2.

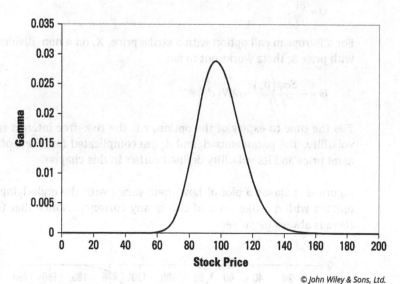

FIGURE 11-2: Gamma of a call option with a strike price of £100.

The chart has a big hump around the strike price of £100 showing that at-the-money options have a large gamma. Delta therefore changes rapidly with changes in the underlying asset price and so at-the-money options are costly to hedge because of the need to rebalance more frequently.

The gamma value of an underlying asset is zero because the second derivative of S with respect to S is zero. This fact means that you can't adjust the gamma of an option portfolio by buying or selling the underlying asset. You can, however, change it by buying or selling other options. A bank that sells over-the-counter options can potentially hedge its portfolio using exchange-traded options so as to make its portfolio *gamma neutral* – in other words, make the overall value of gamma for its portfolio equal to zero.

The advantage of a gamma-neutral portfolio is that the delta hedging can be less frequent as the portfolio value is initially independent of the underlying asset price. The snag is that options have higher transaction costs than the underlying asset so that achieving gamma neutrality by buying or selling options can be costly.

Theta

Theta (Θ) is the rate of change of option value with respect to time. If V is the value of a call or put option, theta is defined by the equation:

$$\Theta = \frac{\partial V}{\partial t}.$$

For a European call option with a strike price, X, on a non-dividend paying stock with price S, theta works out to be:

$$\Theta = -\frac{S\sigma\varphi(d_1)}{2\sqrt{T}} - rXN(d_2)e^{-rT}.$$

T is the time to expiry of the option, r is the risk-free interest rate and σ is the volatility. The parameters d_1 and d_2 are complicated functions of the underlying asset price and its volatility defined earlier in this chapter.

Figure 11-3 shows a plot of how theta varies with the underlying stock price for options with a strike price of 100 in any currency. Notice that for a call option theta is always negative.

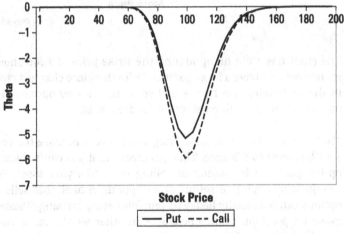

FIGURE 11-3: Variation of theta with stock price for European put and call options with a strike price of £100.

© John Wiley & Sons, Ltd.

REMEMBER

As the time to maturity gets shorter and shorter, the value of an option tends to decline because the opportunities for a successful exercise become fewer and fewer. Time is on the side of optionality.

Rho

Rho (P) is the rate of change of the value of an option with respect to the risk-free interest rate. The risk-free rate is often quite stable over the life of an option, so rho is of less significance than the other Greeks.

You can calculate the value of rho from the Black–Scholes solution in much the same way as for the other Greeks. For a European call option on a non-dividend paying stock with strike price X and time to expiry T, rho is given by $\rho = XTe^{-rT}N(d_2)$.

Vega

Vega (v) is the rate of change of the value of an option with respect to the volatility. V is the value of an option or a portfolio of options:

$$v = \frac{\partial V}{\partial \sigma}.$$

For a European call option with time to expiry, T, on a non-dividend paying stock with price, S, vega is given by the formula: $v = S\sqrt{T}\varphi(d_1)$.

In a way, vega doesn't make sense because sigma is assumed to be constant in the Black–Scholes analysis. However, analysis with more complex models that don't assume constant volatility shows that the vega derived from the Black–Scholes equation is a reasonable approximation to a more realistic model. But beware! Figure 11-4 shows a plot of vega against the stock price for a non-dividend-paying call option. Note the peak around $S = 100$, which is the strike price. This figure shows again that options that are out of the money or well in the money are much easier to hedge as they have much less sensitivity to the volatility of the underlying asset.

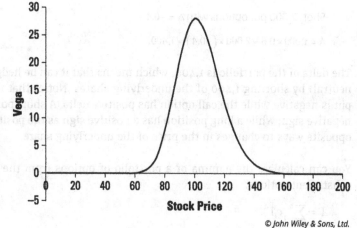

FIGURE 11-4: Variation of Vega with the underlying stock price for an option with a strike price of £100.

© John Wiley & Sons, Ltd.

Relating the Greeks

From the Black-Scholes equation, you know that:

$$\frac{\partial V}{\partial t} + \frac{\sigma^2 S^2}{2}\frac{\partial V}{\partial S^2} + rS\frac{\partial V}{\partial S} - S = 0.$$

You can certainly find an equation relating the value of the Greeks because all the terms in the Black-Scholes equation are, in fact, Greeks. So you can rewrite the equation using theta (Θ), gamma (Γ) and delta (Δ):

$$\Theta + \frac{\sigma^2 S^2 \Gamma}{2} + rS\Delta = rV.$$

For an option or a portfolio of options that's delta neutral, this formula simplifies to:

$$\Theta + \frac{\sigma^2 S^2 \Gamma}{2} = rV.$$

Rebalancing a Portfolio

You can calculate the delta of a portfolio of options from the deltas of the constituent options. If the portfolio consists of n options each in a quantity c_i, then the delta of the portfolio is given by:

$$\Delta = \sum_{i=1}^{n} c_i \Delta_i.$$

For example, in a portfolio consisting of options in the same stock:

Long 1,000 call options with $\Delta = 0.6$

Short 2,000 put options with $\Delta = -0.4$

$$\Delta = 1,000 \times 0.6 - 2,000 \times (-0.4) = 1,400.$$

The delta of the portfolio is 1,400, which means that it can be hedged (made delta neutral) by shorting 1,400 of the underlying shares. Notice that the delta for the put is negative while the call option has positive delta. A short position is given a negative sign, while a long position has a positive sign as the positions respond in opposite ways to changes in the price of the underlying share.

You can calculate the gamma of a portfolio of options from the gammas of the constituent options:

$$\Gamma = \sum_{i=1}^{n} c_i \Gamma_i.$$

Imagine that you have a short position in a call option with a delta of 0 but a gamma of –1,000. You want to make this position both gamma and delta neutral. To do this, you can buy traded call options in the same underlying asset with a gamma of 0.25 and a delta of 0.5. You need to buy 4000 of these options to make the position gamma neutral as $4000 \times 0.25 = 1,000$ neutralises the gamma of the original option. Now, however, your position has a delta of $4000 \times 0.5 = 2000$. To neutralise this, you have to short 2000 shares in the underlying asset. Because the gamma of the underlying asset is always zero, this doesn't affect the gamma of the overall position and so you're now delta and gamma neutral. The final position is short call position with

$$\Delta = 0$$

$$\Gamma = -1,000$$

4,000 call options with $\Delta = 0.5$ and $\Gamma = 0.25$

Short position in stock of 2,000.

Troubleshooting Model Risk

Models such as Black–Scholes, but certainly not limited to Black–Scholes, are used extensively by financial institutions such as banks. This use presents risks to the institutions because each model comes with its own assumptions and limitations. Some of these assumptions and limitations may not be as well understood as the ones for Black–Scholes. A lot of potential exists for the misapplication of formulae from quantitative finance because of the proliferation of financial contracts.

WARNING

As an example, the Black–Scholes equation cannot be applied to bonds. Sovereign bonds are redeemed at a known date in the future for an amount guaranteed by a government. The bond price therefore converges to this amount. The assumption of geometric Brownian motion used in the Black–Scholes analysis doesn't apply because it produces a large variation in possible prices at the redemption date and not a fixed value.

Because of the risks of using models, banking regulators such as the Office of the Controller of Currency in the United States now provide guidance on how to manage model risk. Model risk can arise because

>> The concept behind the model is wrong.

>> The data used to determine the model parameters has errors.

>> The model is misapplied.

>> Incorrect computer code is used.

A few ways to mitigate these risks include

>> Control risk at the source by using a controlled framework for model development with good documentation.

>> Do independent model validation and testing.

>> Have an ongoing review process of model performance.

>> Change the management process for models.

These statements may seem like simple common sense, but in practice banks sometimes get the application of quantitative finance badly wrong. A disciplined and structured approach is needed for the development, deployment and maintenance of complex models.

IN THIS CHAPTER

Using caps and floors to limit interest-rate risk

Examining single parameter interest-rate models

Understanding arbitrage free models of the yield curve

Chapter 12

Gauging Interest-Rate Derivatives

nterest-rates are key quantities in finance because they define the cost of borrowing money. Financial market participants naturally want to protect themselves against changes in the interest-rate.

Interest-rates themselves are not tradable financial instruments. However, instruments such as bonds or swaps are closely connected to interest-rates, and so options on these contracts can be used to manage interest-rate risk.

REMEMBER

When dealing with interest-rates, you must look at the yield curve for loans of all maturities, not just one maturity. Strong connections exist between the interest-rate of one maturity and the interest-rate of another maturity so that the rates at different maturities don't change in time independently of one another. In practice, modelling the entire yield curve is a tall order, and market practitioners fall back on familiar models such as Black-Scholes (explained in Chapter 10). However, in the last section of this chapter I give you a flavour of the models for the entire yield curve that you can use to price interest-rate derivatives consistently with market prices.

Unlike for equity markets where the geometric Brownian motion is considered a good model for the movement of stock prices, there is no clearly favoured model for interest-rates. A variety of models are used, and most of them show some form of mean reversion. Some of these models can be solved exactly and used to price options on zero-coupon bonds.

Looking at the Yield Curve and Forward Rates

Before diving into interest-rate derivatives, you do well to know a bit more about bonds and interest-rates themselves. Chapter 4 gives you definitions of interest-rates and also an introduction to bonds and to bond yields. In this section, I give you more about the yield curve and how to work out bond yields.

Funnily enough for a section about interest-rates, a zero-coupon bond doesn't pay any coupon. Instead, you pay an amount, Z, for the bond now, and on maturity you receive back £1. So, normally, Z is less than £1. Instead of being paid interest in cash, the holder of a zero-coupon bond receives a return on his investment through the capital repayment on redemption. The formula $Z = Z(t, T)$ indicates that the price of the zero-coupon bond depends on both the current time, t, and the maturity date, T, when you get your £1 back. In Chapter 4, I show that you can use the time value of money to work out the value of the zero-coupon bond as $Z(t, T) = e^{-y(T-t)}$, where y is the yield to maturity of the bond.

The yield to maturity is a way of expressing the capital return of the zero-coupon bond as an interest-rate. Zero-coupon bonds with many different maturities exist, and the yield to maturity depends on the maturity date so that $y = y(T)$. However, if you know the yield for a two-year investment and also the yield for a one-year investment, you must know the yield for a one-year investment starting in a year's time. That's a bit amazing. The yield curve seems to be saying something about the future course of interest-rates.

Before doing the maths, let me provide a couple definitions:

» The **spot interest-rate** for an n year investment is the interest-rate for an investment beginning now and lasting for n years.

» A **forward interest-rate** is the interest-rate for an investment beginning at a time in the future. Normally forward rates are inferred from the spot rates for investments of different maturities.

If you invest your money in a zero-coupon bond at a rate of y_1 for T_1 years or y_2 for T_2 years, in both cases starting from now, then you can work out the forward rate, F, for a period starting after T_1 years. Using the equation for the time value of money, and assuming that $T_2 > T_1$, you can write $e^{y_2 T_2} = e^{y_1 T_1} e^{F(T_2 - T_1)}$.

By investing now at a rate of y_2 for a period of T_2, the return is the same as for investing now at a rate of y_1 for a period T_1 and then the remaining $(T_2 - T_1)$ years at the forward rate of F.

To help with the upcoming algebra, it's handy to remember that $e^{A+B} = e^A e^B$.

Gathering together the exponents in the interest-rate equation, you can rearrange them to get $F = \dfrac{y_2 T_2 - y_1 T_1}{T_2 - T_1}$.

If $T_1 = 1$ year, $T_2 = 2$ years, $y_1 = 0.5\%$ and $y_2 = 1\%$, then $F = \dfrac{2 - 0.5}{2 - 1} = 1.5$.

So, the forward one-year rate is higher than the spot one-year rate.

Forward rates aren't always higher than the spot rates but often are. Usually, the yield curve slopes upward and forward rates are higher than spot rates but occasionally that situation reverses. When short maturity rates are higher than long maturity rates, the yield curve is said to be *inverted*. Sometimes, you get a hump in the yield curve for intermediate maturity bonds. Figure 12-1 shows a schematic chart of yield curves. The short rate, for a maturity near 0, is 2 per cent for all the curves and is shown as 0.02.

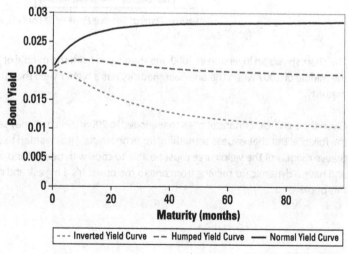

FIGURE 12-1:
Possible shapes
of yield curves.

© John Wiley & Sons, Ltd.

LOOKING AT US TREASURY YIELD CURVES

Economic folklore has it that an inverted yield curve is the sign of an upcoming recession. The figure here shows constant maturity US Treasury yields. These yields are calculations based on traded instruments that allow time series to be plotted when the maturity is always the same.

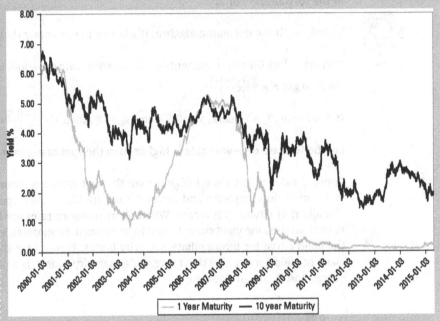

Source: Federal Reserve Bank of St Louis Economic Database

The chart shows an inversion in 2000 and then again from the middle of 2006 until the middle of 2007 when the one-year maturity has a higher yield than the ten-year maturity.

Given the significant financial crisis that ensued in 2008, this chart may seem to prove the folklore. But that issue is something for economists. I just wanted to show that quantitative models of the yield curve must be able to cope with normal and inverted shapes and have a dynamic for moving from one to the other. It's a big ask and not included in this book!

The equation for the forward rate, F, can be rewritten as $F = y_2 + (y_2 - y_1)\dfrac{T_1}{T_2 - T_1}$.

This equation makes it clear that if the yield curve is sloping upward with $y_2 > y_1$ then the forward rate, F, is greater than the interest-rate for the longer maturity loan at y_2. If you make the time period from T_1 to T_2 smaller and smaller by making $T_1 \to T_2$, then y_2 tends towards y_1 and the equation can be rewritten using derivatives as:

$$F = y + T\frac{\partial y}{\partial T}.$$

This rate is now the *instantaneous forward rate* as it applies for a short time period in the future at time T.

TECHNICAL STUFF

You can write this equation in a different way as I describe later in this chapter, so I need to explain it here. The forward rate is often written using the price of a zero-coupon bond Z as:

$$F = -\frac{\partial}{\partial t}\ln Z.$$

If the zero-coupon, at time $t = 0$, has a yield to maturity of y, then $Z = e^{-yT}$.

If you now take the logarithm and differentiate this equation, you get back to the equation in the previous paragraph.

Forward rate agreements

A *forward contract* is an agreement in which you promise to buy from or sell to the counterparty a financial asset, and the counterparty promises to sell to or buy the asset from you at a specified future date at a price agreed today. That makes them similar to futures contracts, which you can read about in Chapter 6.

An example of a forward contract, a *forward rate agreement (FRA)* is an agreement between two parties that a specified interest-rate will apply to a specified principal amount at a future start date and for a specified period.

REMEMBER

The main difference between forward contracts and forward rate agreements is that forward contracts are less standardised and tend to be traded over the counter rather than on an exchange.

The principal amount in a FRA is *notional*, meaning that the amount is never exchanged between the parties and is used only to calculate the magnitude of the interest payment between the parties. The following terms show how an FRA works:

- ≫ **$T = 0$:** The FRA is agreed with notional amount P, forward interest-rate F, start time T_1 and maturity date T_2.

- ≫ **$T = T_1$:** The FRA is for a notional loan of P starting at T_1 ending at T_2. The value of the notional loan is –P while it has to be paid back at T_2 with interest determined by the forward rate agreed at $T = 0$. The repayment of the notional loan is at T_2 and so has to be discounted at the interest-rate prevailing at T_1. This interest-rate is normally the LIBOR rate r_L applicable for the period T_1 to T_2. The cash settlement amount is therefore: $e^{F(T_2-T_1)}e^{-r_L(T_2-T_1)}$. (I talk about LIBOR in Chapter 4.)

- ≫ **$T = T_2$:** End of the maturity period. This date is only used for the purpose of calculating the settlement amount. The contract is settled in cash. If $r_L = F$, then the cash amount is zero and nothing has to be paid. However, if the interest-rate for the period T_1 to T_2 turns out to be greater than the forward rate when the contract was agreed and so $r_L > F$, then the payment is negative. In other words, the party who was long the loan and wanted to fix his interest-rate at F receives a cash payment to compensate for the rise in the interest-rate for the period from T_1 to T_2.

Interest-rate derivatives

The figure in the nearby 'Looking at US Treasury yield curves' sidebar shows time series for the 1-year US treasury yield and the 10-year US treasury yield. In both cases, they vary in time quite strongly. This variation presents risks to market participants exposed to these interest-rates especially to businesses borrowing at a variable rate. An interest-rate derivative contract designed to deal with this situation is the so-called *cap*. It does what is says and places an upper limit on the interest-rate paid by a business with a floating rate loan. An interest-rate that would otherwise be variable is capped. The floating rate used in the loan is normally LIBOR. This rate is reset after a period of a month, three months or longer and then the new LIBOR rate applies for the next period. Interest is paid at the end of each period until the loan expires.

WARNING

Realistically, a loan is at a higher rate than LIBOR as banks like to make a profit. For example, a loan maybe quoted as three-month LIBOR + 1.5 per cent.

A *cap* provides a payoff for any period of the loan for which the interest-rate exceeds the cap rate. Each of these payments for a period is called a *caplet*. Caps are valued by summing the value of all their caplets. If the principal of the loan is P, the reset period τ, LIBOR rate of r_L and cap rate of r_C, then the payment for each caplet is: $C = \tau P \max(r_L - r_C, 0)$.

The *max* function indicates that the payment is the maximum of the two quantities between the brackets separated by a comma.

An analogous product to a cap is a *floor*. Floors work by limiting the interest-rate on a floating rate loan from below. Similar to caps, the cash flows are subdivided into *floorlets* and are given by: $C = \tau P \max(r_F - r_L, 0)$.

A portfolio consisting of a long cap and short floor where the cap rate has the same value as the floor rate is: $C = \tau P \max(r_L - r_C, 0) - \tau P \max(r_C - r_L, 0) = \tau P(r_L - r_C)$.

The combination of a cap and short floor converts the floating rate loan at LIBOR into a fixed-rate loan at the cap rate, r_C. However, this conversion is the same as the interest-rate swap contract from Chapter 4. You can write this as an equation: Cap price = Floor price + Swap price.

Another important type of interest-rate derivative is the *swaption*. You've guessed that this derivative is a swap option, and you're right! (Chapter 4 explains what a swap is.) So a swaption gives the holder the right but not the obligation to enter into a swap contract at a defined time in the future. This kind of optionality is useful to a company that knows it may want to borrow money in the future and wants to fix the rate in advance. A possible reason is a business deal that may or may not happen.

Many other kinds of interest-rate derivatives exist and especially bond options. Some of the most popular are exchange-traded contracts for US T-Notes (ten-year bonds) where the underlying is a T-Note futures contract rather than the bond itself.

SEEING HOW CAPS PLAY OUT

A business wishes to take out a five-year loan for £10 million to fund its expansion. Its bank offers it six-month LIBOR plus 2 per cent, resetting every six months and payable in arrears. The company wants to limit interest-rate costs to no more than 4 per cent and so buys a cap from its bank to fix the maximum borrowing rate at 4 per cent. At the start of the loan, six-month LIBOR is at 1.75 per cent so the company is paying 3.75 per cent on its loan. However, at the end of the first six months, six-month LIBOR is at 2.25 per cent, so the loan rate is at 4.25 per cent, which is above the cap rate of 4 per cent. The bank pays the company a sum of $(4.25\% - 4\%) \times £10 \text{ million} \times \frac{6}{12} = £12,500$.

So, the company is effectively paying 4 per cent on its loan. At the end of 12 months, 6-month LIBOR has dropped back to 1.75 per cent and then declines further so there are no further payments from the cap.

Black 76 model

In 1976, Fischer Black (the co-author of the Black-Scholes equation) worked out a model for pricing options on futures contracts. Futures options, as these are called, are popular in the energy markets but also in the fixed-income market. Most bond options are, in fact, options on a futures contract for a bond. In this section though, you see how to price caps and floors using the Black 76 model.

Black's equation for the price, V, of an option on a futures contract with price F, risk-free rate r and volatility σ is:

$$\frac{\partial V}{\partial t} + \frac{\sigma^2 F^2}{2} \frac{\partial^2 V}{\partial F^2} = rV.$$

This equation comes from taking the Black-Scholes equation for a dividend-paying stock (see Chapter 10 for information on stocks) and setting the dividend rate, q, equal to the risk-free rate, r. A futures price can be treated in a similar way to a dividend-earning stock at a rate, r, when derivatives are being valued. You can find the solutions for the price of call and put options by putting $q = r$ in the solution equations from Chapter 10:

$$V = C = e^{-(T-t)} \left(FN(d_1) - FN(d_2) \right)$$

$$V = P = e^{-(T-t)} \left(XN(-X_2) - XN(-X_1) \right).$$

Now the constants d_1 and d_2 are given by slightly simpler formulae because some terms nicely cancel out when you set $q = r$:

$$d_1 = \frac{\ln\left(\frac{F}{X}\right) + \frac{\sigma^2}{2}(T-t)}{\sigma\sqrt{T-t}}$$

$$d_2 = d_1 - \sigma\sqrt{T-t}.$$

This (fairly) simple model can be used for pricing interest-rate derivatives such as caps and floors. I start with caps but the solution for floors follows in a similar way.

The reset period for the loan is τ, so resets happen at $k\tau$ where $k = 1, 2, 3, \ldots, n$. For example, for the five-year loan in the previous section with six monthly resets, $n = 9$ because the last reset is six months before the end of the loan. At the first reset at time τ, you normally get no payoff from the cap as the initial rate is known when you enter the contract. At subsequent resets at time $k\tau$, the cap holder will receive a payoff at time $(k+1)\tau$. The idea is to value the cap by valuing each of these caplets separately using the Black 76 model. The strike price, X, in the model is going to be the cap rate, r_C. That's because the forward price I'm using in the model is the forward interest-rate for the given reset period. I denote this rate by F_k. Equally, a volatility exists for this period, which I denote by σ_k. The cash payment (if any) from a caplet is received at the end of the reset period. To value the caplet correctly, you need to calculate the present value of this payment. The present here means the time at which the cap was sold at the beginning of the first reset period. The interest-rate you need to use is the yield of a zero-coupon bond with a maturity equal to the time of the cash payment, that is $(k+1)\tau$. I write this rate as $y((k+1)\tau)$. The value of a caplet, using again the notation N for the standard cumulative normal distribution, is:

$$C_C = \tau P e^{-y(k+1)\tau}\left[F_k N(d_1) - r_C N(d_2)\right] \text{ where}$$

$$d_1 = \frac{\ln\left(\dfrac{F_k}{r_C}\right) + \dfrac{1}{2}k\tau\sigma_k^2}{\sigma_k\sqrt{k\tau}}, \quad d_2 = d_1 - \sigma_k\sqrt{k\tau}.$$

The value for a floorlet is given by a similar equation using the put formula P from Black's 76 model:

$$P_f = \tau P e^{-(k+1)\tau y((k+1)\tau)}\left[r_f N(-d_2) - F_k N(-d_1)\right] \text{ where } d_1 \text{ and } d_2 \text{ are given by the}$$
same expressions as for the caplet.

Figure 12-2 shows a schematic chart of how the forward volatilities, σ_k, depend on maturity. It shows that a hump appears at an intermediate maturity, which is often at around two to three years. One explanation is that for short maturities rates are hugely influenced by the central bank and so tend to be stable. For long maturities, the mean-reversion of interest-rates dampens down the volatility leaving the intermediate maturities with the highest volatility.

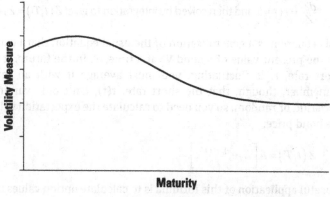

FIGURE 12-2:
Volatility hump of the forward volatility measure.

In this section, I make the assumption that the distribution of the interest-rate is lognormal so that Black's model can be applied. In addition, I assume a constant interest-rate for discounting the payoffs back to the present time. This assumption is a bit inconsistent with the assumption of stochastic interest-rates to calculate the payoff (that's why caps and floors exist!), but in practice it seems to work.

Bond pricing equations

In this section, I assume that the interest-rate is time dependent. This assumption leads to some useful formulae for the price of bonds and some equations that can be helpful for pricing interest-rate derivatives by simulation. The interest-rate I focus on is the *short-term interest-rate*, r(t). You can think of this as the interest-rate prevailing on a specific day. Sometimes this rate is called the *spot interest-rate*. This name is potentially confusing though as I use *spot rate* to distinguish interest-rates applicable now from forward rates. So I use the phrase *short rate* to refer to r(t).

If the short rate depends on time, then so must bond prices. I use t to refer to the current time and T for the maturity time of the bond. So the bond price is $Z = Z(t,T)$.

REMEMBER

The equation $Z = Z(t,T)$ just means that Z is a function of (depends on) t and T. The equation is a way of letting you know that you must pay attention to both the current time, t, and time to maturity, T, when pricing a bond.

Bonds offer investors fixed returns and so compete directly with bank deposits offering returns at the short rate r(t). As far as cash flow concerns, they're identical. Therefore, the change in the value of a bond dZ in a short period of time, dt, is given by the equation: $dZ = r(t)Z\,dt$.

So, the instantaneous return from the bond is proportional to the short rate r(t). The equation can be rearranged as:

$\frac{dZ}{Z} = r(t)dt$ and then solved by integration to give: $Z(t,T) = Z_T e^{-\int_t^T r(\tau)d\tau}$.

This equation is a generalisation of the usual equation that I explain in Chapter 4 for the present value of a bond V_T at a time, T, in the future. It shows that if the short rate, r, is fluctuating, you must average it with an integral over time. Remember, though, that the short rate, r(t), isn't only varying in time but is *stochastic*, or random, so you need to calculate the expectation value of Z(t,T) to get the bond price:

$$Z(t,T) = E\left[Z_T e^{-\int_t^T r(\tau)d\tau}\right].$$

A useful application of this formula is to calculate option values using Monte Carlo simulation in a similar way to the explanation in Chapter 10.

You can price bonds another way that leads to an equation similar to the Black-Scholes equation for option pricing. It seems strange to write about pricing bonds. After all, bonds are traded in their own right with quoted prices not too dissimilar to equities. They're not derivatives like options. However, the thought is that the short-term interest-rate r(t) is the key quantity and longer maturity bonds have prices derived from r(t). This suggests the idea of constructing a hedged portfolio of bonds of different maturity say T_1 and T_2, where the bond prices are $Z_1(r,t;T_1)$ and $Z_2(r,t;T_2)$ and there are Δ of the latter bond compared with the first bond. The value of this portfolio is: $\Pi = Z_1 - \Delta Z_2$.

Over a time period, dt, this portfolio changes by an amount dΠ. To calculate changes in the bond prices, Z, though, you need to know how the short rate, r, changes as Z is dependent on r. A simple model to express how r changes with time, t, is to assume that it drifts at a rate, m, and is subject to Brownian disturbances, X, with a standard deviation of $\sigma\, dr = m\, dt + \sigma\, dX$.

With this equation, you can now write an equation to show how the portfolio changes in value as the short rate changes with time. For a single zero-coupon bond, the change in value in a time step dt, which also entails a change in the short rate dr, is:

$$dZ = \frac{\partial Z}{\partial t}dt + \frac{\partial Z}{\partial r}dr + \frac{1}{2}\sigma^2 \frac{\partial^2 Z}{\partial r^2}dt.$$

To work out this equation, I used Ito's Lemma, which I talk about in Chapter 10.

REMEMBER

The reason for the extra term in dZ depending on σ^2 is that if you expand dZ using terms of second order (mathematicians call this situation a *Taylor expansion*), then the term dr² turns out to be partly linear in dt. This result is because, on average, for a Brownian motion: $dX^2 = dt$. The portfolio with the two bonds will change by an amount $d\Pi = dZ_1 - \Delta dZ_2$.

This portfolio will, though, depend on the stochastic variable dr, which isn't good since the whole idea of hedging is to get rid of risk, thus you'd like the return of the portfolio to be r(t). However, if I set $\frac{\partial Z_1}{\partial r} - r\Delta \frac{\partial Z_2}{\partial r} = 0$, then dΠ won't depend on dr at all and so will be risk free. Then: $d\Pi = r\Pi dt$.

Using the equations for both Π and dΠ in terms of Z_1 and Z_2, this equation turns out to look like:

$$\frac{\frac{\partial Z_1}{\partial t} + \frac{1}{2}\sigma^2 \frac{\partial^2 Z_1}{\partial r^2} - tZ_1}{\frac{\partial Z_1}{\partial r}} = \frac{\frac{\partial Z_2}{\partial t} + \frac{1}{2}\sigma^2 \frac{\partial^2 Z_2}{\partial r^2} - tZ_2}{\frac{\partial Z_2}{\partial r}}.$$

The left side appears to depend on the maturity date T_1 while the right side appears to depend on T_2. This situation is inconsistent and suggests, in fact, that both sides are independent of the maturity date. They must then only be a function of r and t. Usually the equation is written as $a(r,t) = \sigma\lambda(r,t) - m(r,t)$ in terms of the volatility of the short rate σ, the drift m(r, t) of the short rate and a new function λ, which is often called the *market price of risk*. The bond pricing equation is then:

$$\frac{\partial Z}{\partial t} + \frac{1}{2}\sigma^2 \frac{\partial^2 Z}{\partial r^2} + (m - \lambda\sigma)\frac{\partial Z}{\partial r} - r\lambda\sigma.$$

This equation can be used to work out the price of zero-coupon bonds under various assumptions about the governing equation for the short-term interest-rate r.

The market price of risk

The bond pricing equation from the previous section contains a function, λ, which is a bit mysterious. One way to make it clearer is to write the change in a bond price as: $dZ = m_B Z\, dt + \sigma_B Z\, dX$.

This equation defines an average bond return, m_B, and the volatility of the bond. You can now compare this equation with the equation for dZ, used to work out the bond pricing equation. By equating the coefficients of both dX and dt, you find out after a bit of algebra that $m_B = r + \lambda\sigma_B$.

This equation is saying that the average return on a bond is equal to the short-term interest-rate r plus a term that is proportional to the volatility of the bond. The second term represents the additional return a bond holder can expect to earn above the short-term rate for taking on the additional risk of holding a longer-term bond.

Modelling the Interest-Rate

Interest-rates are stochastic, or random. In this section, you see models where this fact is explicitly taken into account so there is hope of building pricing models of interest-rate derivatives that make fewer assumptions than, for example, in the section 'Black 76 Model'. This section begins with the equilibrium models that use a stochastic equation for the short-term interest-rate, r, and ends with an arbitrage-free model where the prices of the bond contracts themselves are modelled.

Stochastic is another word for random used especially for a process such as an interest-rate that changes with time.

The Ho Lee model

A simple model for the stochastic dynamics of the short-term interest-rate, r, is: $dr = \eta\, dt + \sigma\, dX$.

In this equation, t is time as usual and X is a Brownian increment. The two parameters are η and σ. The first parameter defines the average direction in which the short rate moves. The second parameter is the standard deviation of the short-term interest-rate, r. The Ho Lee model can be made more general by allowing η to be time dependent. Doing so allows you to fit its prediction for zero-coupon bond values for different maturities to actual market rates, which means that you can then – hopefully accurately – value interest-rate derivatives such as bond options.

However, other aspects of the model aren't so satisfactory. For example, the standard deviation of forward rates is predicted to be independent of maturity. In practice, that doesn't hold. Although the model can indeed be used to value various interest-rate derivatives, other models have become more prevalent.

The one-factor Vasicek model

One of the problems with the Ho Lee model for interest-rates is that it doesn't show *mean reversion*. This subject was introduced in Chapter 3 and refers to behaviour in which, if the interest becomes high, it's pulled back down to a long-term average value. Equally, if it's particularly low, the interest-rate tends to be drawn back up to the long-term average value. Reflecting this, the Ho Lee equation (see the previous section) is modified with an extra parameter – γ:

$$dr = (\eta - \gamma r)dt + \sigma\,dX.$$

Now, the interest-rate tends towards the value $\frac{\eta}{\gamma}$ in the long run. If it deviates from this value, it reverts at a speed given by γ because this term in the equation is the only one dependent on the interest-rate. There will always be fluctuations around the long-run value because of the Brownian term dX. Figure 12-3 shows a chart of these patterns and compares the Vasicek model with the Ho Lee model.

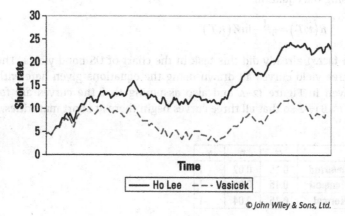

FIGURE 12-3: Movement of short rates for Ho Lee and Vasicek models with the same random impulses.

© John Wiley & Sons, Ltd.

REMEMBER

In this Vasicek model , nothing prevents the interest-rate from going to a negative value because the random term, σdX, has a constant standard deviation. So, even if the interest-rate is low, it can still fluctuate by the same amount. Also, the drift term with dt has a coefficient that can be negative.

The Vasicek model has been criticised because of the possibility that it can create negative rates, but, in fact, interest-rates (yields) on short-term government bonds do go to negative values. That happens if investors like the safety of a government guarantee (compared with depositing money in a bank) even if they get less back from their bond than they pay for it. However, you can see in the chart of one-year US government bond yields in the 'Looking at US Treasury yield curves' sidebar earlier in the chapter, that the short-term interest-rate stays just above zero for a long time without crossing below zero. So, interest-rates or government bond yields like to stay above zero. Negative bond yields quickly become unattractive as simply storing cash under the mattress or perhaps more safely in a bank vault should lead to smaller losses.

Using the bond pricing equation with $m = \eta - \gamma r$ from the Vasicek model, you can work out the value of zero-coupon bonds. To do this, assume that $Z(t;T) = e^{A(t;T)-rB(t;T)}$ and substitute into the bond pricing equation. The maths is complicated so best to leave that for a rainy day. The results are that:

$$B = \frac{1}{\gamma}\left(1 - e^{-(T-t)}\right)$$

$$A = \frac{1}{\gamma^2}\left[B(t;T) - T + t\right]\left[\eta\gamma - \frac{\beta}{2}\right] - \frac{\beta B(t;T)^2}{4\gamma}.$$

From these equations, you can now draw charts of yield curves (yield as a function of the maturity, T) and see how they change as you vary the parameters γ and η. The interest-rate or yield for a maturity of T is found from the value of a bond using the equation:

$$R(t;T) = \frac{1}{T-t}\ln Z(t;T).$$

In fact, I already did this task in the chart of US bond yields. There you can see three yield curves all drawn using the equations given here with the constants given in Figure 12-4 and also assuming that the curves are for $t = 0$. I chose $r(t = 0) = 2$ so that all three curves begin there at short maturities.

FIGURE 12-4: Parameters for the Vasicek yield curves.

The yield curves in the chart in the 'Looking at US Treasury yield curves' sidebar all have the same values for σ and γ but have different values for η. When the short rate, r, is lower than the long-term rate, η, you can see a normal upward sloping yield curve.

Arbitrage free models

The models introduced so far in this section start with an equation for the short rate r(t). From this, you can work out expressions for the price of zero-coupon bonds of different maturities. However, you have another way of developing models for the yield curve that allows much more flexibility to create a model that fits the actual yield curve on a given day. This way is important if you wish to price derivatives such as bond options using the yield curve.

You start with an equation for the zero-coupon bond price itself with a usual factor depending on the short rate, r(t), but also with an additional term representing Brownian noise:

$$dZ(t;T) = r(t)Z(t;T)dt + \sigma(t,T)Z(t;T)dX.$$

This equation can be transformed using Ito's lemma (see Chapter 10) to an equation for the forward rates F(t; T). The calculation here is similar to the one in Chapter 3 for equities:

$$dF(t;T) = \frac{\partial}{\partial T}\left(\frac{1}{2}\sigma^2(t,T) - T(t)\right)dt - \frac{\partial}{\partial T}\sigma(t,T)dX$$

$$= \sigma(t,T)\frac{\partial}{\partial T}\sigma(t,T)dt - \frac{\partial}{\partial T}\sigma(t,T)dX.$$

In this equation, I used the fact that:

$$F(t;T) = -\frac{\partial}{\partial T}\ln Z(t;T).$$

This equation is explained at the end of the section 'Looking at the Yield Curve and Forward Rates' at the beginning of this chapter. If I now write:

$$\upsilon(t,T) = -\frac{\partial}{\partial T}\sigma(t,T),$$

then the equation for dF can be simplified (a little) to:

$$dF(t;T) = m(t,T)dt + \upsilon(t,T)dX \text{ where } m(t,T)dt = \upsilon(t,T)\int_t^T \upsilon(t,s)ds.$$

Now the equation is in a useful form because only a single function υ exists to describe its dynamics. Also the expression for the drift, m(t,T), is an integral that can be easily done numerically. The equation for dF is then a good starting point for modelling the forward curve and pricing derivatives.

5
Risk and Portfolio Management

Chapter 13

Managing Market Risk

Market risk is what happens when a market price goes against you, whether it goes up or down. *Credit risk* is a similar form of financial accident that happens when a company or nation defaults on a loan. Banks are primarily exposed to credit risk. For financial institutions that invest or trade in financial assets on behalf of others, managing market risk is a crucial task.

Market risk is distinct from *operational risk*, which is about failures with people, processes and systems. If market risk gets out of hand, it can lead to *financial instability*, which happens when firms are no longer able to perform critical financial services such as buying and selling shares. This chapter introduces ideas about market risk and the following two chapters extend the analysis with detailed ways of building portfolios to reduce risk.

Investing in Risky Assets

The reason for investing in risky financial assets is to make a profit, or to earn a return in excess of what you can get by depositing money in a bank or lending money to a government in the form of short-term loans (treasury bills). Low or even negative deposit rates can intensify the search for investments with higher risk and higher return. Indeed, the purpose of low or negative interest rates is to encourage money to move out of safe bank deposits into business investment so as to stimulate the economy.

For most investment companies, and that includes insurance companies with large investment portfolios, the key to managing risk is *diversification,* or investing in a wide range of different assets. The idea of diversification isn't to boost performance. In fact, if you invest over a wide range, you're guaranteed to invest in some lower-performing, lower-return assets. Diversifying doesn't guarantee you against losses, but it certainly increases your chances of achieving a positive return.

REMEMBER

Diversification is a simple technique to achieve a better outcome with risky investments – an example of the homespun wisdom of not putting all your eggs in one basket.

As an example, imagine lending money to N companies. Each loan of £1 is for a year and has an interest rate of ten per cent. The default probability is two per cent for each company. (A *default* is when a borrower is no longer able to make interest payments or pay back the principal on a loan.)

Start by assuming that $N = 1$. You have a 2 per cent chance that the loan defaults and you get nothing in return but a 98 per cent chance that the company survives the year and your return is 10 per cent. The average return is $0.98 \times 1.1 + 0.02 \times 0 - 1 = 0.078$, or 7.8 per cent. The first term in this formula is the probability of not defaulting (0.98) multiplied by the total value of your investment at the end of the year which is £1 plus 10 per cent interest or £1.1. The second term in the formula is the default probability (0.02) multiplied by the value of your investment (zero) at the end of the year. I've then subtracted the initial value of your investment (£1) so that you're left with the return of 7.8%. If $N = 2$, the chance of both loans defaulting is $0.02 \times 0.02 = 0.0004$, which is a small number. Now, however, one or both loans can default, so you have a $2 \times 0.02 = 0.04$, or 4 per cent, chance of one loan defaulting leaving you with an almost 50 per cent loss (but not as bad as a 100 per cent loss). The non-defaulting loan earns 10 per cent.

So, as N gets bigger, the chance of a total loss gets smaller and smaller. You can't possibly earn more than 10 per cent and the expected return is 7.8 per cent no matter how many companies you lend out to.

However, the distribution of returns becomes different as N gets bigger. Figure 13-1 shows the probability of ending the year with a given amount of capital from $N = 100$ loans of £1 at 10 per cent per annum to companies with a default probability of 2 per cent.

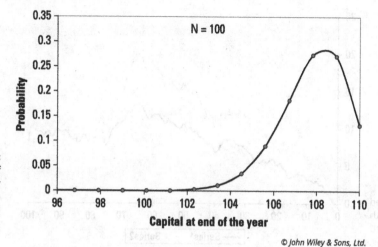

FIGURE 13-1:
Probability of
end-of-year
value for a
large diversified
portfolio of loans.

© John Wiley & Sons, Ltd.

With a big N, you have almost no chance of getting back less than £100. Getting back 10 per cent is unlikely but possible. Far more likely is getting back around £108 after sustaining a couple of defaults. This outcome seems much more satisfactory than exposing yourself to a 100 per cent loss with a single loan.

This example is helpful in understanding portfolios of loans but not so useful for equity portfolios. For one thing, equities don't default, and for another, they tend to be highly correlated. (*Correlation* is a statistical measure of the extent to which asset prices move together or not. Chapter 9 explains how to calculate correlations.) By paying attention to the correlation between the assets, you can reduce the overall risk of the portfolio. You can read more about portfolio risk in Chapter 14.

WARNING

If two time series are correlated, you may be tempted to think that they must look the same, but that's not always the case. Figure 13-2 shows a chart of two time series created using the same random numbers so that the correlation coefficient of the returns of the time series is exactly equal to 1. Upward moves in one series are matched by upward moves in the other, and likewise for downward moves. But for an extended period, series 2 drifted higher than series 1.

Series 2 was generated using random numbers, ε_n from a standard normal distribution in the equation:

$$P_{n+1} = P_n + \varepsilon_n + 0.1.$$

Series 1, on the other hand, was generated using the equation:

$$P_{n+1} = P_n + \frac{1}{2}\varepsilon_n + 0.1.$$

Correlation tells you something about the similarity of short-term movements but nothing about longer-term movements.

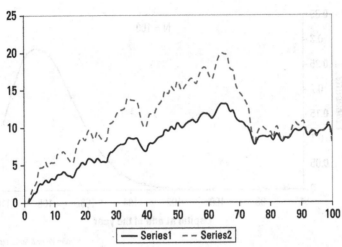

FIGURE 13-2:
Two simulated
time series with
exactly correlated
returns.

| —— Series1 | - - Series2 |

Stopping Losses and other Good Ideas

If a financial asset is risky, nothing is simpler than just selling it if its price declines more than a given amount. Deciding the price at which you'll sell the asset is called setting a *stop loss*. The stop loss can be an absolute price at which you'll sell or it can be set relative to the most recent high price of your asset. Then you decide to sell if the asset declines more than a set percentage from the most recent high price, which means that if your asset continues to rise in price from the date at which you bought it, your stop loss rises in price and is called a *trailing stop loss* because it follows behind a rising price.

Although it appears to be sure and simple, the stop loss mechanism has drawbacks:

>> If you set the stop loss close to the current price, the stop loss is likely to be activated by a random fluctuation in the market. In that case, a stop loss is likely to increase your trading costs, especially if the stop is activated during a time when trading volume is low and the difference between the buying and selling prices in the market is high.

>> Even if the stop loss is set a good distance from the current price, there's no guarantee that it will actually protect you from a large price movement. Often these occur overnight in a big jump so you can't execute the stop loss immediately.

TIP

Careful use of stop losses can be beneficial, but mostly setting them increases trading costs. Other methods of managing risk are often preferable.

Hedging Schemes

Risk can be reduced by *hedging,* which is buying (or selling) an investment so as to offset the risk in another investment.

Hedging is routinely used by commodity producers and consumers using the futures market to reduce exposure to changes in the price of the commodity. Clearly a producer wants protection from a fall in the commodity price while a consumer wants protection from a rise in price. (Chapter 6 gives a detailed explanation of futures.)

For the producer who is long the commodity and short the future, the change in the value of her position, ΔP, depends on changes of the futures price, F, the spot price of the commodity, S, and the size, h, of the futures position:

$$\Delta P = \Delta S - h\Delta F.$$

The delta symbol indicates a change in the following quantity. In this case, the change is due to prices changing with time.

For a consumer with a long futures position and short the commodity, the equation is:

$$\Delta P = -\Delta S + h\Delta F.$$

I define risk as the variance, V, of the change in value of the positions, P.

Chapter 2 explains random variables and some of their properties. In this chapter, you need to work out what happens when you add two random variables – x and y. Using x and y makes the equations simpler and clearer, and you can then use the result in other contexts.

Let $z = x + y$. Then $E(z) = E(x) + E(y)$ where E indicates the expected value of random variable. The variance, V, of a random variable x is V(x):

$$V(x) = E\left(\left(x - E(x)\right)^2\right) = E(x^2) - E^2(x).$$

A similar equation holds for y. Now if you replace x with x + y in the preceding equation you get:

$$V(z) = V(x + y) = E\left(\left(x + y - E(x) - E(y)\right)^2\right).$$

After a little bit of algebra, and using the equation for V(x) and V(y), this equation becomes:

$$V(z) = V(x) + V(y) + 2(E(xy) - E(x)E(y)).$$

The last term is the same as 2cov(x, y), or twice the covariance between x and y. *Covariance*, a measure of the extent of the relationship between two random variables, is discussed in Chapter 9 and is defined using the expectation operator, E, as:

$$cov(x, y) = E\left[(x - E(x))(y - E(y))\right],$$

which simplifies to the expression in the equation for V(z). So:

$$V(z) = V(x) + V(y) + 2cov(x, y).$$

Remember also that [writing the correlation between x and y as corr(x, y)]:

$$\sigma^2(x) = V(x) \text{ and that corr}(x, y) = \frac{cov(x, y)}{\sigma(x)\sigma(y)}.$$

Phew!

Writing the correlation between x and y as ρ, you can see that for both the consumer and producer the variance of the hedged position is:

$$V(P) = \sigma_S^2 + h^2\sigma_F^2 - 2h\rho\sigma_S\sigma_F.$$

The standard deviation of the spot price is written as σ with a subscript for the spot price, S, and the futures price, F. The variance of the hedged position depends on the size of the futures position in a non-linear way (there is a term with h^2).

Differentiating V(P) with respect to h and setting the resulting equation to zero, you can find the location of the minimum variance:

$$\frac{dV}{dh} = 2h\sigma_F^2 - 2h\sigma_S\sigma_F = 0.$$

The value of h that solves this equation is:

$$h = \rho\frac{\sigma_S}{\sigma_F}.$$

So, the best way to reduce the variance of the hedged position isn't necessarily to have your futures and physical positions matched in size. You should use the calculated value of h for your futures position size. Clearly, though, if the correlation, ρ, is one and the standard deviation of the spot price is equal to the standard deviation of the futures price, the best value of h is one.

Commonly, you don't use exactly the same commodity for the futures as the spot. The reason is partly because of the restricted range of futures contracts compared with the number of commodities in the world, but also because a hedger often likes to use the most liquid (heavily traded) futures contract so that she can reduce or increase her position at low cost.

Betting without Losing Your Shirt

You may have noticed that financial markets have something in common with casinos or betting in general. That common element is the random nature of the outcome of trades and bets. In this section I show you how to find a way to optimise bets or investments, despite this randomness, so as to maximise your long-term average growth rate. You find out just how useful probability is!

REMEMBER

In gambling activities such as casino games, the house makes the rules and those rules are in favour of the house – of course. On average, bettors lose as the casino intends to make a profit. In the stock market, over time and on average, prices rise because of economic growth, and investors probably get a good return. But the stock market is volatile, and in the short run, you can easily lose money. The foreign exchange market is much more like a casino though. You bet against other participants in a zero-sum game, apart from some interest payments. Systematically making gains is unlikely.

If you make a sequence of bets (or trades if you prefer financial markets), each bet has an uncertain outcome. You start with an amount of capital, P. The idea is to grow this money at the highest rate you can without going bust – in other words, without your account going to zero.

You have a probability, p, of winning each bet and a probability, $(1-p)$, of losing it. If you place a stake of $1, you get f dollars if you win and nothing if you lose. Win or lose, you also lose your stake, so f must be greater than 1 for the gamble to make any sense. If f is less than 1, you're certain to lose money on every bet. However, if fp is greater than 1, your expected return on each bet exceeds your stake, so, on average, you come out winning.

That sounds good, but accidents still happen. For example, by bad luck, you may have a losing streak to begin with and run out of capital before you can start making money. You need to place bets of the right size so as to conserve capital and be able to withstand the downturns that inevitably happen just by random chance. Of course, if your bet size is too small, you won't benefit from the positive expected return from your bets. So, you need to work out the optimum size of bet to capture the positive returns available without exposing yourself to too much risk.

Assume that you bet a fixed fraction, α, of your capital each time. If you start with P, after the first bet you have:

$$P_1 = (1 - \alpha + \alpha X)P.$$

The random variable, X, takes the value f with probability p and the value zero with probability $(1-p)$. If X equals zero, you have $(1-\alpha)P$ of capital left because you've just lost a fraction $-\alpha-$ of it. On the other hand, if you win, and X equals f, the formula for P_1 splits up into the capital you held back $(1-\alpha)P$ and your winnings $(\alpha f P)$. After placing n bets in sequence, you have an amount of capital P_n remaining given by the following formula. I added a subscript to X to indicate that it's not always the same outcome:

$$P_n = (1 - \alpha + \alpha X_1) \times \cdots \times (1 - \alpha + \alpha X_n)P.$$

The $\times \cdots \times$ in the middle of the formula indicates that lots more terms like the first and last ones exist. In fact, a term exists for each of the n bets.

I take the logarithm of the formula for P_n because I'm expecting the gambling to turn out well with exponential growth. The logarithm should be connected to the growth rate of the account:

$$\frac{1}{n}\ln\frac{P_n}{P} = \frac{1}{n}\sum_{j=1}^{n}\ln(1 - \alpha + \alpha X_j).$$

By writing $\frac{1}{n}$ on each side of the equation (that's allowed!), the right-hand side looks just like the average value of the quantity inside the brackets. Using the probability, p, and the payoff, f, you can now to write the equation as:

$$\frac{1}{n}\ln\frac{P_n}{P} = p\ln(1 - \alpha + \alpha f) + (1 - p)\ln(1 - \alpha).$$

Calling this quantity γ, a little algebra gives you:

$$P_n = Pe^{\gamma n}.$$

So γ is the growth rate of the account. To find the value of α that maximises the growth rate, differentiate the equation for γ with respect to α to get:

$$\frac{p(f-1)}{(1-\alpha+f\alpha)} - \frac{(1-p)}{(1-\alpha)} = 0.$$

You can solve this for α to get:

$$a^* = \frac{pf-1}{f-1}.$$

This is the optimal fraction of your account to bet each time so as to achieve the highest growth rate. It shows, for example, that if $pf < 1$, then the growth rate is negative, which is to be expected.

Figure 13-3 shows a chart of the result of making 200 bets with $p = 0.4$ and $f = 3$. The optimal value of α is 0.1 (you can check this value using the previous formula). However, I also plotted the account values for twice this value (0.2) and half this value (0.05).

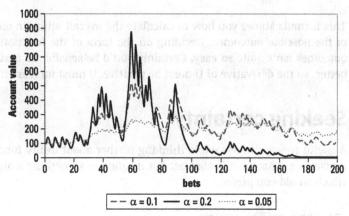

FIGURE 13-3:
Betting with medium, large and small fractions of your wealth.

Legend: $-- \alpha = 0.1$ $— \alpha = 0.2$ $\cdots \alpha = 0.05$

If you choose $\alpha = 0.1$, the account grows as expected but is quite volatile. If you choose $\alpha = 0.2$, you have an exciting time but end up with almost nothing. By contrast, if $\alpha = 0.05$, which is half the optimal value you calculated, the account isn't volatile and actually ends up higher than for $\alpha = 0.1$, but most of the time is beneath the curve for $\alpha = 0.1$. The growth rate for $\alpha = 0.05$ is slightly less than for $\alpha = 0.1$, but the returns are less volatile, so you've good reason to choose a value of α less than the optimal value. This statement is certainly true if you're unsure of the values for p and f.

Evaluating Outcomes with Utility Functions

When it comes to money, the common factor in most people's minds is that more is better. That seems to be universally true, but money, or more generally wealth, is held in many different forms, and they all have different risk characteristics. Investments such as stocks have high risk and high returns while cash has low risk and low return. How then to make the best decision about allocating investments or making financial decisions?

A common framework is to use *utility functions*. These functions assign a number, U, to an amount of wealth, W. The preferred outcome of any financial decision is always the one with highest utility. In a financial decision, outcomes with probability, p_i, result in wealth, W_i. The expected utility is calculated by weighting the utility of each of the n possible outcomes of your decision by its probability. For an investment, P, you can write this as:

$$EU(P) = \sum_{i=1}^{n} p_i U(W_i).$$

This formula shows you how to calculate the overall utility in terms of the utility of the possible outcomes. Deciding on the form of the function U for individual outcomes isn't quite so easy. Certainly you'd be sensible to assume that more is better, so the derivative of U must be positive. U must increase if W increases.

Seeking certainty

A useful concept to use while thinking further about utility functions is *certainty equivalence*. That sounds abstract but it refers to something simple. For example, which would you prefer:

>> Choice A: £50 for certain

>> Choice B: £100 if a coin turns up heads but nothing if it turns up tails

Say that the utility, U, is a simple linear function of W, so $U = W$. This fact satisfies the 'more is better' rule of money. It also means that the utility of £50 for certain is exactly equal to the utility of £100 with probability 50 per cent assuming that the coin is fair. Most people prefer choice A to choice B. The risk of coming out with nothing makes them prefer the first option.

To make both choices have the same utility, the value of option A must be a lot less than £50. This value is the certainty equivalent of the 50 per cent bet on £100. Figure 13-4 shows a possible curve for the utility as a function of wealth.

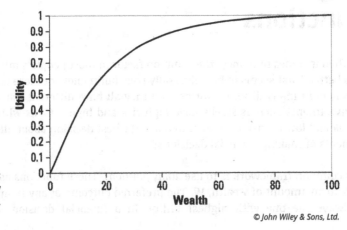

FIGURE 13-4: Convex utility function.

$U(100) = 1$, so the utility of winning £100 with 50 per cent chance is 0.5. However, the chart shows that the utility of £50 is more like 0.9 and so the curve shows a clear preference for £50 with certainty. However, the utility of £15 is approximately 0.5 and so is the same as £1,000 with 50 per cent. £15 is the certainty equivalent of the £100 gamble with this utility function.

The fact that the certainty equivalent of the risky bet is less than its expected value means that the gambler (investor) is *risk averse*. Some investors, however, are *risk loving* and place a higher certainty equivalent value on a bet than its expected value. Gamblers who enjoy the pleasure of betting are risk loving.

The certain equivalent, C, of a risky bet can be worked out from the formula for the expected utility:

$$U(C) = \sum_{i=1}^{n} p_i U(W_i).$$

Notice that the slope (the first derivative of U) of the chart in Figure 13-4 gets less and less as W gets bigger. This fact means that the second derivative, or *curvature*, of U(W) is negative. In maths, you can write this as:

$$\frac{d^2U}{dW^2} < 0.$$

This formula is the condition for what is called a *convex function*. The shape of the curve shows that there is diminishing utility to extra wealth when you become wealthy. Intuitively, this statement makes sense. The extra utility you gain by increasing your wealth beyond your current level is called *marginal utility*. This phrase is economists' jargon, but it's helpful because it reminds you to think about changes in wealth and utility and not just absolute values. Most financial decisions are made with reference to your current position rather than the absolute position.

Because the curvature of the utility function in Figure 13-4 is negative, it is always true that a risky bet with the same expected value as a certain bet has lower utility. A risky bet has to have a higher payoff than a certain bet to have the same expected value because of the reducing value of the slope of the utility curve. By the same argument, the certainty equivalent of a risky bet is always less than the expected value of a risky bet if the utility function is convex (has negative curvature). A convex utility curve is therefore linked directly with risk aversion. In a way, the convexity of the utility curve and the diminishing marginal utility explains risk aversion.

Modelling attitudes to risk

Different forms of the utility function are used to model different attitudes to risk. In the previous section, 'Betting without Losing Your Shirt', I took the logarithm of the wealth after the nth bet and maximised that. The logarithm is another common utility function and, in fact, one of the first ever used.

It should be clear that I could have chosen a different utility function – for example, one that would have reduced the fluctuations in the account value. Rarely does an organisation adopt a risk-loving utility function in making financial transactions. Systematic gains could be made by offering the organisation transactions that result in losses. To be sure, judging what level of risk is safe is the hardest thing.

Avoiding risk always

A special group of utility functions that prove useful are those that show *constant absolute risk aversion*, which have the property that if C is the certainty equivalent of a risky amount of wealth, W, you can say the same thing even if you shift both values by delta, Δ. So then $C + \Delta$ is the certain equivalent of $W + \Delta$.

This property means that when considering a new risky investment, what matters is the change in utility and wealth. You don't need to know the initial wealth. This makes intuitive sense as most investors are looking for gains in wealth irrespective of their starting points. The only function that satisfies this and also shows risk aversion is the exponential utility function:

$$U(W) = 1 - e^{-W}.$$

The simple form of this equation makes it well suited to practical problems in optimising investment portfolios.

Becoming risk loving with prospect theory

In the previous section, 'Seeking certainty', I offer a simple risk experiment that involves choosing between a certain gain and a risky gain. Here, I present a similar choice, but this time about losing money not gaining money. Which do you prefer?

> » Choice A: A certain loss of £50.
> » Choice B: A loss of £100 if a coin turns up heads but no loss if the coin turns up tails.

The expected loss from B is £50 if the coin is fair, which is the same as the certain loss in A. However, most people prefer option B. The prospect of a certain loss is painful and most people gamble on avoiding the loss. Suddenly, they become risk loving rather than risk averse. Figure 13-5 shows a possible utility function to model this effect. The model is convex for positive values but concave for negative values. For gains in wealth, it represents risk aversion while for losses it represents risk loving.

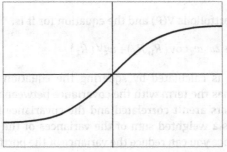

FIGURE 13-5:
Utility function
showing both
risk-averse and
risk-loving
behaviour.

REMEMBER

Prospect theory is a more general view on utility functions in which the peculiarities of human behaviour are taken into account. It includes the effect that people can become risk loving when faced with only losing prospects.

Using the Covariance Matrix to Measure Market Risk

The *covariance* is a measure of the extent of the relationship between two random variables – normally, asset returns.

The *covariance matrix* is the combination of many random variables, not just two. You may encounter a covariance matrix if you're looking at the returns of all the assets in a portfolio.

In all cases, you find the correlation by dividing the covariance by the standard deviation of both of the variables being correlated. This division ensures that the correlation lies between –1 and 1 and that the correlation is a good indicator of the short-term relationship between the two variables.

To keep things simple, I assume that your portfolio contains just two stocks. I denote the returns on these stocks by R_1 and R_2. You have an amount, w_1, of the first stock and w_2 of the second stock. The return for the portfolio is R. The return for the portfolio is the weighted average of the return for the individual stocks:

$$R_P = w_1 R_1 + w_2 R_2 \quad \text{with} \quad w_1 + w_2 = 1.$$

The second equation just shows that the proportions of the stocks in the portfolio add up to one, which is just common sense.

The variance of the portfolio is V(P) and the equation for it is:

$$V(P) = w_1^2 V(R_1) + 2w_1 w_2 \operatorname{cov}(R_1, R_2) + w_2^2 V(R_2).$$

Because the variance is calculated by squaring the equation for the portfolio returns, the formula has the term with the covariance between the returns of the two assets. If the assets aren't correlated and the covariance is equal to 0, the portfolio covariance is a weighted sum of the variances of the stocks. However, with negative covariance you can reduce the variance of the portfolio significantly. This point is when diversification can be particularly powerful and reduce the risk of investing.

Estimating parameters

By estimating the expected covariance of the assets in your portfolio, you can work out how much risk (portfolio standard deviation) you're exposing yourself to. By finding assets with negative covariance (correlation), you can reduce the risk a lot. Any parameter (such as the covariance) that's calculated from market returns, however, is only an estimate. Even if your two assets have a stable (constant) correlation over time, you can still calculate the correlation only from a sample of data points. If the correlation changes with time, you may want to calculate the correlation from a smaller sample of points.

More worrying is that if your portfolio has M assets, where M is a big number such as 500, you have many correlations to calculate. In fact, an accumulation of errors is evident, and you're unlikely to get an accurate covariance matrix unless you have an extremely large number of historical data points.

Shrinking the covariance matrix

Using a covariance matrix estimated from sample data in a calculation is potentially dangerous. If you're trying to reduce the variance of your portfolio, you may end up increasing the variance if many of the values of the matrix are inaccurate. The presence of errors can produce misleading results. A way to avoid this problem is to use a technique called *shrinkage*. In this technique, you create a weighted average of the sample covariance matrix, C, calculated from your data and a target matrix, T. The target matrix is normally chosen to be a simplified diagonal matrix. If I is the unit diagonal matrix and σ_{av}^2 is the average value of the variances of the variables in your data set, a good choice is:

$$T = \sigma_{av}^2 I.$$

Using a factor Δ, the shrinkage estimator for the covariance matrix is:

$$\Sigma = (1 - \delta)C + \delta T.$$

DOING THE STATISTICS

When you calculate a statistic such as an average from market data, the numerical value of the statistic itself is uncertain – you need statistics for the statistics. Here, you can find out how to calculate the variance of an average.

If you have a quantity X_{av} that's the average of N random variables, each with mean μ and standard deviation σ, then:

$$X_{av} = \frac{1}{N}\left(x_1 + x_2 + \ldots + x_N\right).$$

Assuming that the variables are uncorrelated, the variance of X_{av} is just the sum of the variance of the terms on the right side:

$$V\left(X_{av}\right) = \sum_{i=1}^{N} V\left(\frac{x_i}{N}\right).$$

But the variance is calculated by taking squares, so you can rewrite this equation as:

$$V\left(X_{av}\right) = \frac{1}{N^2}\sum_{i=1}^{N} V\left(x_i\right).$$

The variance of each variable (N of them) is σ^2, so this formula simplifies to:

$$V\left(X_{av}\right) = \frac{\sigma^2}{N}.$$

This formula gives you a measure of the variance on your estimate of the average. You can find the standard deviation of your average by taking the square root of the equation to get $\frac{\sigma}{\sqrt{N}}$. The standard deviation of the average is $\sqrt{N}$ smaller than the standard deviation of each data point. This fact is why taking averages is a good idea: it reduces the error on the estimate of a quantity. However, some error is still left.

You can do similar but more complicated calculations for the correlation ρ. If the number of samples N is large, then the standard deviation of a correlation is:

$$\sigma_\rho = \frac{1-\rho^2}{\sqrt{N-1}}.$$

Chapter 14

Comprehending Portfolio Theory

This chapter talks about trying to obtain as much return as possible from risky assets at minimum overall risk. This endeavour is a bit like having your cake and eating it, too, but such is the magic of diversification. By investing in risky assets, you gain the possibility of earning higher returns at the expense of higher risk. You can then lower this risk by careful portfolio construction and making best use of diversification.

To do so you need to use *optimisation*, which is the mathematical process of finding the maximum or minimum value of a function of many variables. In portfolio theory, optimisation involves minimising risk as a function of the amount of each asset. Often you need to apply *constraints*, restrictions on the possible amount of each asset. Normally, common sense guides your constraints – ensuring that the total value of the portfolio adds up to the correct amount, for example.

If the assets in your portfolio are *correlated* (meaning that price movements of one asset are closely related to price movements of other assets), and they normally are, then you need to calculate a correlation matrix for the returns of your assets. The correlation matrix contains the correlation between each of the assets in your portfolio. You also need to estimate the expected returns of your assets. That's not at all easy because of the ups and downs in markets, so you'll need a lot of data to do this accurately. Portfolio theory then shows you how to build the optimum portfolio by trading off risk against return.

In this chapter, risk is the same as the *volatility* (the standard deviation of the returns) of the portfolio. This statement assumes that the fluctuations in the market are Gaussian, or have a normal distribution. While this assumption does not take into account rare events, it can be a good starting point for investigating portfolio construction.

Diversifying Portfolios

Diversification is the process of building a portfolio in a way that reduces exposure to any one asset or risk. Usually this is done by investing in many assets whilst ensuring that those assets are not all exposed to the same risk factors. In this section I talk about a portfolio, N, with risky investments such as stocks but no correlations between the assets. Such a portfolio is a bit unrealistic but it makes the maths easier. I assume that a fraction of the portfolio, p_i, is invested in the ith asset so that:

$$\sum_{i=1}^{i=N} p_i = 1.$$

The return of each asset is r_i so that the return of the portfolio, r_p, is

$$r_p = \sum_{i=1}^{i=N} p_i r_i.$$

If all the assets are independent, then the total variance of the portfolio is the square of the portfolio volatility, σ_p. You can calculate this total variance from the formula:

$$\sigma_p^2 = \sum_{i=1}^{i=N} p_i^2 \sigma_i^2.$$

The chart in Figure 14-1 shows the result of a simulation of 100 such uncorrelated assets. The price of the ith asset on day t is $P_{i,t}$ and I generated the numbers using the formula:

$$P_{i,t} = P_{i,t-1} e^{\varepsilon_{i,t-1}}.$$

ε is a random number drawn from a Gaussian distribution. I've chosen the standard deviation of the numbers to be 0.0126 and the mean to be 0.0008. Using the square root of time rule, which I cover in Chapter 7, I calculate that the annual volatility is 0.2 or 20 per cent. The average return is $250 \times 0.0008 = 0.2$, which is again 20 per cent. The price series for each of the 100 assets are shown as light grey lines.

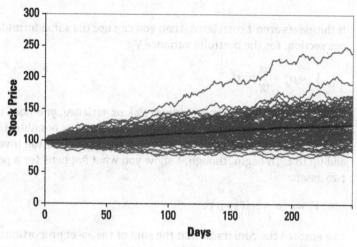

FIGURE 14-1:
Simulation of
uncorrelated
portfolio of
assets.

The black line in the middle of the tangle of grey lines is the price series for a portfolio that is equally invested in the 100 assets. This portfolio is much less volatile than any of the individual stocks. In fact, using the formula for the variance of the portfolio shows that because the portfolio holds each asset in equal proportions, $p_i = 1/N$, and because the volatility of each asset is the same:

$$\sigma_p^2 = N\frac{1}{N^2}\sigma^2 = \sigma^2\big/N.$$

So the volatility of the portfolio is $\sqrt{N}$ – smaller than the volatility of the individual assets, which is a big reduction!

Most stocks have a correlation of about 0.5, so the benefits of diversification are less than shown in the preceding example. However, long-term government bonds with a maturity of ten years or greater often have a negative correlation with stocks. They can provide powerful diversification and so in managing a portfolio one of the most important decisions is to work out how much money to allocate to bonds.

Minimising Portfolio Variance

In statistics, *variance* is a measure of how dispersed numbers are. If the variance is zero then there is no dispersion and all of the numbers are the same. In this section I assume that you have a portfolio of N risky assets as I did in the preceding section, but now I try to minimise the variance of the portfolio.

If the assets aren't correlated, then you can use the same formula as in the previous section: for the portfolio variance V_p:

$$V_p = \sigma_p^2 = \sum_{i=1}^{i=N} p_i^2 \sigma_i^2.$$

To find the portfolio with minimum risk or variance, you need to find the values of the asset proportions, p_i, that make V_p as small as possible. However, in doing this calculation, you need to ensure that the sum of all the invested proportions add up to 1. To begin, though, I show you what happens for a portfolio with only two assets:

$$V_p = \sigma_1^2 p^2 + \sigma_2^2 (1-p)^2.$$

I've ensured the constraint that the sum of the asset proportions must add up to 1 by writing the proportion of the second asset as $1 - p$. So now you have only one variable, p, available to minimise the portfolio variance. You can work out the value of p to minimise the portfolio variance by calculating its derivative with respect to p:

$$\frac{\partial V_p}{\partial p} = 2\sigma_1^2 p - 2\sigma_2^2 (1-p) = 0.$$

With a little bit of algebra you can solve this equation for p to get the following:

$$p = \frac{\sigma_2^2}{\sigma_1^2 + \sigma_2^2}; \quad 1-p = \frac{\sigma_1^2}{\sigma_1^2 + \sigma_2^2}.$$

The numerator (top line!) of these equations shows that if σ_1 is bigger than σ_2, the portfolio has the second asset in a higher proportion than the first asset. This is how the variance is minimised – by increasing the proportion of the asset with lower volatility.

Substituting the value for p into the equation for V_p gives the value of the variance at the minimum, written as V^*_p:

$$V_p^* = \frac{\sigma_1^2}{\left(1 + \sigma_1^2 / \sigma_2^2\right)}.$$

This equation shows that V^*_p is always less than σ_1^2 because the denominator (bottom line) is greater than 1. So the portfolio always has lower variance than the individual stocks.

Using portfolio budget constraints

A portfolio of stocks can have many constituents in an effort to benefit from diversification. As more and more stocks are added to a portfolio, the variance of the portfolio can, in principle, get lower and lower if the stocks are not correlated. In practice, the majority of the benefit of diversification is achieved well before even 100 stocks are in the portfolio.

Optimising a portfolio of this size isn't as straightforward as a simple portfolio with just two assets. In this section, I show you some smart maths that can help you sort out problems of this kind.

The variance, V_p, of your portfolio, N, of risky assets depends on what proportion, p_i, of your fund is invested in each asset. These proportions must add up to 1. A technique called Lagrange multipliers minimises the portfolio variance while respecting the constraint that you remain 100 per cent invested.

The first step in using Lagrange multipliers is to build the function you want to minimise. I call it L:

$$L = V_p\left(p_1, p_2, ..., p_N\right) + \lambda\left(1 - \sum_{i=1}^{i=N} p_i\right).$$

The constant, λ, is the Lagrange multiplier. At the moment, you don't know its value but by doing a little maths you discover it. The term in brackets following the multiplier is just the constraint that the proportions add up to 1. The idea of Lagrange is to minimise this new function, L, which builds in the *constraint* (the condition that the proportions p_i must add up to 1) that you want to hold. You minimise in exactly the same way as before – by differentiating with respect to the proportions, p_i. The result is

$$\frac{\partial L}{\partial p_i} = 2p_i\sigma_i^2 - 2\lambda = 0.$$

LAGRANGE AND HIS FUNCTIONS

Joseph-Louis Lagrange was an 18th century Italian mathematician who made important contributions to many areas of maths and physics. He spent most of his time working in Berlin in what is now Germany and later moved to Paris where he worked on the decimal system.

His most famous work is on calculus and how to use it to minimise and maximise functions and even functions of functions. Physicists use his methods all the time because many laws of nature are principles about minimising or maximising something. Economists and quants have followed their lead when they saw that they could minimise risk using Lagrange's method .

You can solve this equation easily to find that

$$p_i = \lambda / 2\sigma_i^2.$$

But, λ is still unknown. No worries, though. You can substitute this equation for p_i back into the constraint equation to get the following:

$$\sum_{i=1}^{N} \frac{\lambda}{2\sigma_i^2} = 1.$$

To simplify the subsequent algebra I introduce a new quantity, Z, which is defined by the equation:

$$Z = \sum_{i=1}^{i=N} \frac{1}{\sigma_i^2} = 2 / \lambda.$$

Using Z, which you can calculate from the volatilities of your assets, you can find λ and also each of the p_i. They're given by the equation:

$$p_i = \frac{1}{Z\sigma_i^2}.$$

REMEMBER

A portfolio's asset proportions depend inversely on the square of the volatility of the assets. Highly volatile assets need significantly smaller weight in a portfolio even if, like in this example, they're uncorrelated with the other assets.

Using the formula for the value for p_i, the total variance of the minimum variance portfolio comes out as 1/Z. However, if all the variances of the assets are around the same value, say σ, then $Z \approx N / \sigma^2$. The variance of the optimal portfolio is then approximately σ^2 / N. A portfolio of N assets with no correlation and similar volatility has a total variance N times smaller than for any of the individual assets.

Doing the maths for returns and correlations

A theory about portfolios has to go beyond just looking at the variance of the returns of the portfolio and the assets of the portfolio. In the previous section, I show the benefits of diversification if the stocks are uncorrelated. However, most often stocks are correlated, meaning that if one stock rises in value then it's very likely (but not certain) that the other stocks will rise in value. And likewise, if one stock falls, the others are likely to fall. In addition, investors are concerned about the returns from their portfolios. You can try to maximise your returns while also benefiting from the risk reduction from diversification. Good has just got better. So, you need to include returns and correlations and not just variances.

Just like patting your head and rubbing your tummy at the same time, it can be tricky to maximise returns while minimising risk. Different people have different ways of doing it but I choose a straightforward method.

The idea is to use a utility function that incorporates the risk and return of an investment. Using an exponential utility function, which I talk about in Chapter 13, the certainty equivalent C_p (subscript p is for portfolio) for an investment portfolio with mean return, r_p, and return variance, σ_p^2, is

$$C_p = r_p - \frac{\lambda}{2}\sigma_p^2.$$

λ is a parameter that expresses your aversion to risk.

TECHNICAL STUFF

The exponential utility function for an amount of wealth, W, has the formula:

$$U(W) = -e^{-\lambda W}.$$

By making an assumption that the wealth, W, is a Gaussian random variable with mean r_p and variance, σ_p^2 you can work out that the certainty equivalent of such a portfolio is given by the preceding formula for C_p. Remember that you define the certainty equivalent C (Chapter 13 has more detail) using the expectation, E, for the portfolio with wealth, W, by the equation:

$$U(C) = E(U(W)).$$

The proof now involves calculating the expected value of the exponential of a random variable so I'll skip it here. The constant λ in the exponential utility function is the coefficient of *absolute risk aversion*. If you choose a high value of λ, then the optimal portfolio will have a low variance.

REMEMBER

The *utility function* assigns a value to any investment amount. However, this value depends on the probabilities of the investment ending up with a specific value at the end of the investment period. The *certainty equivalent* of an investment is the amount of money that has the same utility as the expected value at the end of the investment period. It's the cash equivalent of an investment.

If the portfolio variance, σ_p^2 is large, then any increase in it significantly reduces the utility C_p because of the negative sign in front of the λ. So a high value of λ means less chance of risky, high-variance stocks in the portfolio. With a small value of λ, risky stocks will not be penalised much. The parameter λ, therefore, controls the trade-off between risk and return.

To demonstrate how to use the formula for C_p, imagine a portfolio with only a single stock but also invested in cash, a risk-free asset. The proportion of the portfolio in the risky stock is p. The risk-free return on cash is r and the return on the stock is d. The portfolio return is r_p:

$$r_p = pd + (1-p)r.$$

If the volatility of the stock is σ, then the portfolio volatility is

$$\sigma_p = p\sigma.$$

The portfolio volatility is solely due to the risky asset but depends on its proportion p in the portfolio. You can now build the certainty equivalent utility C_p:

$$C_p = pd + (1-p)r - \frac{1}{2}\lambda p^2 \sigma^2.$$

To maximise C_p, just differentiate with respect to p and set the result equal to zero:

$$d - r - \lambda p \sigma^2 = 0$$

so that:

$$p = \frac{(d-r)}{\lambda \sigma^2}.$$

This formula shows several things:

>> The numerator is the *risk premium,* which is the yield of the risky asset in excess of the risk-free return, r. The higher the risk premium, the higher the proportion of the portfolio you should invest in the risky asset.

>> High volatility assets have a low weighting in the portfolio.

>> If you're risk averse with a high value of λ, then you put a lower amount into the risky asset.

This example shows how to use the certainty equivalent, C_p, for a risky asset and cash. Now I use the same method for a portfolio of N correlated assets. I call the correlation matrix for the assets $C_{i,j}$. (Chapter 9 explains correlation matrices.) The portfolio variance is now:

$$V_p = \sigma_p^2 = \sum_{i,j=1}^{N} p_i p_j C_{i,j}.$$

Using the portfolio proportions, p_i, the expected return for the portfolio, r_p, is

$$r_p = \sum_{i1}^{i=N} p_i r_i.$$

The constraint equation in which the portfolio proportions add up to one is

$$\sum_{i=1}^{i=N} p_i = 1.$$

REMEMBER

Because this analysis includes both the mean portfolio return and variance, you often hear it called *mean–variance analysis*.

The next step is to work out what to maximise so as to find the best portfolio to balance risk with reward. Unlike the previous example with a single risky asset and cash, you now have a number of risky assets, N, whose proportions must add up to one. You can do this with Lagrange multipliers as in the previous section 'Using portfolio budget constraints'. So, in fact, what you need is a Lagrange multiplier that's the certainty equivalent with the budget constraint term added. The certainty equivalent formula for C_p is taken from the previous section, but now you need sums over all of the N assets in the portfolio to work out the risk and the return terms. You also need to include the correlation matrix to work out the portfolio variance, and don't forget the budget constraint term beginning with γ! Putting all of that together you get

$$L = \sum_{i=1}^{i=N} p_i r_i - \frac{\lambda}{2} \sum_{i,j=1}^{N} p_i p_j C_{i,j} + \gamma \left[1 - \sum_{i=1}^{i=N} p_i \right].$$

The Lagrange multiplier for the budget constraint (to keep the sum of asset proportions equal to one) is γ and, again, the risk aversion parameter is λ.

TECHNICAL STUFF

You can now maximise this intimidating looking equation by taking derivatives with respect to the portfolio proportions, p_i, just as in the 'Minimising Portfolio Variance' section earlier in the chapter:

$$\frac{\partial L}{\partial p_j} = r_j - \lambda \sum_{i=1}^{i=N} C_{i,j} p_i - \gamma.$$

This set of N equations has N + 1 unknowns: the N portfolio proportions and the Lagrange multiplier γ.

By including the budget equation for the proportions, you get one more equation so you now have N + 1 equations and N + 1 unknowns. You can find the portfolio proportions from the equation:

$$p_i = \frac{1}{\lambda} \sum_{j=1}^{j=N} C_{i,j}^{-1} \left(r_j - \gamma \right).$$

Substituting this into the budget constraint for the proportions, you can then find the Lagrange multiplier, γ:

$$\gamma = \frac{-\lambda + \sum_{i,j=1}^{N} C_{i,j}^{-1} r_j}{\sum_{i,j=1}^{N} C_{i,j}^{-1}}.$$

The first of these equations gives you the asset proportions, p_i, for the portfolio that best balances risk and return. The second equation gives you the value for γ to ensure that you satisfy the budget constraint. Both equations depend on a given level of risk aversion determined by the parameter λ.

WARNING

Remember that $C_{i,j}$ is a matrix. So, to solve the equations, you need to use specialist software, although many spreadsheets include functions to invert matrices such as the correlation matrix $C_{i,j}$.

TECHNICAL STUFF

Although I used a Lagrange multiplier, γ, to enforce the budget constraint that the proportions of the assets must add up to one, the solution I've given is sometimes called the *unconstrained solution* because there's no constraint to ensure that the proportions are less than one and greater than zero. If you're able to sell assets short though, you won't need these constraints because – in effect – you can then have negative amounts of an asset. Also, if you can borrow money, then you can also have more than 100 per cent of an asset! More complex maths is needed to impose constraints – be happy that I'm not going there!

Building an efficient frontier

The equations for determining the proportion of each financial asset in a portfolio are best solved numerically. The process goes as follows:

1. **Calculate your expected returns, r_i, and the covariance of returns, $C_{i,j}$.**

2. **Decide on your value for risk aversion, λ.**

3. **Calculate the inverse of the covariance matrix.**

    You can find functions for this inverse in most spreadsheets.

4. **Calculate gamma from the formula:**

$$\gamma = \frac{-\lambda + \sum_{i,j=1}^{N} C_{i,j}^{-1} r_j}{\sum_{i,j=1}^{N} C_{i,j}^{-1}}.$$

5. **Calculate the portfolio proportions using the solution for p:**

$$p_i = \frac{1}{\lambda} \sum_{j=1}^{j=N} C_{i,j}^{-1} \left(r_j - \gamma \right).$$

6. Calculate the return and risk (portfolio standard deviation) using the equations:

$$r_p = \sum_{i1}^{i=N} p_i r_i$$

$$V_p = \sigma_p^2 = \sum_{i,j=1}^{N} p_i p_j C_{i,j}.$$

Figure 14-2 shows the result of a few calculations like this. It shows a curve called the *efficient frontier*. Portfolios that are optimal in the sense that they maximise the expected utility lie on the frontier. Other, less efficient, portfolios lie beneath the frontier with lower returns. Alternatively, you can stay to the right of the frontier with the same return but higher risk. Figure 14-2 shows that for high values of the risk aversion parameter, λ, the variance, σ_p^2, of the optimal portfolio has low variance or risk and the returns are low. On the other hand, if the risk aversion parameter λ is low then the optimal portfolio has high variance and high returns.

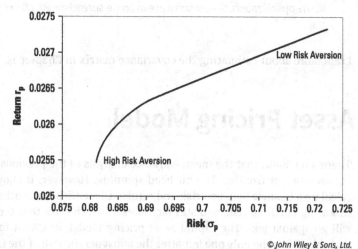

FIGURE 14-2: An efficient frontier curve using the parameter for risk aversion.

Dealing with poor estimates

Now's the time to own up: Mean-variance analysis often doesn't work well. This kind of analysis is the mathematical foundation of portfolio theory but when it meets the real world problems happen. Sound familiar? The concepts in the theory such as diversification are important, but some of the actual predictions are dodgy. The reason is that the parameters you need for the model, the correlation matrix and the expected returns especially are difficult to estimate.

You can find ways of dealing with the problem:

>> **Don't use historical data to make estimates.** These data is likely to be unreliable especially if you've calculated it from short time series.

>> **Use shrinkage.** Doing so is probably essential. The covariance is notoriously difficult to estimate, so if you try to optimise a portfolio using poor values, the predicted proportions may be way out. Best to be conservative and shrink the covariance matrix towards a diagonal matrix.

>> **Use a different utility function.** I've used an exponential utility function but you don't have to do that. You can use a utility function that includes both risk-averting and risk-loving behaviour. The problem is that other utility functions lead to much more complicated maths so maybe leave this problem to experts.

>> **Use constraints.** Sometimes the analysis can give poor answers perhaps with excessive weight in one stock. A solution to this problem is to use constraints in the optimisation. Solver software in some spreadsheets allows you to do this.

I talk more about estimating the covariance matrix in Chapter 13.

Capital Asset Pricing Model

There's no doubt that the mean-variance analysis in the previous section 'Building an efficient frontier' is a bit head spinning. However, it shows that you can calculate a balance between risk and return. Diversification works. But even after balancing portfolio risk, you still face *market risk*, the risk that the overall market will go against you. The capital asset pricing model, or CAPM for short, asserts that this risk is the only one left after the idiosyncratic risk of the individual stocks has been diversified away. This view is quite an extreme one that has been shown to be incorrect (it doesn't fit the data) but remains influential because of its simplicity. CAPM achieves maximum simplicity by treating the overall market as the only significant factor in the performance of investments. There can be some subtleties in using it, for example in deciding what the market portfolio is.

In 'Building an efficient frontier', I show what happens when you invest a portfolio of stocks. Now I turn to the slightly more complicated case when you can also invest in cash or some other risk-free asset such as a treasury bill (short-term loan to the government). I show the results of these calculations in Figure 14-3. The dashed line goes through the return axis at the value of the risk-free rate and touches the efficient frontier tangentially. This line is called the *capital market line.*

The point where this line touches the efficient frontier is called the *market portfolio*. Mixtures of the market portfolio and cash lie on the capital market line. Portfolios to the left of the market portfolio are in the region of high risk aversion (refer to Figure 14-2) and so are combinations of lending at the risk-free rate and the market portfolio. Portfolios on the capital market line to the right of the market portfolio are in the region of low risk aversion and are combinations of borrowing at the risk-free rate and the market portfolio.

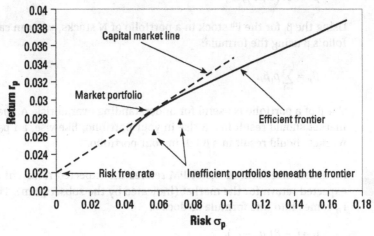

FIGURE 14-3:
Efficient frontier and the capital market line.

Because in CAPM the only risk is assumed to be due to the market, you can write the returns, R_t, for a given stock in a portfolio as a linear function of the market returns X_t:

$$R_t = \alpha + \beta X_t + \varepsilon_t.$$

This equation has two parameters:

REMEMBER

> » α is the mispricing of the stock relative to the market. α should be 0 if the market is efficient.
>
> In an efficient market, you can't do better than the market itself. If α is greater than 0, returns will clearly exceed that for the market.
>
> » β is the sensitivity of the stock to the market. If β is greater than 1, then the stock is high risk and its returns (positive and negative) are higher than that for the market. If β is less than 1, the stock is low risk and its returns are lower than that for the market.
>
> » In addition, ε is the residual risk for the specific stock. It's assumed that this risk can be diversified away by investing in many stocks.

REMEMBER

α and β have become iconic parameters in the vocabulary of hedge fund managers. If the returns, R_t, are for an investment or trading strategy, then α represents the extra return that the manager is generating from his activity. β measures the risk that can't be diversified away.

You can calculate β for a stock from the covariance, $\mathrm{cov}(R,X)$, between the returns of the stock and the returns of the market and the variance, σ_X^2, of the market:

$$\beta = \mathrm{cov}(R,X)/\sigma_X^2.$$

Using the β_i for the ith stock in a portfolio of N stocks, you can calculate the portfolio's β using the formula:

$$\beta_p = \sum_{i=1}^{i=N} p_i\beta_i.$$

The β of a portfolio is useful for understanding overall risk. A 1 per cent rise in the market should result in a β rise in your portfolio; likewise, a 1 per cent fall in the market should result in a β fall in your portfolio.

TIP

An alternative form of the CAPM relates the expected return of a stock, μ, to the expected return for the market (indicated by the subscript m). The risk-free rate, r_f, comes into this formula as does β:

$$\mu = r_f + \beta(\mu_m - r_f).$$

Assessing Portfolio Performance

Figuring out which investments to make and comparing the performance of investment funds is no simple task. However, investment managers need informative performance indicators to make good decisions. In this section, I show you how to do this task with some simple indicators of risk-adjusted return.

Sharpe ratio

The first and probably most important measure of portfolio performance is the Sharpe ratio. This ratio is an example of a *risk-adjusted performance measure* because both portfolio returns and volatility are used in the calculation. If the risk-free interest rate is r_f and the portfolio return r_p, then the Sharpe ratio, S, is defined as:

$$S = \left. (r_p - r_f) \middle/ \sigma_p \right.$$

The denominator is the annualised portfolio volatility and the returns are annual returns.

TIP

If the returns and volatility are both calculated from daily data, then you need to make a correction to annualise the Sharpe ratio. The returns should be multiplied by T, the number of trading days in the year, and the volatility must be multiplied by $\sqrt{T}$. This is, yet again, the square root of time rule. So, doing a little bit of algebra in your head (don't worry I won't ask you to do this again), you need to multiply the daily Sharpe ratio by the $\sqrt{T}$ to get the normal annual Sharpe ratio.

Referring to Figure 14-3, the slope of the capital market line is the Sharpe ratio of the market portfolio. Remember that the y-axis on the chart is returns and the x-axis is risk or σ. Also, because the line drawn is the steepest possible line starting at the risk-free interest rate and intersecting the efficient frontier, the market portfolio is the point on the efficient frontier with the highest Sharpe ratio. In risk-adjusted returns terms, the market portfolio is the best portfolio.

An investment with a Sharpe ratio of 1 is considered to be excellent, and you need a good trading strategy to achieve this. Let me know if you work out how to do this task, please!

The stock market has a Sharpe ratio of around 0.3. However, Sharpe ratios are numbers calculated from the historical performance of a fund. They're actually estimates of the Sharpe ratio calculated from a sample and so have a margin of error. You can get an idea of this error by using formulae from Chapter 13. The error on an average calculated from N data points is

$$\frac{\sigma}{\sqrt{N}}.$$

It turns out (although I'm not going to prove it here) that this is the main error – not the error from the estimate of the standard deviation of the returns – for small Sharpe ratios. So the error in the estimate of the Sharpe ratio, ΔS, is

$$\Delta S = \frac{1}{\sqrt{N}}.$$

The σ has cancelled from the formula. Thinking now of the annual Sharpe ratio where there are n years of trading data so that N = 250 × n, the error in the annual Sharpe ratio is

$$\Delta S_{annual} = \sqrt{\frac{250}{N}} = \frac{1}{\sqrt{n}}.$$

This means that for an equity strategy with a low Sharpe ratio of around 0.3, the error in the annual Sharpe ratio is almost as large as the Sharpe ratio itself even with ten years of data.

Be sceptical of claims about the performance of hedge funds and mutual funds!

Drawdowns

You may be wondering about volatility-adjusted returns, thinking that surely only the average returns matter. In practice, the volatility affects investors greatly. Figure 14-1 shows the portfolio rises steadily, almost like a bank account. A volatile investment has significant drawdowns. A *drawdown* is a decline in the price of an asset or portfolio of assets from its current value. If the probability of a large drawdown is high, that's bad news for the portfolio. Nobody wants an investment worth substantially less than what it was or indeed what he paid for it. After time, T, the price of an asset that follows the geometric Brownian motion described in Chapter 3 is P(T). I denote the average return by r and the volatility by σ as usual. ε is a Gaussian noise with a mean of 0 and standard deviation of 1:

$$P(T) = P(0)e^{rT + \varepsilon\sigma\sqrt{T}}.$$

In this formula, I use the square root of time rule again (see Chapter 7). For the expected returns to be more important than the Gaussian fluctuations, the first term in the exponent must exceed the second term so that:

$$rT > \sigma\sqrt{T}.$$

You can rewrite this formula as:

$$T > \sigma^2 / r^2.$$

which shows that, for times longer than this, the probability that P(T) is less than P(0) is small. That's because, for longer times, the growth from the expected returns overcomes the fluctuations. I write this characteristic time scale as $\underline{T}$. The typical decline, D, in the asset price that occurs in this timescale is yet another application of the square root of time rule. The volatility gets multiplied by the square root of the typical time scale:

$$D = \sqrt{\sigma^2 \underline{T}} = \sqrt{\sigma^4 / r^2} = \sigma^2 / r.$$

(Please don't yawn; you're just getting good at this!)

This calculation is based on general principles so as to show how the typical drawdown depends on the volatility and mean return. A more accurate calculation shows that:

$$D = \sigma^2 / 2r.$$

An excellent investment fund with a Sharpe ratio of 1 with, say, $\sigma = 0.2$ and $r = 0.2$ has $T = 1$ year. A drawdown lasting much longer than a year would be unusual. So, even for an excellent fund, drawdowns can be unpleasant and unnerving. Also, a more typical investment such as an equity fund with $\sigma = 0.2$ and $r = 0.1$ has $T =$ four years. You may have a long wait before your fund gets back above water.

Going for risk parity

Risk parity is a way of constructing investment portfolios that emphasises balance between different investment classes such as equities, bonds and commodities. It recognises that correlations can be unstable and so a more fundamental and less mathematical approach to portfolio construction can work.

REMEMBER

The correlation measures the strength of the statistical relationship between two assets. Its value is between -1 and 1. If the assets tend to move together, the correlation is close to 1, whilst if one moves up whilst the other moves down, then the correlation will be close to -1. You need a correlation matrix if you have many assets because you can then calculate the correlation between each of the assets in the portfolio.

That's despite the fact that Harry Markowitz, who invented it, won a Nobel prize for his work. Portfolio optimisation is probably more craft than science. Estimating correlations is fraught with difficulty because they're unstable.

REMEMBER

During most periods of time, government bonds are anti-correlated with equities. This situation happens when economic growth and inflation pick up, which is good for equities but bad for bonds. If investors like what they see, they buy equities to increase the growth potential of their portfolio and fund that purchase by selling bonds. Note that the reverse is true as well – investors sell equities and buy bonds if they see the promised growth stalling for some reason.

However, the market doesn't stay in the same condition forever. If a situation arises when the market expects inflation to start falling, then both equities and bonds tend to do well. That's because the present value of their dividends or coupons suddenly becomes more valuable because the interest rate tends to be low if inflation is low. In this new situation, bonds and equities can become correlated. That's the opposite of the situation with rising growth and inflation. Worse is that the market can flip quickly from a correlated to an anti-correlated state. Creating a portfolio that is robust to these changes isn't easy but makes a lot of sense.

Another way of building a portfolio is to ignore the correlations (which may change soon anyway) but pay attention to the risk. In fact, I do that earlier in the chapter in the section 'Using portfolio budget constraints'. The result shows how to weight portfolio assets depending upon their volatility. The risk parity approach to portfolio construction takes this weighting further and ensures that different asset classes (equities, commodities, stocks or even property) all have the same risk allocated to them. In other words, the fluctuations in the asset value of the portfolio can be equally attributed to all the asset classes.

The concept of risk parity can be taken a stage further. By placing equal amounts of risk into different asset classes, your portfolio is more likely to achieve a consistent performance. However, potentially it can be made more robust still by considering that inflation and economic growth are the main influence on portfolio performance. More accurately, it is unexpected changes in inflation and growth that can influence your portfolio because expected changes are already reflected in current prices.

TIP

Split your portfolio into four quarters, with each quarter designed to do well in a specific market condition – rising inflation, falling inflation and rising growth and falling growth. This split means that the portfolio can do well consistently over time irrespective of market conditions and not fall dramatically if an unexpected event occurs.

Chapter 15

Measuring Potential Losses: Value at Risk (VaR)

Just how bad can things get? That is the question that the value at risk (VaR) measure attempts to answer. Losing money is never fun so getting a heads-up on the scale of potential losses is a great idea. However, doing so is never going to be easy.

Getting down to the maths, *VaR (value at risk)* is defined as the maximum loss a portfolio will experience at a specified confidence level over a specified time horizon. Sometimes VaR is written VaR^α and the confidence level is indicated as a superscript, α.

The chief executive of JPMorgan Chase & Co, one of the largest investment banks in the United States, once said, 'I don't pay that much attention to VaR'. So why should you? Well, VaR is used extensively for internal risk management by many financial institutions and has been part of financial regulation for many years. Although it has defects, VaR is still a useful statistic. The scepticism of JPMorgan's chief executive is probably based more on an understanding of the measure's weaknesses than on recklessness. This type of scepticism is healthy as it leads you to question the assumptions used in risk models and to devise better ways to test them.

The Basel Committee of the Bank for International Settlements (often called the central bankers' bank) makes specific recommendations for the use of VaR and other similar methodologies, such as stress VaR and expected shortfall. Remember, though, that before the ink is dry on any new regulation someone, somewhere, will be working out ways to circumvent it, and new forms of risk will be being created. The hunt for profits drives this.

In this chapter, I explain VaR and touch on its strengths and weaknesses. It's a ubiquitous tool in finance used for managing risk by financial managers working at trading desks or for large portfolios with a diverse range of instruments. It's also used for calculating *regulatory capital* – the amount of capital banks are required to hold to cover for unexpected losses.

Controlling Risk in Your Portfolio

Risk can be controlled by a financial institution, such as a bank, in a number of ways. The most important is by hedging. Chapter 5 gives you the lowdown on *hedging*, which is simply trading designed to protect against adverse price movements.

You can quantify the effect of changes of market prices or volatility on your portfolio. That's helpful, but most large institutions hold many different financial instruments that can't all be characterised by the same parameters. One of the big benefits of VaR is that it simplifies risk monitoring by providing a single number irrespective of what the asset is. So VaR can calculate risk in an interest-rate derivative, a bond or a futures contract.

In addition, VaR can be *aggregated* (a fancy word for adding up everything that affects what you're interested in, which, in this case, is risk) across products and currencies to give an overall measure of the riskiness of an institution's positions. This measure is especially important as diversification is one of the key ways to reduce risk. By holding a large portfolio of instruments, you can reduce risk. (See Chapter 14 for more about diversification.) VaR gives you a good way of monitoring a large diverse portfolio of financial instruments.

A key application of VaR is by banking regulators to determine how much capital banks must hold for the risks they're taking. This subject is constantly evolving. You can check in at www.bis.org, the website for the Bank for International Settlements, to get the latest update.

Defining Volatility and the VaR Measure

Financial risk is often quantified by volatility. Chapter 7 tells all about *volatility*, which is the standard deviation of the returns of a financial instrument and is easy to calculate. But volatility does have a few drawbacks:

>> Volatility is calculated by summing the square of the returns of an asset, irrespective of whether they're positive or negative, and then taking the average. This calculation gives equal consideration to both gains and losses, which doesn't correspond with what most financial professionals think of as risk: financial people consider losses as risk; they don't think of gains as risk.

>> Volatility is a parameter closely associated with the normal, or Gaussian, distribution of returns. In fact, the volatility gives an indication of the width of the distribution and so tells you mostly about small values for returns around the centre of the distribution. However, what's important for risk managers are large losses, which are shown in the tails of the return distribution.

>> Extreme events can lead to bad estimates of the volatility. If you calculate volatility with a simple moving average and miss out some recent large losses then you can badly underestimate risk.

REMEMBER

Value at risk is about the probability of losing an amount, X, over a period of N days in which the portfolio isn't managed. Your VaR is X if the probability of losing an amount X or more over the next N days is α per cent. To correctly specify VaR, you need to give both the holding period, N (usually in days), and the significance level, α.

>> The holding period (N) depends on why you're calculating VaR. If you're managing a desk trading government bonds, N may be just one day; if you're managing a less frequently traded instrument or corporate loans, N may be as long as a year.

>> The significance level, α, is also determined by the purpose of calculating VaR. Bank regulators want to be sure that their banks don't run into problems so they often specify $\alpha = 0.01$. If you're running a trading desk, then $\alpha = 0.05$ may be more appropriate.

Normally α is a small number such as 1 per cent or 5 per cent. VaR is usually quoted as a positive number even though it refers to losses.

TIP

A good alternative to using α is to use $1 - \alpha$. $1 - \alpha$ is the confidence level that your loss will be no worse than VaR. For example, if $\alpha = 0.01$, then you have a 99 per cent confidence that your loss would be less than VaR.

If the probability density function for returns over a period of N days is $P_N(x)$, you can express this definition for VaR using an equation. Chapter 2 has the full explanation probability density functions. In summary, though, if P(x) is a probability density function then P(x)dx is the probability that the random variable x lies in a range of width, dx, around the value x:

$$\int_{-\infty}^{x} P_N(x)dx = \alpha.$$

This equation means that if you integrate the probability density function from the far left (−∞) up to a loss of X, the area (= probability) is α. The shaded area of the probability distribution function in Figure 15-1 indicates the fraction of the returns that are greater than the loss X.

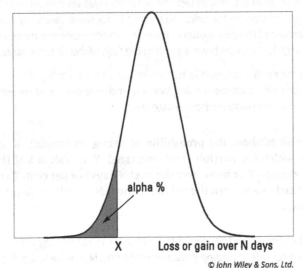

alpha %

X   Loss or gain over N days

© John Wiley & Sons, Ltd.

FIGURE 15-1:
A probability
density function.

As an example, if α = 0.01 (or 1 per cent), then you'd only expect a loss greater than X once every 100 days. As the holding period in the definition of VaR increases, then VaR increases. It does so because with more time available losses are more likely. But, as the significance increases, the VaR must decrease because more frequently occurring smaller losses must be included.

It's worth knowing that in the next time period of N days you also have the possibility of a loss of X. So losses can potentially pile up.

TIP

Also worth noticing is that the definition of VaR refers only to the end point of the time period of N days. It doesn't take into account the maximal loss during the time period.

Another way of showing VaR is by using a cumulative distribution function, as shown in Figure 15-2, which shows VaR(X) at α level of significance. Here, α appears on the y axis rather than as the area of a shaded region.

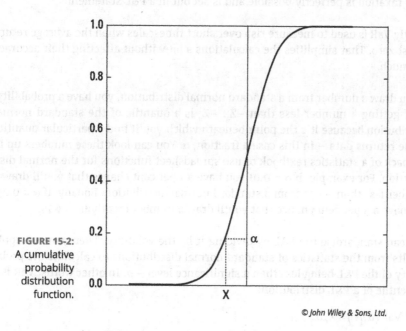

FIGURE 15-2:
A cumulative
probability
distribution
function.

Constructing VaR using the Covariance Matrix

In a world where you assume that financial returns are governed by the normal distribution, you can calculate the VaR directly from the variances and covariances of the assets in a portfolio. You also need to know how much of each asset is in the portfolio.

REMEMBER

The *variance* is the square of the standard deviation. It's the average of the squared deviations from the average value. The *covariance* is a statistical relationship between two variables and is a measure of how much they move together.

The value of a portfolio now at time, t, is P_t and the value at the end of the N day period is P_{t+N}. Then your profit and loss (P&L) is $P_{t+N} - P_t$. The assumption in this method of calculating VaR is that this P&L is normally distributed with an average of μ and volatility σ.

TECHNICAL STUFF

Profit *and* loss (P&L) is slightly confusing terminology because you make a profit *or* a loss – not both. But the expression comes from accounting where a number of figures are presented. For example, making a profit before taxation but a loss after taxation is perfectly possible and is set out in a P&L statement.

Mostly VaR is used to measure risk over short timescales when the average return is just zero. That simplifies the calculations a bit without affecting their accuracy too much.

REMEMBER

If you draw a number from a standard normal distribution, you have a probability, α, of getting a number less than $-Z_\alpha$. $-Z_\alpha$ is a quantile of the standard normal distribution because it's the point beneath which you'll find a particular quantity of the returns data – in this case a fraction, α. You can look these numbers up in the back of a statistics textbook or use spreadsheet functions for the normal distribution. For example, if $\alpha = 0.01$ you have a 1 per cent chance that you'll draw a number less than -2.33 from a standard normal distribution. Equally, if $\alpha = 0.05$, you have a 5 per cent chance that you'll draw a number less than -1.645.

You can standardise the P&L by dividing it by the volatility. Then you can apply results from the statistics of standard normal distributions to calculate the probability of the P&L being less than a significance level – α. In other words, VaR is a percentile of a P&L distribution:

$$\mathrm{VaR}(\alpha, N) = Z_\alpha \sigma.$$

In this formula, the values of α and N are in brackets to remind you that VaR is always specified by the level of significance and the time period.

Calculating a simple cash portfolio

To calculate VaR for a single asset such as a stock, start with the N = 1 day VaR. You can then use the square root of time rule to calculate the N day VaR.

Say you have €5 million in BMW shares. The daily volatility is 1.8 per cent. The standard deviation in the daily value of this position is 1.8 per cent of €5 million or €90,000. Using the formula for VaR from the previous section, the one-day VaR at a significance level of 1 per cent is 2.33 × 90,000 = €209,700. If you now want to calculate the N-day VaR for this position, you just have to multiply by √N. For example, 10-day VaR for BMW is:

$$\mathrm{VaR}(\alpha = 0.01, N = 10) = \sqrt{10} \times 2.33 \times 90{,}000 = 663{,}130.$$

Using the covariance matrix

You can also use the statistics of normal distributions to calculate the VaR of portfolios with more than one asset. To do this, you need the covariance matrix $C_{i,j}$. This matrix is introduced in Chapter 9. You calculate the standard deviation of a portfolio with N stocks from the formula:

$$\sigma_p^2 = \sum_{i,j=1}^{N} p_i p_j C_{i,j}.$$

This formula is for the standard deviation of the portfolio price changes $P_{t+N} - P_t$ and the p_i are the nominal amounts (amounts expressed in currency units such as dollars) of each stock. For a portfolio with only two stocks, you can use the definition of the correlation ρ (see Chapter 9):

$$C_{1,2} = \rho \sigma_1 \sigma_2$$

to write the formula for the portfolio standard deviation (squared) as:

$$\sigma_p^2 = p_1^2 C_{1,1} + p_2^2 C_{2,2} + 2\rho p_1 p_2 \sigma_1 \sigma_2 = p_1^2 \sigma_1^2 + p_2^2 \sigma_2^2 + 2\rho p_1 p_2 \sigma_1 \sigma_2.$$

The covariance, $C_{1,1}$, is the square of the volatility of the first share while $C_{2,2}$ is the square of the volatility for the second share. I use that after the second equality sign.

As an example of using this formula, I expand on the example used in the previous section. So, in addition to 5 million € in BMW shares, your portfolio has 10 million € in Daimler Benz shares. The correlation between the shares is 0.87. That's a high number because both BMW and Daimler make cars. Their share prices respond to the same risk factors, such as the unemployment rate and oil price, so they both tend to rise and fall together.

You can now use the formula for the portfolio standard deviation. I abbreviate numbers – 5 million as 5m, for example – so as to keep the arithmetic on a single line:

$$\sigma_p^2 = \left(15m \times 0.018\right)^2 + \left(10m \times 0.017\right)^2 + 2 \times 0.87 \times 5m \times 0.018 \times 10m \times 0.017.$$

If you do the arithmetic, it comes out at 252,234€. To get the one-day VaR, you now just multiply this value by 2.33 to get:

One day VaR at 1% significance = 252,234 × 2.33 = euros 587,705.

Estimating Volatilities and Correlations

In Chapter 7 on volatility, I show how you can estimate the volatility using an exponentially weighted moving average. To remind you, I show the equation below so that you can compare with the equation for the covariance:

$$\sigma_{i,t+1}^2 = \lambda \sigma_{i,t}^2 + (1-\lambda) r_{i,t}^2.$$

The index, i, indicates that the equation is for the ith asset in the portfolio and the t indicates the day. The parameter λ is a smoothing parameter. You can also use this technique to calculate the covariance matrix and the correlations. I write the covariance between asset i and asset j at time, t, as $C_{ij,t}$. The return for asset i at time t is $r_{i,t}$. Now you can write the formula for the covariance in terms of the covariance for the previous day:

$$C_{ij,t+1} = \lambda C_{ij,t} + (1-\lambda) r_{i,t} r_{j,t}.$$

This formula for the covariance is of the same form as the formula for the volatility and with the same value for the smoothing parameter λ. In fact, in the equation for the covariance, if you set i = j, then it's the same as the equation for the volatility provided that:

$$C_{ii,t} = \sigma_{i,t}^2.$$

The volatility is just a special case of the covariance, the diagonal elements of the covariance matrix as shown in Figure 15-3.

FIGURE 15-3:
A covariance
matrix has
diagonal
elements equal to
squared volatility.

$$\begin{pmatrix} \sigma_1^2 & \cdots & C_{1,N} \\ \vdots & \searrow & \vdots \\ C_{N,1} & \cdots & \sigma_N^2 \end{pmatrix}$$

To calculate the correlation, ρ, between two assets, all you have to do is divide the covariance by the volatilities for both asset i and asset j. In this formula, I dropped the subscript t as it is the same for all terms in the equation:

$$\rho_{ij} = \frac{C_{ij}}{\sigma_i \sigma_j}.$$

Simulating the VaR

In the section 'Constructing VaR Using the Covariance Matrix' earlier in this chapter, I show how you can work out VaR if you know the covariance matrix of assets in your portfolio. This relies on the assumption that the distribution of returns is normal. You can, however, break free of this assumption by making use of historical returns data. Doing so has the additional benefit of using data that directly reflects the correlations between the returns of the assets.

Using historical data

The historical simulation of VaR does what it says on the can and uses historical data to simulate the empirical probability density for the portfolio P&L. To get reliable results, you need at least a year's worth of daily data, but more is better and five years of data would be safer.

For a portfolio with N stocks and (M+1) days of data, the following is what you need to do to calculate VaR:

1. **For each of the N stocks, calculate the M values for the returns starting from the second day in your data set.**

Call these $r_{i,j}$. That's the return on the ith stock on the jth day.

2. **Using the portfolio amounts, calculate the portfolio value on the last day of the data set.**

Assume that this is the current day, and you want to know the one-day VaR so that you can figure out what your losses may be tomorrow. If you have n_i shares in the ith stock and its price is $p_{i,j}$ on the jth day, then the portfolio value, P, on the last day M+1 of the data set is:

$$P(M+1) = \sum_{i=1}^{N} p_{i,M+1} n_i.$$

3. **Using the returns calculated in Step 1, starting from day j = 2, calculate the price for each stock on day M+2:**

$$p_{i,M+2} = (1 + r_{i,j}) p_{i,M+1}.$$

In doing this, you're assuming that the returns process for tomorrow will be similar to the historical returns process from the data set.

4. From these calculated prices for the stocks on day M + 2 from Step 3, you can now calculate the portfolio value on day M + 2 using exactly the same numbers, n_i, as you used to calculate the original portfolio value:

$$P(M+2) = \sum_{i=1}^{N} p_{i,M+2} n_i.$$

5. Repeat Step 4 for the remaining M − 1 values for the returns for each stock so that you now have M values for the portfolio on day M + 2.

6. Put these portfolio values into ascending order, starting from the worst loss.

   If you want to calculate the VaR at a significance level of α, then find the number in this sequence of portfolio values.

   This number is the VaR for this level of significance because, given this data set, there is a probability of α of getting a loss less than this number.

The nice thing about this method is that you're using real data, so it exactly reflects the correlations between the asset returns.

WARNING

Some potential pitfalls come with this method of calculating VaR. In particular, the data set you choose may represent a period when the market was in a definite trend not representative of how it will be in the future. Going further back in time can help as can selecting a specific period in the past when the market was stressed.

Spinning a Monte Carlo simulation

The Monte Carlo simulation method of calculating VaR is, in a way, a hybrid between using historical data and the method described in 'Using the covariance matrix' earlier in the chapter. You can find out more about this technique in Chapter 10.

This method also requires a covariance matrix calculated from historical data. However, after you calculate the covariance matrix, you use it to generate simulated price series for all of the assets in your portfolio assuming that the returns follow a Gaussian process.

The Monte Carlo simulation must use random numbers that have the same covariance as the historical data. To do this, you need to use the Cholesky decomposition of the covariance matrix. This decomposition needs to be done using maths software such as Matlab, R or the SciPy module for the Python programming language.

TECHNICAL STUFF

If you have a covariance matrix, V, the Cholesky decomposition of V is the matrix C such that $V = CC^T$. Remember that both V and C are matrices, so in the formula you use matrix multiplication and not ordinary multiplication. Also, the T superscript indicates that you have to calculate the transpose of that Cholesky decomposition matrix. Now, to use the Cholesky decomposition:

1. **Generate N random numbers from a standard normal distribution.**

   A standard normal distribution has a mean of zero and a standard deviation of one. I'll call the N random numbers that I generate from the standard distribution X. X is a vector because there are N numbers.

2. **Multiply X by C to get N numbers that reflect the covariance of your data.**

   In other words – and this is the clever bit – you calculate y = CX. Remember this formula involves matrix multiplication because there are N random numbers.

TIP

The advantage of using a Monte Carlo simulation is that it generates a price time series for each asset. If your portfolio contains assets such as options that depend upon the path the price takes, you can value these assets with this method.

The disadvantage of using Monte Carlo simulation is that it assumes that the returns distribution is normal. It can also be time consuming to generate the large volume of random numbers needed.

Validating Your Model

The Bank for International Settlements (BIS) sets out an approach for banks to calculate their *minimum regulatory capital*, defined as the amount of capital a bank needs to be considered a viable concern by its creditors and counterparties. Normally, these capital requirements are calculated using measures such as VaR, so banks need to check these calculations thoroughly.

TECHNICAL STUFF

So what is a bank's capital? Usually the capital is a mixture of equity, debt and retained profits that banks hold in reserve to support their business. The regulator distinguishes between Tier 1 and Tier 2 capital: The main difference is that Tier 1 is a more sure and certain form of capital such as retained earnings and largely excludes innovative forms of capital constructed from risky loans.

Backtesting

Backtesting is a form of reality check on VaR calculations. You can check out how well your VaR predictions would have worked in the past. The loss given by VaR should be exceeded only α per cent of the time. So, if you go back in time with your data, work out how many times the actual loss exceeded the VaR from your model. When this situation occurs, it's called an *exception*.

WARNING

If your VaR significance is five per cent but you have exceptions ten per cent of the time, then you probably have a problem with your model.

Stress testing and the Basel Accord

The Bank for International Settlements has introduced a new form of VaR called *stress VaR*, or simply *SVaR*. In concept, SVaR is simple: Calculate VaR using data from a period of extreme volatility – for example, the credit crisis during 2007 and 2008.

The point is to avoid *pro-cyclical* estimates of VaR. Sometimes markets can enter a phase of overconfidence. Participants believe that things are going well but they've only forgotten how bad things can get. Volatility is low and VaR estimates are low. This situation encourages even greater risk-taking just before a crash happens.

SVaR is a good reality check to make. The Basel committee recommends using a significance of one per cent and a time horizon of ten days. To ensure that your volatility does indeed reflect the stressed days during the period of the data set, you're best calculating it using a simple standard deviation of the returns and not an exponentially weighted moving average (EWMA). The EWMA may inadvertently give low weights to the stressful days.

Including the Average VaR

The definition of VaR I use in the previous sections of this chapter is widely used, but it has defects. VaR refers to losses that occur with a probability of α but doesn't say anything about losses with a smaller probability, which means that there may be the possibility of a rare event with particularly high losses that wouldn't affect the VaR number.

Say you have a portfolio of £100 million and the one-day 5 per cent VaR is £1 million. Every 20 days you stand to lose £1 million or more. Don't despair though; remember that markets go up as well as down! However, now you have a new possibility of losing £5 million or more with a probability of 1 per cent. Sadly, the 5 per cent VaR figure didn't say anything about the magnitude of the losses you may experience except that they're bigger than £1 million. If you knew they could be £5 million every 100 days, you'd reconsider this investment.

To illustrate this problem with the definition of VaR, take a look at Figure 15-4. It shows two statistical distributions of returns with an equal value of VaR, which you can tell because the shaded areas are of equal size. The VaR is 2 for both cases as the shaded regions both extend to −2. (Remember that VaR is quoted as a positive number.) However, a big difference exists between the distributions. The graph in Figure 15-4 b has a blip at the large value of −4 and so potential losses are much larger. VaR tells you nothing about this blip, so it can be misleading.

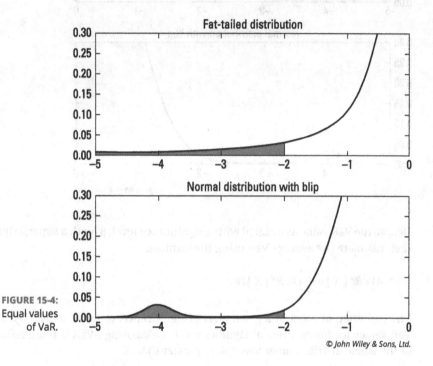

FIGURE 15-4:
Equal values
of VaR.

© John Wiley & Sons, Ltd.

If I'd chosen a smaller value of α in Figure 15-4 – about half the value in fact – the value for VaR would have turned out differently. That's because of the different shape of the probability distributions in the left tail associated with large losses. I show this different shape in Figure 15-5, which shows that for the same value of the significance (equal shaded areas), the VaR for the blip distribution is 4 while for the fat-tailed distribution the VaR is only 3. The VaR figure can be a bit misleading depending on the shape of the probability distribution.

A proposed solution for this problem with VaR is to use another risk measure called *expected shortfall*. As if to confuse the unwary, this shortfall is sometimes called *conditional VaR* or just *Average VaR* (abbreviated to *AVaR* normally). This measure answers the question, 'If things get bad, how much can we expect to lose?' It does this by taking an average value of the VaR.

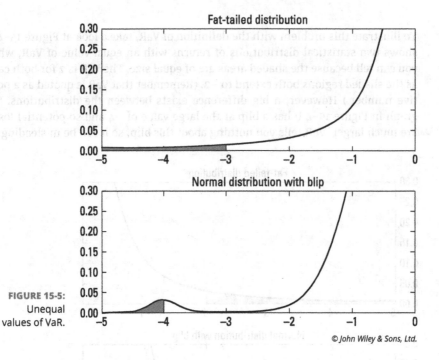

FIGURE 15-5:
Unequal
values of VaR.

© John Wiley & Sons, Ltd.

Denote the VaR value associated with a significance level, β, with a superscript and then calculate the average VaR using the formula:

$$AVaR^\alpha(X) = \frac{1}{\alpha}\int_0^\alpha VaR^\beta(X)d\beta.$$

The definition of AVaR at a given level of significance, α, takes an average of the VaR values for lower levels of significance, β. Calculating AVaR is more reflective of the whole distribution at loss values greater than X.

TECHNICAL STUFF

An advantage of using expected shortfall, or AVaR, is that it satisfies the condition of *subadditivity*, or the advantage of diversification you get when you combine investments. In other words, diversifying lowers your risk. Mathematically this condition states, for a risk measure, ρ, that:

$$\rho(X+Y) \le \rho(X) + \rho(Y).$$

Surprisingly, the simple VaR risk measure doesn't satisfy subadditivity. Intuitively, it's a condition you'd like a risk measure to satisfy because only then is the risk of two combined investments less than the sum of the individual risks of each investment. You want your risk measure to reflect this reality. The Basel committee of the BIS introduced the use of expected shortfall after the credit crisis of 2007/2008. Better late than never!

Estimating Tail Risk with Extreme Value Theory

It somehow makes sense to focus on exceptional or extreme losses rather than common or garden losses. Most market participants are used to their portfolio moving up and down in value by small amounts and take that in stride. What they really want to know, however, is what the big loss might be like. A special form of statistics looks at the frequency of these large losses (and gains) and is called *extreme value statistics*.

The normal probability distribution predicts that large market moves are much less frequent than they actually are. The world's a more exciting and dangerous place than statistics textbooks would have you believe.

A way of looking at this situation is to work out the probability distribution of the maximum value of N independent and identically distributed (sometimes abbreviated *iid*) random numbers. These independent distributions don't have to be normal, and so the results of extreme value theory are quite general. I define

$$X = \max\left(X_1, X_2, \ldots, X_N\right).$$

THE RARITY OF BLACK MONDAY

On Monday, 19 October 1987, stock markets across the world suffered one of their worst days ever. In the United Kingdom, the FTSE 100 index declined by 10.8 per cent from 2301.9 to 2052.3. No wonder that day's now called Black Monday. Even worse was that on the following day, the FTSE 100 fell by another 12.2 per cent.

In the previous year, the standard deviation of daily returns (here I'm defining return as price today minus price yesterday, not taking a ratio with the previous day's price) on the FTSE 100 index had been approximately 15. So, the fall of almost 250 points on 19 October was more than a 10 standard deviation event.

According to the normal distribution, these events should be so rare you'd have to wait for longer than the age of the universe (14 billion years) before one comes along. So the stock market crash on Black Monday was a bit more than bad luck. It shows that the normal distribution does not apply to these kinds of extreme events and that a better form of statistics is required to understand tail events.

Then, if X is standardised by subtracting a location parameter, α, and dividing by scale parameter, β, so that:

$$Y = (X - \alpha) / \beta,$$

then the approximate distribution function of extreme values y is

$$F(Y) = \text{Probability}(y > Y) = \exp\left(-(1 + \xi y)^{-1/\xi}\right).$$

The parameter ξ is typically positive for distributions that occur in finance and is called the *tail index*.

Using a distribution of this kind is probably best left to experts. It can be difficult to fit and apply this distribution to a diversified portfolio, but it's good to know that someone's thought about measuring what's happening in the tail of returns distributions.

6

Market Trading and Strategy

Chapter 16

Forecasting Markets

I s it possible to forecast markets? If markets are efficient and correctly reflect current information, it should be impossible to accurately predict their movements. In an efficient market, each price change is independent of earlier price changes. Prices should be like random numbers, not capable of being forecast.

However, many market participants definitely don't see things that way. For a start, many hedge funds and active fund managers charge their customers a lot of money to anticipate market movements. Some fail but others are systematically successful. High frequency traders attempt to exploit market inefficiencies on particularly short timescales down to microseconds. Some of their successes may be due to having better hardware (faster computers and communication links) than their competitors but they also rely on good predictive models of markets.

In this chapter, I look at well-established ways of trying to forecast markets. Some involve using charts, others use maths and statistics. In both cases, you need lots of data.

A commonly used mathematical method is to try to detect patterns in the historical price movements of an asset and see whether those patterns persist into the future. Another method is to try to discover a *leading indicator*, an economic factor used to predict a market price before it changes. This indicator defies the efficient market hypothesis (EMH) but doesn't stop people from trying methods like these.

REMEMBER

The *efficient market hypothesis (EMH)* says that financial asset prices fully reflect available information. In principle this makes gathering information such as leading indicators futile because the information should already be incorporated into prices.

The efficiency of markets means that your model needs to predict just a small fraction of the market movements for it to be useful. Indeed, that's all you're ever likely to achieve. With just this small advantage though, you can be ahead of other participants and able to show them the star that you are. Financial trading is both art and science and requires experience to be successful. This chapter is intended to give you a start. Don't expect to find the Holy Grail here, but I hope you find some useful tools.

Measuring with Technical Analysis

Technical analysis involves analysing price and trading volume data with the purpose of forecasting prices and establishing good (profitable!) times to buy or sell an asset. It has a strong visual element and often relies on the use of price charts.

Technical analysis is often criticised as a form of voodoo science because most of the analyses don't have a firm grounding in statistics. That's to miss the point, though, of some of these techniques. A lot of science started with empirical observations and only later was rationalised by the use of statistics and mathematics. You can get inspiration from some of the ideas and take on some of the clever ways of presenting market data.

Constructing candlesticks

No, that section heading wasn't caused by a rogue spellchecker. Candlestick is the name given to a special diagram first used by Japanese rice traders.

Candlestick charts are useful because they show more information than a regular line chart or bar chart. The chart is made up of a candle for each trading day or time period. The body of the candle is shaded white if the stock's closing price is higher than its opening price and black if the closing price is lower than the opening price. The lines above and below the body are called *shadows* and indicate the high and the low prices. Figure 16-1 shows examples of two candlesticks.

Experienced traders use candlestick charts to identify configurations that are either bullish or bearish.

REMEMBER

An event or signal is said to be *bullish* if it suggests that the market will subsequently rise. A bull market is a rising market. An event or signal is said to be *bearish* if it suggests that the market will subsequently fall. A bear market is a falling market.

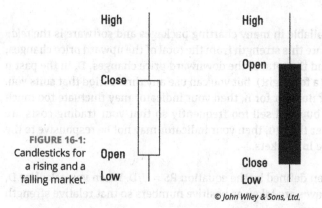

FIGURE 16-1:
Candlesticks for a rising and a falling market.

High

Close

Open

Low

High

Open

Close

Low

© John Wiley & Sons, Ltd.

Figure 16-2 shows two commonly identified candlestick patterns. The hammer pattern can occur at the bottom of a bear market while the shooting star is associated with the top of a bull market.

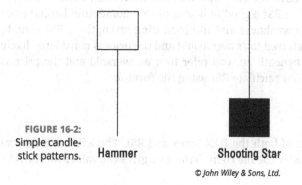

FIGURE 16-2:
Simple candlestick patterns.

Hammer

Shooting Star

© John Wiley & Sons, Ltd.

The hammer pattern has a closing price which is the high for the day indicating the possible end of a bearish trend. The shooting star pattern has a closing price that's the low for the day indicating the possible end of a bullish trend.

WARNING

They may have exciting names, but candlestick patterns are likely to be insufficient in themselves to detect useful trading opportunities. Traders use many different patterns and lots of experience.

Relying on relative strength

Examining charts of prices is helpful if you're trying to figure out how they might go in future or how the price might be related to another quantity or price. However, you can get a real boost of insight by calculating an indicator. An *indicator* is calculated from historical prices (and sometimes trading volume as well) and is designed to tell you something about how the price is trending.

A popular indicator available in many charting packages and software is the *relative strength*. You calculate this strength from the total of the upward price changes, U, in the past n days and the total of the downward price changes, D, in the past n days. Typically, n = 10 (a fortnight), but you can use any time period that suits you. If you choose a smaller number for n, then your indicator may fluctuate too much and encourage you to buy and sell too frequently so that your trading costs are high. If n is much higher than 10, then your indicator may not be responsive to the changes that take place in markets.

Relative strength is then defined by the equation RS = U/D. When you calculate D, the downward price moves are taken as positive numbers so that relative strength is always a positive number.

A more convenient number to use than the RS is the *relative strength index,* or RSI. The RSI is a number that lies between 0 and 100. If RS is large because there have been few downward price moves, then RSI is almost equal to 100. By contrast, if RS is small because there have been few upward price moves, then RSI is going to approach 0. This fact makes RSI a good indicator of the momentum behind price changes with 0 indicating weakness and 100 indicating strength. If RSI is high, say over 80, this level is referred to as *overbought* and the price is considered likely to fall; if RSI is low, say beneath 20, you refer to it as oversold and the price is considered likely to rise. You calculate RSI using the formula:

$$RSI = 100\left(\frac{RS}{1+RS}\right).$$

Figure 16-3 shows a chart of both the DAX index and RSI. The left-hand vertical axis gives the values for RSI while the right-hand axis gives the values for the DAX Index.

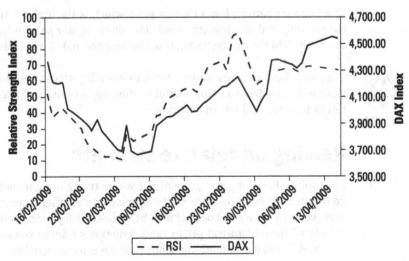

FIGURE 16-3: RSI overlaid on a chart of the DAX Index.

© *John Wiley & Sons, Ltd.*

You can certainly see that at the low point of the index, around 6 March, RSI is at a low point beneath 20, so is probably oversold. In other words, RSI appears to be signalling a profitable buying opportunity here. However, to determine whether RSI really systematically signals good buying and selling opportunities, you need to do a detailed statistical analysis using a lot of historical data.

WARNING

This chapter gives you a short introduction to technical analysis, mainly to show you the ingenious, and to some extent alternative, ways some traders examine market behaviour. *Technical Analysis For Dummies* by Barbara Rockefeller (Wiley), gives the lowdown on these techniques for those who want to do it for real. If you decide to use these signals, you need to carry out extensive checks before trading with real money. These checks should include backtesting with historical data and then paper trading the system for some time. By *paper trading*, I mean that you follow how successful trades would have been without actually making the trades. This activity allows you to check whether the trading signals work on data that was not used, and indeed not seen, when you developed the system. The next chapter, Chapter 17, gives you more detail about backtesting.

RSI is an example of what's called an *oscillator* because the signal moves up and down around a midpoint value. In the case of RSI, that value is 50. Figure 16-4 shows a plot of the oscillations in the RSI value for the DAX index for the past five years.

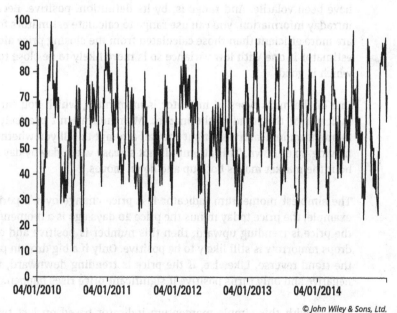

FIGURE 16-4: RSI for the S&P 500 Stock Index.

© John Wiley & Sons, Ltd.

For values over 70 the stock is overbought and due for a fall, so you should sell. For values of RSI less than 30, the stock is oversold and is due to bounce back up so you should buy. As shown in the chart, frequently the value of RSI is around 50 and in these situations keeping out of the market could be a good idea.

Checking momentum indicators

Traders have constructed many different indicators from historical price data. Some of these indicators don't use just the closing price for a time period but also the high and low prices. Others use the trading volume as well.

REMEMBER

Stock markets across the world commonly provide open, high, low, close and volume data for every trading day. This data set is a rich one in that it provides much more information than just the closing price for the day. The trading volume tells you how many shares were traded in a day and is potentially indicative of the significance of a price change. If a price starts rising with particularly high volume, the reason is because some traders have strong convictions and are buying a lot. This rise can be a good indicator that the price will rise even further.

The high (H) and low (L) prices for the day can tell you something about the volatility. In fact, the *range*, R = H − L, is a good substitute for the volatility. If the high for the day is well above the low, the price has been moving round and must have been volatile. And range is, by its definition, positive. Because it includes intraday information, you can use range to calculate estimators for volatility that are more efficient than those calculated from the closing price alone. An efficient estimator is one with low variance so is more likely to be close to the true value, which is good.

One of the main types of indicator is *momentum*, which you can think of as an indicator of the trend of the market. Momentum isn't precisely defined; many momentum indicators exist but they all attempt to tell you whether the market is moving up or down. This attempt is not so easy when day by day or even hour by hour the market makes both up and down moves.

The simplest momentum indicator is a price change over a period of time. For example, the price today minus the price 20 days ago is a momentum indicator. If the price is trending upward, then this number is positive and even if the price drops tomorrow is still likely to be positive. Only if a big drop in price occurs does the trend reverse. Likewise, if the price is trending downward, this indicator is negative and only turns positive if significant price rises happen.

A snag with this simple momentum indicator based on just two prices is just that − the indicator is based on only two prices. So, its value is quite strongly dependent on the two prices you choose. Much better to use an indicator calculated from many prices. In Chapter 8 I explain how to use the exponentially weighted moving average (EWMA) to create an average of historical prices in which greater weight is given to more recent prices.

REMEMBER

To calculate an exponentially weighted moving average, or EWMA, from prices p_n, you can use the formula

$$P_n = (1 - 1/\lambda) P_{n-1} + p_n / \lambda.$$

In this formula, the capital P indicates the EWMA of the prices. The constant lambda, λ, determines how responsive the EWMA is to recent changes in price. If lambda is large, say 128, then the EWMA isn't responsive to recent prices and prices from over 128 days ago are contributing. On the other hand, for a small value of λ, such as 4, then only recent prices are contributing.

You can create a momentum indicator from these averages by taking the difference between two of them. You do this calculation by subtracting an EWMA with a large value of λ from an EWMA with a small value of λ. By using EWMAs, the indicator becomes more efficient, or less susceptible to the random noise that comes naturally with market prices.

Momentum indicators created by subtracting two EWMAs are often called oscillators because they switch between positive and negative values depending on whether the price trend is going up or down.

If trends in prices are indeed evident, then momentum oscillators such as the one calculated by subtracting two EWMAs can be predictive to some extent of future prices. These oscillators are also known by the name MACD indicator – moving average convergence/divergence.

WARNING

Just to keep you on your toes, remember that if a financial market is efficient, then it doesn't have any price trends. In this theory, each new day is a fresh start with no memory of the past, and each price change is like a random number. Active traders, by what they're doing, don't believe in this theory. Theories are not written in stone.

Blending the stochastic indicator

The popular stochastic indicator is similar to both the relative strength oscillator that I talk about in 'Relying on relative strength' earlier in the chapter and the momentum oscillator from the preceding section. But the stochastic indicator uses the high and low values of daily prices, which can be helpful in assessing whether the most recent price has broken new ground and moved beyond the highest high or the lowest low of recent times.

I use C to denote today's closing price and L(n) to denote the lowest low price in the past n days. R(n) is the range of prices in the past n days and is the difference between the highest high and the lowest low of the past n days. If H(n) is the highest high from the past n days, then R(n) = H(n) − L(n). The stochastics indicator is denoted by K and is normally expressed as a percentage so you must multiply by 100. To calculate it:

$$K = 100 \times \frac{C - L(n)}{R(n)}.$$

The numerator is positive (any price is higher than the lowest low!) and never higher than the denominator (no price is higher than the highest high), so K is a percentage figure between 0 and 100. K approaches 100 when the price is shooting up and approaches 0 when the price is plunging down.

Traders use the stochastic indicator in different ways. For example, if the stochastic indicator reaches a high value near 100, a trader may enter a short position anticipating that the price will move down. Contrariwise, if the stochastic indicator falls near 0, a trader may enter a long position.

Stochastic indicators are frequently calculated smoother than the one I calculated here. The indicator jumps around less than the raw value K and can be a better signal to use for trading. For example, if I now call this K_t, then I can calculate a smoothed version D of the stochastic indicator with this formula:

$$D = \frac{K_t + K_{t-1} + K_{t-2}}{3}.$$

Breaking out of channels

In this section, I explain a chart that's useful when a market is moving in a narrow range and then manages to break out to higher or lower values. I define a trend, M_t, using a simple moving average calculated from the high, H, low, L, and closing price, C, on day t. I also define a simple moving average of the range R_t of the daily price. You calculate these moving averages from the prices from the previous n days using the equations:

$$M_t = \frac{1}{3n} \sum_{i=1}^{n} \left(H_{n-i+1} + L_{n-i+1} + C_{n-i+1} \right)$$

$$R_t = \frac{1}{n} \sum_{i=1}^{n} \left(H_{n-i+1} - L_{n-i+1} \right).$$

You can use these quantities by plotting them on a chart with the closing price and *channel boundaries*, which are defined by adding and subtracting the range from the trend. Figure 16-5 shows an example in which I label M as the mid-band. The upper band is indicated using a long dashed line and the lower band with a shorter dashed line. Together they define a channel through which the stock price moves until it breaks out.

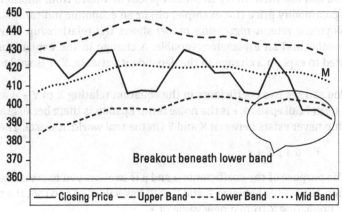

FIGURE 16-5: A sell signal from a channel breakout.

Chart legend: — Closing Price — – Upper Band - - - - Lower Band ····· Mid Band

Chart label: Breakout beneath lower band, M

If the price breaks out beneath the lower band, then it can be a good idea to sell the stock. Alternatively, if it breaks out above the upper band it can be a good idea to buy the stock.

WARNING

Before embarking on any such strategy, you really need to thoroughly backtest it. I cover backtesting in Chapter 17.

Making Predictions Using Market Variables

Market prices are subject to many different influences so it's unlikely (but not impossible) that you can find one variable that can predict them. Even if you can, it might not be too helpful. For example, a collapse in the price of oil almost certainly leads to a fall in the share price of oil companies, but the price of oil is as unpredictable as a share price. However, knowing how sensitive the share price of an oil company is to the price of oil might be interesting and useful. In these sections, I investigate relationships like this.

If you're ambitious, you can try to find leading indicators yourself. Bond yields are often considered a leading indicator of the stock market, so that might be a place to start. Good luck!

Understanding regression models

Linear regression models are among the most commonly used models in finance. You can use them to try to predict prices or values from another variable such as a commodity price (for example, oil) or an economic indicator such as the unemployment rate. A regression model shows the relationship between a *dependent variable* and an *explanatory variable*. A change in the explanatory variable, X, is used to explain a change in the dependent variable, Y. Y is said to depend upon X.

You can see two coefficients in the equation relating X to Y – α and β. In addition, a term I call epsilon, ε is the noise term. Epsilon is there because an exact relationship never exists between X and Y (in the real world at least). The equation is then

$$Y = \alpha + \beta X + \varepsilon.$$

The purpose of the coefficients α and β is to allow you to create as good a relationship as possible between X and Y with low values of ε so that the model is effective at predicting Y from a new value of X.

TIP

Both X and Y represent lots of data. I could have used little subscripts on X, Y and ε to indicate this but doing so can be distracting. You can build models from any amount of data, so X and Y might just have 10 data points or 10,000 or even 10 million. Statistical methods are applicable in diverse circumstances.

The equation is *linear* because on a graph the relationship between X and Y is like a straight line. It's an assumption that the relationship between X and Y is linear and quite a big one. Statisticians argue big time whether this is the best way of modelling data. They call it *parametric* statistics because it starts with parameters such as alpha and beta and a choice of equation.

Another method is to use *non-parametric* statistics, which is much more open about the form of the equation. You use the data to guide you. The snag with non-parametric statistics is that you may need more data; the good news is that you can end up with a better model.

Figure 16-6 shows scatterplots of data used to build models like this. Scatterplots are useful to visually investigate the relationship between two variables. The X values are the daily price return values for the DAX index whilst the Y values are the daily price return values for the stocks Fresenius Medical and BASF. In Figure 16-6a, the data just looks like a blob with no discernible structure while Figure 16-6b shows a fairly clear pattern with most of the data lying near a line running from the bottom left to the top right of the picture. If you look a little bit more carefully at Figure 16-6a, however, you can see that, in fact, the data clusters around a line just like in Figure 16-6b, but is much more dispersed. This degree of dispersion around the line is called R-squared. It's the epsilon term in the equation at the top of this section that represents this dispersion. If there was no epsilon term, then the equation would produce a nice straight line. But that's not the way the data is: there's no exact relationship between the returns of either of the stock with the returns of the DAX. But there's a statistical relationship and the strength of it is measured by R-squared. The plots show clearly that BASF has a much stronger connection with the DAX index than Fresenius Medical.

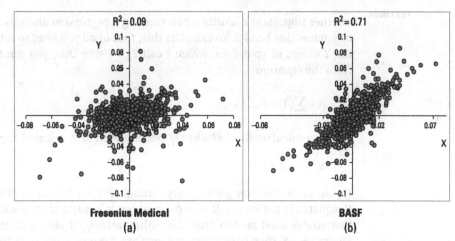

Source: Deutsche Borse

FIGURE 16-6: Scatterplots of data for two regression models.

For the stock in Figure 16-6a, Fresenius Medical, R squared is 0.09 whilst for BASF in Figure 16-6b, it is 0.71. Both of these stocks are components of the DAX index so that X represents price returns of this index for both charts.

Books such as *Statistics II For Dummies* by Deborah Rumsey-Johnson and *Analysis of Financial Data* by Gary Koop (both published by Wiley) give lots of detail on the maths of regression. Here, I give you a heads-up on just some key details.

I rewrite the equation for linear regressions slightly, adding the subscript i now to indicate that there are many data points X and Y:

$$\varepsilon_i = Y_i - \beta X_i - \alpha.$$

You may be wondering how to calculate the parameters alpha and beta in this equation. The classic way is to use the method of *least squares*, in which you take the errors, ε, for each value of i, square them and add them all up. This is the residual sum of squared errors and is often called delta because it is a measure of the difference between the data values Y_i and the predicted values for Y using alpha and beta. The big sigma sign, Σ in the formula, indicates a summation starting from the first data point i = 1 up to the last data point i = N. In the previous example this would mean that you have data for N days for both stocks and the DAX index:

$$\Delta = \sum_{i=1}^{N} \left(Y_i - \beta X_i - \alpha \right)^2.$$

You now do some heavy maths and figure out the values of alpha and beta that make the value of delta as small as possible. I'm going to spare you the heavy maths, though you can find the equations in the books I mention earlier.

All spreadsheets have functions to calculate regression coefficients, so you can easily run these regressions on your computer with your own data.

Another important quantity when running a regression analysis is the total sum of squares that I call S. To calculate this, first of all you need to find the average of the Y values of your data, which I call Y_{avg}. Using this, you can then calculate S from the equation:

$$S = \sum_{i=1}^{N} \left(Y_i - Y_{avg}\right)^2.$$

You now calculate the *coefficient of determination* or R-squared from the formula

$$R^2 = 1 - \Delta / S.$$

If your regression line goes exactly through all the data points, then delta is 0 and R-squared is 1. This result sounds great but is really a bit of a warning: it's likely that you've used far too little data. Alternatively, if your data is a big blob like Figure 16-6a, then both alpha and beta are close to 0 and so both S and delta are the sum of the squared values of the data points Y_i.

For a big data blob as in Figure 16-6a, the average value of Y, Y_{avg}, is particularly close to 0. The equation for the sum of squares, S, then shows that S is the sum of the squared values of Y_i.

Now S and Δ are approximately the same value, so R-squared becomes equal to 0. When R-squared is close to zero, you have a poor fit to data. Don't despair, most of the time in finance the fit of data to models is poor because financial markets are almost completely random. Certainly if you have a model to try to predict how prices will change in future, then expect a low R-squared near zero. For a model like the one in this section where you're trying to find how prices for one asset are related to another at the same time, you can expect a higher R-squared such as the value of 0.71 for the model relating BASF to the DAX index.

Forecasting with regression models

When you've built a regression model, you'd like to use it to make predictions on new data values. To make a prediction, Y_{pred}, for Y given a new explanatory value x, you just plug this value into the regression equation but set epsilon to equal zero so that

$$Y_{pred} = \alpha + \beta x.$$

However, now you need to know how good this prediction is. The first thing is to calculate an estimate for the standard deviation, σ, of the measurements of the dependent variable, Y. You can calculate this variable from the residual sum of squares, Δ:

$$\sigma = \sqrt{\Delta/N}.$$

This value of σ isn't the standard deviation of the Y values but of their deviation away from the regression line. If the model to predict stock returns from index returns is good, then this value of σ is low. Another thing you need to know is the variance of the X data, which is called V(X). (I talk about variance in Chapter 2.) Finally, you need to calculate the average of the X values, X_{avg}. The variance of the predicted value for Y is

$$V(Y) = \frac{\sigma^2}{N}\left[\frac{(x - X_{avg})^2}{V(X)} + 1\right].$$

This formula looks complicated but the following explanations should help:

» The variance of Y gets smaller as the amount of data gets bigger. This makes sense and is a good reason to work with a lot of data.

» If your regression model is poor with a high value of σ, then your extrapolations are going to be poor.

» The further your new data point x is from the centre of your data cloud, X_{avg}, the worse your predictions become.

Again, this makes sense. If you have to extrapolate to points far from where you had any data, you probably won't get good predictions. However, what really matters is how this deviation from the centre of your data cloud compares with the dispersion of your data along the x axis. That's why the squared deviation away from X_{avg} is divided by the variance of the X data. If your prediction point, x, is well within the data cloud, then $x - X_{avg}$ will be small compared with $\sqrt{V(X)}$, and your predictions should be good. If not, then you may have a problem with large prediction errors.

REMEMBER

To be able to extrapolate well and use your regression formula over a wide range of values of x, you want V(Y) to be small.

Predicting from Past Values

The idea of predicting the future from the past is an appealing one. The sense that history repeats itself is a common one. In this section, I show you a few ways to attempt to predict the future using mathematics – not just by looking at charts. These methods focus on how the recent past might affect future price changes.

The efficient market hypothesis (EMH) suggests that using past price values to predict the future is impossible. Remember, though, that the efficient market hypothesis is just that – a hypothesis that may not be true.

Some financial assets, such as the shares of multinational companies, are traded frequently, which makes it unlikely that you can predict even a small fraction of the next day's price change since almost all available information is incorporated into the price. However, for less frequently traded assets, or during turbulent times when strong trends can develop because market participants become governed by fear or greed, it's sometimes possible to predict some of next day's price change.

Defining and calculating autocorrelation

The *autocorrelation* of a price time series is a quantity that tells you the degree to which past values are related to current values. That makes it different from the more common *cross-correlation*, or simply *correlation*, which shows how much one price series is related to another price series.

If you have a time series of price data, p_n, then the first thing to do is to calculate the returns $r_n = (p_n - p_{n-1})/p_{n-1}$ because the returns are almost completely random, so you should definitely check just how random they are. Also, generally, profit-hunting traders and investors are interested in returns. Alternatively, you can use the natural logarithm ln and the definition $r_n = ln(p_n/p_{n-1})$.

I first calculate the *auto covariance*, which is the same as the covariance between the price returns of two assets (see Chapter 9) excepting that it relates price returns of an asset with earlier price returns of itself. It is then a simple step to calculate the autocorrelation. You calculate the auto covariance, γ, using the expected value, E, for the product of the return on day k with the return on the previous day k − 1. As a formula, this is

$$\gamma = E\left(r_k r_{k-1}\right).$$

I'm assuming here that the average returns are 0. Otherwise, you must subtract the average of the returns from r_n before using this formula. If you have N historical data values on the price returns, then you can estimate the expected value E using the formula:

$$\gamma = \frac{1}{N} \sum_{k=1}^{N} r_{n-k+1} r_{n-k}.$$

The formula for γ looks complicated, but it finds the average value for the product of return values with a one-day time lag between them. If a high value of return tends to be followed by another high value, then γ is positive. On the other hand, if a high value of the return tends to be followed by a loss (negative return), then γ is negative. Finally, (you thought I'd never get to the point) you calculate the autocorrelation by dividing the auto covariance by the variance of the historical returns you used to calculate the auto covariance. So, the autocorrelation, ρ, is

$$\rho = \gamma / V(r_n).$$

Downloading price data from Yahoo Finance, I calculated the autocorrelation for the jet engine manufacturer Rolls Royce using this formula and it comes out as −0.003. The data I used starts in 1988 and goes up to August 2015. This autocorrelation does indeed seem small. Is it possible that it may be 0 just as the EMH says? If I'd used another set of 7,000 data points, I might have gotten a slightly different answer (and with another set yet another answer).

REMEMBER

The autocorrelation is a statistic. You cannot be certain of its value. In fact, the autocorrelation is distributed like the normal distribution. This fact means that if you calculate the autocorrelation to be −0.003 based on some real data, then the true value of the autocorrelation lies in a range around −0.003. The width of this range is given by the standard deviation of the distribution for the autocorrelation. You can find out about the normal distribution in in Chapter 2.

Clever statisticians have worked out what the variance (the square of the standard deviation) is of statistics such as the autocorrelation. They tell us that if you calculate an autocorrelation with N data points, the variance is 1/N. In the example, I used 7,000 data points to calculate the autocorrelation and so the variance is 1/7,000 = 0.000143. Remember that this figure is the variance of the autocorrelation and not the variance of the data used to calculate an autocorrelation from data! If I now take the square root of this figure, I get the standard deviation to be 0.012.

With a measured autocorrelation of −0.003 and a standard deviation, σ, of 0.012, it becomes clear that a likely true figure for the autocorrelation is 0.

For a normal distribution, 95 per cent of measured values lie within ± 2 σ of the true value. An autocorrelation of −0.003 is consistent with a true value of zero as the efficient market hypothesis suggests.

Getting to know autocorrelation models

In this section I show you a model that you can use if your data is autocorrelated. Autocorrelation is what happens if a price, an interest rate – or any other market variable for that matter – has values now that show some statistical relationship with earlier values. Normally, this situation doesn't happen because markets are efficient. They're supposed to react immediately to fresh information. Each day is a new day and regret and memory are assumed not to play a role. You've probably guessed I'm a bit sceptical about this, and you're right. Price returns, especially on a daily frequency, have low autocorrelation but at intraday frequency are often autocorrelated. That's a reason for the popularity of high frequency trading in banks and hedge funds.

The model I use is for the financial return, r_n, on day n and with the autocorrelation a. The equation for this model is

$$r_{n+1} = ar_n + \varepsilon_n.$$

In this equation, the mysterious-looking ε_n represents a number drawn from a normal distribution. The equation is therefore saying that the return on day n is related to the return on the previous day but some random noise is given by the ε term, which means that the returns on successive days are never precisely related by the constant a. If the constant a is 0, the equation just says that the return r_n is given by a random number drawn from a normal distribution. That's exactly what I found in the previous section 'Defining and calculating autocorrelation' for the Rolls Royce share price and is consistent with an efficient market.

A consequence of this simple equation for the returns. r_n, is that they become autocorrelated not just from day to day but over many days (or over many seconds or milliseconds if you're using intraday data). You calculate the autocorrelation with a time lag of n days by a little change to the definition introduced in the preceding section. Now the definition is

$$\rho(n) = E(r_k r_{k-n})/V(r_k).$$

Again, the auto covariance is divided by the variance of the returns to generate the autocorrelation. In fact, you now have an *autocorrelation function* because it depends on n, the time lag between the two return days that you want to see whether they're related. Figure 16-7 is a picture of the autocorrelation function for the simple model in this section. Even if the value of a is large (I used the value 0.7 for this chart), the autocorrelation function declines exponentially so that no relationship exists between the returns of days separated by a time lag of more than about 15 days.

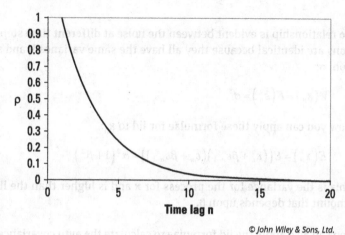

FIGURE 16-7:
Autocorrelation
function for a
simple model of
correlated
returns.

Moving average models

In the preceding section, I introduce a model that relates the returns of a financial instrument from one day to another. The random term ε means that you can never know today's return exactly from yesterday's return. In fact, because the relationships between the returns on different days are usually so weak, they're normally swamped by the random term. However, another way of building models in this way can, in some situations, work better than the autocorrelation model. This model is the *moving average model* in which the modelled variable is influenced both by the random term ε and the random error from earlier days or hours. In other words, the moving average model has a memory of previous random impulses. It only has one parameter, which I call β. I call the variable being modelled x as often this model is applied to variables other than returns. The equation then is as follows:

$$x_{n+1} = \varepsilon_n + \beta \varepsilon_{n-1}.$$

Now, the variable x is equal to a random number, ε, at time n but with the addition of another random noise from the previous time period. If you take x_n to be a return at time n then, according to the efficient market hypothesis, β should be zero because the market should have no memory of the past. The term with β means that what happened in the previous time period affects changes in the current time period.

You can check this property by calculating the autocorrelation function for the process x_n. To do this, you make use of the fact that the random numbers are taken from *identical independent distributions*, or iid for short. Random variables are iid if each random variable has the same probability distribution and they are mutually independent (have no correlation). The distributions are independent because, for a lag k:

$$E(\varepsilon_n \varepsilon_{n-k}) = 0.$$

No relationship is evident between the noise at different time steps. The distributions are identical because they all have the same variance V and standard deviation, σ:

$$V(\varepsilon_n) = E(\varepsilon_n^2) = \sigma^2.$$

Now you can apply these formulae for iid to x_n:

$$E(x_n^2) = E((\varepsilon_n + \beta\varepsilon_{n-1})(\varepsilon_n + \beta\varepsilon_{n-1})) = \sigma^2(1+\beta^2).$$

This is the variance for the process for x and is higher than the iid process by an amount that depends upon β.

You can also apply the iid formulae to calculate the auto covariance with a time lag of 1:

$$E(x_n x_{n-1}) = E((\varepsilon_n + \beta\varepsilon_{n-1})(\varepsilon_{n-1} + \beta\varepsilon_{n-2})) = \beta\sigma^2.$$

This result comes out because only one product term is not zero and it's the one where both ε terms have the subscript n – 1. You can then use the formula for the variance of ε to get the result.

As a brain teaser, try to calculate the auto covariance: $E(x_n x_{n-2})$. Don't be afraid to use pencil and paper. You can do the calculation in exactly the same way as for a time lag of one and you should find that the answer is zero because there is no product term where the ε noise terms have the same subscript. Because the noise is independently distributed, in this model the auto covariance has a short range. The autocorrelation with a time lag of one is the auto covariance divided by the variance of x_n^2 and is

$$\rho = \beta\sigma^2 \Big/ \sigma^2(1+\beta^2) = \beta \Big/ (1+\beta^2).$$

The autocorrelation can be positive or negative depending on whether β is positive or negative.

As an example of a moving average model, I use some data on trading volume. Trading volume V_n is a measure of how many contracts (futures or stock or bonds) are traded in a time period such as a day. When major events happen, volume can be high as market participants adjust to news. The data I use is for the DAX stock index. Similar to using price returns, I calculate the change in trading volume from one day to the next so that $x_n = V_n - V_{n-1}$. Now using the formula for $\rho(n)$ shown earlier in this section, I can calculate the autocorrelation function. The result is shown in Figure 16-8.

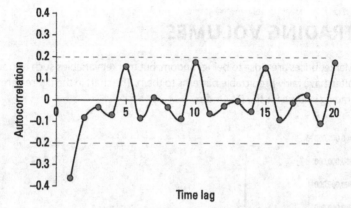

FIGURE 16-8: Autocorrelation function for volume difference for the DAX index.

The two horizontal dashed lines indicate approximately how well you can estimate the autocorrelation function. The values of the autocorrelation function for time lags of two and higher are within the band defined by the dashed lines, so there's no reason to believe the autocorrelation function is other than zero. However, for a time lag of one the autocorrelation is quite negative. The autocorrelation function is consistent with the moving average model with a value of β around –0.7.

Mentioning kernel regression

A final way to build a model describing the relationship between an explanatory variable X and a dependent variable Y is to use *kernel regression*. This regression is similar to a technique I use in Chapter 8 in explaining smoothing with kernels, so I just give a summary here. Just as in the earlier section 'Understanding regression models' you have data X_i and Y_i. Now, however, the idea is to avoid assuming that the relationship between X and Y is linear. It's okay to assume a quite general form, which I call f, so that

$$Y_i = f(X_i) + \varepsilon_i.$$

A way to build this function f is to use a weighted average over the data points Y_i. The formula for this is:

$$f(x) = \frac{\sum_{i=1}^{N} K_h(x - X_i) Y_i}{\sum_{i=1}^{N} K_h(x - X_i)}.$$

The function K_h is the kernel, and the subscript indicates the *bandwidth*, h. The *bandwidth* is the width of the region over which the kernel function k is different from zero.

TRADING VOLUMES

Market prices are close to being random, but market variables such as trading volume often have fairly predictable patterns to them. The chart in the figure here shows the trading volume for the DAX index.

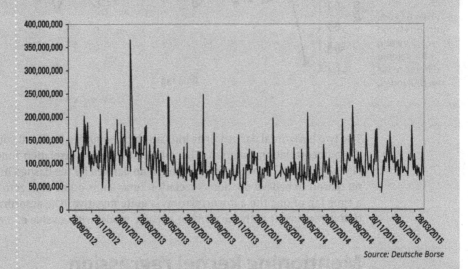

Source: Deutsche Borse

The spikes in the trading volume at fairly regular intervals are due to the expiry of futures contracts for the DAX. (See Chapter 6 if you're not familiar with futures contracts.) Index futures are cash settled based on the value of the index at a specific time of the last trading day of the futures contract. Normally, that's on the third Friday of the contract month. This situation gives rise to arbitrage opportunities to sell the index future and buy the underlying cash equities if the futures contract is more expensive than the cash equities, which traders happily take up and generate high volume.

Other predictable patterns are evident such as higher volume on Mondays but are not so easy to see on this chart.

For example, a common choice for Kh is the Gaussian distribution function where the role of the bandwidth is taken by the standard deviation. This equation averages over the Yi values in the vicinity of the point x where you want to predict the function f. However, it does it in a way where only the points in a region within a distance h play a significant role.

Chapter 17

Fitting Models to Data

Quantitative finance deals in models – hopefully, good models. Complicated equations may look good in a thesis, but do they stack up when they're faced with real-life data? And if you do find a model that you think fits the data, are you just fooling yourself? In this chapter, I talk more about how to fit your data to models and how to decide whether the model you're using is a good one. Models are ubiquitous in quantitative finance. In Chapter 10, I look at some specialised but important models for pricing options. In Chapter 7, I introduce several models for calculating the volatility of prices. However, many other examples of models are available in quantitative finance. For example, banks find it important to have a good model for the yield curve of bonds.

This chapter is quite mathematical and general but the results can be applied to trading models. These are models that (hopefully!) have some predictive power for the future return of an asset. Because financial markets are almost efficient, it's a big ask to develop a model like this. That's why careful testing is essential.

Modelling has certain darker arts as well, such as calibrating option pricing models so that they fit market price data. *Calibrating* an option model can involve adjusting parameters, such as volatility, assumed to be constant when the model equations were derived. Calibration is an example when quantitative finance practitioners prefer to use simple, familiar models over more complex ones, even if using them involves a slight inconsistency of assumptions. So this chapter is very much about the practical application of mathematical theory to financial data.

Another word for calibration is *estimation*. It's exactly the same process but estimation is the word preferred by statisticians. Saying *estimation* emphasises that any parameters that you calculate are just that – estimates. The value of the parameters depends on which data you use and so there is always some *dispersion* in the values of the parameters.

Maximising the Likelihood

I use the method of maximum likelihood a couple of times already in this book (for example, in Chapter 8), but here I take you through it a bit more slowly as you'll benefit from knowing it in some detail. The value of having an estimation of a quantity (such as a volatility) that is more likely rather than less likely is clear.

The starting point is the probability density function for your data, X_i. Start by estimating a parameter such as the volatility, which I call *a* as it could be anything. For a dataset with N points in it, the likelihood, L, is defined as:

$$L(X_1, X_2, ..., X_N; a) = \prod_{i=1}^{i=N} P(X_i, a).$$

REMEMBER

The symbol Π is a Greek P and stands for *product*. It indicates that you must multiply together all the terms to the right of the symbol starting from i = 1 and continuing until i = N.

The *likelihood* is the product of the probabilities of all the data points X_i. I'm making the assumption that the data is *independent and identically distributed,* or *iid,* so that the probability of the data set (that is, of the values being X_1, X_2 and so on) is the product of probabilities of the individual data points.

The idea now is to maximise likelihood. That's a bit strange to maximise the probability of the data, but using Bayes' theorem shows that it's linked to finding the most probable value of the parameter a, which seems more intuitively sensible.

You'll often find it more convenient to maximise the logarithm of the likelihood rather than just the likelihood itself. The reason is because the logarithm of a product is equal to the sum of the logarithms and so:

$$\ln L = \sum_{i=1}^{i=N} \ln P(X_i, a).$$

APPLYING JUST ONE PARAMETER

You can use maximum likelihood for a probability function with only one parameter. As an example I look at the probability, P, of a loan not defaulting before a time, t, given that it's not defaulted now. The formula for this is given by an exponential function (indicated by the usual letter e) and with a constant, τ, the mean time to default:

$$P(t;\tau) = (1/\tau)e^{-t/\tau}.$$

This formula makes some assumptions, such as that there is a constant in time probability of default, but the model is still a reasonable one. To estimate what τ is using maximum likelihood I use some data on N defaulting loans. Records indicate the default time, t_j, of the N loans so that the log likelihood is:

$$\ln L = \sum_{j=1}^{j=N} \left(\frac{1}{\tau} e^{-t_j/\tau} \right) = -\sum_{j=1}^{j=N} t_j / \tau - \ln \tau.$$

To maximise ln L, you need to use a bit of calculus. Don't panic! Ln L reaches a maximum when its slope is equal to zero, which means that you have to differentiate it with respect to τ. The derivative of ln τ is just $1/\tau$. So:

$$\frac{d \ln L}{d\tau} = \sum_{j=1}^{j=N} \left(\frac{t_j}{\tau^2} - \frac{1}{\tau} \right) = 0.$$

Note: When you differentiate a function and set it to zero as I did here, you don't always get the maximum value. In fact, you may get a minimum value! To check whether you've found a maximum, you really need to find the second derivative of the function and check to see that it's negative.

Now, by doing a little bit of algebra – multiply the equation by τ squared and remember that the summation of N τs is just Nτ – you get that:

$$\hat{\tau} = \frac{1}{N} \sum_{j=1}^{j=N} t_j.$$

The hat on top of τ is to show that this is an estimate of τ. You may be underwhelmed by this formula because the result shows that the maximum likelihood estimate for τ is just the average of the observed default times. However, this example shows how to make the connection between maximum likelihood and common estimators such as the average.

REMEMBER

Figure 17-1 shows a chart of the logarithm function. This function is a continuously increasing one as the probability increases from zero to one so that the maximum value of ln L corresponds to the maximum value of L. The peculiar placement of the x-axis is because the logarithm of a number between zero and one is always negative.

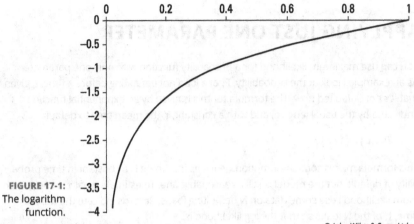

FIGURE 17-1: The logarithm function.

Minimising least squares

In the previous section, I discuss the likelihood function for finding a parameter, τ, to describe a data set. I now take another very common case and assume that the probability distribution function for the data points is given by the Gaussian (normal) distribution, which means that the probability function is given by:

$$P\left(X_i;\mu,\sigma_i\right)=\frac{1}{\sigma_i\sqrt{2\pi}}e^{-(x-\mu)^2/2\sigma_i^2}.$$

This example is made a little bit complicated because I use two parameters – μ, the mean, and σ, the standard deviation – instead of just one. If you look a little bit closer, you see that the σ has a subscript, i. This subscript is because I'm allowing the standard deviation to vary from one data point to the next.

REMEMBER

Financial markets are inherently unstable. The *volatility* (the standard deviation of the returns) is constantly changing as the market becomes more or less jittery. This change can be due to the arrival (or non-arrival) of important news or simply a change in mood of market participants.

For now, though, I'm going to maximise the likelihood by varying just the mean, μ.

Using the formula for the log likelihood from the previous section, 'Maximising the Likelihood', you can write it as:

$$\ln L=-\sum_{i=1}^{i=N}\ln\sigma_i\sqrt{2\pi}-\sum_{i=1}^{i=N}\frac{\left(X_i-\mu\right)^2}{2\sigma_i^2}.$$

The first term in the equation for ln L depends on the standard deviations, which are fixed constants and so play no role when you try to maximise ln L with respect to the mean. The second term is the squared difference between the data and the mean, μ. However, it comes with a negative sign in front, and so to maximise ln L, you need to minimise the term with the squared differences.

Maximising a function, f, is the same as minimising the function $-f$.

To minimise the squared term, you differentiate it with respect to μ and set the result to zero. This gives you the following equation for the value of μ:

$$\sum_{i=1}^{i=N}\left(\frac{X_i - \mu}{\sigma_i^2}\right) = 0.$$

A little algebra gives the result:

$$\hat{\mu} = \frac{\sum_{i=1}^{i=N}\left(X_i/\sigma_i^2\right)}{\sum_{i=1}^{i=N}\left(1/\sigma_i^2\right)}.$$

I put a hat on μ to show that it's an estimate from the data.

This formula shows that to estimate the mean, the data values, X_i, can usefully be weighted by the square of the standard deviations, σ. The most uncertain data points with high values of σ are given the least weight. That makes sense and reflects the importance of σ when you're fitting models.

So far I've looked at a data set X_i and used maximum likelihood to estimate the mean value. Now the time is right to do something a bit more complicated. I'm going to assume that Y can be quite a general function, $f(X_i)$. The log likelihood now becomes

$$\ln L = -\sum_{i=1}^{i=N}\ln\sigma_i\sqrt{2\pi} - \sum_{i=1}^{i=N}\frac{\left(Y_i - f(X_i;\alpha)\right)^2}{2\sigma_i^2}.$$

The σ are constants again, and so maximising ln L is equivalent to minimising:

$$\chi^2 = \sum_{i=1}^{i=N}\left(\frac{Y_i - f(X_i;\alpha)}{\sigma_i}\right)^2.$$

The sum of squared differences is given the special name of *chi-squared*. Because chi-squared needs to be minimised so as to maximise the log likelihood, using this frequently used method to fit a function to data is often called the *method of least squares*.

After you minimise chi-squared by finding the best values for the parameters, α, the values of f(;) won't be exactly equal to the data values, Y_i. You have a small mismatch called the *residual*. You can write an equation for the data values showing this. I call the residuals ε and put a hat on the data values because these parameters have been adjusted to minimise chi-squared:

$$Y_i = f\left(X_i; \hat{\alpha}\right) + \varepsilon_i.$$

To be a good model for your data, you want the residuals, ε, to be small. But that isn't quite sufficient. Ideally, they should be normally distributed and have no autocorrelation. If the residuals are autocorrelated, then it suggests that the choice of the function, f, is not quite right.

REMEMBER

Autocorrelation, γ, is the relationship between the values of a time series now and the values in the past. If you have N data points it's defined by the equation:

$$\gamma = \frac{\sum_{i=1}^{i=N} \varepsilon_i \varepsilon_{i+1}}{\sum_{i=1}^{i=N} \varepsilon_i^2}.$$

It's just like the correlation that you may have encountered in Chapter 9 except now it's the correlation between a time series and earlier values of the same time series. Chapter 16 explains more about the autocorrelation.

REMEMBER

Anti-correlated means that an increase in a time series value is more likely to be followed by a decrease than another increase.

Using chi-squared

If you minimise chi-squared with N data points and m parameters in the model, there are n *degrees of freedom* where n = N − m. The chi-squared distribution has a mean of n and a variance of 2n. So if chi-squared differs markedly from n, something is probably awry with your fitting process. The book *Numerical Recipes in C: The Art of Scientific Computing* by William H. Press et al (Cambridge University Press) is a great resource on data fitting. The author includes more detail on the chi-squared distribution and also includes computer code that you can use.

Comparing models with Akaike

You may have two competing models that you'd like to compare. There's always someone who says she has something better . . . . In this situation, you can use the Akaike information criterion, or simply AIC for short.

If L_{max} is the maximum value of the log likelihood that you got from your fitting process, and m is the number of parameters in your model, then AIC is defined as:

$$AIC = -2L_{max} + 2m.$$

Select the model with the smaller value of AIC. This means that models with few parameters are favoured as are models with large values of the log likelihood.

To directly compare two competing models, always use the same sample so that the playing field is level.

AIC is not the only criterion that you can use for selecting models. Another popular criterion is the Bayesian information criterion or BIC for short. BIC is defined by the equation:

$$BIC = -2L_{max} + m \ln N.$$

BIC penalises the number of parameters more strongly than AIC and so there is less chance of overfitting (which is discussed in the next section) a model if you use BIC.

Fitting and Overfitting

When statisticians talk about *goodness of fit*, they're not referring to their jeans but to their data and models. (Thank you, by the way, to Deborah Rumsey-Johnson for her humour in *Statistics For Dummies*; It's good to share jokes.) To be serious though, fitting data to models can be tricky, and in this section, I show you some of the pitfalls.

If you have data X_i and Y_i, and you want to fit a model so that Y is a function, f, of X (which I'll write later as Y = f(X)), then you need to know how many parameters to use in your model. For example, if you choose to use a linear model, then Y = mX + c, and two parameters exist – m and c. No model, however, is perfect. When you fit a model, you have a mismatch between the actual Y value and the predicted Y value. You try to improve the fit by adjusting some parameters. I call these parameters α in the following equation. There may just be two of them, as for the linear model with a single variable, or there may be many more for a complex model. Calling the function used to model the data as f, the equation is

$$Y_i = f(X_i; \alpha) + \varepsilon_i.$$

The numbers ε represents are the residuals of the model. In the earlier section 'Minimising least squares', I show that you can fit a model by minimising the sum of the squares of the residuals. However, if you add more and more parameters to your model, you can potentially achieve a close match between X and Y, especially if you use a complicated function for f. But doing so may not be a good idea.

Goodness of fit can look impressive (like those well-fitting jeans), but it can cause problems because, even if the model fits the data well, when you use the model on new data it can fail badly. This is the problem of *overfitting*. Overfitting is serious because the main point of developing models is to tell you something you didn't know about new data.

I created a simple data set with just seven points in it. The X values are the integers from one to seven. The Y values are also the integers from one to seven but with a little bit of random noise added. You can see a chart of this data set in Figure 17-2.

Without the added noise, the data can be fitted exactly by the simple model Y = X because the X values are identical to the Y values. The random noise changes that

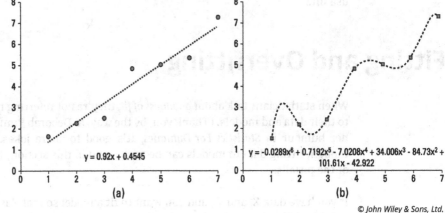

FIGURE 17-2: Fitting data to a straight line and a polynomial.

a bit. Figure 17-2a shows that a straight line is still a good-looking fit to the data. In Figure 17-2b, though, I fitted the data exactly to a polynomial. The equation for the curve is given at the bottom of the plot.

Now, use the fitted equations to calculate the value of the function for X = 0. For the straight line, the answer is 0.4545, which is close to the expected value of zero, which you can see either by setting X = 0 in the equation for the straight line next to the axis or by running your eye along the fitted (dotted) line to see where it intersects the *y* axis. However, for the polynomial fit, you can see that the curve will intersect the *y* axis at −42.922, again by substituting X = 0 into the equation. This answer is way off and highly misleading. The polynomial curve is overfitted.

TIP

A good technical term for new data is *out of sample*. The data you use to build a model is the sample, so any new data is out of sample. Also good to know is that the process of fitting a model and determining the parameters, α, is sometimes referred to as *calibration*, although statisticians prefer to use the word *estimation*.

The most persuasive solution to overfitting is *cross-validation*. It may sound complicated, but in fact you've already seen how it works in the previous example. In steps, the cross-validation procedure goes like this:

1. **Split your data sample into two parts.**

The first is the calibration sample and the second is the test sample.

2. **Build your model using the calibration sample.**

You know what your parameters, α, are from using least squares minimisation. (See the section 'Minimising least squares' earlier in the chapter.)

3. **Apply your model to the test data samples.**

In other words, predict the Y values from the X values for the test samples.

4. **Compare the residuals from the calibration samples with the residuals from the test samples.**

If you find a significant difference, then your model is likely overfitted (or perhaps underfitted if the model you used is too simple). The performance on the test samples is likely to be worse than that on the calibration samples but should still be satisfactory.

Cross-validation gives you an idea of whether your model will work well in practice. You have to decide how much of your data set to place with the calibration samples and how much in the test samples. As a rough guide, 50:50 is a good balance. That's quite conservative, so extending the calibration set to 70 per cent of your data is okay, too.

Popular too is *miss-one-out cross-validation* when you leave out a single data sample and then use the resulting model to predict the Y value for this sample. The advantage of this technique is that you can repeat the process for every sample in the data set. The amount of calculations required can be rather large (and time-consuming), but it can give you a very good idea of the quality of your model.

WARNING

You need to resist a temptation when using cross-validation. If you choose a function, f, to model your data and it turns out to be poor when you do cross-validation, then you may go on to try another function, g. This function can lead to iterative attempts at fitting your model, which can be a source of overfitting on its own. In other words, you may just stumble on a function that happens to work with the test samples but is not, in fact, a good model for your data. This situation is inevitable when building models to try out several ideas, but you reach a point when doing so becomes dangerous. If the model you've built is a time-series model in which the data starts in the past and goes up to the present, then a sure way of testing it is to apply your model to new data as it becomes available. This process may be time-consuming if you're trying to predict quarterly gross domestic product (GDP), but is great for, say, intraday stock prices.

Gross domestic product (GDP) is the total output of an economy. If successive drops in GDP occur, an economy is said to be in recession so is watched closely by the media and politicians.

Applying Occam's Razor

Fitting a model to data is tricky and often leads to the problem of overfitting. Cross-validation is a good way of checking for this problem. In addition, you can use the principle of *Occam's razor*, which states that if you have two competing models that make similar predictions, then you should choose the simpler one. In the dismal style of economists, Occam's razor is also called the *principle of parsimony*.

William Occam (or Ockham) was a 14th-century Franciscan friar more interested in theology than quantitative finance, but he had a nice insight on how to acquire useful knowledge.

You can relate Occam's razor to the Akaike information criterion (AIC) from the previous section 'Comparing models with Akaike' (or indeed the Bayesian information criterion BIC). AIC is a way of fitting models, similar to least squares, but with a penalty for selecting a model with more parameters. AIC, therefore, naturally selects simpler models according to the principle of Occam's razor.

Occam's razor is well worth keeping in mind when you're developing a trading model. Simplicity is an asset. If you use a complex model to try to forecast financial returns, then you're likely to be just fitting equations to noise, so that when you use it to make forecasts, they can go badly wrong. With a simple model, you can be much surer whether it works or not and avoid some painful losses.

Detecting Outliers

An *outlier* is an observation in your data set that's markedly different from the other observations. It's the oddball data point that's out of whack with the rest. An outlier can raise tricky issues and lead to lots of debate. You'll see recommendations in statistics books to find outliers. Others recommend you include them but to use robust methods that can cope with them. A *robust method* is one that gives you the same answer even if you add a bit of dodgy data.

TIP

Here are a few straightforward tips for dealing with outliers:

>> Many outliers are the result of crass mistakes in data collection or processing. Are the units correct? Perhaps dollars were confused with cents. Is the data for the correct asset? Perhaps you confused Man Group plc (hedge funds) with Man SE (trucks). This level of data checking is crucial and can avoid many problems down the line.

>> Subtle errors can lead to big problems, even after carefully checking the origin of the data. If you're already using some models for, say, option prices, you may be confusing market prices with model prices. So you have the asset and units correct, but the nature of the data is different. Equally, you can find many different definitions of interest rate (maturity of loan, secured or unsecured), and you need to check that you've got that right.

>> Other details in financial data are worth paying close attention to, especially the time stamp. Sounds obvious but is easy to get wrong, especially if you're using data from different time zones.

This process of checking your data is often called *data cleaning*. Often, you spend a large fraction of time on a modelling project cleaning data, so you're well advised to establish some steps in the process. The result should be clean, usable data. Hopefully, if you detected and replaced bad data, your clean dataset is no smaller than your original dataset. Deleting data should be a last resort.

Even with reliable, carefully checked sources of data, there can be problems. Getting data from multiple sources is a good way of thoroughly cross-checking data.

WARNING

You can use standard statistical tests to decide whether a data point is an outlier or not. However, these methods often rely on the assumption that the distribution of the returns is normal, or Gaussian. That isn't the case for financial markets. Major market events, such as the stock market crash in 1987, shouldn't have happened according to normal statistics. However, as we know, it did happen. Events like this crash look like outliers in many models.

TECHNICAL STUFF

From January 1987 until October 1987, the standard deviation of the simple returns (closing price today/closing price yesterday) on the FTSE100 index (Financial Times Stock Exchange 100 Index) was approximately equal to 20. However, on 19th October 1987, the FTSE 100 index dropped almost 250 points, which is over 12 standard deviations. Even a 5-standard deviation event is exceptionally unlikely, so a 12-standard deviation event is essentially impossible according to normal statistics. The 1987 crash is stark and frightening evidence that financial markets are not normal – in both the statistical and usual sense of the word!

The Curse of Dimensionality

When you build a model, you're trying to find a relationship between a variable, X, and something you'd like to predict, often called Y. But what happens if you think that Y depends on much more than just X? That's a common situation as the financial markets are complex with many different assets, currencies and interest rates. In one dimension (with just one variable X), you'd like the data to be uniformly spread along a line of length, say, ten. If variable X is dollars, that means you have data for prices from zero up to $10. For data that is well spread out, you can then reliably build a model and detect the shape of the function even if it is curved. With two variables, you can think of the data as lying on a square with a side length of ten. The area of the square is $10^2 = 100$. So you need much more data in two dimensions (with two variables) to build a good model. I show this process in Figure 17-3.

For more dimensions (variables), the problem gets even worse. In three dimensions, you need to use $10^3 = 1,000$ data bins. This problem of the exponentially increasing amount of data you need to build good models with more than one variable is the *curse of dimensionality*.

WARNING

When you're building models, you can always *scale* your data. In other words, you can multiply your data by a constant factor so that the numbers lie in a convenient range. This process is just like changing the units in which the data was measured. For example, changing from cents to dollars is like dividing prices by 100. You can also shift the origin of the data axis for your variables by adding or subtracting a constant number from the data.

TIP

If you scale data, you need to undo the scale change after you finish building your model so that you get back to the original data scale. If you multiplied your data by C, then you need to undo it by dividing by C.

If you try to build a model with three variables, you need even more data if you want a good model that you're confident with. In three dimensions, the cube-shaped grid should consist of 1,000 little cubes. In general, if your model has predictor variables, D, then you need a grid with 10^D D dimensional cubes for your data.

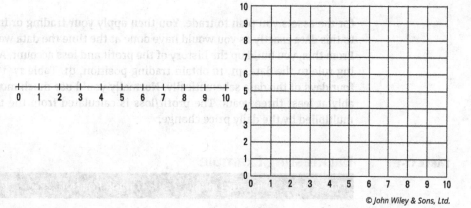

FIGURE 17-3:
Data grids for
one- and
two-dimensional
models.

TIP

Thankfully, a few get-arounds are available for the curse of dimensionality:

>> Assume that the variables in the model are continuous to make life easier for yourself. If Y is large when X = 5, then you're reasonable to assume that it'll be quite large when X = 4 or 6.

>> Assume that the variables are all linear. It's potentially dangerous to do this, especially if you have many variables, but it is effective.

>> Reduce the dimensionality of your data by using techniques such as Principal Components Analysis. This technique is a powerful one explained fully in Chapter 9.

Seeing into the Future

If I could have seen into the future, I wouldn't have sold that flat in London I owned 25 years ago. Trading and investment are the two branches of finance in which you'd most like to have a crystal ball. You'd like to show that your strategy or portfolio will do well in the future and persuade investors to put their money into it. Given the random nature of financial markets, persuading investors of the soundness of your plan isn't easy, but you can attempt it in two main ways: backtesting and out-of-sample validation. They can both be misleading so the next sections give you a guide.

Backtesting

Backtesting is a technique widely used to test trading and investment strategies for profitability. The idea is simple: You start with a database of historical prices for the assets you plan to trade. You then apply your trading or investment rules to this data exactly as you would have done at the time the data was first released. From this, you build up the history of the profit and loss account. Apply your trading rule to the data, p1, to obtain trading position, q1. Table 17-1 shows the first four days of the data schematically. Normally you'd use much more data, preferably at least three years. The profit/loss is calculated from the trading position multiplied by the daily price change.

TABLE 17-1   ## Backtesting Example

Date	Historic Data	Trading Position	Profit/Loss
Day 1	p1	q1	
Day 2	p2	q2	q1*(p2–p1)
Day 3	p3	q3	q2*(p3–p2)
Day 4	p4	q4	q3*(p4–p3)

WARNING

Backtesting works only for strategies that are completely rule-based, so that given historical price and fundamental data, the trades are exactly specified. By *exactly specified*, I mean that the trade is a buy or sell and the trade quantity is known.

TECHNICAL
STUFF

Financial traders often distinguish between *fundamental* and *technical* strategies. *Technical strategies* use only historical price data and perhaps trading volume data. They stem from the idea that past price patterns can tell you something about future price patterns. *Fundamental strategies,* by contrast, use information on events that are understood to cause price changes. For example, employment data is a closely observed piece of fundamental data as are profit announcements of companies. Fundamental strategies trade using underlying causes while technical strategies are more about market reaction to these causes.

Backtesting is useful to test out whether an investment or trading idea would have worked in the past. Yet, this test is no guarantee that it will work in the future.

WARNING

Some important dangers come with the technique: Software is available that allows you to automate backtesting. That's great, but if you end up testing a large number of potential systems and selecting the one with the best performance, you're probably guilty of overfitting. The best system possibly worked on your data set just by random chance.

Make sure when doing a backtest that you include a sufficient number of different market regimes. These regimes should include bear markets when prices are trending down and bull markets when they're going up. Ideally, there should also be a period when prices are range bound. Realistically, this means having a lot of data to do an adequate backtest.

Out-of-sample validation

Out-of-sample validation is the most powerful way of checking whether a model is any good. You check the predictions of the model using data that wasn't used to build it. In effect, you use the model for real and see whether it works well.

Out-of-sample validation is different from *cross-validation*. In cross-validation, you split the data set into two parts: a *calibration set* and a *test set*. The earlier section 'Fitting and Overfitting' explains this process in detail. A lot of potential exists, though, for iteratively modifying your model in a cycle from the calibration set to the test set. If the test results aren't good, you change the model and try again. This modification can lead to overfitting, especially if you iteratively try to select predictor variables.

You absolutely must, therefore, test a model with genuinely unseen data. This test can be done as some form of acceptance test, but for a trading model, you normally use a period of paper trading in which you follow the predictions of the model in time and see if they're profitable.

Chapter 18

Markets in Practice

W hen you start in quantitative finance, you may easily get the impression that it's just some fancy mathematics to do with random walks. But you need to understand a little bit more about what goes on behind the scenes when a market comes up with a price.

All markets have unique features and the regulations governing them are constantly changing, often in response to dramatic events such as the flash crash of 6 May 2010 when some prices on the New York stock exchange plunged down almost to zero and then mysteriously jumped back up to where they were all within 36 minutes. This kind of thing isn't how things are supposed to go, and it certainly isn't possible to model them using the random walks conventionally used in quantitative finance. Trying to understand events like this one isn't for the faint hearted but these events show that the details of trading rules are important for the behaviour of markets.

In this chapter, I take you through the mechanisms by which market participants come to an agreement about price and how, sometimes, these mechanisms go wrong. I also talk about bid and ask prices and the market impact of trades. This chapter shows you that quantitative finance and market modelling has a wild frontier with some unanswered questions that many participants struggle with.

Auctioning Assets

In the supermarket, prices are clearly labelled and you have no scope to haggle over prices. That's handy when you're buying a tin of tomatoes as it saves time. Also, if you don't like the price, you can go to a competitor. But financial markets don't work that way.

Financial markets are auctions; they work more like flea markets than supermarkets. You may be familiar with auctions if you've ever purchased something via an Internet auction. In most cases, auctions are effective at finding a fair price because of the presence of competitive bidding. Because the final price depends on demand from buyers, you can get a bargain if too few buyers turn up or make bids. But these attractive prices then attract other buyers. Therefore, auctions have a natural dynamic that has made them a permanent feature in many markets across the world.

Auctions work in many different ways. Some of the basic forms they take include:

>> **Dutch auction:** The price of the items start at a level higher than anyone is prepared to pay. This judgement is made by the auctioneer. The price is then reduced in steps until someone decides he wants to buy. He indicates this decision to the auctioneer and the auction then finishes. The most famous example of this kind of auction is the Aalsmeer flower market in Holland.

A Dutch auction is a successful mechanism for quickly selling large amounts of goods. When the auction stops, the winner states how much of the consignment he wishes to take. The remaining part of the consignment is then put up for auction. Presumably buyers who wish to buy large quantities wait until they see an indication of (higher) prices from smaller volume buyers to make their bids.

>> **English auction:** The auctioneer starts at a minimum reserve price and solicits bids at higher increments. Buyers indicate their willingness to buy by waving a numbered paddle or nodding their heads. The auction ends when there are no further bids at the next price offered by the auctioneer. The item then goes to the highest bidder. Art auctions are the classic example.

A slight variation of this auction is the *open outcry auction* in which bidders are allowed to shout out their bids and don't have to obey the fixed increments offered by an auctioneer.

>> **Double-sided auction:** Financial markets, such as stock exchanges, operate this way: Traders post bids to buy stock at a specified price and for a given quantity; other traders post offers to sell stock at a specified price and for a given quantity. At any moment in time, this combination of bids to buy and offers to sell is called the *order book*.

TECHNICAL STUFF

The *bid price* is the price at which you can sell shares on a stock exchange (or any other kind of exchange for that matter). The *ask price* is the price at which you can buy shares on a stock exchange.

Prices change rapidly from millisecond to millisecond as orders are matched by algorithms run by the exchange.

Two major forms of double-sided auctions exist:

- **Quote driven:** In this system, market specialist traders called *market makers* post bid and ask prices before orders are submitted.

- **Order driven:** Orders are placed and only then are prices determined by a matching algorithm. Most of these orders are *limit orders* – requests to buy or sell at a stated price and in a stated amount. No guarantee exists that limit orders will be executed because bids may be at too low a price and offers at too high a price. You also have no guarantee that there'll be sufficient volume of orders at the stated price.

>> **Sealed bid auction:** Popular before the advent of the Internet, in these auctions, bidders submit their bids by mail. At the close of the auction, the envelopes containing the bids are opened and the highest bid declared the winner.

An interesting variant of this kind of auction is the *second price sealed bid* auction. The winner (highest bidder) doesn't pay the high winning bid, but the next highest bid. The advantage of this system is that it encourages truthful bidding in which bidders place bids they believe reflect the value of the item for sale. Normally, bidders tend to reduce their bids for fear of overpaying for the item – a practice called *bid shading*. This practice makes bidding tricky and can potentially discourage participants. Second price auctions are more economically efficient in that prices reflect the beliefs of the bidders more closely.

Selling on eBay

eBay is probably the most familiar of all auctions. It works much like a second priced sealed bid auction in which the winning bidder pays the price of the next highest bidder plus a small bid increment. This small increment by which prices increase in the auction is the equivalent of the *tick size* in financial markets. In addition, an automatic bidding system bids on behalf of the buyer by the minimum amount to outbid other buyers up to a secret maximum bid specified by the buyer.

An interesting feature of eBay is that there tends to be an avalanche of bids at the end of auctions. Bidders probably don't like to reveal their interest early so as to try and avoid a *bidding war*, in which competing buyers successively outbid each other and rapidly force up the price. Most stock markets experience a large increase in trading volume towards closing time possibly for similar reasons.

Auctioning debt by the US Treasury

Perhaps the most significant auctions are for sovereign debt. The participants in these auctions are mostly banks or specialist dealers in government bonds. The scale of these auctions can be awesome with many billions of dollars' worth of bonds offered in a single auction. They do, however, work in comparatively straightforward ways.

In the US, bids can be competitive or non-competitive. With a *non-competitive bid*, the bidder is guaranteed to receive the amount he specified but accepts the yield determined by the competitive auction bids. Non-competitive bidding is intended for individuals, and the amount available for issue in this way is strictly limited so as not to interfere with price formation by competitive bidding.

REMEMBER

The yield of a bond is the annual return taking into account both the coupons and the redemption value. Chapter 4 has more on this.

Competitive bids are ranked by the yield specified by the bidder. They're then accepted in full, starting from the lowest yield until the total value of awarded bids equals the offered amount of security (for example, a Treasury Note). Importantly, the yield on all the issued securities is exactly the same and equal to the highest accepted bid. Each bidder is allowed to bid on only up to 35 per cent of the offered amount. The reasoning is to prevent a situation in which a single bidder can determine the outcome of an auction in his favour.

The key result from debt auctions such as for US Treasury Notes is the yield. But investors also follow the *cover*, which is the ratio of the total amount of bids to the offered amount. The cover is used as a measure of the amount of investor interest in an auction.

On the 26th January 2016, the US Treasury auctioned $26 billion in two-year Treasury Notes. They were issued on February 1st 2016 and will be redeemed on January 31st 2018. $75.3 billion was tendered, and so the cover ratio was $75.3/$26 = 2.9 which shows the popularity of US Treasuries despite an auction yield of 0.75%.

MAKING SURE THAT YOU DON'T NEED TO CALL SAUL – OR ANY LAWYER

Financial transactions are subject to many types of deception, some with interesting names. Making a shill bid or being a front runner aren't things you want to do.

Auctions are open events so as to encourage wide participation and accurate price formation. But this openness can also potentially encourage abuse. Most abuses centre around bids that aren't genuine in some way, often for the purpose of artificially increasing a price.

On eBay you can place a bid on your own auction so as to give the illusion of interest in the auction. This type of *shill bid* is illegal as the objective is to deceive other participants. Similar behaviour is possible on financial markets and especially in high frequency trading (HFT). In HFT you can place and then cancel limit orders with the purpose of misleading others. This is called *spoofing* and has sometimes been raised as the cause of the 2010 flash crash. Regulations now forbid it.

At a major theatre in London at the moment, they advertise a *front runner membership* that gives preferential access to tickets. However, in finance, front running is something quite different and quite illegal. Many financial markets operate with intermediate dealers who buy and sell on behalf of their clients. If a dealer receives instructions from a client knowing that a buy order will increase the price of the asset, the dealer could buy the same asset for his own account in advance of buying for his client. After the purchase for his client has moved the price up, he could then sell his own position for a nice profit. Brokers have a duty to put client interests ahead of their own.

Balancing supply and demand with double-sided auctions

In this section, I give you more detail of how double-sided auctions work. Figure 18-1 shows a snapshot of the order book for the Chi-X Europe exchange. On the left side, the orders are split into Asks and Bids. The *asks* are orders to sell the asset that, in this instance, is shares in the oil company BP. The *bids* are orders to buy shares in BP. From the centre line, the asks are listed in ascending order while the bids are listed in descending order. The centre line is where the lowest ask meets the highest bid and is where trades can take place. The list of the last ten trades on the right shows that the latest trade took place at the lowest ask price.

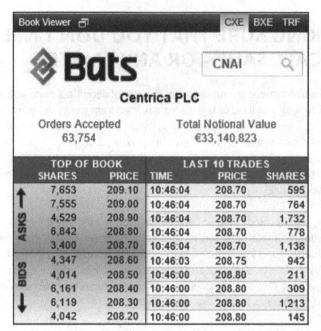

FIGURE 18-1:
View of an
exchange
trading book.

	TOP OF BOOK		LAST 10 TRADES		
	SHARES	PRICE	TIME	PRICE	SHARES
ASKS ↑	7,653	209.10	10:46:04	208.70	595
	7,555	209.00	10:46:04	208.70	764
	4,529	208.90	10:46:04	208.70	1,732
	6,842	208.80	10:46:04	208.70	778
	3,400	208.70	10:46:04	208.70	1,138
BIDS ↓	4,347	208.60	10:46:03	208.75	942
	4,014	208.50	10:46:00	208.80	211
	6,161	208.40	10:46:00	208.80	309
	6,119	208.30	10:46:00	208.80	1,213
	4,042	208.20	10:46:00	208.80	145

Source: www.BatsTrading.co.uk

The majority of the orders in an order book are limit orders. However, you can also place a *market order*, which is an order to trade straight away at the best price. A market buy order is executed at the best ask price while each market sell order is executed at the best bid price. Because market orders are executed immediately, the transaction price is recorded as the *last trade price*.

Limit orders are placed at a range of distances from the last trade price in the order book – some close and some far. Aggregate information on all of these orders is referred to as the *market depth*. Market depth gives an indication of the size of an order needed to move the market price by a given amount. If a market is deep, it needs especially large orders to move the price.

Stock markets operate in a continuous fashion during the day with limit orders arriving all the time and market orders being executed as soon as possible. In addition, most stock markets operate discrete opening and closing auctions that establish the opening and closing prices separately from the normal continuous auction. Various reasons can be given for this practice but one of the main reasons for the closing auction is to establish as fair a price as possible given the linkage with other products, such as futures and options, that are settled using closing stock market prices.

PICTURING THE ORDER BOOK

Limit orders and market orders are constantly being added to the order book. Market orders are executed by being matched with a limit order at the market price at the centre of the order book. That's where the highest bid meets the lowest ask as shown in Figure 18-1. You'll find it useful to know the *shape* of the order book or, in other words, how many shares are in the queue to be executed. Knowing the shape can tell you something about the future movement of prices because the shape is related to order imbalances.

The shape is influenced by a couple of factors:

- Most orders are received around the current price

- Orders near the market price are most likely to be executed and disappear from the order book

The result of these two factors is that the order book is typically hump-shaped with the peak a short distance away from the market price. The humps on the buy and sell sides are symmetrically positioned, as shown here:

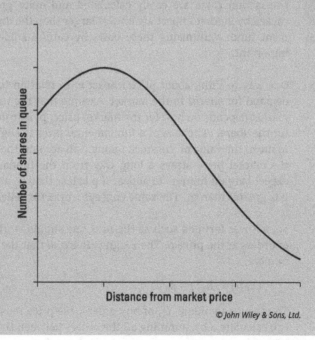

© John Wiley & Sons, Ltd.

Settlement is when cash payment is finally made for a financial asset.

REMEMBER The aim of the closing auction is to match up as many of the outstanding buy and sell orders as possible. Each stock market has its own rules, but most of these auctions terminate at a random time at a price that maximises the number of trades. The random timing minimises the possibility of the price being manipulated by a trader for his advantage.

Looking at the Price Impact of a Trade

The *price impact* of a trade is the relationship between that trade and the subsequent price change. If you're trading frequently or splitting up a large order into many smaller orders, then price impact is important for you. Although you can think of price impact as a form of friction when you're trading, it's really the basic mechanism by which markets adjust to new information.

Price impact is quite different from *direct costs* such as commission and fees. Those transaction costs are easily calculated and quite predictable. The *indirect costs* caused by market impact are always larger than the direct costs for a large investment fund. Minimising these costs by careful trade management is therefore important.

REMEMBER

One way to think about price impact is in relation to the balance of supply and demand for shares in the market. Assume that the total volume of buyers in the market depends on how far the market price, p, is from the fundamental price, p_0, for the share. (The idea of a fundamental price is slightly nebulous, but is meant to mean the value of the stock taking into account the company's profitability.) If the market price strays a long way from the fundamental price, then you can expect bargain hunters to appear if p is less than p_0 and profit-takers to appear if p is greater than p_0. The same concept works for sellers.

So, a linear formula such as the next one should work, where V(p) is the volume of orders at the price p. The ± sign is there so that the volume is always a positive number.

$$V_{\pm}(p) = \pm b_{\pm}(p - p_0).$$

To execute a volume, Q, of buy orders, the price must rise by an amount, Δ. You can calculate Δ by summing all the orders between the price p_0 and $p_0+Δ$ using an integral:

$$Q = \int_{p_0}^{p_0+\Delta} V(p)\,dp = \int_{p_0}^{p_0+\Delta} b_+(p - p_0)\,dp = \frac{b_+}{2}\Delta^2.$$

Rearranging this formula to solve for Δ, shows that the price impact depends on the square root of the order size, Q:

$$\Delta_{\pm} = \sqrt{2Q/b_{\pm}}.$$

In practice, this formula works well. You can check it using detailed trade data from a broker. The results of that analysis show the square root rule for the dependence of the price impacts on order size, and also show an additional dependence on the volatility, σ, of the market and V, the *average traded volume*. *Average traded volume* is exactly what it sounds like: the number of shares traded in a day for any stock varies, sometimes depending on whether there is any significant news for it; V is the average of this number. The constant, C, in the formula varies from stock to stock but is approximately equal to 1:

$$\Delta = C\sigma\sqrt{Q/V}.$$

This formula tells you that if the volatility of the market rises, then the price impact will rise. It also says that if the average traded volume of a stock rises, then the price impact declines. Both are intuitively sensible. If volatility is high and the market is fluctuating a lot, then you expect an extra trade to have a bigger than normal influence. Equally, if you typically find a large amount of trading in the stock you'd like to buy or sell, then the impact of your additional trade doesn't affect the price much.

As an example of this formula, assume that you have a trade, Q, with one-hundredth of the daily volume, V, so Q = V/100. Also assume that the constant C = 1. Now you can calculate Δ:

$$\Delta = \sigma\sqrt{\frac{V/100}{V}} = \sigma/10.$$

A trade with one-hundredth of the average daily volume will move the market by a tenth of the daily volatility. This amplification is huge and shows the need for careful trade management to avoid high cost from price impact.

Being a Market Maker and Coping with Bid-Ask Spreads

A market maker stands in the middle between trades. He's there to facilitate the buying and selling of financial assets such as stocks. The market maker offers to sell stock at the ask (or offer) price and to buy at the bid price. His plan is to make money by charging a higher price to sell than to buy. So quoted ask prices are always higher than the bid prices, which sounds simple.

In the jargon of finance, a market maker is a *liquidity provider*. I talk about liquidity in the upcoming section 'Exploring the meaning of liquidity'.

REMEMBER

Electronic market making is different than old-fashioned market making by humans with obligations to provide quotes both ways. Now traders can buy in one venue and sell in another, so the traditional model doesn't work. Most markets are order driven. Anyone placing limit orders is a market maker rather than a market taker (who uses market orders).

The *bid-ask spread* is the difference between the bid price and the ask price. The spread can vary in time and according to the stock involved. During the noughties, bid-ask spreads declined significantly, a move often attributed to the growth of high-frequency trading, or HFT. The presence of automated or algorithmic dealers increased the competition in the markets between market makers and forced a reduction in asking prices and an increase in bid prices.

You'd think that the difference between an asking and a bid price would just reflect transaction costs in the market or some form of commission, but more subtle ideas have emerged to explain how dealers operate. These ideas centre around the idea of informed and uninformed traders. *Informed traders* know valuable information. If the information is good news for the stock, they buy; if it's bad news, they sell. An *uninformed trader* trades by necessity, not in response to useful information. For example, the manager of a mutual fund may need to make a trade because a client sold his holding and the manager has to sell the corresponding shares.

For a market maker posting both buy and sell orders in the market, informed traders are a danger. They know more than he does and so his posted prices may prove to be incorrect. The market maker then pays too much to buy or receives too little when selling and loses money. This situation is sometimes called the *adverse selection*.

Adverse selection – buying too high or selling too low – happens in many different markets where an asymmetry of information is evident. That's when one person knows more than another person. Customers who buy insurance products are probably those with the greatest need of them and so present an above-average risk to the seller. This has to be factored into the price offered.

Because of the presence of large numbers of informed traders in the market, the bid-ask spread can change throughout the day as market makers protect themselves against adverse moves in prices.

Exploring the meaning of liquidity

Mostly, liquidity is considered to be a good thing for a market. *Liquidity* is defined as the ability to execute large trades rapidly at low cost and with limited impact on prices. Liquidity exists because speculators are prepared to absorb excess demand for a financial instrument in exchange for compensation given by a price change in their favour.

Liquidity can also refer to the volume of orders placed in a market. This is an expression of a willingness by market participants to trade in the market and is indicated by the presence of large numbers of limit orders. Limit orders can be cancelled, so liquidity can disappear quickly. High trading volume isn't necessarily a good indicator of market liquidity.

It's also possible to measure liquidity by the bid-ask spread. A market that's particularly liquid has a narrow bid-ask spread. But the spread is dependent on the trade size. The bid-ask spread for large trades is higher than for small trades. Market makers can also increase the bid-ask spread to large values if they believe that traders are much more informed than they are. This increase can have the undesired effect of stopping trading altogether and leading to a market collapse.

WARNING

Liquidity is a double-edged sword: While it's great for most investors most of the time to have rapid and cheap access to the stock or bond market, those investors can take flight quickly and cause rapid downward (or, indeed, upward) spirals in prices. So, liquidity can vanish just when you need it most. The credit crisis of 2008 is an example of that outcome. An even worse outcome was the flash crash of 2010 when liquidity vanished in a matter of moments as the algorithms of high-frequency traders switched off in response to already sharp falls on the New York Stock Exchange.

Because of the potential for liquidity drying up and prices plunging, many stock exchanges have what they call *circuit breakers* – rules that prevent percentage moves of stock prices lying outside of specified bands. These bands are placed above and below the average price for the previous five minutes of trading. If the stock price doesn't move back into its band, trading is stopped for a period of five minutes or more. Rules of this kind are referred to as *limit up-limit down* mechanisms.

Making use of information

In this section, I show you how a market maker adjusts his asking and bid prices using the Bayes theorem. Imagine that you're a market maker. Your job is to continuously quote prices to buy and sell shares. To do this, you have to update your bid and ask prices to reflect new information and changing market prices given by actual trades. Your plan is, of course, to make a profit. If you ask too much, though, nobody will buy from you, and if you ask too little, you won't cover the cost of buying the stock in the first place. So you need some maths to tell you how to set your bid and ask quotes that reflect your current knowledge of the market price and anticipate informed participants who may know more than you do.

To start, you're not a 100 per cent sure of the value of the stock you're trading. The value is fluctuating, so it may be at a high price, η, of $101 or a low price, λ, of $99. Now a sale comes through. That tells you that someone thinks the stock may be worth less than it was. To quantify this, you can use Bayes' theorem. You want to know price, P, P(λ|Sale) and P(λ|Buy). Assume that initially you have a 50 per cent chance the price is η and 50 per cent that the price is λ.

The process uses the Bayes theorem, which uses the formula:

$$P\left(A|B\right) = \frac{P\left(B|A\right)P\left(A\right)}{P\left(B|A\right)P\left(A\right)+P\left(B|\overline{A}\right)\left(1-P\left(A\right)\right)}.$$

In this first part, A is the conjecture that the stock's value is λ. B represents the information you've received on the market – whether the last transaction was a sale or a purchase.

Using the Bayes theorem I can write the following formula for the probability that the price of the stock is λ = $99 given that you've just observed a sale in the market. In the formula η = $101.

$$P\left(\lambda|Sale\right) = \frac{P\left(Sale|\lambda\right)P\left(\lambda\right)}{P\left(Sale|\lambda\right)P\left(\lambda\right)+P\left(Sale|\eta\right)P\left(\eta\right)}.$$

You already know that P(λ) = P(η) = 0.5, but the conditional probabilities are a little bit trickier to calculate.

Assume that half of the traders in the market are informed and half are uninformed. An uninformed trader is as likely to sell as he is to buy. However, an informed trader who knows that the stock is at the low value of $99 (you don't) will sell for sure. Contrariwise, an informed trader who knows that the stock is at the high value of $101 will not sell. To use these results, you need another formula from probability theory. The symbol ♦ indicates an informed trade and the same symbol with a bar on top indicates an uninformed trade:

$$P\left(Sale \middle| \lambda\right) = P(\blacklozenge)P(Sale|\blacklozenge) + P\left(\overline{\blacklozenge}\right)P\left(Sale \middle| \overline{\blacklozenge}\right).$$

The arithmetic is

$$P\left(Sale \middle| \lambda\right) = \tfrac{1}{2} \times 1 + \tfrac{1}{2} \times \tfrac{1}{2} = \tfrac{3}{4}.$$

Now you just need to calculate P(Sale|η):

$$P\left(Sale \middle| \eta\right) = \tfrac{1}{2} \times 0 + \tfrac{1}{2} \times \tfrac{1}{2} = \tfrac{1}{4}.$$

Putting all of these results together, you can now calculate the *posterior probability* (the probability after relevant evidence is taken into account) that the true share price is λ given that a share sale has just happened.

$$P\left(\lambda \middle| Sale\right) = \frac{\tfrac{1}{2} \times \tfrac{3}{4}}{\tfrac{1}{2} \times \tfrac{3}{4} + \tfrac{1}{2} \times \tfrac{1}{4}} = \frac{3}{4}.$$

It makes sense that seeing a share sale in the market strengthens your belief that the true value of the stock is at the low value of $99. Given that, in this model where I'm assuming the price can only be $99 or $101, then P(η|Sale) = 1/4. The sale reduces your belief that the true value of the share is at the high end.

The next part of the calculation is to figure out what happens if you first observe a buy trade in the market. These calculations mirror the previous ones starting with the Bayes theorem again:

$$P(\lambda | Buy) = \frac{P(Buy | \lambda)P(\lambda)}{P(Buy | \lambda)P(\lambda) + P\left(Buy \middle| \eta\right)P(\eta)}.$$

In addition, splitting up the probability of buying given that the price is low into the two possibilities of an informed or an uninformed buyer gives you this equation:

$$P\left(Buy \middle| \lambda\right) = P(\blacklozenge)P(Buy|\blacklozenge) + P\left(\overline{\blacklozenge}\right)P\left(Buy \middle| \overline{\blacklozenge}\right).$$

Using the same 50 per cent probability of an informed buyer, you get that

$$P\left(Buy \middle| \lambda\right) = \tfrac{1}{2} \times 0 + \tfrac{1}{2} \times \tfrac{1}{2} = \tfrac{1}{4}.$$

The zero is there because an informed buyer recognises that a low true value for the stock implies bad news, so he refuses to buy. However, for a high value, an informed trader will certainly buy because it must reflect good news and so:

$$P\left(Buy|\eta\right)=\frac{1}{2}\times1+\frac{1}{2}\times\frac{1}{2}=\frac{3}{4}.$$

Putting these values into Bayes' theorem, you get

$$P\left(\lambda|Buy\right)=\frac{\frac{1}{4}\times\frac{1}{2}}{\frac{1}{4}\times\frac{1}{2}+\frac{3}{4}\times\frac{1}{2}}=\frac{1}{4}.$$

Putting all of these results together, you can now use Bayes' theorem to calculate the probability of the high price, η, given that you've observed a buy trade:

$$P(\eta|Buy)=\frac{P(Buy|\eta)P(\eta)}{P(Buy|\lambda)P(\lambda)+P(Buy|\eta)P(\eta)}=\frac{\frac{3}{4}\times\frac{1}{2}}{\frac{1}{4}\times\frac{1}{2}+\frac{3}{4}\times\frac{1}{2}}=\frac{3}{4}.$$

A buy trade indicates that the higher price is the one more likely to be correct.

Calculating the bid-ask spread

After you modify your view about the price of the stock based on observing the order flow, you now need to do something about it. You can set the ask price for the stock by calculating your expectation, E, from the probabilities of the high and low prices – η and λ – given that you've just observed a buy order. Do this using the formula:

$$ask=E\left(V|Buy\right)=\lambda P\left(\lambda|Buy\right)+\eta P\left(\eta|Buy\right).$$

Using the values for the conditional probabilities from the preceding section, you get

$$ask=\$99\times\frac{1}{4}+\$101\times\frac{3}{4}=\$100.5.$$

Likewise, the bid price is given by:

$$bid=E\left(V|Sell\right)=\lambda P\left(\lambda|Sell\right)+\eta P\left(\eta|Sell\right).$$

And the arithmetic goes like this:

$$bid=\$99\times\frac{3}{4}+\$101\times\frac{1}{4}=\$99.5.$$

As you'd expect, the market maker is asking a higher price if you want to buy from him than if you want to sell to him.

These prices are consistent with the market maker's prior belief about the value of the stock and the information from the market implied by the arrival of buy or sell orders. As further orders arrive, a market maker continuously modifies his bid and ask prices in an effort to not lose any money.

Trading Factors and Distributions

In this book, I show you that the distribution of the returns of a financial market aren't consistent with a simple Gaussian (or normal) distribution.

The Gaussian distribution often comes up in science when many factors are influencing the outcome of an experiment. If you ask all the students in your class to measure the length of a piece of string, they'll all give different answers. And that's not just an urban legend or something to do with perfidious students. If you take all of these measurements and count how many you have for each length, the distribution looks like a Gaussian distribution. However, financial returns aren't distributed like that.

REMEMBER

Financial returns are influenced by the behaviour of traders and investors who are knowing participants in the market. This influence leads to two key features of real markets:

>> The distribution of returns in financial returns have fat tails. Far more large rises and large falls in the market exist than you'd expect from a normal Gaussian process. In Chapter 2, I show that the distribution of the returns for a stock index has far more large positive and negative values than you'd expect from a Gaussian distribution.

>> There's a significant autocorrelation in the volatility. The market is often in a quiet state with low volatility and few large price changes – either positive or negative. However, it can switch fairly quickly to a state with high volatility. These correlations in volatility are not what you'd expect from a market following Gaussian returns. If the returns of a financial market are Gaussian, then you'd expect the volatility to be constant and with no correlation.

Several explanations are possible for these behaviours; the most likely ones are

>> **Feedback with past price changes:** Just as you can use feedback to create strange distortions with an electric guitar, feedback in financial markets can potentially create strange effects. For example, if the market falls for some reason, the fall may trigger algorithms to sell. These sales reduce the price further and lead to an avalanche of sell orders, and ultimately, the market crashes. I illustrate this in Figure 18-2.

TECHNICAL STUFF

An *algorithm* is a computer program that can send orders to an exchange to buy or sell stocks. Many algorithms use historical price data at intraday frequencies as input. Other data feeds such as prices from related markets and news in computer-readable format can be used as well.

>> **Traders directly influence one another:** Traders sharing information through chat rooms or other forms of interchange can lead to herding behaviour. An opinion or view can propagate rapidly and lead to an imbalance in the market. If each trader in the market wants to buy or sell an amount, φ, of a financial asset where φ can be +1, 0 or –1 depending upon whether the trader wants to buy, hold or sell the asset, then the price impact, δp, is related to the net order imbalance by the following equation where k is a constant that depends on the liquidity of the market:

$$\delta p = \kappa \sum_{i=1}^{N} \varphi_i .$$

If a net order imbalance caused by a herding of opinions exists, then there'll be a price impact. Moreover, if some traders are influenced by the market impact itself and change their view based on this, a feedback effect can accentuate the market impact.

>> **Large orders split into many small orders so as to reduce market impact:** The section 'Looking at the Price Impact of a Trade' in this chapter gives more detail on this. The impact of even a small order on prices can be large, so large investment funds split their trades into smaller trades to lessen this impact. This generates correlation in market activity and so in the correlation of volatility.

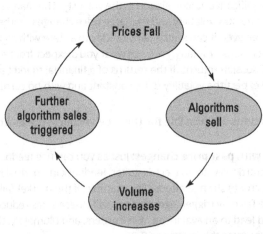

FIGURE 18-2: Schematic of a market feedback loop.

7

The Part of Tens

Find an executive summary of the book's key points.

Recognise the basic unpredictability of markets.

Put some important concepts to use to avoid losing money.

Get hot tips on what to do if you're keen to develop a career in quantitative finance.

Chapter 19

Ten Key Ideas of Quantitative Finance

I n the ten short summaries in this chapter, I explain some key ideas of quantitative finance. I made some hard choices about what to include: some of the points are obvious and useful but easy to ignore; others are subtle ideas that take time to absorb. All are designed to give you some quick insight into quantitative finance. This isn't a substitute for reading the book, but if you only have time for one chapter, make it this one.

If Markets Were Truly Efficient Nobody Would Research Them

The *efficient market hypothesis* that the market knows best has become widely accepted and is the basis behind passive investing strategies such as index tracking.

REMEMBER

An *index-tracking fund* aims to closely follow a public index such as the S&P 500 or the Hang Seng Index. The fund manager's only aim is to achieve a market-average investment performance. The fund manager offers investors low costs in exchange for the modest performance promise.

If the market were truly efficient, and all publicly available information was incorporated in prices, there would be no incentive for anyone to acquire information. Funny then that major companies that sell just that information are thriving. If everyone is uninformed and acts passively like the manager of an index-tracking fund, it pays for someone to become informed. There cannot be an equilibrium in the market, and information seeking will always be a key feature of markets.

One way of putting this is that markets are *almost* efficient. Assuming efficient markets works well for index trackers because the low cost for the clients is attractive and can be achieved by low expenditure on information and research. And the lack of false promises is also popular with clients. Acting as though the market is efficient works if you're happy with being no better than average.

But there are pockets of inefficiency in the market; they're not easy to find, but they do exist. The existence of consistently profitable trading and investing firms provides some evidence for this. Academic research also shows up inefficiencies in markets. For example, evidence shows that *value stocks*, outperform the market. *Value stocks* are those in which the assets (for example buildings and machinery) of the company exceed the value of all of the shares in the company. Many companies like this aren't very glamorous and so are overlooked and under priced by investors.

There's also good evidence of a *momentum* effect in markets. Financial assets tend to follow their recent history. Of course, there are turning points in markets, but all trading strategies realise losses sometimes. Betting on the continuation of a trend works for many investment firms despite some losses due to changes in trend.

The Gaussian Distribution is Very Helpful but Doesn't Always Apply

Many calculations in quantitative finance rely on the assumption of a Gaussian (normal) distribution, which I discuss in Chapter 2. This assumption is a good one, but many studies show that it's not the whole story. The returns of most financial assets are influenced by many factors, so the Gaussian assumption should be a good one. However, knowing participants can influence markets through their actions. So the returns distribution isn't as simple as what you get from the distribution of measurements of the length of a piece of string, for example. Financial returns typically have far more small returns near zero and also far more large returns – both negative and positive – than a normal distribution. You can correct for a lack of normality in most models, so the Gaussian viewpoint is still a good one to maintain but be aware of its limitations!

Don't Ignore Trading Costs

You can easily get carried away by the beauty of some of the models in quantitative finance, but don't stray too far from reality! Automation has greatly reduced trading costs but has not entirely eliminated them. If you ignore trading costs, you can end up taking substantial losses. After all, many market participants still earn their living by being intermediaries between trades.

There will always be friction in markets. The price to buy a financial asset (the *ask price*) will always be higher than the price to sell it (the *bid price*). So if you do a *round trip*, in which you buy and sell an asset very quickly, you'll lose out unless the market is quicker than you and you're lucky. Be aware of it and try to come to good estimates of its magnitude. The model presented in Chapter 18 for the bid–ask spread is a good start. It shows clearly that the bid–ask spread is not constant, so it's costly to trade sometimes and cheap at other times.

And if you work for a large investment company or bank, the market impact of your trading is important. In a way, this is the point of capitalism. Prices respond to supply and demand and act as signals to others. If you start buying (selling) a financial asset, the price will start to rise (fall) as other participants respond to what's happening.

Know Your Contract

This seemingly obvious advice doesn't apply only to quantitative finance, but is especially important for quantitative finance because there are so many complex contracts to get your head around. After all, quants invented the term *plain vanilla* to describe the simplest form of option.

You need to keep an eye on many details in the underlying equity, bond and foreign exchange (FX) markets. For example:

>> **Equity market:** Most equities pay out dividends. When the stock goes ex-dividend and the buyer is no longer entitled to the dividend, the share price drops sharply. Published share prices are often adjusted accordingly, so that's something to watch for.

>> **Bond market:** The maturity and coupon dates are key, as are the coupon amounts. For callable bonds, know what premium is paid if your bond is called.

>> **Futures market:** With its diversity of contracts, you do well to pay attention to the details of the futures market. Some are cash settled, others are physically settled. Delivery terms vary from exchange to exchange and need to be examined carefully – especially for timing and quality. You need to know the contract size. For example, crude oil contracts (Brent or WTI) are for 1,000 barrels. Also, check out carefully which months are traded. This affects any strategy for rolling the contracts.

>> **Options market:** This market has the most complexity. Some options depend on multiple underlying assets. Know what they are. So-called knock-out barrier options pay out only if a specific level is *not* reached. If the barrier is reached, then the option becomes worthless. You need to know these contract terms exactly.

Understanding Volatility is Key

Volatility is arguably the most important quantity in quantitative finance. Volatility is important for pricing options, sizing positions in trading strategies and in monitoring risk of investments. Randomness is the key property of financial price series, and volatility is the measure of randomness.

Many academics have devoted their careers to the study of volatility, so many models are available. Chapter 7 gives a summary of the most robust and popular models. If you haven't read that chapter already, read it now. Get to know some models of volatility and how to use them. Don't be seduced by complex models that are hard to fit.

You Can Price Options by Building Them from Cash and Stock

An *equity call option*, which is a contract giving the holder the right but not the obligation to buy stock at a certain price at a certain future date, can be synthesised from a position in both stock and cash (see Chapter 5 for more detail on options). To see this, imagine holding a position of one call option and a short position in the underlying stock. A *short position* in a stock is like holding a negative amount of stock: if the price rises, the short position value declines; if the price falls, the short position value rises. A short stock position is, then, like betting that the stock will fall. But the call option is like a bet that the stock will rise.

By combining call options and short stock positions in the correct ratio – called delta (Δ) – you can come up with a risk-free position. In other words, the value of the combined position is independent of the stock price for the length of the position. Because this combined position is risk free, it can be valued using the risk-free interest rate.

This way of arriving at pricing formulae is called *arbitrage pricing* because it uses the principle that there should be no arbitrage opportunities left. (Chapter 10 on pricing options gives more details.) Arbitrage pricing is a generally powerful tool because riskless ways of making profits in financial markets are rare.

Finance Isn't Like Physics

In physics, you have immutable laws (do you remember action = reaction from your school days?) that are the same this year and next. In finance, you find few such laws . . . although the formula for compound interest may count. Finance is about human constructs, contracts such as bonds or options and human behaviour, so you can't pin it down with universally true laws.

Innovation in finance is much easier than in other industries (no need to build big factories), so change can be rapid. So rapid in fact that regulators can find it hard to keep pace. Darwin's theory of evolution is probably more relevant to the financial marketplace than Newton's laws of motion.

Many very detailed studies have been carried out on the statistics of financial assets, and you do indeed find many common features such as fat tails and volatility clustering, but so far no universal laws and certainly no causative laws like those of Newton. The adaptive human behaviour that drives markets seems to preclude that. Treat all market models with healthy scepticism.

Diversification is the One True Free Lunch

Holding individual financial assets, whether they're stocks or bonds, is risky. There's a good chance that on selling the asset you will receive less than you paid for it. In the worst case, the company goes bust or defaults on its debt and you get nothing or close to nothing. However much you research the assets you purchase, you always face risk because the future is unknowable. Careful analysis can help you avoid risky stocks or bonds but only ever reduces the risk fractionally.

The one big thing that can help you to reduce risk is to *diversify* – to buy many assets and to buy assets as unlike each other as possible. Doing two unrelated things reduces the chance of both of them going wrong compared to either one of them considered separately. What it says is that markets are efficient and that the price of risk has already been included in the price of the assets you buy. It also asks you not to think that you know more than you really do – overconfidence in your views is dangerous when the reality is that most market price changes are random. Because the returns from a diversified portfolio generally aren't correlated the value of one asset often drops when another asset rises in value.

The risk adjusted return of a diversified portfolio isn't just the same as the risk of a single asset. The return from a portfolio of N assets increases as N increases. However, the risk of a diversified portfolio will increase with $\sqrt{N}$. This means that the return per unit of risk from a diversified portfolio increases as N divided by $\sqrt{N}$ which is $\sqrt{N}$. In other words, the risk-adjusted return from a diversified portfolio can be $\sqrt{N}$ larger than for a single asset.

Be aware that you have many choices in building a diversified portfolio. An index-tracker fund invests its capital according to the size or capitalisation of the constituent companies. This may reduce the diversification of the portfolio if the index is dominated by very large companies. Better, in the long run, to allocate with equal weights, so that the variance attributed to each asset in the portfolio is the same, and to avoid concentrating risk.

A diversified portfolio isn't a get-rich-quick strategy (I wouldn't be writing this book if I knew how to do that!) but it should give you good steady performance and enable you to sleep at night.

Find Tools to Help Manage All the Data

Finance is one of the industries in which data and computing take centre stage. Money and financial instruments are traded constantly throughout the day with prices quoted every millisecond or even more frequently. With the proliferation in the number of financial assets such as bonds, options and stocks, the amount of data available is enormous. Not just price data: news agencies now provide computer-readable feeds so that you can attempt to analyse the impact of almost any factor of a financial asset.

Mastering the tools that help you assimilate as much of this data as possible gives you a big advantage. These tools are not necessarily complex or difficult. A simple scatterplot is a powerful and underestimated tool for investigating the relationship between two variables and also for checking the integrity of the data.

REMEMBER

A *scatterplot* is a graph in which the values of two variables are plotted on two axes, often called the X and Y axes. A scatter chart is visual, can be used on large datasets and can guide you in building a good model. Refer to Chapter 9 for a good example of a scatterplot.

Another powerful tool for big data sets is Principal Components Analysis (PCA). It lets you see what is important in your data and allows you to reduce the dimensionality of your models. Moreover, it has its own sets of scatterplots, the score and loadings plots, that let you build intuition about your dataset. Find out about PCA and use it in your analysis.

Don't Get Fooled by Complex Models

Data is abundant, as is computing power, so it's natural to combine them and try to build complex predictive models.

You can't avoid some complexity. For example, to analyse the risk of a large portfolio of stocks, you need to know the correct prices of the constituent stocks. That may sound simple, but to carry out historical simulations you need historical data going back many years. So for each stock (and there may be hundreds of them), you need to account for price events such as dividends, stock splits and special dividends. You need to incorporate this level of complexity into models if they're to be credible.

However, you may introduce other forms of complexity during your analysis because the complex model is hard to implement and requires time-consuming calculations, and that can be potentially quite dangerous. For example, in a large dataset with data for hundreds of assets going back many years, introducing a GARCH volatility model (see Chapter 7), which requires an optimisation to fit it, may greatly extend the runtime for any portfolio calculations. Sticking to a robust exponentially weighted moving average model, which I also talk about in Chapter 7, may be the better choice.

WARNING

A dangerous form of complexity occurs when you use many variables to try to predict financial returns. The snag here is that you'll end up fitting your model to *random noise* (price fluctuations with no trend) rather than uncovering a meaningful relationship. This is called *overfitting*. The model will appear to be excellent for the data points you're using to build the model. However, for out-of-sample data, your model will probably be worse than useless and make very poor predictions. Improved statistical tests for goodness of fit are helpful, but you still need to be aware of the danger of using them in a selective way that invalidates the conclusions.

TIP

An important technique for avoiding overfitting is cross-validation. In this technique, you split the data set into a training set you use to build your model and a validation set you use to evaluate your model. As you increase the complexity of your model the measure of lack of fit (such as a sum of squared errors) will decrease for both the training and validation sets. At some point however, the lack of fit for the validation set will start to increase even as the fit continues to improve for the training set. This is because your model has begun to fit to the noise (random fluctuations) in the training set. It's at this point that you need to stop adding variables or parameters to your model.

Chapter 20

Ten Ways to Ace Your Career in Quantitative Finance

A sking questions and building your own models is the best way to find out what to do next in your quest to become a quantitative finance guru. The tips in this chapter offer additional suggestions.

Follow Financial Markets

Being good at maths and computing is great, but following what's happening in the real world is also a big help.

It can seem weird picking up a pink newspaper, but that's a price you have to pay for being in finance. The tables of numbers in these journals can tell a story and some of the articles are interesting.

Only when you start following some data and the story do you begin to get a deeper understanding of what's going on. If something is of special interest to you, you can always investigate further with a few of the many publicly available data sources, including the following:

>> *Yahoo Finance* (www.finance.yahoo.com) has extensive stock market data to download. The Python computing language also has software tools to automate this.

>> The Federal Reserve Economic Database (FRED) at www.research. stlouisfed.org has excellent data on US bonds and interest rates.

>> The US Energy Information Administration (www.eia.gov) has good data on the oil and gas markets.

Read Some Classic Technical Textbooks

If you're keen to get into more detail on some of the topics of this book, then the best places to go are classic textbooks such as *Options, Futures and Other Derivatives* by John C Hull (Pearson Education). This book has stood the test of time and is used as a course book by many universities. The book is now into its eighth edition and has a global edition for non-US readers. The focus of the book is on derivatives pricing but it also has good coverage of risk management.

Market Models: A Guide to Financial Data Analysis by Carol Alexander (Wiley Finance) is also an excellent book and with much more focus on data analysis techniques rather than derivatives pricing. The author has excellent chapters on volatility models and principal components analysis.

If you're feeling feisty, you can try the more up-to-date four-volume series *Market Risk Analysis* also by Carol Alexander (Wiley Finance). It covers most of the topics of her earlier book but in much greater depth.

Read Some Non-technical Books

You may not want to start working on a derivatives pricing desk at a bank or do any quantitative trading yourself, but you'd like to know more about the quantitative way of seeing the world. You can find great books on the subject. *My Life as a Quant* by Emmanuel Derman (Wiley Finance) is the autobiographical story of how the author went from researching esoteric physics to working in bulge bracket banks on Wall Street. Along the way he met Fischer Black, one of the authors of the famous Black–Scholes equation. The personal reminiscences are insightful.

Another good read is *The Black Swan: The Impact of the Highly Improbable* by Nassim Nicholas Taleb (Penguin). Taleb also wrote the bestseller *Fooled by Randomness*, a primer on problems of luck and uncertainty. *The Black Swan* is more philosophical as it includes the author pondering the dysfunction of markets and human nature.

Take a Professional Course

Courses are available in quantitative finance so that you can become accredited and hopefully use your expertise to get a job. The best known is the Certificate in Quantitative Finance provided by Fitch Learning. Head to www.cqf.com. The course is delivered online and requires six months of study. The team of lecturers is led by Paul Wilmott, who is also the author of several textbooks on quantitative finance.

If your interest is more in investment management than derivatives pricing, then the Chartered Financial Analyst qualification from the CFA Institute (www.cfainstitute.org) is worth considering. The Professional Risk Managers International Association (PRMIA) at www.prmia.org offers a variety of graduate-level courses in risk management.

Attend Networking Meetings and Conferences

Getting to know other quants is sure to give you inspiration and maybe even help with a career move. A good way to do this is to attend conferences and networking meetings including:

>> The two-day MathFinance Conference (www.mathfinance.com) is held every year in Frankfurt, Germany. Renowned academics give keynote lectures while practitioners share their insights in roundtable discussions. The conference even includes a conference dinner when you can have more extended conversations and enjoy local hospitality.

>> In the United States, the Advanced Risk Management and Portfolio Management one-week boot camp is a way to learn lots in a week. See www.symmys.com for details.

>> The Thalesians (www.thalesians.com) organise Meetup talks with respected speakers in financial centres around the world on a regular basis. They also publish quantitative strategy notes.

Participate in Online Communities

If you're studying on your own and need some help or just want to find out what others are thinking, then participating in an online community is an idea. The Wilmott Forum at www.wilmott.com and Quantnet at www.quantnet.com are dedicated to quantitative finance and have many deep experts contributing as well as newbies.

If you're looking for a job, then try using LinkedIn at www.linkedin.com, if you're not doing so already. Make sure to join groups such as Algorithmic Trading to keep you better connected.

Use resources such as Stack Overflow (www.stackoverflow.com) if you're struggling with some programming. The chances are that your question has already been asked and answered. If not, you can always ask your own.

Study a Programming Language

Reading a book (especially this one) is a great start, but to really get stuck into quantitative finance you have to become good at computer programming.

Spreadsheets are a good place to start, especially if you make use of the macro languages available behind them. You can easily generate random numbers to carry out the simulations you need to price even quite complex options. In addition, any spreadsheet has enough mathematical functions to calculate the formulae from the solution of the Black-Scholes equation. Even with a megabyte of data, spreadsheets are still manageable and that's enough for decades of daily price data.

However, spreadsheets are not the best tool for quantitative finance. Handling big data sets with spreadsheets is hard, and if you use formulae in the spreadsheets themselves rather than in macro code, you may easily get confused. Specialist programming languages such as Python and R have much better provision for mathematical projects and have extensive packages with mathematical, statistical and graphical routines. Python modules such as pandas were designed with financial time series in mind and have solutions to common problems in dealing with this data such as missing data.

For programs that need to run in real time, such as for trading, or if you just need to do lots of calculations fast, then C++ is still the most commonly used language. Python and R offer greater flexibility during development, but it's also possible to run C++ from within Python and R if you need to.

Go Back to School

Many universities across the world offer a masters program in finance, but you can also do courses such as a masters in mathematical and computational finance that offers in-depth training in all the subjects covered by this book. They also come under the description of financial engineering or just computational finance. The website www.quantnet.com gives some rankings for US universities.

Many of the courses are expensive and are a major time commitment but should significantly boost your chances of landing a good job.

Apply for that Hedge Fund or Bank Job

If you feel that you've really mastered quantitative finance, then it's time to apply for a job. Many, many, recruiters exist in the field so take your time to find one that you feel can help you. Make sure that you use LinkedIn and create a good profile.

Specialist websites such as www.efinancialcareers.co.uk are helpful. The book *Frequently Asked Questions in Quantitative Finance* by Paul Wilmott (Wiley) gives detailed advice on preparing for an interview at a bank.

Take Time to Rest Up and Give Back

Don't forget that with all this hard work studying mathematics and finance, you need a rest sometime. Take a break. Chill. And don't forget – if you make a pile with that job on Wall Street, be generous with the loot. It's good for you, and good for others – and you don't need a complicated math model to prove that!

Glossary

algorithm: A term from computer science meaning a set of rules followed in a calculation. In finance, it has come to mean a set of rules used to execute trades automatically, and normally, at minimum cost.

arbitrage: Exploiting price anomalies to make a risk-free profit. In classical financial theory there aren't supposed to be any arbitrage opportunities. It's assumed someone else always got there first. Example: buy stock in one trading venue at a low price; sell it in another venue at a high price. Unlikely but possible.

autocorrelation: The correlation of a time series with itself at different time steps. Day to day, price returns are almost independent of each other because of the efficiency of markets, so the autocorrelation is almost always equal to 0. However, at shorter time intervals, intraday autocorrelation may not be 0.

autocovariance: A measure that gives an indication of the connection between a random variable at a given moment in time with itself at a specified earlier moment in time.

backtesting: Testing a trading strategy by applying it to historical data.

backwardation: A condition in the futures market in which near futures, close to expiry, are more expensive than far futures. Backwardation is normally associated with high demand for a commodity such as crude oil. The opposite of backwardation is *contango*.

bid-ask spread: The difference between the price quoted for an immediate sale (bid) of a financial asset and the price (ask) for an immediate purchase of a financial asset.

Black-Scholes equation: A partial differential equation for the price of an option in terms of the underlying asset price, the risk-free interest rate and the volatility of the underlying asset.

big data: Data that can't be captured and manipulated by standard tools such as spreadsheets because there's so much of it.

Brownian motion: See *geometric Brownian motion*.

carry trade: A trading strategy that involves borrowing money in one currency at a low interest rate to invest it in another at a high interest rate.

calendar spread: A position in the futures or options market consisting of two contracts, one long and the other short, with different expiries. Example: if the crude oil market is in backwardation but you think supply will be released from storage, then you can sell the front month future and buy the second month future.

call option: An option to buy an underlying asset such as a bond or a stock.

close out: To place a trade opposite in sign to your existing position so that your resulting net position is zero. For example, if you're long ten oil futures contracts, then you can close out this position by going short ten oil futures. The short positions must have the same expiry as the long position to close out the overall position. If not, you have a *spread position*.

contango: A condition in the futures market in which the near futures, close to expiry, are cheaper than the far futures. Contango is normally associated with weak demand and high levels of storage of a physical commodity such as crude oil.

correlation: A statistical relationship between two variables. Correlation is a number between –1 and 1. If it's –1, then the first variable rises when the other falls. If it's +1, then the first variable rises when the other variable rises. They also fall together.

coupon: Interest payment from a bond.

covariance: A statistical relationship between two variables similar to *correlation*. The covariance gives an indication of how closely connected the variables are. You calculate the correlation between two variables from the covariance by dividing by the standard deviation of each of the variables. The correlation is a kind of normalised covariance.

data: A set of measured values.

default: A situation in which a country or company that's issued bonds goes bankrupt and can no longer make regular coupon payments.

delta (Δ): The rate of change of the price of an option with the price of the underlying asset.

derivative: A financial instrument whose price is derived from the price of another financial instrument.

Dow Jones Industrial Average (DJIA): A stock market index which indicates the price performance of 30 of the largest companies listed on the New York Stock Exchange. It includes a wide range of companies representative of the US economy.

drawdown: The peak-to-trough decline in the value of an investment.

efficient market hypothesis (EMH): The theory that financial asset prices reflect all available information. According to this theory it should not be possible to beat the market and manage a portfolio of stocks that performs better than an index.

eigenvalue: A characteristic value for a matrix and in finance especially the covariance matrix. The covariance matrix for N assets has N eigenvalues when N is an integer.

exponentially weighted moving average (EWMA): A method of smoothing (averaging) a time series by weighting the most recent values more highly than the later values. The weighting is done in a particular way with weight values that decline by a constant factor with each time step into the past.

expiry: The time by which an option must be exercised. For a futures contract, expiry is the date when the holder must make or take delivery.

exotic option: An option more complex than the usual *plain vanilla option*. An exotic option may depend on multiple underlying assets or have a payoff that depends on a more complex condition than just the underlying asset price at expiry.

fat tail: A large positive value for the *kurtosis* meaning that the probability of extreme events is far more likely than expected from a *Gaussian distribution*. Sometimes referred to as a heavy tail.

financial asset: An asset whose value comes from a contractual claim such as a bond or a stock.

financial instrument: A tradable financial asset.

fitting: The process of adjusting the parameters in an equation so that the calculated values of the equation are as close as possible to some measured data. Fitting is an important step in creating a working mathematical model.

forward curve: The curve drawn using futures (or forward) market prices for contracts with different expiry.

front month: The *futures contract* closest to expiry.

FTSE 100 Index (the Financial Times Stock Exchange 100 Index): A stock index consisting of the 100 largest stocks by market capitalisation on the London stock exchange.

futures contract: A contract to buy or sell a commodity, or *financial asset,* such as a bond, at a specified time in the future and at a specified price.

gamma (Γ): The second derivative of an option's price with respect to the price of the underlying asset.

GARCH (generalised autoregressive conditional heteroskedastic): A model for volatility that can capture the effect in financial markets when tranquil periods of small returns are interspersed with volatile periods of large returns.

Gaussian distribution: The standard bell-shaped curve from statistics.

geometric Brownian motion: A model for stock prices that assumes that each price change is random and independent of all previous price changes.

hedge: A trade designed to protect against adverse price movements.

high frequency trading (HFT): Trading using mathematical algorithms running on computers. High frequency can mean holding periods of less than a second and often much less.

implied volatility: *Volatility* calculated from the market price of options.

interest-rate swap: A financial instrument that permits the holder to exchange a fixed rate of interest for a floating rate of interest on the same notional amount of principal.

in-the-money option: An *option* that has intrinsic value.

in sample: A term used in statistics to mean the data used to build a model. Contrast this term with *out of sample,* which is data used to test a model.

intrinsic value: The value an option would have if it were exercised immediately. With stock price S and *strike price* X, the intrinsic value of a call option is S – X if S is larger than X. Otherwise, the option has no intrinsic value. For a put option, the intrinsic value is X – S if S is less than X and is 0 otherwise.

kernel: A function that enters a statistical calculation to smooth out noise from data. Kernel smoothing is a technique that can be used to build non-linear relationships between random variables. See also *noise.*

kurtosis: A measure of the fatness of the tails of a statistical returns distribution. In maths language, kurtosis is the fourth central (calculated from the mean) moment of the distribution divided by the square of the second central moment. You then subtract 3 so that the kurtosis of the normal distribution is 0. See also *fat tail.*

limit order: An order placed in a market to be executed at a specified price or better.

liquidity: The extent to which a financial asset can be quickly bought and sold without affecting the price.

LIBOR (London Interbank Offer Rate): An indication of the interest rate at which a bank can obtain funding for a specified maturity and in a specified currency. LIBOR is calculated for seven maturities and five currencies.

long position: A holding in a financial asset that will profit when the asset rises in price.

maturity: The end of the life of a contract. This term is used especially for bonds.

mean: Mathematical average.

mean reversion: The tendency of an asset price or interest rate to move back to its average price over time. Mean reversion models are often used for interest rates and commodity prices. The *geometric Brownian motion* used to model stock prices does not mean revert.

model: A mathematical representation of the real world.

moving average: An average calculated only from the most up-to-date points in a time series and not from all of the data available. Thus, the average moves as more data becomes available. A moving average is calculated from N data points in a time series that has many more than N points. The average can then be recalculated by adding one point at the front and dropping a point at the end. The moving average is then indicative of the average of the time series at a particular point in time and not of the whole time series.

noise: Unexplained variation or randomness in a *time series.*

normal distribution: See *Gaussian distribution.*

option: A contract that gives the holder the right but not the obligation to buy (or sell) an underlying asset at a time in the future at a price agreed now.

order: An instruction to buy or sell in a trading venue such as a stock market.

out of sample: Data not used while building a model that can be used to reliably test the model.

out-of-the-money option: An option that has no *intrinsic value.*

overfitted: A model that has too many parameters or is too complex and so tends to describe *noise* rather than signal. An overfitted model makes poor out-of-sample predictions.

PCA (Principal components analysis): A mathematical method of finding the most important sources of correlated information in a multivariate model. You can use PCA as a way to reduce the number of variables in a multivariate model.

plain vanilla option: A standard *option* contract.

Poisson distribution: A statistical distribution commonly used to describe discrete events, such as the number of trading orders, within a period of time.

portfolio optimisation: Adjusting the proportions of the assets in a portfolio so as to improve the returns and reduce the risk of the portfolio.

present value: The current worth of a future sum of money, such as a coupon payment. The relationship between the two quantities is defined by the interest rate for the period of time until payment.

principal component: A constrained linear combination of variables in a large data set with the maximum variance.

put option: An option to sell an underlying asset.

random walk: A mathematical construction based on a sequence of steps each of which is in a completely random direction independent of the preceding step.

redemption: The repayment of the principal value of a bond at or before maturity.

regression: A statistical relationship between two or more variables. Especially common is the linear regression in which the parameters in the model occur only to the first power; in other words, there are no squared or higher terms in the parameters.

return: The change in the price of a financial asset. The *simple return* is the price now less the price in the previous time period. The *relative return* is the simple return divided by the price in the previous time period.

risk: The standard deviation of the returns of a portfolio of financial assets; more generally, risk is to do with the potential of losing something of value. Often risk is broken down into components such as market risk, legal risk, operational risk and credit risk.

risk-free rate: The interest rate for an investment considered to have no risk. Often this rate is taken to be the yield on a three-month US Treasury Bill.

risk parity: A method of building an investment portfolio based on the allocation of risk rather than capital and creating a balance between different asset classes such as bonds and equities.

Standard and Poor 500 (S&P 500): A stock market index that indicates the price performance of 500 of the largest companies listed on either the New York Stock Exchange or the Nasdaq Exchange. It has a very diverse range of constituents and because of that is considered an accurate marker of the performance of US equities. It's used as the underlying asset for some of the most popular derivatives contracts, such as the S&P 500 Futures.

skew: A measure of the asymmetry of a statistical distribution. In maths terms, skew is the standardised third central moment of the distribution (calculated from the mean). An asset with positive skew has more chance of a large up move while an asset with negative skew has a higher chance of a large down move. A trading strategy with negative skew may be profitable but consists of lots of small gains interspersed with occasional large losses.

short position: A holding in a financial asset that will profit when the asset falls in price.

Sharpe ratio: A measure of the performance of an investment fund. Sharpe ratio is the average daily return divided by the standard deviation of the daily returns. Multiply by the square root of 250 (the number of trading days in a year) to get the annual Sharpe ratio. A stock index typically has an annual Sharpe ratio of around 0.3 while a particularly good investment fund may have a ratio of 1.

sigma (Σ): The standard deviation of the returns of a financial asset and the symbol used for *volatility*.

spoofing: Placing orders not intending to execute them. The orders are intended to give other participants a false indication of supply and demand.

spot price: The cash price for a commodity or currency for delivery now.

spread position: Holding equal and opposite positions in the futures or options markets. A *calendar spread* is when the opposing positions have different expiries.

standard deviation: A measure of the dispersion of a data set around its average value. Standard deviation is the square root of the average of the squared deviations from the average value.

stochastic: Randomly determined, especially in time.

strike price: The price at which the holder of an option can buy or sell.

time series: A set of data points consisting of measurements taken at successive times.

time value: The value an option has by virtue of the time left until *expiry*. Time value is the options market price less its *intrinsic value*.

trend following: A trading strategy that emphasises past price movements and bets that the price will continue to move in that direction.

value at risk (VaR): The loss in a portfolio that will not be exceeded at some specified confidence level and over a specified time horizon.

variance: The square of the standard deviation. Variance is the average of the squared deviations from the average value.

volatility: The standard deviation of returns.

yield curve: A curve that shows the interest rate for bonds of different maturity.

Index

contracts, 18–19, 349–350
controlling
  about, 9
  data, 352–353
  risk, 22–24
  risk in portfolios, 276
convenience yield, 110
converges, 32
convertible bond, 86
converting
  percentages to fractions, 194
  volatility, 210
convex function, 251
convexity, 178
correlated, 257
correlations
  about, 243, 306
  calculating, 262–266
  defined, 362
  estimating, 282
coupon, 17, 76, 362
coupon-bearing bonds, 75–76
covariance, 246, 253, 279, 362
covariance matrix
  constructing VaR using, 279–281
  measuring market risk with, 253–255
  using, 281
cover, 332
covered positions, 211
covered-call writing, 94
creating
  distributions with random variables, 35–38
  income, 23
  models with principal components analysis (PCA), 180–182
  portfolios, 23–24
  random numbers on computers, 54–58
  VaR using covariance matrix, 279–281
credit risk, 241
credit-default swap, 19
cross-correlation, 306
cross-validation, 174–176, 321, 327, 354

cryptocurrency, 16
CSCO (Cisco Systems), 163
cumulative distribution, 152
curse of dimensionality, 324–325
CVX (Chevron), 163

D

data
  big, 361
  defined, 362
  identifying clusters of, 180–181
  managing, 352–353
  one-dimensional, 140, 150–151
  putting into bins, 140–143
  reducing amount of, 160–176
  standardising, 166–167
  weighting equally, 124–125
data analysis
  about, 139
  data smoothing, 139–149
  estimating distributions, 149–151
  modelling non-normal returns, 151–158
data cleaning, 323
data frames, 160
data matrices, analysing
  see principal components analysis (PCA)
data matrix, 160–161
data smoothing
  about, 139–140
  with kernels, 143–146
  putting data in bins, 140–143
  using moving averages as filters, 147–149
DAX, 73, 105
day vol (daily volume), 89
DD (DuPont), 163
debt, auctioning by the US Treasury, 332
decomposition, 170–172
'deep out of the money,' 91–92
default, 18, 74, 242, 362
defensive stocks, 181

I

IBM (International Business Machines Corp.), 163
ICE (Intercontinental Exchange), 96, 100
icons, explained, 3
identical independent distribution (iid), 309–311, 314
identifying clusters of data, 180–181
identity matrix, 169
iid (identical independent distribution), 309–311, 314
implied volatility, 364
in sample, 364
'in the money,' 91
income
  earning from options, 94–95
  generating, 23
index arbitrage, 108
index futures, 105–106
index-tracking fund, 347
indicators, 295–298, 299–300
indirect costs, 336
infinity (∞), 36
informed traders, 338
instantaneous forward rate, 227
INTC (Intel Corp.), 163
integrals, calculating, 202
Intel Corp. (INTC), 163
Intercontinental Exchange (ICE), 96, 100
interest. *See also* bonds; shares
  about, 16, 67, 68
  accrued, 78–79
  compounding, 68–71
  fixed rates compared with floating rates, 81–84
  London Interbank Offer Rate (LIBOR), 79–80
interest rate futures, 106–107
interest rates
  central banks and, 71
  constancy of, 196
interest-rate derivatives
  about, 223–224
  forward rates, 224–234
  models, 234–237
  yield curve, 224–234
interest-rate swap, 17, 81, 364

International Business Machines Corp. (IBM), 163
International Swaps and Derivatives Association (ISDA), 81, 96
Internet resources
  Advanced Risk Management and Portfolio Management boot camp, 357
  Bank for International Settlements, 276
  CFA Institute, 357
  Cheat Sheet, 2–3, 4, 109, 122, 154
  efinancialcareers, 359
  Federal Reserve Economic Database (FRED), 356
  Fitch Learning, 357
  International Swaps and Derivatives Association, 81
  LinkedIn, 358
  MathFinance Conference, 357
  Professional Risk Managers International Association (PRMIA), 357
  Python, 170
  Quantnet, 358, 359
  Stack Overflow, 358
  Thalesians, 358
  US Bureau of Labor Statistics, 13
  US Energy Information Administration, 356
  Wilmott Forum, 358
  Yahoo Finance, 356
in-the-money option, 364
intrinsic value, 91, 364
inverse-transformation method, 56
inverted, 225
investing, in risky assets, 241–244
investment grade, 74
investment trusts, 72
irrational exuberance, 14–15
ISDA (International Swaps and Derivatives Association), 81, 96
iterating, 126

J

Johnson & Johnson (JNJ), 163
JPMorgan Chase & Co. (JPM), 163
junk grade, 74

marking to market, 101–102

Markowitz, Harry (inventor), 273

mathematics, of quantitative finance, 8–9

MathFinance Conference, 357

maturity, 75, 364

max function, 229

maximising

expectations, 153–158

likelihood, 314–319

MB (megabyte), 161

McDonald's Corp. (MCD), 163

mean, 41, 44, 364

mean reversion, 62–64, 138, 235, 364

means of exchange, as a function of money, 15–16

measuring

autocorrelation, 306–307

bid-ask spread, 342–343

correlations, 262–266

exponentially weighted moving average (EWMA), 299

integrals, 202

market risk with covariance matrix, 253–255

parameters, 191–192

potential losses. *See* value at risk (VaR)

principal components, 173–174

proportion of assets in portfolio, 266–267

returns, 262–266

simple cash portfolios, 280

with technical analysis, 294–301

volatility, 128–132

meetings, networking, 357–358

megabyte (MB), 161

Merck & Co. Inc. (MRK), 163

method of least squares, 317

Microsoft Corp. (MSFT), 163

Microsoft Excel, 55–56, 174

minimising

least squares, 316–318

portfolio variance, 259–268

minimum regulatory capital, 285

miss-one-out cross-validation, 321

mixing Gaussian distributions, 149–150

MMM (3M Corp.), 163

models

about, 313–314

autocorrelation, 308–309

backtesting, 325–327

binomial, 187–192

binomial tree, 192–195

Black 76, 230–231

building with principal components analysis (PCA), 180–182

capital asset pricing, 268–270

comparing, 318–319

complexity of, 353–354

defined, 364

detecting outliers, 322–324

dimensionality, 324–325

fitting, 319–322

interest-rate, 234–237

interest-rate derivatives, 234–237

maximizing likelihood, 314–319

moving average, 309–311

non-normal returns, 151–158

Occam's razor, 322

out-of-sample validation, 327

overfitting, 319–322

regression, 302–304, 302–305

validating, 285–286

Vasicek, 235–237

modern portfolio theory (MPT), 23

momentum, 12

momentum effect, 348

momentum indicators, checking, 298–299

money, functions of, 15–16

Monte Carlo methods, 54–58, 200, 206–207, 284–285

mortgage-backed securities, 20

moving average crossover, 148–149

moving average models, 309–311

moving averages

defined, 364–365

using as filters, 147–149

MPT (modern portfolio theory), 23

real distributions, 41–44

rebalancing, 216, 220–221

recognising Gaussian (normal) distribution, 40–41

redemption, 75, 365

redemption yield, 76

reducing
  amount of data, 160–176
  covariance matrix, 254
  risk, 23–24

regime switching, 136

regression
  defined, 365
  kernel, 311–312

regression models, 302–305

regulatory capital, 276

relative strength index (RSI), 295–298

Remember icon, 3

resources, Internet
  Advanced Risk Management and Portfolio Management boot camp, 357
  Bank for International Settlements, 276
  CFA Institute, 357
  Cheat Sheet, 2–3, 4, 109, 122, 154
  efinancialcareers, 359
  Federal Reserve Economic Database (FRED), 356
  Fitch Learning, 357
  International Swaps and Derivatives Association, 81
  LinkedIn, 358
  MathFinance Conference, 357
  Professional Risk Managers International Association (PRMIA), 357
  Python, 170
  Quantnet, 358, 359
  Stack Overflow, 358
  Thalesians, 358
  US Bureau of Labor Statistics, 13
  US Energy Information Administration, 356
  Wilmott Forum, 358
  Yahoo Finance, 356

returns
  about, 20–21
  calculating, 262–266

defined, 47, 366
  weighting, 125–127

rho (P), 219

risk. *See also* market risk
  attitudes to, 251–253
  controlling portfolios, 276
  defined, 92, 366
  hedging, 92–93
  managing, 22–24
  market price of, 234
  reducing, 23–24
  troubleshooting for models, 221–222

risk averse, 251

risk loving, 251

risk parity, 273–274, 366

risk-adjusted performance measure, 270

risk-free rate, 16, 97, 186, 366

risk-neutral probability, 188–191

robust method, 323

Rockefeller, Barbara (author)
  Technical Analysis For Dummies, 297

rolling positions, 112–114

RSI (relative strength index), 295–298

Rumsey-Johnson, Deborah (author)
  Statistics For Dummies, 319
  Statistics II For Dummies, 303

running calculations, 126

Ryan, Mark (author)
  Calculus For Dummies, 9

S

sales of stocks/commodities, effect on stock/investment commodity price of, 46

scatterplot, 24, 353

Schatz, 75

Scholes, Myron (economist), 197

sealed bid auction, 331

seasonality, in futures prices, 117–118

second price sealed bid auction, 331

secondary market, 75

securities, 74

selling, on eBay, 331–332

Notes

Notes

Notes

Notes

About the Author

Steve Bell is a physicist who has spent much of his career working on scientific applications of mathematics and statistics for international companies such as ABB. Just in time for the financial crisis of 2008, he managed to switch into finance: he worked for one of the biggest hedge funds in Europe developing quantitative trading strategies, specializing in energy markets. He now works as a statistical consultant in his company Research in Action Ltd. He has a D.Phil. in theoretical physics from the University of Oxford and is a fellow of the Royal Statistical Society. In his leisure time he enjoys gardening, walking in the mountains of Scotland and generally avoiding email and technology.

Dedication

To my family and friends.

Author's Acknowledgments

Firstly, I'd like to thank Annie Knight at John Wiley for inviting me to write this book. The opportunity is very much appreciated. Thanks to my project manager Chad Sievers for keeping me on my toes and to my editor Kathleen Dobie for improving the readability of the book in so many ways. Also, to all of the other members of the Wiley team who helped with the book. I am very grateful to Piotr Fryzlewicz at the London School of Economics for his insightful comments as technical editor.

This book was mostly written in libraries. I'd like to thank the Bodleian Library, University of Oxford for issuing me with a reader card. The Guildhall Library in the City of London gave me some inspiration to write about finance. I also enjoyed using the Bishopsgate Institute. The Royal Statistical Society kindly permitted me to use their fellow's suite for many afternoons and made me feel welcome.

I'd like to thank people who read and commented on chapters of the book. Special thanks to former colleague Boris Afanasiev who read and helped me to improve many of the mathematical chapters and for some interesting discussions about probability theory. Oliver Maspfuhl of Commerzbank AG commented on two of the chapters on risk, and Oleg Soloviev of Econophysica made suggestions on the table of contents. I had many interesting discussions about quantitative finance with Oliver Brockhaus of MathFinance AG, and he also helpfully checked some equations. Dave Rendell was very helpful with his detailed reading of Chapter 1.

Lastly to Ulrike, Emily and Mariella for having to put up with a grumpy husband and dad during the difficult chapters. Thank you so much for your love and support.

Publisher's Acknowledgments

Executive Editor: Annie Knight

Project Manager: Chad R. Sievers

Development Editor: Kathleen Dobie

Copy Editor: Kim Vernon

Technical Editor: Piotr Fryzlewicz

Art Coordinator: Alicia B. South

Production Editor: Kumar Chellappan

Cover Image: ©iStock.com/PashaIgnatov

Take Dummies with you everywhere you go!

Whether you're excited about e-books, want more from the web, must have your mobile apps, or swept up in social media, Dummies makes everything easier.

FOR DUMMIES®

A Wiley Brand

BUSINESS

978-1-118-73077-5

978-1-118-44349-1

978-1-119-97527-4

MUSIC

978-1-119-94276-4

978-0-470-97799-6

978-0-470-49644-2

DIGITAL PHOTOGRAPHY

978-1-118-09203-3

978-0-470-76878-5

978-1-118-00472-2

Algebra I For Dummies
978-0-470-55964-2

Anatomy & Physiology For Dummies, 2nd Edition
978-0-470-92326-9

Asperger's Syndrome For Dummies
978-0-470-66087-4

Basic Maths For Dummies
978-1-119-97452-9

Body Language For Dummies, 2nd Edition
978-1-119-95351-7

Bookkeeping For Dummies, 3rd Edition
978-1-118-34689-1

British Sign Language For Dummies
978-0-470-69477-0

Cricket for Dummies, 2nd Edition
978-1-118-48032-8

Currency Trading For Dummies, 2nd Edition
978-1-118-01851-4

Cycling For Dummies
978-1-118-36435-2

Diabetes For Dummies, 3rd Edition
978-0-470-97711-8

eBay For Dummies, 3rd Edition
978-1-119-94122-4

Electronics For Dummies All-in-One For Dummies
978-1-118-58973-1

English Grammar For Dummies
978-0-470-05752-0

French For Dummies, 2nd Edition
978-1-118-00464-7

Guitar For Dummies, 3rd Edition
978-1-118-11554-1

IBS For Dummies
978-0-470-51737-6

Keeping Chickens For Dummies
978-1-119-99417-6

Knitting For Dummies, 3rd Edition
978-1-118-66151-2

FOR DUMMIES

A Wiley Brand

SELF-HELP

978-0-470-66541-1

978-1-119-99264-6

978-0-470-66086-7

LANGUAGES

978-0-470-68815-1

978-1-119-97959-3

978-0-470-69477-0

HISTORY

978-0-470-68792-5

978-0-470-74783-4

978-0-470-97819-1

Laptops For Dummies 5th Edition
978-1-118-11533-6

Management For Dummies, 2nd Edition
978-0-470-97769-9

Nutrition For Dummies, 2nd Edition
978-0-470-97276-2

Office 2013 For Dummies
978-1-118-49715-9

Organic Gardening For Dummies
978-1-119-97706-3

Origami Kit For Dummies
978-0-470-75857-1

Overcoming Depression For Dummies
978-0-470-69430-5

Physics I For Dummies
978-0-470-90324-7

Project Management For Dummies
978-0-470-71119-4

Psychology Statistics For Dummies
978-1-119-95287-9

Renting Out Your Property For Dummies, 3rd Edition
978-1-119-97640-0

Rugby Union For Dummies, 3rd Edition
978-1-119-99092-5

Stargazing For Dummies
978-1-118-41156-8

Teaching English as a Foreign Language For Dummies
978-0-470-74576-2

Time Management For Dummies
978-0-470-77765-7

Training Your Brain For Dummies
978-0-470-97449-0

Voice and Speaking Skills For Dummies
978-1-119-94512-3

Wedding Planning For Dummies
978-1-118-69951-5

WordPress For Dummies, 5th Edition
978-1-118-38318-6

Think you can't learn it in a day? Think again!

The *In a Day* e-book series from *For Dummies* gives you quick and easy access to learn a new skill, brush up on a hobby, or enhance your personal or professional life — all in a day. Easy!

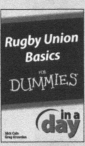

Available as PDF, eMobi and Kindle